THE BEAUTIFUL FALL

THE BEAUTIFUL FALL

—◆—

LAGERFELD, SAINT LAURENT,
AND GLORIOUS EXCESS IN 1970S PARIS

ALICIA DRAKE

Little, Brown and Company
New York   Boston   London

Little, Brown and Company
Hachette Book Group USA
1271 Avenue of the Americas, New York, NY 10020
Visit our Web site at www.HachetteBookGroupUSA.com

First Edition: September 2006

Excerpt from "Early Success" by F. Scott Fitzgerald, from *The Crack-Up*, copyright 1945 by New Directions Publishing Corp. Reprinted by permission of New Directions Publishing Corp. and Harold Ober Associates, Inc.

ISBN 0-316-76801-4/978-0-316-76801-6
LCCN 2006929786

10 9 8 7 6 5 4 3 2 1

Q-FF

Printed in the United States of America

for Rupert

How 'ya gonna keep 'em down on the farm (after they've seen Paree)?
Sam M. Lewis and Joe Young, song title, 1919

CONTENTS

———◆———

Foreword

1974

Café de Flore was the essence of all that was desirable on the Rive Gauche of Paris. It stood on the corner of Saint Germain life, an irresistible mix of café society, surging with literary, artistic, wanton and fashionable ambitions. It was a mirrored place of entrances and encounters.

That afternoon in 1974 a young man pulled open its wrought-iron and glass-fronted door and paused to watch his beauty take effect. He was dressed incongruously for town and for his age. He wore an open-neck sailor shirt with a blue-striped silk cravat knotted as a tie at his neck. He had on long cream shorts, leaving his legs bare and boyish, and in his hand he carried a slim volume of Montesquiou's poetry. His schoolboy pose was countered by a moustache, a Proustian affectation that swept from his upper lip in a manicured brush-stroke.

He stepped through the Flore afternoon, careless of but not oblivious to the accelerated voices and blatant stares, to take his seat on the leather banquette before a brass-framed mirror.

His reflection was flushed and exultant. He had spent the morning sitting for David Hockney in his studio on the Cours de Rohan, not far from the Flore. Hockney was living in Paris and sketching a series of friends and personalities that included studies of the American painter Shirley Goldfarb, herself an habitué of the Flore. And now there was to be a portrait of him, neither friend nor yet personality, but possessed of a certain timely allure.

Jacques de Bascher de Beaumarchais was the name he had chosen to make his entrance on the Parisian *monde*. He arrived in Paris with all the ravenous social ambition of Balzac's Eugène de Rastignac, only to discover he had arrived a century too late. The Faubourg Saint-Germain, that geographical stretch of elegance and intrigue that once described the salons and rituals of the grand aristocracy of Paris, was by now more of a nostalgic whim to indulge than a ruling class to conquer.

Paris society, like the rest of the world, was turning inexorably in favour of celebrity and youth. And in this new social order there was a new and thrusting arrival – fashion. Ironically the new fashion elite was consumed by all the familiar obsessions of the fading aristocratic *monde*: narcissism, devastating rivalry, power and wealth, although fashion took on an additional obsession: the insecurity of the parvenu.

By the early 1970s fashion designers in Paris were shedding their status as purveyors of grand wardrobes for elegant ladies and beginning to emerge instead as stars in their own right: puissant style arbiters and creators of fame, sex appeal and glamour that was accessible to all. They were years behind London and New York in making that transformation; they did, however, possess the profound advantage of being part of the myth and mystery that is Paris couture.

Designers, models and muses all came seeking attention at the Flore. There, bathed in the sunlight, were Betty Catroux, Loulou de la Falaise and Clara Saint, the female triumvirate of the most powerful and seductive fashion designer in Paris, Yves Saint Laurent. Yves himself was rarely seen at the Flore, although that never prevented the breathless expectation that today he might be.

On the other side of the room, behind the potted palms, sat a dazzling throng of Americans: model Pat Cleveland, Corey Tippin, Juan Ramos and illustrator Antonio Lopez, who captured the self-conscious enchantment of the Flore with pencil and sketch pad. And opposite Jacques sat Karl Lagerfeld, German ready-to-wear designer, lavish in wing collar and monocle, a fashion force in the making.

Jacques saw the arch glamour of fashion and he, like so many others, was captivated. Beyond its creativity, renewal or money, it is glamour that proves fashion's perpetual seduction: glamour and its reflex of idealisation on to which every hope and fantasy can be projected; glamour and its implicit promise of a life devoid of mediocrity.

Jacques could not create, he could not design, but he had youth and beauty, of which fashion requires a constant supply. Designers do not create in a vacuum; they need relentless stimulation, innovation and objects of fascination to stir the mind. To be that object of fascination is a coveted and hazardous place to be. At the age of twenty-two, Jacques de Bascher chose Paris fashion on which to stake his life's ambition.

Chapter 1

1954–58

Standing on stage were the three winners of the International Wool Secretariat fashion design competition of 1954. Two of them were young men dressed almost identically: dark suits, dark ties, white shirts, the very image of apprenticeship propriety. Yves Mathieu-Saint-Laurent, as he was called then, was aged eighteen, recently arrived from Oran, Algeria and winner of the first and third prizes in the dress category. He stepped forward to accept his prizes with all the paddock tremors of a race-horse, one hand leaping up spasmodically to hide one eye, obscuring half the world.

Beside him was Karl Lagerfeld, aged twenty-one, from Hamburg and winner of the coat category. He talked fast and in French, nervously licking his lips as his words spilled out like marbles. He clasped his hands awkwardly in front of him. At the far end of the group stood Colette Bracchi, winner of the suit category and seemingly the most self-assured of the three. She would henceforth disappear into fashion oblivion.

These three represented the best of young Paris fashion talent. Poised to enter the rarefied world of haute couture, they were, as the man handing out the prizes told the audience, 'already on the road to success'. Their winning designs had been picked from an entry of six thousand anonymous sketches, which made Saint Laurent's feat of having two sketches selected all the more extraordinary. Added to his success was the fact that Yves had come third in the previous year's competition.

The competition was only in its second year, but already highly prestigious. Its objective was to promote wool in fashion, so the rules stipulated that every design entry should be intended for wool fabric. The jury included Hubert de Givenchy and Pierre Balmain, and the previous year Christian Dior had been a judge. There was substantial prize money but, more importantly, each first-prize winner had their sketch made up into an outfit by one of the Paris haute-couture houses.

That meant by the time of the awards ceremony in December the winners were all accompanied on stage by a model wearing their design. Karl's coat was made of daffodil-yellow wool and followed straight lines. It finished primly on the calf and, as if to compensate, was cut low across the collarbone and then dipped into a V at the back. It was an appropriate coat for a blue-chip wife to wear to lunch.

Yves Saint Laurent's cocktail dress was pert and enticing, a black sheath that wrapped around one shoulder, exposing the other to a passing caress. A black veil fluttered across the model's face, suggesting the seductive whimsy expected of a Parisienne. 'Elegance,' said the breathless teenage Yves, 'is a dress too dazzling to dare to wear twice.'

Yves Saint Laurent and Karl Lagerfeld stepped on to the Paris fashion stage together as equals. And yet from the very start Yves walked an apparently charmed path. He was the youngest of the three winners by three years; his first and third prizes in the dress category defined him as a boy wonder; and he was French Algerian, which meant the French could claim his victory as their own. Most subtle and yet most marked was the distinction that Saint Laurent won the dress category and, within the world of haute couture, dresses carried utmost prestige.

They would become rivals, but first they were friends, which was hardly surprising, for Yves and Karl had much in common. Both were the only, cherished sons of prosperous, middle-class families. Their fathers were successful businessmen who provided for their families, aspiring wives and bourgeois lifestyles. Both fathers conducted an entirely courteous and caring, if distant, relationship with their sons, which was perhaps characteristic of their generation. Both boys were homosexual and aware of their sexual orientation from an early age. They loved to sketch and in particular they loved to sketch dresses. They were both boys from the provinces, dreaming of Paris.

★

Yves was brought up bathed in white light and hero-worship, at least within his family. He was born on 1 August 1936 in Oran, a major port town of Algeria and – as it was described at the time – the fifth largest town in France, for Algeria was a French colony and had been so since 1830. There were nearly one million French settlers living there and they were known as *pieds-noirs* – black feet, for their shiny black shoes that stood out against the bare feet of the Algerians.

In the desert the French settlers had built themselves a proud, provincial town worthy of the *métropole*, as mainland France was known. There was *lycée* and cathedral, prefecture and town hall. Many, the Mathieu-Saint-Laurent family among them, had arrived in Oran as refugees from their homeland. Through generations of hard work, the settlers had carved out a life of warm beaches and comfortable homes from the rocks and dust they had found there, and it was perhaps this exile-turned-good that gave Oran its atmosphere of blessed sanctuary.

'Our world at the time was Oran, and not Paris,' Yves would later write. 'Not Algiers, the metaphysical city of Camus with its white truths, nor yet Marrakech with its remarkable pink magic. Oran, a cosmopolitan centre of tradesmen and merchants who came from everywhere and above all from elsewhere, a glittering city in a patchwork of a thousand colours under the calm sun of North Africa.'

It was the one town in North Africa where the European population outnumbered the Arab population. Unlike Algiers, which was overwhelmingly French in outlook, Oran had a Spanish feel to its culture, architecture and way of life, a vestige of the two-hundred-year Spanish occupation of the town that began in the sixteenth century. The population was multi-ethnic and vivacious – Arabs, Jews, French, Alsatians, Bretons, Spanish and Italians lived alongside one another, although they were divided by an intransigent class structure of which the French occupied the apex. Oran's diversity spilled out all over: in the many languages, dialects and everyday life of a city that mixed Spanish fort, archbishop, Arab market and synagogue with palm trees and *blanquette de veau*. The *pieds-noirs* had their own distinctive accent and a particular sharp-sided wit that was honed by the inferiority complex of the French colonies.

Oran's charm lay in its Mediterranean light and laughter, in the yellow dunes underfoot and the evening surge of faces on the Boulevard Séguin.

'There were more beautiful women per square metre in Oran than anywhere else,' remembers Yves' youngest sister Brigitte Bastian with pride and nostalgia. 'The men from Algiers came to Oran to find their girlfriends.' The Oranais woman was admired for her panache, always dressed up whatever her budget and promenading by the beach in the latest look copied from Paris with gloves, hat and bag to match. Palm Sunday was the excuse for a whole new outfit to be purchased and paid back, in Oranais speak, 'little by little', meaning on credit.

Yves' mother Lucienne kept up with the best of them. She was spoilt, cosseted by her indulgent husband. She ran the house and her wardrobe. 'They called my mother *la gato* – the cat in Spanish – because of her eyes. She was a beauty,' remembers Brigitte. 'All the men thought so.' There was a strong vein of coquetry running through the family. The dressmaker came to the house once a week and as a small boy Yves sat and watched the fittings, discussing the new styles he had seen in the fashion magazines and periodicals from Paris. From the age of four he was telling the women in the house how they should dress. His mother remembers Yves not liking an aunt's outfit and telling her so. 'I think he made her change her dress and accessories at least five or six times before he was satisfied, while we all waited,' his mother later said. 'He had such authority and was so sure of himself that we accepted it from him.'

Yves' father's ancestors had settled in Oran having fled the Prussian occupation of Alsace–Lorraine in 1870. They were a family of magistrates and lawyers who changed their name from Mathieu de Heidolsheim when they left Alsace. Yves' father Charles made his money in Oran through an insurance company that he set up with a business partner, as well as real-estate dealings. He also managed a chain of cinemas operating in Algeria, Morocco and Tunisia, which was a source of delight to his three children as they got to see all the latest films for free.

The Mathieu-Saint-Laurent couple socialised with the provincial heights of Oran. *Préfets* and *notaires* came to the house and drank aperitifs on the terrace before paella was served on the best family porcelain. They were members of the lawn tennis club. Yves' younger sisters Michèle and Brigitte were born in 1942 and 1945. Not even the war could mar their years of idyll. The family spent the summers at their villa in Trouville, a seaside town fourteen kilometres to the west of Oran and a resort frequented by the Oranais bourgeoisie. Summer holidays lasted three months.

Yves grew up charming his family and their friends with his precocious talent and imagination. Late at night he pushed handwritten invitations under the doors of his sisters' bedrooms, inviting them as privileged clients to his spring/summer couture show. 'He would make dresses from bits of old fabric, a theatre with paper cut-out dolls; he transported us into this fairy-tale world,' says Brigitte.

At the age of twelve Yves saw a production of Molière's *L'Ecole des Femmes* that was playing at the Oran theatre. Louis Jouvet was both directing and starring in the play and Christian Bérard had designed the set. The production was highly influential on Yves' burgeoning aesthetic. Yves' mother Lucienne later described it as 'a revelation for Yves'. Bérard was a hero of 1930s and 40s decorative arts in Paris, designing exceptional sets and costumes for the ballet, theatre and films, as well as drawing gorgeous fashion illustrations for French *Vogue* and *Harper's Bazaar*. He was nicknamed Bébé for his baby face and gestures. He was large and bearded, tramp-like in his dress, lyrical in his talent with a melancholic charm that was offset by an opium habit. He was a central figure in the pre-war Parisian set of genius, style and dissipation, a friend of Cocteau, Chanel and Marie-Laure de Noailles. Yves loved Bérard's style, both his fashion illustration and his set design and costumes, and he imitated his drawing style for years to come. After seeing the *L'Ecole des Femmes* performance, according to Yves' mother, 'Theatre was all he could think or talk about. We let him turn an empty room in the house into a theatre. He wrote and directed plays, designed and made all the sets and costumes, with his sisters and cousins as actors.'

The house was full of friends and women, aunts, mothers, grandmothers and sisters, and among them Yves was, says his sister, 'The infant king. I was brought up in absolute admiration for my brother; he was kind, funny, a prankster, he loved pulling practical jokes,' remembers Brigitte. 'He was wily and crafty.' He was full of boyish tricks, teaching his youngest sister to ring up stray telephone numbers. They would take it in turns to ask the unsuspecting person at the end of the line, 'Good morning, Madam, have you received the box?' 'Which box?' came the bemused reply. 'Why, the box to pack your bottom in,' Yves or Brigitte would say. It was a joke reliant on the rhyming of *caisse* and *fesse* in

French and one that inevitably ended with the slamming-down of the telephone and uncontrollable hilarity.

On Sunday evenings Yves attended 6 p.m. mass at the cathedral of Sacré Cœur, which was near to the house, and returned home afterwards to find his audience always waiting. He would remove the sheaf of papers from his jacket with a mischievous smile and show Michèle and Brigitte his newest caricatures of members of the congregation sketched during mass. Madame le Long Bec or Mrs Long Beak was Brigitte's favourite. 'Yves was the hero at home,' says Brigitte. 'That was the way it was in our home. In Algeria the eldest brother counts, he is important to us.'

At home he was the hero of a female and fantastical world, at school he was the outcast. From the age of eight until sixteen Yves attended a Jesuit boarding school in Oran, the College Sacré-Cœur, where he stuck out from the start as a dayboy and a fop. Among the confident, laddish, football-crazy adolescents, he was nervous, highly strung and ostracised. 'It was Calvary for him,' says François Catroux, who was a pupil of Sacré-Cœur at the same time and would later become friends with Saint Laurent in Paris. 'The school chapel had very low windows and during recreation, while all the other boys were playing football, Yves was always sitting there on the window ledge of the chapel. He was terrified that the boys would touch him. Everyone said horrible things to him, called him names. Physically he was already a little odd, always dressed up and wearing a tie. He was already closed in on himself. They called him every name under the sun, you know, young people are cruel and Yves felt that intensely. He seemed so very anxious, he must have been aged about fourteen.'

There were other homosexuals at school, but Yves stuck out for his essentially effeminate way of being. 'Yves was thin, elegant, feminine-looking and the others were macho or at least looked like they were,' says Brigitte. 'You have to remember, Oran was a town of machos. It was an extremely sensitive issue to be a homosexual there at that time, you were in hiding.'

Growing up a homosexual in the 1940s in most places carried an overwhelming burden of guilt, self-hate and shame; perhaps not for everyone, but certainly for Yves. 'He was someone who couldn't admit his sexuality to begin with; perhaps he didn't even know it then or at

Yves Saint Laurent as a teenager on the tennis courts of Oran.

least he wasn't completely conscious of it, and yet he was already ashamed of what he was,' says François Catroux. 'And that wasn't because of the school; you know, he wasn't the only boy in school who was homosexual, there were others who were entirely at ease with their sexuality. It was only Yves who was so ashamed and that has to do with this side to Yves whereby he likes sorrow. He likes to be unhappy. It is as if it is only in this state of sorrow that he truly finds himself.'

His sexuality became a long-term focus for his neurosis and sense of isolation. 'I wasn't like the other boys, you see. I didn't conform. No doubt it was my homosexuality . . . my classmates could see that I wasn't the same as them,' said Yves, looking back some forty years later in an interview with *Le Figaro*, 'and so they made me into their whipping boy. They beat me up and locked me in the toilets. During playtime I would hide in the chapel – I was at a religious college – or I would arrange it so that I could stay alone in class . . . I was full of sadness, fear and terror. Every morning before I had to go off to school I was sick. It was psychological torture; children, you know, they forgive nothing. As they bullied me, I would say to myself over and over, "One day, you'll be famous." That was revenge.'

Back home at night Saint Laurent retreated into his world of fantasy, cutting out his mother's old dresses, drawing intricate stage backdrops and costumes for his theatrical productions. His family were aware of his sexuality from an early age and his father tacitly accepted it, although he never discussed it with his wife or Yves. Yves' mother tried to disguise it in euphemisms. 'Maman tried to hide everything,' says Brigitte, 'And we knew it all along.' Brigitte fought with children at school who called her brother a 'tapette', a vulgar, pejorative name meaning 'poof'. 'I asked my mother whether it was true. She said to me, no, he's like an angel; they are neither one sex nor the other. That's what Maman told me.'

And according to his family, Yves never mentioned the day's anguish at school. 'We never knew,' says Brigitte. 'He would come home and it would be play-acting, crazy fun. He must have suffered terribly, but he never told us.'

In 1953, having won third prize in the International Wool Secretariat competition, Yves took the plane to Paris for the first time to receive his award. He travelled with his mother and the trip had a dual purpose, for, as well as the prize-giving, he also met with Michel de Brunhoff, the powerful and connected editor-in-chief of French *Vogue*. Yves' father had arranged the meeting through a family contact without Yves knowing and De Brunhoff had promised to look over Yves' sketches with the intention of helping him find his way into fashion or costume design. Yves had not yet sat his *baccalauréat* examinations, nor did he want to. Edmonde Charles-Roux, who was De Brunhoff's assistant at the time, remembers the rather peculiar visitor: 'He was very tall with huge glasses. Very, very, very shy. He didn't open his mouth; it was his mother who did all the talking for him. Then suddenly he exploded, telling us why he didn't want to stay at school and why he didn't want to sit his *baccalauréat* but would rather go straight into fashion. You felt he had a will. He was shy, yes, but he wasn't timorous or afraid. You could feel the strength of character.'

Yves possessed self-belief from the very start. During that same Paris trip, he walked with his mother along the Avenue Montaigne, staring into boutique windows, furriers and couture houses, observing the glow of luxury. He came to a halt outside number 30, looked up at the lit windows of Christian Dior — which was at the time the greatest Parisian couture house — turned to his mother and said, 'Maman, it won't be long before I'm working in there.'

He followed De Brunhoff's instructions and returned to Oran, where he took and passed his bac in June 1954, and in September he enrolled at the Ecole de la Chambre Syndicale de la Couture Parisienne. This was the couture-industry school on Rue Saint Roch, and at the time anyone aspiring to a career in couture studied there to learn the technique and craft. In the mid-1950s there were dozens of pupils like Yves, young men fresh from adolescence and flushed with fantasies of haute couture and ambitions of dressing the Comtesse de Paris. One of those other pupils was Karl Lagerfeld. He was not in the same class as Yves, but he was studying at the Ecole de la Chambre Syndicale and it is here that the two young men first met.

Even among the Chambre Syndicale students, Yves Saint Laurent's talent was outstanding. Fernando Sanchez was a young Belgian student who had been brought up in Spain and was in the same class as Yves. 'I remember the first time I saw his drawing. He was a star and it shone from him – a pure talent.' Anne-Marie Muñoz, who would meet him months later, shared a similarly revelatory reaction on seeing Saint Laurent's sketches for the first time. 'It wasn't even a question of thinking whether I liked them or not, it seemed so obvious. It was something evident, a sort of perfection, a beauty and intelligence to the clothing and how easy it looked. The greatest quality in them was the emotion they evoked.'

At the Ecole Chambre Syndicale Yves' mind was already racing with fantasies of success. He committed his schoolboy yearnings to paper, writing an imaginary newspaper's rave review that he later gave to friend and Dior model, Victoire. 'Contrary to what happens every season, this time the bomb, whether it be qualified as A or H, did not explode in the salon of Monsieur Christian Dior,' wrote Yves, referring to the previous triumphant A and H lines or silhouettes of Dior, 'but rather for the launch of a young couturier, Yves Mathieu-Saint-Laurent, who, with one collection, hoisted himself in one bound to the ranks of the greatest.'

He stayed only three months at the couture school before slipping into boredom and gloom. His father was so worried about his son's morale that he wrote to De Brunhoff asking if there was anything he could do for Yves. In the spring of 1955 Yves returned to De Brunhoff's office. 'He was very unhappy at the couture school; he said it was worth nothing, which is proof in itself that he was not scared,' says Edmonde Charles-Roux, 'He didn't believe in it; he found it too traditional, not enough action for him. That was the kind of young man he was, very impetuous.'

As well as the complaints, he handed over a batch of fashion silhouettes he had been working on to De Brunhoff. Edmonde Charles-Roux remembers her delight at the charm of the sketches, which was matched by De Brunhoff's incredulity that the sketches were 'practically identical to the collection Dior would present fifteen days later', even though Saint Laurent could not have known this. De Brunhoff was impressed by Saint Laurent's style and his ability to pick up on fashion's feeling, and according to Charles-Roux he did what he had never done for anyone before: he put the sketches under his arm and went round to show them to his old friend Christian Dior and recommended that he meet Saint Laurent. Yves took up a post as assistant in the studio of

Monsieur Dior in June 1955, leaving behind the Ecole de la Chambre Syndicale after only a term there.

From the start there was this fairy-tale fait-accompli quality to every step Yves Saint Laurent made in fashion, as if his career path was already mapped out in history. Wherever Yves went a door seemed to swing open before him. Was it some predestined stroke of fate, or was it Yves Saint Laurent constructing his own fame and destiny as he went, forcing open the doors that blocked his way?

The house of Dior stood on the corner of Avenue Montaigne and Rue François Premier, a fashion landmark where the world's celebrity couturier ruled over his empire of 1,400 workers. Dior was plump and shiny-cheeked, revered by clients and seamstresses alike for his ability to express the postwar hunger for a voluptuous femininity and French elegance. His public persona was carefully constructed to match his idealised Dior woman: Monsieur Dior was the epitome of bourgeois provincial decorum; he was known for his exquisite manners and modesty, the good taste of a well-brought-up boy from Normandy. His taste, like that of so many couturiers, was based on nostalgia and his mother. He was a lover of women, if not carnally then at least in the ideal.

Yves Saint Laurent started work in the studio of Christian Dior. In the tyrannically hierarchical and segregated ethos of the couture house, the studio is the tabernacle; it is here that the creative design takes place. Yves stuck out straight away, both because of his talent and his isolation from others. 'He was already formed by the time he arrived at Dior: the drawing style, his eye, everything,' says André Levasseur, who was working for the boutique line at Dior, 'but his shyness was desperate. He hugged the walls as he walked.' Yet there were also hints of the power Yves could wield through this shyness. Tan Giudicelli was also working as an assistant in the Dior studio at the time and remembers Yves was 'like a little girl, he was very odd. He was someone who never spoke, always silent. It is strange but when you are passive to that extent, you can dominate.'

It was while he was working as an assistant at Dior that Yves was asked to design the head-dresses for a costume ball that Baron Alexis de Redé threw in 1956, called 'Le bal des têtes'. Yves sketched a series of feathered, flowered and utterly romantic concoctions for the ladies and this was a significant introduction to fashionable Paris.

Across the road from Dior, at 44, Rue François Premier, Karl Lagerfeld was at work as an assistant at the less illustrious house of Pierre Balmain, which he had joined in 1955. Balmain was the couturier responsible for making up Lagerfeld's prize-winning sketch into a coat and he subsequently offered Karl a job. There is a certain dramatic symmetry to Yves and Karl's starting point in fashion, for Christian Dior and Pierre Balmain had themselves worked together at the house of Lucien Lelong at the beginning of the 1940s and their careers. At one time they even talked of going into business together, but then Pierre Balmain left to open his own house in 1945. A year later Dior founded his house with the huge financial backing of France's greatest textile industrialist, Marcel Boussac.

Dior's very first collection or 'New Look', as it was famously dubbed, was a runaway, phenomenal success. To a bruised and humiliated nation, Dior restored pride and seduction in the form of a new silhouette of pleated, flowing, calf-length skirt, tiny waist and upholstered bosom. He used twenty yards of fabric per skirt that dropped to the calf in soft folds of extravagance and delighted his cotton-king boss, Boussac, as the looms began to whir again. After years of boxy shoulders and short, straight skirts, the sound of a Dior skirt literally swooshing round your legs as you walked was quite some sensation.

With his New Look, Dior became fashion's superpower, the 'saviour' of post-Occupation Paris couture and his couture house evolved into a highly lucrative business with licences and hit perfumes. He conquered America, appearing on the front cover of *Time* magazine, while his friend Pierre Balmain enjoyed a rather more bite-sized success. Balmain serviced a loyal clientele of what he called the 'jolie madame' while enjoying a chic social life among European royalty, but he lacked the high-octane celebrity and glamour of Dior. He did not lead fashion. Later Karl explained: 'Balmain made me an offer, I didn't choose him. I didn't really know very much about all these things at the time. I was there to learn something and not to act the genius. Being at Balmain was not like being at Dior or Balenciaga, which were chapels. I said to myself I was there to learn, and I was sufficiently detached.'

Despite the status differences between couture houses they all shared one common characteristic: they were rife with petty jealousies and spite. The new boy from fashion school was always a prime target, as

Karl himself experienced. Many years later he remembered: 'My first day in fashion, at Balmain in the '50s – it was terrible! If that is fashion, I thought, I better go back and finish high school. Today, nobody would accept the work conditions and the money we had to accept at that time. Yves and I were lucky, because our families had money. But one would not believe how humiliating the atmosphere was then in the fashion houses, how mean the people were. It would be illegal today.'

If Karl was jealous of Yves' head start at Dior, he didn't let it show. During these years of apprenticeship Karl and Yves saw each other constantly. During the day Karl was to be found at the Bar des Théâtres on Avenue Montaigne, where all the young apprentices and house models working in the couture houses came to gossip and smoke and flirt on red velvet banquettes. Karl always seemed to be there, sitting in a booth, hair impeccably shined and sculpted, lips pursed, surrounded by mannequins, buying them coffee.

Karl had the car and so at night he and Yves drove round Paris, heading to La Closerie des Lilas on the Boulevard Montparnasse for dinner or later on for drinks at La Coupole. Youths of the 1950s, both Yves and Karl were steeped in nostalgia, trying hard to conjure up the heady extravagance of 1920s and 30s Paris between the wars. Their favourite bar was Le Bœuf sur le Toit, precisely because it had been the cult piano-cabaret bar of Cocteau, Picasso and Chanel after the First World War.

Saint Laurent lived in a room that he rented from an old lady on the Boulevard Pereire and had done up in navy-blue velvet. He regaled friends with comical tales of her spying on him through the keyhole at night as he undressed. Karl had started life in Paris staying at the threadbare Hôtel le Gerson, which was a modest student-hostel-type hotel just down from the Sorbonne on a narrow backstreet in the *quartier latin*. By now he was installed in an apartment on the Rue de Tournon in the sixth *arrondissement* leading to the Jardin du Luxembourg. Above his fireplace hung a sketch by Yves of a ballet décor. Sometimes Fernando Sanchez would join them at night. 'Karl was the only one with any money so we would spend all our time round at his apartment,' remembers Fernando. Karl's father Otto Lagerfeld funded him at the time. 'My uncle Otto was managing director of Glücksklee,' said Karl's cousin, the late Kurt Lagerfeld, 'and he kept having to stump up money for Karl.

He drove a flash Mercedes sports car that Uncle Otto had paid for.' Glücksklee was the German brand name for condensed milk produced in Germany for the American Milk Products Corporation.

Yves had become friends at Dior with Victoire, who was one of the star mannequins there, and she soon became an integral part of their night-time sorties. Victoire was very different from the other angular beauties that had epitomised 1950s couture with their haughty, touch-me-not perfection. Victoire was sexy. She had breasts and bottom, cheek-bones and black eyes, and an incredible mouth that cracked open to reveal huge teeth. She was flesh and exciting. When she walked into the Dior salon wearing a deep-*décolleté* black cocktail dress, there was a palpable temperature change among the powdered ladies and their husbands as Victoire flashed the teeth, mouth and eyes and sashayed her way among them. It was Monsieur Dior who had transformed her fortunes by changing her name from Jeanne to the triumphant Victoire.

Like schoolboys with a pounding crush, both Yves and Karl contested hotly for her attention. Yves gave her a porcelain doll dressed in an emerald-green silk crinoline that he had bought at the flea market; not to be outdone, Karl turned up weeks later with a doll's china tea-service that he had come across in the attic at his family home in Hamburg. They were gifts of homage mixed up with a strange yearning. When they went out at night together Victoire felt that Yves desired her but he did not seem able, or did not dare, to make a physical move. She sensed that Karl had similar feelings for her and yet he too seemed inhibited by his own desires. After late nights out on the town, they sometimes ended up all three of them sleeping beneath a Turkish rug on the floor of Karl's apartment.

It was Yves who held the ultimate chip in the quest for Victoire's attention, for by 1957 he had been promoted and named assistant to Christian Dior, which meant he was designing many of the dresses that she would model throughout the season. And Victoire, like every model, always wanted the most beautiful outfit that would assure her pre-eminence in the shows.

There was a fourth integral member of the Yves and Karl gang and that was Anne-Marie Poupard (later Anne-Marie Muñoz), who was working as a junior assistant at Dior. She had entered the house as the niece of composer Henri Sauguet, who was one of Christian Dior's oldest and greatest friends and a member of his artistic inner circle. She had started there in 1954 with a lowly position in the atelier, where the seamstresses sew and put together the dresses, but by this time Anne-Marie was working in the boutique.

Anne-Marie was a counter-balance to the three other rival egos in the gang. She had come to Paris to see and meet people; her ambitions were limited. She did not threaten Victoire's diva status; instead she observed the manoeuvrings of vanity, possession and control within the set. It was Yves who set the day-to-day agenda. 'Yves was just the same as he is now: he never wanted to go out, yet at the same time it was always Yves who was the boss in the group. Whenever we were choosing the restaurant it was Yves who would decide between one place and the other, quite naturally. There was a force to him,' comments Anne-Marie Muñoz.

Yves chose outings to L'Hélicoptère or Le Fiacre, both of which were tiny gay nightclubs on the Rive Gauche where boys danced the Charleston. Le Fiacre was a famous bar and restaurant on the Rue Saint Sulpice where on summer nights the scene got so crowded customers spilled out on to the street. There were pockets of homosexual life and men cruising all over Paris, but Saint Germain in the 1950s was known for its *folles*, the name used to describe camp gays of the moment who were recognised by their bottom-swivelling walk and deliberately effeminate ways, including a habit of high-drama shrieking.

Downstairs at Le Fiacre Yves danced cheek-to-cheek with Victoire, Karl drank Coca-Cola, Anne-Marie watched. They each returned home alone. Whatever his longings were, Yves was not yet fulfilling them. His life was tame and repressed. He was infinitely demanding, with the high-pitched sense of humour of a child. 'Every night when we went out it would be, "Ooh là là, watch out! Watch out!" or, "Help, protect me, have you seen that one over there!"' remembers Victoire. 'If I grabbed his arm and twisted it, he would cry out, but he was delighted,' she continues. 'Yves was always someone who wanted to be thrown on a bed, so to speak.'

By the summer of 1957, the group that had been together two years began to vibrate with jealousies and intrigue. Victoire flirted with others at the house of Dior, enraging Yves, who wanted sole possession of her beauty. She had had a short affair with a young assistant at the house called Gaston, who, although she did not know it at the time, was Monsieur Dior's boyfriend, and she also had her own boyfriend, who was pressing for marriage. Karl invited Victoire – or Vishnou, as he used to call her – out for a secret breakfast rendezvous at the Ritz, vying for her favour by presenting her with a sketch of herself dressed up in fashions of different ages, from flapper girl to belle-époque lady. Yves fought back by giving her a pastel drawing of a cocktail dress he had designed and dedicated to 'the woman that wears my dresses so well'.

The four of them – Victoire, Yves, Karl and Anne-Marie – drove up to the coast of Normandy for a weekend and Yves spent his time sulking on the café *terrasse*. When jealousy flared, Yves would shrink from contact with the others; he would close in upon himself so entirely that he was sealed off, seemingly absent from the proceedings. It was a state of mind that brought – and would always bring – people running to him.

By this time Yves was designing some forty dresses for each collection in his role as Dior's assistant. In the run-up to the collection he would go home to Oran to work on his sketches, where his return was fêted with whoops of praise. Yves was doing so well in Paris and his mother invited all their friends to the house so that they could admire his success. 'It was revolution in the house when he came,' remembers Brigitte. 'The cook didn't know what to do with herself trying to come up with dishes to please him. She wanted to spoil him rotten. He adored sole so we ate sole, there were fresh fruit juices; we lived only for Yves, every one of us.'

Lucienne's dressmaker dropped by to be shown Yves' sketches for Dior. Brigitte was there to run his errands. 'He was marvellous, but he could also be diabolical, oh yes. I was at his service when he was at the house,' says Brigitte, who by this time was twelve. 'He would send me off to Victorine, which was a haberdashery on a little street nearby, and I would go to buy his pencils, his drawing paper, all that.'

In autumn 1957 Christian Dior left town for a stay at the spa of Montecatini for another of his habitual and drastic attempts to lose weight. He suffered a heart attack and died at the age of fifty-two on 24 October 1957. Although his solo fashion career spanned only ten years, there was huge and tender affection for this couturier who, it seemed, had restored elegance and a romantic pleasure to Paris fashion. Both the couture house – the outside of which was draped in black –

and France were devastated. Parisians now mourned the public Monsieur Dior: the laughter and jollity, dapper suits and goddess dresses. Few people knew about Dior's private reality of depression, insomnia, compulsive eating, private debt, obsessive superstition and the ever-increasing neurosis of trying to create and renew and outdo the previous season's silhouette.

Dior's financial backer, Marcel Boussac, was left with a 60-million-franc fashion business to keep afloat. And after the emotion of the funeral had subsided and the wreaths of lily of the valley were removed from around the Arc de Triomphe, photographers and press were summoned to Avenue Montaigne to hear how he was going to do it. From the very start Dior had employed a business manager, Jacques Rouët, whose job it was to carry out the business offensive while Dior's aura of divine creativity was preserved intact. This was a business model Yves Saint Laurent would later adopt himself. Jacques Rouët announced a creative team of four people, all of whom had worked with Monsieur Dior. There were three women: Raymonde Zehnacker, Marguerite Carré and Mitza Bricard, who had been Dior's director of design studio, technical director in charge of the workrooms and muse. They formed a powerful cabal, draped in mink, pearls and mutual envy, that had protected and upheld the myth of Dior during his lifetime. They were a highly predictable choice: each had worked with Monsieur Dior since the establishment of the couture house and were the closest Rouët could get to reviving the sensibility of the man. The fourth person in the team was Yves Mathieu-Saint-Laurent, aged twenty-one.

It is perhaps hard now to recapture the shock at the idea that a 21-year-old was going to be the couturier of France's richest and most prestigious couture house. Fashion has since become a youth industry, but back in the 1950s haute couture was designed by people called Madame, Monsieur or Mademoiselle, in the over-fifty age bracket and catering to a similar clientele. And here was this young man, six foot two and jangling with nerves, looking every inch the first violinist in the school orchestra, being asked to design haute couture for the world's biggest couture house.

If there was one person not surprised by the appointment it was his doting mother. Shortly before his death, Dior told Yves that he wished to see his mother. Lucienne turned up to the couture house to meet the couturier in a fluster of powder and rouge and, according to her memory during their brief encounter, Dior named Yves as his successor.

In December 1957 Saint Laurent returned home to his family in Oran, where he took to his bedroom and sketched a frenzy of ideas and dresses. 'I was in a state of complete euphoria preparing that collection. I knew I was going to become famous,' he later said. After three weeks he flew back to Paris. 'He showed us his sketches; he had a whole suitcase full of sketches,' remembers Anne-Marie Muñoz. 'There was the Trapèze shape, there was lace, there were pleats. He had tried everything, the way you do at that age. After, it was the ladies who made the choice of which sketches were to be made up into the outfits for the show.' From now on, twice a year, Yves would hide himself away and sketch one thousand drawings in the space of two frenzied weeks. It was a crazy pace for a young man of his age to work at. From the abundance of these ideas, there would emerge two hundred outfits for the collection.

For this first collection Mesdames Zehnacker, Carré and Bricard performed major editing on Yves' young exuberance, whittling down the suitcase of sketches he brought back from Oran to 178 outfits and choosing the one silhouette that was to be the message for the fashion season.

On 30 January 1958 Yves Saint Laurent, as he was now known having dropped the Mathieu, showed his first collection in the dove-grey salons of the house of Dior. 'Trapèze' was the name he gave to his new silhouette of dresses that fitted at the breast and then flared out, studiously ignoring the waistline, to end below the knee. By acting as if the waist didn't exist, in a couture house that had built its fortune on the eroticisation of the New Look waist, Yves Saint Laurent threw down a gauntlet to the couture world. Most importantly, it was a younger look than the house of Dior had shown in years and both customers and press were transfixed by what they called 'the little-girl dresses'. The Trapèze was still a classic couture silhouette but was made radical by the way Saint Laurent had removed much of the famous Dior body-padding and construction for the very first time. In previous years a Dior dress could practically stand up on its own, it had so much whale-boning and corseting inside contrived to reshape and enhance the silhouette of the Dior lady; added to that was the weight of the lining and the thickness of the fabric and padding, which made the dress into a kind of sculpture. Yves made the clothes free-flowing and gave them youth and spirit by literally lightening them up and shortening the hemline.

And yet the collection still followed in the Dior tradition of a new and changing silhouette for each season, a design stipulation that Christian Dior had implemented with huge success initially, creating excitement and hype around the unveiling of each season's collection. It was a fashion tactic that incensed the other couture houses, not least Chanel, who was infuriated by what she perceived as needless manipulation of hemlines. Ultimately it became a curse for Dior himself, who was terrorised by the pressure and constraint of creating a new look each season.

At the end of the three-hour presentation as the last mannequin left the salon, Yves Saint Laurent stepped out to a standing ovation. There was sobbing, a shrill burst of both grief and euphoria as the audience was transported by the energy of youth and beauty. 'I never saw a better Dior collection,' wrote *New York Herald Tribune* editor Eugenia Sheppard in the following day's newspaper. 'Everybody was crying. It was the emotional fashion binge of all time.' The outpouring was as much a celebration of Yves Saint Laurent's talent as of high-finance relief. In the weeks since Dior's death there had been considerable speculation about the fate of the house and Dior licensees had lobbied hard for Boussac to appoint a successor and not to close Dior. 'Everybody in Paris will sleep better for the success of the House of Dior,' wrote Sheppard.

It was as if the wellspring of sentimental affection that had surrounded Christian Dior was transferred in one swift and painless transfusion to Yves Saint Laurent – to stay with him for ever. But with the affection came the expectation too. Saint Laurent was now the youngest couturier in the world and heir to the kingdom of Dior. How strange, how vertiginous to be aged twenty-one and watch your dreams already rushing to fulfilment, dreams that you are still dreaming.

Yves Saint Laurent walked from the salon up to the second floor and out on to the wrought-iron balcony on the corner of Avenue Montaigne, the same balcony from which Dior used to take his bows. The cameras captured the image of triumphant couturier and applauding crowd below. John Fairchild, Paris bureau chief of *Women's Wear Daily* at the time, was there for the balcony scene and questioned whether it was indeed spontaneous or rather, as he suspected, a clever trick by the Dior press officer who ordered the Dior seamstresses to appear and cheer below on the street. But it only takes one silent image to make a fashion myth and it has remained in the collective memory as the moment of Yves Saint Laurent's coronation in Paris.

'Yves Saint Laurent – *le nouvel enfant triste*,' trumpeted the next day's headline in *L'Express*, hailing Saint Laurent as the 'new sad child', that peculiarly French perception of 1950s youth. Below the story read: 'Three hundred people plus several television cameras rushed to the corner where Yves Saint Laurent had just emerged from the models' *cabine* and one felt sure this young man, only just made famous, would die of suffocation – not least because he doesn't look at all solid. He is tall, thin, a little stooped, short-sighted with large, melancholy, periwinkle-blue eyes staring out from his kind and skinny face. It is the skinny face of a well-brought up child who must so often have said, "No, I swear *Maman*, really I am not hungry."'

In public situations Yves was so introverted and contorted by his timidity that it was crippling not only for him, but also for the person trying to communicate with him. Years later Yves described himself during the Dior years as looking like a 'studious schoolboy'. Around the world the newspaper journalists and radio commentators seized upon the same vocabulary of childlike defencelessness: 'narrow-shouldered, a sad look behind huge glasses', 'sickly child', 'too serious', 'shy and stooped', 'skinny', 'a faun in the forest'. The image conjured up of Yves Saint Laurent was from the very beginning that of victim in victory, of a youth sacrificed for fashion. This would be the highly emotive vernacular that would stay with him and describe him throughout his career; fragile and vulnerable was how the world perceived him. Few people saw the incandescent ambition and violent creativity that was also Yves Saint Laurent.

One man at least sensed Saint Laurent's intensity: Bernard Buffet, who at that time in France was regarded as the most brilliant young painter of his generation and another *enfant triste*. He was there at the Trapèze collection in 1958 and later the same year he sketched the young couturier. Yves Saint Laurent loved Buffet's drawing; he kept it in his bedroom for many years and later it hung on the wall behind his desk

in his studio at Avenue Marceau, where it still hangs today. Buffet drew
a Saint Laurent on the cusp of manhood, that moment in life when the
face is still a battle of noses and chins, before all the features accept their
role and agree to fit. Buffet captured the tapered fragility of Yves that
everyone was struck by. But he also saw beyond it. He saw the vast
plain of a forehead, the monumental and wilful chin, the etched lines
of neurosis and the Saint Laurent eyes, at once seeking glory, observing
and filtering reality, shuttering his inner self from the outside world.

Bernard Buffet's portrait of the young Yves Saint Laurent.

Chapter 2

1958–66

The extraordinary high of his first acknowledged success excited every desire Yves Saint Laurent possessed for recognition. 'I began uniquely for fame,' he would admit ten years later. 'Fame is rather flattering . . . and this is a trade that's essentially [built] on that.'

Several days after the presentation of his first Dior collection, society hostess Marie-Louise Bousquet threw a dinner at a restaurant in honour of the new star and there Yves met with his destiny – Pierre Bergé, short and bristling and lethal. Bergé was twenty-seven at the time and the lover and business manager of Bernard Buffet.

He was already an ambitious operator around town; he had been there at Yves' Trapèze show at Dior and he had attended Dior's funeral, as had Yves. At dinner Saint Laurent and Bergé were seated opposite each other, Bergé vibrating with energy, scintillating in his conversational thrust and parry before the mute and watchful Saint Laurent.

Bergé was a man of modest beginnings intent on an extraordinary life. He was born on 14 November 1930 in Saint-Pierre d'Oléron, which is the main town of the small Ile d'Oléron, located off the west coast of France in the Charente. He was the eldest of two boys and his mother worked as a schoolteacher, his father as a tax inspector.

The family moved to Lisieux in Normandy and Pierre attended the local school, where his mother taught. He was bright, learned to read early, grasped things straight away and then set about disrupting the rest of the class by being loud and obnoxious. He jumped a class and was

aged six among seven- or eight-year-olds, who, as his mother remembered over fifty years later, 'were not exactly bright sparks as they were
the children of alcoholics'. He became such a distraction to the others
that when he was in his mother's class she made him sit up at the front,
by her side.

He read Victor Hugo's *Les Misérables* at the age of eight or nine,
which perhaps provided inspiration for the life he was to lead. 'He never
bent to school discipline. Never. He was not a worker. He was very
unstable, very restless. He was happy with getting by,' recounts his
mother. He had not yet harnessed his energy, but the famous Bergé
temper was already much in evidence. When Pierre was a pupil at *lycée*,
aged seventeen, a teacher slapped him. He was so livid that he hung
out by the school gates waiting for the teacher the next day, having
forewarned all his friends to be there to witness the action. As the
teacher rode out on his bike, Pierre grabbed the bicycle and slapped
the man twice about his face. The idea of a pupil hitting his teacher in
1947 France is almost inconceivable, in a country where unquestioning
obedience before the teacher was, and still is, the rule.

He was, concludes his mother, 'lazy and undecided at school', but
not so in adult life. At the age of seventeen he left home and La Rochelle,
where his father had been posted. 'I left the provinces to come to Paris
and find freedom,' he says fifty-eight years later. He was already fascinated by the celebrities of the Parisian *monde* and most of all by its
artistes. As a teenager he wrote fan letters to Jean Giono and André
Gide.

'I came to Paris in order to stop writing to people and to start
meeting people,' says Bergé. 'Sometimes it worked, sometimes it didn't,
that's another story. But that was my ambition: to be close to the *faiseurs
de feux* or fire-makers, to watch, to be a witness and above all not to
be sitting on the verge when there was a road being forged ahead.'

He had ideas of a career in journalism, worked briefly for writer
Maurice Rostand, who was son of Edmond Rostand, author of *Cyrano
de Bergerac*, and famously met with Gary Davis, an American ex-bomber
pilot turned ardent pacifist who was in Paris publicising his Citizens of
the World movement. Bergé joined the movement and set up a newspaper called *La Patrie Mondiale* to write about the cause in 1949, although
it was to close after two issues due to lack of funds.

Bergé was above all a realist and when the journalism did not work out, he turned to second-hand book dealing to make his way, which in those days in Paris was also an effective way of meeting people. He was aged eighteen when he met the artist Bernard Buffet by chance in a bar in Saint Germain and they embarked on a heady eight-year affair. Bergé, as he himself admits, did not know much about art. He was young, up from the provinces and convinced that Buffet was the creative genius he had come to Paris to find. He thought, as he has often said, that he had met his Rimbaud.

And so he devoted the next eight years to selling the man and his art. Victoire remembers an opening night for an exhibition of paintings by Buffet in 1954, where she watched fascinated and somewhat appalled as a terrier-like man in an ill-fitting suit dragged Bernard Buffet round the room by his jacket arm, propelling him from one potential client to the next with the words, 'Now, Bernard, you must meet Madame so and so.' It was Bergé, as she later found out.

Recalling these years in his memoirs, Bergé remembers, 'Life revolved around Bernard's work.' It was to be the story of Pierre Bergé's life, revolving about and exalting a creative talent that was not his own. And Bergé was ready to do that, to be the kingmaker but with the essential quid pro quo that he had to believe in the man's talent.

Over the years Bergé's high expectations and zealous faith in Buffet turned to disillusion and resentment as the artist fell from the ranks of the avant-garde. He became a celebrity painter, repeating his signature style and characters until his paintings became hackneyed and their value – financial and artistic – plummeted. 'I had been an accomplice, probably guilty,' writes Bergé in his memoirs, remembering his role in Buffet's meteoric rise. 'I had believed so much in his genius.'

It was a strange and bilious break-up and the exact circumstances are muddied. Buffet was drinking; perhaps Bergé was all too aware of Buffet's falling star. Buffet announced his surprise engagement to Annabelle Schwob de Lur, a black-haired, bohemian model, whom he would marry in 1958. And Pierre and Yves collided in an intense love affair.

From the start Pierre Bergé was mesmerised by Saint Laurent. 'I saw in him someone with an immense talent,' says Bergé of that first encounter. 'He is an extremely mysterious individual, very introverted and with many different facets and secrets. I understood all that – the talent and the enigma – very quickly.' But Pierre was also intrigued by Yves' acutely strung otherness and many years later he would remember Yves during that time as 'a strange, shy boy. He wore very tight jackets as if he was trying to keep himself buttoned up against the world – he reminded me of a clergyman, very serious, very nervous.'

And Yves, what attracted him to Pierre Bergé? Was it the compelling sexual force of the man or the powerful mind? Or did Yves Saint Laurent see before him the man who would make him king? There was six years' difference in age between them and Bergé entered Yves' life with an already established reputation as both rainmaker and dominator in the Parisian *monde*. 'Everything I didn't have, he had,' said Yves forty-three years later to explain Bergé's appeal. 'His strength meant I could rest on him when I was out of breath.'

Bergé's ruthless potency was a source of some considerable fascina-tion among men in Paris. In August 1959 journalist and writer Matthieu Galey had a brief summer liaison with Bergé that he wrote about in a series of revealing entries in his diary, which was later published. It was a time when the affair with Saint Laurent was new and the break-up with Buffet was still causing waves throughout Paris. 'This quarrel has now spilled out into the newspapers, publicity which is mostly unpleasant,' writes Galey of Bergé and Buffet's fall-out. 'Pierre couldn't care less, or even rejoices in it, keeping business and sentiment separate. It's good for business, this row . . . But if Pierre has chosen to erase the friend from the hard years from his life, the works of art remain: the apart-ment on the Rue Saint-Louis-en-l'Ile is a veritable Buffet museum. Most of the canvases, the most beautiful, the earliest, bleak, miserable, enraged, accusing, are dedicated to him by name.' Galey records how the paintings are everywhere – on the walls, in the cupboards, in the corridors, in the hall – and that their omnipresence does not seem to bother Bergé in the slightest. Galey wonders aloud: 'Is this the insensi-tivity of a brute, or a magnanimity that is greater than all bust-ups? Hard to say. Pierre is a force, a torrent, a bull. Nothing holds out against him. Perhaps not even rancour.'

Galey did not hold out against Bergé and the following entries allude to their affair and Galey's realisation that he is just 'an amusing digres-sion in his [Bergé's] busy summer'. By September the heat of the affair has passed and Galey has succeeded in breaking the spell. He can breathe again. 'As for Pierre, he has renounced his Pygmalion role for me, and the little mouse is no longer hypnotised by the terrible cobra *dominateur*.' The diary entries are important for what they reveal about Pierre Bergé's powers of enthrallment, but also his overwhelming impulse to direct the talent of other men.

Saint Laurent designed six collections for the house of Dior, but his tenure there was never easy. Madame Raymonde Zehnacker, Dior's confidante and heir, fought to perpetuate her influence in the house and over the young designer. She would shout and bully Yves and he took to hiding from her in the little office behind the studio where Dior used to take his naps. When it came to design, however, Yves imposed his own will. His profound conviction in his own talent was remarked upon early in his career. André Levasseur remembers even before Saint Laurent got the big job in the days when he was still an assistant: 'He was already very assured of his own talent. I remember he showed me some theatre-costume drawings he had done and asked what I thought of them, and I looked at them and said, "You'd be better off making them less Bérard in style," and he replied, "But no, I don't agree with you at all." He already had a high opinion of what he was meant to do.' Edmonde Charles-Roux recalls that 'he never listened to any advice you might give him, he did what he wanted to – but in life he was very vulnerable.' A year into his job at Dior Yves Saint Laurent took the winter collection and sixteen mannequins to England for a society fashion show held at Blenheim Palace in the presence of Princess Margaret. Aged twenty-two, Saint Laurent might have been a little intimidated or at least in awe of the English royalty, but not a bit of it. When asked by a journalist what he thought of Princess Margaret he remarked that she was charming, but that 'her dress was too short'.

His will was never more evident than in his final collection for the house of Dior, the so-called Beat collection of July 1960, in which Yves was inspired by Juliette Gréco and the beatnik scene of Saint Germain. It was the strongest design statement of his career so far, with younger looks than usual in the collection, including a short alligator-skin jacket with fur trim and abbreviated sleeves which had a sporty cut to it, and a long black voluminous coat, called mischievously 'le Blouson Noir', the name given to young suburban hoodlums in the late 1950s. Not all the silhouettes looked right: Victoire wore a dress by the name of Comédie

Française with a huge balloon skirt in black silk faille. There was a mass of black in the collection, which, combined with its existentialist pose and the dynamic cut of the clothes, all came as a shock to both the house of Dior and its clients.

Although according to the house archives the collection was a commercial success, it was badly received by the Dior management, who deemed it too radical for their clientele. Dior's owner, Marcel Boussac, was not amused by it or its blouson-noir overtones. Saint Laurent's youth and fragility had always been a cause for concern in the house even when Dior was alive. In 1957, Monsieur Dior had contacted Marc Bohan, then a 31-year-old couturier at the house of Jean Patou whose career Dior had been following closely, to offer him a job in the studio. In June of that year Bohan had signed a contract with Dior. 'Yves Saint Laurent was already his assistant,' remembers Bohan, 'but he was, however, young and Dior wanted someone else as well. Dior was feeling worn and he wanted someone stronger and with experience, particularly for the trips to New York and England.'

Christian Dior died the day Marc Bohan was due to take up his post at the house and then weeks later Yves was given the job as designer. But, interestingly, even as Dior management announced Yves Saint Laurent as Dior's successor, they still kept Bohan under contract in secret, as a back-up plan should things not work out with Yves. They didn't know what to do with Bohan so they sent him off on an expenses-paid trip to New York in February 1958, and when he returned at the end of July he was sent to London to design the Dior ready-to-wear.

For a still extremely young man Yves bore enormous responsibilities, including being head of a staff of fourteen hundred people and directing the work of twenty-four different couture ateliers. Dior was an industry with worldwide ambitions. It was not only Yves' youth, fragility and beatnik sensibility that worried the Dior powers; there was, according to some who worked at the house at the time, another cause for concern: Pierre Bergé. He was by now a constant presence in the house of Dior, to be seen chatting up Madame Luling in the press office and hanging out in the salon, although interestingly never present in the studio. He was making demands for Yves, such as a chauffeur-driven car. 'Jacques Rouët was scared of him,' says a Dior employee of the time. 'He took a dim view of Bergé's involvement in the house, his influence on Yves, and in particular feared that he might threaten his own position.'

By this time the euphemistically named 'events' of Algeria had escalated into a terrifying and fatal civil war; indeed Yves could no longer return to his family in Oran because of the danger. The struggle for independence had begun in 1954 when the National Liberation Front (or FLN) mounted an insurrection and France responded with troops and a policy of no compromise. The French government was determined to maintain the unity of the republic, of which they considered Algeria a part, and their refusal to cede was further strengthened by the fact that they had just given up Indo-China, Tunisia and Morocco. Algeria had to be kept at any price.

Over the next seven years the French used censorship, highly controversial methods of brutality and paratroopers to further their cause. They called up national-service youth to fight as well as professional soldiers, which was a hugely unpopular decision. It was a savage and tragic war. By 1959 De Gaulle, newly re-elected as president, had begun leading France towards accepting an independent Algeria, much to the bitter rage and disbelief of the *pieds-noirs*, who regarded Algeria as their homeland and had been responsible for precipitating the return of De Gaulle. They viewed his policy of self-determination for Algeria as treachery and they formed their own Secret Army Organisation (or OAS) to continue the fight for what they felt was rightfully theirs.

Yves Saint Laurent, aged twenty-four and himself a *pied-noir*, was of the age of conscription. The house of Dior had already manoeuvred once to avoid his first calling-up, but this time Dior allowed Saint Laurent's conscription to go ahead. Was it their way of easing the designer out of the main job? By this stage in the war even those who had already done their national service were being recalled and conscription was hard to avoid, as Edmonde Charles-Roux makes clear. 'It wasn't enough to say, "Ah, but he makes lovely dresses so he can stay here." It needed Monsieur Boussac to say that he needed Saint Laurent. They would have perhaps let him off if he had been deemed necessary to French industry,' she speculates. 'It needed someone highly placed to say, "Listen, this boy is obviously a homosexual, he is not physically capable of being a soldier and if you push him he will fall." But they did not do that.'

Instead Yves Saint Laurent reported for military duties on 1 September 1960, in the 308th week of war in Algeria. He didn't make it beyond the training camp. He broke down and was taken to the Bégin military hospital suffering from mental collapse. He was then transferred to the Val-de-Grâce, the military hospital in the south of Paris, where he stayed until 14 November 1960, when he was released from hospital and all military duties.

It was while Yves was in hospital in September 1960 that it was made known that he would not be returning to Paris as head designer at Dior. Marc Bohan remembers dining with Edmonde Charles-Roux, who by this time was editor-in-chief of French *Vogue*, at Brasserie Lipp that September. Charles-Roux told Bohan that Yves Saint Laurent had been dropped and that the house of Dior was going to hire him as designer.

Bohan, having spent the last two years designing ready-to-wear for Dior in London, had in fact recently resigned from the house to join Revillon. He met almost immediately with Boussac in order to negotiate the contract and he took up position as head designer of the house of Dior by the middle of October 1960. Meanwhile Dior offered Yves the inferior post of designing the Dior ready-to-wear in London. It was an impossible humiliation and one that Yves refused to accept.

Many years later Saint Laurent would say that conscription conjured up for him all the terror and anxieties he had known at school. 'It was a terrible experience. For me it was like going back to school. I said that I was suffering from nervous depression and so they sent me to hospital,' remembered Yves in 1991. There was something inevitable about Yves' breakdown. There was the psychological impossibility of fighting as a *pied-noir* against his homeland of Algeria, plus the physical impossibility of him fighting at all, as his sister Brigitte points out: 'Yves was puny, weedy; he was not cut out to join the army. If I put myself in Yves' position and this is me speaking, not my brother, I see Yves, he leaves Algeria, overnight he has this huge success, then there is the war in Algeria – and you must remember Yves loved Algeria, he loved coming home, all that – and then there was his homosexuality that played a part too. He was apparently treated in an atrocious way by the Val-de-Grâce, far too vigorously. It was shameful, he had electric-shock treatment and it must have shattered him. And at the time we couldn't come to see him – I was too young and my parents couldn't leave Oran because of the war.'

There have been repeated accusations by Bergé and Saint Laurent over the years that Yves was maltreated at the Val-de-Grâce military hospital. Thirty-one years later, in an interview with *Le Figaro* in 1991, Saint Laurent conjured up memories of his time there in strange images that appeared to merge fact with surreal fantasy: 'It was horrifying. They wanted to stop me from getting out and so they gave me tranquillisers to drug me. I was in a room all alone with people coming in and out. Mad people. Really mad people. Some of them caressed me, but I didn't let them take advantage. Others were screaming for no reason. There was everything there to cause you anguish. In two and half months, I only went to the loo once I was so frightened. At the end I must have weighed thirty-five kilos and I had trouble with my brain. The doctor who was treating me told me that he had administered the most powerful dose of tranquillisers that you can give someone. He [the doctor] said to me then: "You will be back, you'll see."'

The memory of treatment at Val-de-Grâce has tended to obscure the devastating effect that Dior's abandonment and Yves' dramatic fall from the heights of fashion must also have had on him. 'Pierre placed so much importance on the Val-de-Grâce episode,' says Victoire, 'but I lived through it with them and the real reason was that Yves had been at the pinnacle, the *petit prince* at the house of Dior, and then all of a sudden he was at the Val-de-Grâce and dropped by Dior and pouff, no one cared about him any more. That is hard for someone so young to bear.'

It is hard to decipher if this was the start of Yves' mental illness, which would become increasingly pronounced in later years, or was rather the first momentous manifestation of an already existing condition. 'I think one has to be very wary of what one says about this subject,' says Charles-Roux. 'No one among us knows what Yves would have been like without this treatment; perhaps he was already a depressive deep down. It's very easy to say it was the Val-de-Grâce that treated him too force-fully, but perhaps he would have been like that anyway without this accident.'

Another old friend, Anne-Marie Muñoz, looks back over the years of Yves' mental tribulations: 'Although I don't think the stay at Val-de-Grâce can have helped things, I think those moments were extremely difficult for him . . .' She trails off before restarting. 'But deep down I have never known him any different. It can be worse, it can be less good, then it can be easy, but there was never one defining moment. He was born that way. Pierre Bergé says he was born with a nervous breakdown and it is true he was, but he was also born with incredible good fortune.'

Yves' mental fragility was alluded to constantly within the fashion press over the ensuing years, but always within a cloud of euphemism. There were references to Yves being found shaking alone in his office or being sickly and unwell, and the American Press talked openly of Yves using tranquillisers during a trip to New York in the 1960s. But it was not until 1976 that Yves' mental condition overflowed in public again.

Yves was forbidden visitors while he was at the hospital of Val-de-Grâce and the only person who succeeded in flouting the ban and gaining access to him was Pierre Bergé, who visited Yves every week and fought to get him out. It was the start of Bergé's fight both to protect Yves and to control access to him, a compulsion which was to last a lifetime.

From 1960 and his exit from the Val-de-Grâce, Pierre directed what was known and not known about Yves Saint Laurent and who should see and who should not see Yves Saint Laurent. He set about shaping and broadcasting information about him, choosing what and where and to whom it should be communicated. He decided what the public should and should not know. From the start he behaved like some sort of zealous eighteenth-century pamphleteer. It was Pierre who ensured that each and every public episode in Saint Laurent's life became a fact, to be recorded, celebrated, annotated and, most importantly, disseminated.

After the disappointment of Buffet, Pierre decided that here was true genius and that he, Pierre, was going to make Yves Saint Laurent. 'That is the great talent of Pierre,' says François Catroux, who by this time was in Paris, making a name for himself as a fashionable interior decorator. 'He has always known how to exploit the talent of others. He knew he wasn't mistaken with Saint Laurent, that he had fallen upon someone who was exceptional within the fashion world, and so from this moment on he fought to disassociate Yves completely from the rest of the profession. He didn't want Yves to be just a colleague among others. He always, always said there is Yves Saint Laurent and then there are the other designers who come a long way after. And so he constructed this kind of personality of Yves Saint Laurent, rather than leaving him to be merely a talented couturier. Pierre wanted to make an artist of him. He wanted to put him up there on a plane with the great artists and that has been his guiding role from the beginning.'

Yves Saint Laurent's every encounter was predestined, every event imbued with mystical significance, and every collection was proclaimed a first – 'the first trousers', 'the first *Smoking*', 'the first transparency', 'the first *Saharienne*' – as Pierre staked Saint Laurent's claim in fashion history. 'The great turning-point in fashion of the entire world was in 1966, because in 1966 Yves invented ready-to-wear!' exclaims Pierre today, which is an absolute distortion of reality – couturiers had been selling their own *prêt-à-porter* since 1950 – but he delivers the statement with such aplomb and conviction that one could for a minute believe him.

Later in Yves' career when there were no more firsts, they would be succeeded in the Saint Laurent official history by the anniversaries: twenty-five years of creation celebrated at the Costume Institute at the Metropolitan Museum of Art; thirty years of the house of Saint Laurent at the Opéra; the World Cup retrospective fashion show; Yves' retirement on the fortieth anniversary of the opening of the Saint Laurent house and the retrospective show at the Centre Pompidou. If Saint Laurent supplied the design genius, it was Bergé who provided the rhetoric.

Even when reduced to solitary confinement, Yves Saint Laurent was planning the victorious comeback. 'There is no other solution; we have to open a couture house,' he told Pierre, while on his back and under sedation at the Val-de-Grâce. When Saint Laurent was released from hospital Bergé flew into battle against the considerable might of the house of Dior, suing for breach of contract and winning the case.

Throughout the following year of recovery, Saint Laurent and Pierre Bergé lived in Pierre's apartment on the Ile Saint Louis. In the summer Bergé rented a *péniche* or houseboat that was moored on the Seine and Pierre, Yves and Victoire hung out together throughout July in a state of magnetic attraction and repulsion. Victoire had married Roger

Thérond, editor of *Paris Match*, in April 1958, but he was caught up in running a magazine and so Victoire sought amusement with her old friends. They spent hot afternoons on deck playing canasta; sometimes Karl would turn up and join them. 'We did everything to distract Yves,' says Victoire. 'Sometimes he would have these intense furies. He would wrap a towel tight round his head and shout, "See, I've got no hair left!" There was this incredible anger against those who had abandoned him. He was like a child with a profound sense of disillusion, a feeling of having been terribly wronged and not knowing how to exteriorise that.'

All that year Saint Laurent was out of work and desperate. He designed costumes for his new friend, the cabaret dancer Zizi Jeanmaire, and a suit for Victoire, which were made up by Victoire's mother, who was a couturière. Both times Victoire persuaded her husband to photograph and publish the outfits in *Paris Match* and keep Yves' name in the public eye.

Pierre was lunching, selling off paintings from his collection, trying to find a backer and refusing to give in. He had rented two modest rooms on the Rue la Boétie as their business premises and Victoire spent her days there in her new dual role of mannequin and *directrice de couture*, beside a telephone that never rang, trying to keep Yves on track. She tried to cheer him up with optimistic assurances of future success, staff and couture dreams, but Yves broke down distraught, crying, 'No, we haven't got anybody, I know it. Pierre will never do it. I am done for, do you hear me? I'm finished!'

Pierre, however, was far from finished. He went forth and found a backer in self-made millionaire Jesse Mack Robinson from Atlanta. Together with his backing of $700,000 and the 680,000-franc damages Yves won from Dior, they opened the house of Yves Saint Laurent on 4 December 1961, moving to other temporary premises. Again it was Victoire who persuaded her husband to publish now-famous photographs of her and Yves preparing the collection at the new couture house, which in reality was just two unfurnished rooms in an attic roof. Taken from outside the office late at night, one of the photographs shows Yves and Victoire in their separate offices. Each figure is framed by a window and the rest of the picture is in darkness, although you can just make out the shutters on the façade of the building. Both Yves and Victoire are lit by identical lamps hanging above their heads. Victoire is seated at a desk, phone to her ear, cigarette in hand, while Yves stands in the next-door office, posing with bolts of fabric on his table. Beyond are bare white walls. The starkness of the setting and the dramatic composition of the photograph express the huge pressure Yves was under to pull the rabbit out of the hat with this collection. It would be all or nothing. They finally moved to the permanent premises of an *hôtel particulier* at 30, Rue Spontini in the sixteenth *arrondissement* the night before the first show.

The next morning was a stampede of expectation. It had been over a year and a half since Yves had shown a collection, and the show took place in the small salon of the couture house, so the guest list was inevitably restricted. Victoire opened the show, walking down the staircase in a pink and green open check wool suit. It set the tone for what was mostly a predictably couture show of sheer-stockinged legs and arms trapped in long satin gloves, Raj coats in silk brocade clasped with a pearl brooch or a dainty cocktail dress with a garland of silk flowers dancing round the hem. But there was one outfit that stood out and was to become an iconic image in the history of fashion: a navy-blue pea-coat, wide white pants and babouche flat slippers worn by Victoire. It was this 'caban' or pea-coat in thick felted wool with fat brass buttons, the sort of jacket worn by sailors to keep the Atlantic gales out, which expressed the modernity and force Yves Saint Laurent would bring to fashion.

At the end of the show Yves' clients and friends erupted in loyal ecstasy, although the daily newspapers were not so effusive. There was a sense of anticlimax, summed up by Patricia Peterson of the *New York Times* when she wrote: 'Everyone wanted this young man to have a staggering success that would make fashion history. It is hard to live up to such high expectations and Saint Laurent, although he produced a very good collection, did not say anything new.'

Yves was not yet ready to break free from the hold that both the late Christian Dior and haute couture still had on him. Although his talent always set him apart, Yves was still a product of his education and considered himself heir to Monsieur Dior. He even kept the couture cane that Dior had used. When Yves had entered the house of Dior in 1955, haute couture was still a world of patrician beauty. It deified a certain posture: static, cream-shouldered, jutting hips, cigarette poised between lipstick and eternity. The couture client was not a woman, but a lady – preferably titled and always chauffeur-driven. She came seeking the grandeur and elegance appropriate to her social status and age. At Dior, Saint Laurent had learned to conjure up mighty dresses for this gracious few, to dictate the changing hemlines and silhouettes that inspired the rest of the fashion industry.

It is true that Yves felt the influence from beyond the couture salon early in his career and much has been made of the 1960 Beat collection, which is frequently cited as an example of his interest in street culture. Yves, like all great designers, sensed the desires and vibrations of change in the air. But nevertheless he was still Monsieur Saint Laurent and he looked out on the street in the same manner as Mademoiselle Chanel – from the lofty heights of the wrought-iron balustrade of a couture house. They both appropriated symbols and clothes from other worlds, which were then digested, transformed and rendered chic to fit the elegant parameters of couture. Saint Laurent's 1960 black alligator jacket had a youthful spirit, but it was worn with pert fur hat, mink trim and kid gloves, and by a millionaire industrialist's wife, not some groovy beatnik hanging out in Saint Germain.

There were rules and codes of elegance and conduct within the couture religion and Saint Laurent was still a staunch believer. In 1963 Yves was sitting at a lunch in the country with the Baroness de Turckheim when Victoire turned up late. By this time their friendship had soured into bitterness and reproach. Victoire felt that Pierre was jealous of her friendship with Yves and that he was doing his utmost to push her away and distort the friendship. There are many who claim that over the years Bergé has sought to distance them from Saint Laurent. But perhaps Victoire wanted to break free herself. She was now twenty-eight, married, and had taken on a level of autonomy that was not conducive to her role as Yves' muse.

That day Victoire stepped out of her red Alfa Romeo with long auburn hair hanging loose around her shoulders. She was not wearing a chignon and, even worse, she was wearing another model's suit from the couture collection. At the beginning of each fashion season every house mannequin was assigned her own outfits to model and Victoire had helped herself to someone else's suit. In couture terms this was rather like using someone else's toothbrush. On her feet were a pair of her own boots, rather than the correct Saint Laurent co-ordinating shoes intended for the outfit. She was flouting every couture-house convention and Yves was white with rage.

As they sat down to lunch a near-hysterical Yves confronted Victoire: 'But that is not your suit! You cannot do that! You should never have done that! The suit is not the right proportion. And your hair worn loose like that, *quel horreur*, it's a vegetable patch.' It was the last straw between Victoire and Yves. The muse had rebelled: she wanted to be provocative and free; the couturier could only visualise her gloved, impeccable and ideal. 'And I thought to myself, that's it, it's over,' remembers Victoire. 'You are a couple of old men, you go worry about your baroness. I've had enough.'

Worrying about baronesses was indeed a preoccupation for both Pierre and Yves. During the 1950s Bergé had got himself on to the inside track of the homosexual literary scene, first as fan, then as friend to Jean Cocteau and Jean Giono. Now he and Yves were conquering new horizons. They cultivated the appropriate society connections to make themselves a feature of the salons of the Faubourg Saint-Germain.

Together they made for a seductive duo. Yves, the new darling of haute couture, such finesse and lovely artistic fingers, those strange opaque blue eyes and his ability to make you look gorgeous in his little black dresses. And Pierre? He was not handsome – too much nose and too little leg – but he had chutzpah and a domineering, dockside charm which, combined with his cultivated conversation and ability to quote liberally from Aragon, kept the *faubourg* thrilled. 'He had this way of making you feel you were the most important person in the room,' remembers Victoire. 'He would sort of half close his eyes as he listened to you as if you were fascinating. He had unbelievable charm.'

The key baroness they were worrying about – indeed that all of Paris was worrying about – was Marie-Hélène de Rothschild, the acknowledged queen of Paris. She had great style, bouffant-blonde charisma and Rothschild wealth, and she ordered a dress from Yves' very first collection. Soon Yves and Pierre were accompanying Marie-Hélène to the Prix de l'Arc at Longchamps to watch her husband's horses win. Hélène Rochas, society beauty and widow of the Rochas fashion house, was also a loyal and early client. Charlotte Aillaud was another important social link in their lives. Wife of architect Emile Aillaud, sister to singer Juliette Gréco, Charlotte Aillaud was a refined Rive Gauche hostess. She had a chic salon where she mixed writers, actors and Paloma Picasso, serving them all chili after the theatre. She met Yves and Pierre at a dinner in the early 1960s and was enchanted by them both, becoming a lifelong friend and client. 'I was completely seduced by Pierre, by his memory, the sense of friendship, the generosity, the enthusiasm, and at the same time his raw force and his unpredictability. And Yves,' says Aillaud, 'Yves then was simply charm personified. You could not resist him.'

It seemed no one could resist Yves. The press fell upon his every collection, delighted to have found a successor to the seventy-some-thing-year-old generation of Balenciaga and Chanel, but more signifi-cantly delighted to have found the Parisian rival to London's growing phenomenon of youthful fashion stars such as Mary Quant and Ossie Clark. He did tweedy Robin Hood suits with shorts that he put with brown-suede thigh boots; he made smock tops and headscarves, then supremely elegant black layered cocktail dresses.

The Americans loved him because he could be relied upon to come up with a new line, a new thought every season that they then copied and sold in the garment district by the thousands under the heading 'fresh from Paris'. The first half of the 1960s was still a period when manufacturers and department-store buyers paid a fee each season to see the couture shows in order to buy clothes and, most importantly, to get the right to copy them. A plane left from Paris every season loaded up with couture outfits, which were then pulled apart on arrival and copied seam for seam on 7th Avenue.

'In those days everybody, press and manufacturers, were all looking for one look: the new look, the maxi, the midi,' says John Fairchild, who was then Paris bureau chief of *Women's Wear Daily*. These were the last years of a monolithic message in fashion, when the couturier still dictated the hemline for the season and – more significantly – women still obeyed. Yves was brilliant at providing the new look. 'When you think about it, he was it!' says Fairchild. 'He was so damn good and there were very few people doing modern then.' André Courrèges was radically modern when he gave Paris couture the miniskirt in 1961 and then followed that three years later with his futuristic fashion style of geometric-cut silver suits and bright white trousers worn with white flat boots that looked like they were clothes to launch a terribly chic space rocket. But although Courrèges really rocked the fashion world for a finite period in the 1960s, Yves offered something longer-lasting and more subtle in his new definition of women's style. 'The word seduction has replaced the word elegance in fashion,' he said. 'I don't like trousers when they are worn as a form of protest, that's to say, "I'm the equal of man", the George Sand, suffragette kind of way. I think quite the opposite. In wearing trousers a woman can develop the maximum of her femininity in the fight against man.'

Ironically, it was just as Yves experienced phenomenal fashion success with his own house that his family lost their home. On 3 July 1962, following a referendum, Algerian independence was declared. In the unbridled violence that ensued, 1,500 *pieds-noirs* were killed in Oran by ALN troops. Yves' father escaped from his office, driving his Cadillac through the mob to rejoin his wife and daughters at their seaside villa in Trouville; there was no choice but to leave Algeria, along with the 120,000 other settlers who fled the country in the months that followed. 'It was, as they say, the suitcase or the coffin,' says Yves' sister Brigitte Bastian.

The daughters, Michèle and Brigitte, were placed on a merchant ship leaving for Boulogne sur Mer, in the north of France, while Yves' father stayed behind briefly to try to liquidate assets. But it came to nothing. He, like most of the *pieds-noirs*, left Algeria with what they could carry in cardboard suitcases, for the shops and bazaars had long since run out of real suitcases to sell. The Mathieu-Saint-Laurent family lost everything. They would never return to Oran.

In France the *pieds-noirs* were met with open hostility. The war had become a source of horror for France with its bloodshed and the army's strong arm of oppression. By 1961 it was the subject of a huge popular backlash. The OAS alliance with the extreme right and its strategy of terrorist attacks within mainland France had drained any sympathy for their cause. Their profound nationalism was a source of embarrassment to the French.

Yves' parents were faced with the unenviable challenge of starting from scratch. His father was aged fifty-three. They split up although they never divorced. Lucienne went to live in a temporary apartment in

Boulogne before moving to the sixteenth *arrondissement*, her lifestyle to be assured by her son and administered by Bergé. The father Charles went first to Antibes to live with Brigitte and eventually to an apartment in Monte Carlo, also provided by Yves. In this way the Saint Laurent family came under the control of Pierre Bergé.

Shortly after Algerian independence, Brigitte came to Paris to see her brother Yves. Aged fifteen and a half, she was actively involved in the French-Algerian fight and the contrast of the bombs and killing she had witnessed compared to the hothouse life of her brother struck her as incongruous. 'When I saw him again in Paris there was something between us, we didn't hit it off,' remembers Brigitte. 'I don't know what it was, well, I think I do know, but anyway . . .' Yves' family have long since learned to weigh their words carefully, so Brigitte does not say it, but it was Pierre Bergé that she felt had come between her and her brother. It was Bergé who was now shaping Yves' horizons. And Yves was retreating from his former life. Victoire was now *persona non grata* in the couture house and in their social life and she had left the house of Saint Laurent. Looking back, over forty years later, Victoire believes the split was deliberate. 'I was the witness of their difficult moment, of Yves' misfortune, of his fall. I knew them before they became the idols of couture. I think Pierre preferred to get me out of the picture.'

Karl Lagerfeld was also a much-reduced figure in their social life. There were no more afternoons of canasta and, although there was still contact with him, the days of Karl and Yves driving around town together were long gone.

Yves and Pierre had moved from the houseboat to a ground-floor apartment on the Place Vauban, a sedate crescent of a place that wraps around the south side of Les Invalides. Their apartment overlooked the gilded dome of the church of Les Invalides, beneath which lies the red porphyry sarcophagus of Napoleon. It was a chic address loaded with republican and *grand-bourgeois* symbolism.

For a man who symbolised the youth of haute couture, who was in his late twenties, Yves was living a controlled and grown-up existence. During the week Yves drove home for lunch from the haute-couture studio in his black VW Beetle, for that was a time when he still drove. He and Pierre met for luncheon at one o'clock, frequently with a select journalist or two who were invited over for an informal briefing. The *maître d'hôtel* served chilled tomato juice, while Pierre fussed over the correct vintage of Château Talbot and revved up for his fashion discourse. They sat on reproduction Louis XVI dining chairs and ate peach Melba beneath the scores of Buffet paintings, which, with their manic, vertical, black brush-strokes, must have only heightened the sense of claustrophobia.

The Saint Laurent group of friends that formed in the mid-1960s was small, closed and predominantly French. Clara Saint was a new and significant arrival to the set, a social and cultural fairy godmother; she began as a friend and in 1968 became the press officer for the Rive Gauche ready-to-wear. She was deliciously witty, with glossy red hair and a penchant for 1940s tweed suits, which she wore throughout the hippie years. She was born in Santiago, Chile, the only child of a Chilean mother and French-Argentine father and she lived in Buenos Aires for the first eight years of her life. When her parents split up, she moved to Paris with her mother. At the age of twenty her father died and she inherited a large Argentinean coffee company, which she sold for a considerable sum of money which she then blew through in just six years, hence the need for a job. She was a social powerhouse with an impressive array of friends spanning social, artistic and political milieus, from Margot Fonteyn to Andy Warhol, and she knew every stroke of gossip in town.

Clara was key to the social rise of Pierre and Yves. It was Clara who was responsible for introducing them to Rudolf Nureyev, whom she had met through Fonteyn. She led the way to the ballet, so dear to Yves and Pierre at that time, arranging dinners with Nureyev and fellow Russian star Maïa Plissetskaïa. 'It was Clara who shed the light on something. "Let's go here, do this",' says Jacques Grange, who was a later entry into the Yves Saint Laurent clique. 'She was an *éminence grise*,' says Argentinean writer Javier Arreyuelo. 'She was the one who gave to what I call the Saint Laurent church so much of its dogma, the dos and don'ts.' She taught them the rules of the social *monde*.

Clara introduced her boyfriend Thadée Klossowski to the Saint Laurent set and he was welcomed with open arms, being a young man of cheekbones and intrinsic chic who was vaulted into the ranks of glamour because he was also the son of the painter, Balthus. Yves' fellow student at the Ecole Chambre Syndicale, Fernando Sanchez was still a great friend, although he had left Paris to work in New York, where he was leading a rather more giddy life of marijuana and Motown.

It was always the same set of people Yves and Pierre saw, over and over and over again. Entry to the set was closely guarded, but by whom? Someone here was constructing a group that resounded with all the right high-minded cultural and social notes. 'It was Clara who cast the group,' says writer Joan Juliet Buck. 'She chose who would be allowed into the Saint Laurent group. She brought in Paloma, with whom she was a friend. She was incredibly close to Pierre.'

On Sundays there were tea parties at the Place Vauban apartment with Thadée, Clara, Fernando when he was in town, Charlotte Aillaud, artists Claude and François-Xavier Lalanne, plus always a couple of hand-some single boys on hand for flirtation. Bergé served mint tea outside in the garden and people sat gossiping and listening to the sounds of Callas on the stereo. Yves lay on the grass doodling and sketching his own hidden thoughts. The afternoons were resolutely genteel and square. Fernando remembers turning up one day: 'I smoked a joint in front of the gang – it was before Loulou arrived – they looked at me like I was on my way to drug rehabilitation.'

Yves and Pierre's social life might have been rather tame, but not so their relationship. Bergé was six years older than Yves and liberated in his homosexuality. Later he would tell Andy Warhol of his penchant for wearing a cock ring, although he was not to know that Warhol would record the fact and publish it in his diaries for all the world to know. Bergé was Yves' first great passion, dominant and forceful, and he pulled Yves out from his years of sexual repression. This sexual dynamic is so often underestimated when assessing their early relationship. Thadée Klossowski says, 'The whole story between Pierre and Yves was a huge sexual success. They had these games, games which were rather violent, and then Yves would be under lock and key but he would escape.' He had a tiny bedroom on the ground floor and he would climb out of the narrow window and run off along the *quais* by the Seine to linger under bridges.

From the start everyone assumed it was Pierre Bergé pushing the reluctant and forlorn Yves to stardom, shackling him to a relentless and lifelong workload. Even those close to Yves and Pierre perceived the balance of power as unequivocal: the overbearing, iron fist clamped around the gentle, creative and trembling butterfly. Few people ever suspected the depth of complicity that linked Yves and Pierre.

Chapter 3

1967–68

It was Clara Saint who suggested the destination for what turned out to be a life-changing holiday for Yves. Pierre and Yves were used to taking holidays in the Canary Islands until Clara persuaded them to go to Marrakech in 1967. For Yves, returning to North Africa for the first time in seven years must have been a highly charged experience. 'I suppose Marrakech was very touching for Yves because it was going back to his childhood and the smells and the colours,' says Thadée, who accompanied Yves and Pierre on that first trip.

Marrakech did indeed echo elements of Yves' memories of Algeria, while at the same time having the appeal of being free from the oppressive connotations those memories may have harboured. Morocco did not suffer the human tragedy of Algeria in winning its independence. Nor did Marrakech life resemble the French middle-class existence of civic success and seaside villas, which Yves had lived in his *pied-noir* childhood. Marrakech at the time was an exotic playground for jet-set hippies and had not yet been discovered by the hitchhiking variety. It was a lush enclave in which to live out fantasies.

North Africa had long held an enchantment in the mind and body of the French homosexual. Historically both Algeria and Morocco were recognised destinations where sexual encounters and unashamed pleasure could be enjoyed, and the Arab youth was an object of fascination, if not obsession, for many French homosexuals. André Gide, François Augiérias, Jean Genet and Roland Barthes all wrote of their sexual encounters in North Africa. Their writing shared common themes: the easy nature of those encounters, the absence of shame and the virility of the Arab male. Their lyrical descriptions of night skies and sensuous abandon conjured up a romanticised, mythologised portrait of North Africa and its male that might have been pulled from a Delacroix painting.

When Yves and Pierre first went to Marrakech there were just a handful of foreign houses forming a tiny and archly sophisticated community of which Talitha Getty – the 26-year-old wife of John Paul Getty – was the night star. Talitha was a turbulent beauty struggling against the tide of her husband's wealth. They had married the year before and lived between Rome, London and Marrakech, where they had bought a nineteenth century palace while on their honeymoon, which their best friend and aesthete Bill Willis had then transformed. Memphis-born and unremittingly social, Willis set the decorative standard for Marrakech with his inspirational merging of haute-bohemian and Oriental style.

Talitha hosted dinners on her rooftop terrace at which she appeared barefoot and ethereal, rings on every finger, kaftan flying, stoned and enchanting. She possessed not just a sexual freedom, but also a freedom about her body that was almost childlike in its candour. She was emblematic of the upper-class hippie movement that defined 1960s London but which Paris had not experienced in the same way. Yves had never seen anyone like Talitha before. Later he admitted, 'When I knew Talitha Getty . . . my vision completely changed.'

She invited all her London friends to stay – Marianne Faithfull, Mick Jagger, Anita Pallenberg – and they arrived in various states of head-spin and decadence. Fashion designer Ossie Clark was there, coked up and dancing on life's edges. He was brittle and brilliant, dreaming up ravishing dresses of chiffon that expressed all the freedom and eroticism of the new rock-and-roll generation.

Yves was entranced. He took in every visual detail. He was struck by the wildness and high sexuality of it all, at that time so alien to Paris couture. It wasn't just the clothes that affected Yves; the Gettys lived with a degree of indulgence and hedonism that he had never witnessed before. 'There was a marvellous secretary,' remembers Valérie Lalonde, whose mother owned a house next door to the Gettys. 'She ran the house to perfection and with such precision, but at the same time she'd also be there cutting up hash cake for us all.' There was hash for the novices, opium for the advanced.

This was a heady new environment for Yves, aged thirty-one, to find himself in. Victoire remembers that when she split with Pierre and Yves in 1963, Yves neither drank nor took drugs. 'In many ways Yves and Pierre were terribly square and French,' agrees Thadée Klossowski. They were repressed, if not sexually, in terms of youth culture. 'He was shocked,' says Thadée of Yves' reaction to Marrakech and its voluptuous scene, 'shocked and immensely titillated.'

On that very first holiday Pierre and Yves found and fell in love with a house that was located within the walled medina and a couple of minutes' walk from the central square of Djeema el-Fna. The house was small, made up of numerous abbreviated staircases, and belonged to a self-proclaimed Vietnamese prince. They gave him cash and bought the house on the spot. It was called Dar el-Hanch, meaning House of the Serpent. Fernando Sanchez bought the house next door as a holiday home. On their second trip Yves and Pierre invited Thadée and Clara, Hélène Rochas and her lover Kim d'Estainville to stay in their new house. Someone stumbled upon a stash of pornographic novels in the medina, hard-core books for legionnaires, and brought them back as prize booty. Every night after dinner they took turns reading passages aloud from the books around the table amid much hilarity. There was always a hot-headed sexiness to the Marrakech holidays, both in conversation and in the possible encounters. And so Yves began dividing his life between the escape of Marrakech and the return to the obligations and ambition of Paris. The contrast between the two existences could not have been greater.

In Paris he was Monsieur Saint Laurent, the young star of haute couture who in ten years had come to be the oracle of fashion, not just for Paris, but for the world. Since the first collection for his own house, Yves had grown in confidence and daring. Every new collection was hailed as ground-breaking and the sheer versatility and range of the man was already astounding. He transposed a Mondrian painting on to a shift dress that was uncompromising in its simplicity, then a year later in 1966 he demonstrated wit and verve with pop-art dresses decorated with funky profiles inspired by Andy Warhol's paintings, as well as putting three-dimensional pink lips on little black dresses. He possessed a lyrical imagination shown in a knitted, cream, Aran bridal dress, which was a cocoon of ribbon and wool shaped like a Russian doll, out of which peeped the bride's face. Two years later he dreamed up an African beaded collection of 1967 that included shimmering 'grass' jackets and jet-beaded dresses with a conical bosom that Jean Paul Gaultier would revisit some twenty years later with his own conical breast corset.

Meanwhile, as Yves created, Pierre Bergé was building both the reputation and business of the house around the cult of the personality. It was a classic Paris haute-couture strategy and one employed by Dior, whereby the couturier is the epicentre of celebrity and glamour around which the stockings, scent and handkerchiefs are sold.

Together Bergé and Saint Laurent launched the first perfume, Y, in 1964, in partnership with Charles of the Ritz, who manufactured and marketed the scent, cutting Yves and Pierre 5 per cent of its sales. The following year the president of Charles of the Ritz, Richard Salomon, stepped up his investment in Saint Laurent by buying J. Mack Robinson's 80 per cent share in the house for a little less than $1 million.

With the considerable investment and industry might of Charles of the Ritz, Saint Laurent launched his ready-to-wear collection in 1966 under the name Rive Gauche, opening the first Saint Laurent ready-to-wear boutique on the Rue de Tournon in September of that year. The Left Bank name and identity was a stroke of genius that set the collection apart from that of couture and gave the ready-to-wear a badge of youth and cool. Fashionable girls and women thronged to buy his sexy safari minidresses that tied low over a plunging *décolleté*.

By 1967 Yves was designing four collections a year, two for ready-to-wear and two for haute couture. He was also highly creative and prolific in designing theatrical and film costume at this time. He designed Catherine Deneuve's wardrobe for Luis Buñuel's film *Belle de Jour*, which won the Lion d'Or at the Venice Film Festival of 1967. The Spanish surrealist's provocative film explored the perversions and erotic fantasies of a blonde bourgeoise wife and opened with the scene of Catherine Deneuve as Séverine daydreaming of being flagellated while bound to a tree. She becomes a call girl available afternoons only while her surgeon husband is off saving lives. Saint Laurent's designs for Séverine pitched subversive chic against a frigid conservatism with devastating success. Both the clothes, including a memorable black vinyl trench coat, and the ensuing long-term, public friendship with Catherine Deneuve were integral elements of the cult of Saint Laurent.

In Marrakech, away from the pressures of fashion, Yves was light-headed and funny, making childish jokes at the expense of others – frequently Pierre, whom he would refer to as 'elle' or she, a habit that drove Pierre to distraction. 'We would laugh endlessly with Yves,' says Thadée, 'he was the funniest person.' Often he was unintentionally funny, like the time he announced to the breakfast table, 'Oh, I woke up in the middle of the night and helped myself to the most delicious exotic fruit that I found in the refrigerator.' No one could quite imagine which exotic fruit Yves was referring to; it turned out he had helped himself to some raw potatoes lying abandoned on the fridge shelf. He was a brilliant mimic, pulling off pitch-perfect impressions, but characteristically only ever within the intimacy of close friends.

For Yves those first years in Marrakech were his happiest. There were picnics in apricot groves and the sound of Verdi in orange-blossom courtyards. There were sexual encounters and trays of kif brought in by a manservant in the evening candlelight. It was a hidden life behind closed doors.

Drugs had been part of the indigenous North African culture since Odysseus and in Marrakech there was a new wave of lotus-eaters. Fernando Sanchez was experimenting with hallucinogens and mari-juana and delighting in the metamorphosis they provoked in him. 'It was never-never land,' says Fernando, who had gone from tame young man in a suit to growing his hair into an afro and wearing flouncy shirts open to the navel. He remembers driving out with Bill Willis and the gang into the desert early one evening to trip on acid and watch the sun go down. The experience was suitably mind-blowing, but as the sun disappeared behind the mountains there was sudden giddy laughter as they realised they were sitting atop a sand dune, out of their minds in the fast-falling night without a clue between them as to how to get back to the car.

'I remember changing from this kind of bourgeois, well-behaved boy that I had been told to be,' says Fernando, 'into someone who started dressing rather outrageously, with pierced ears and boots and kohl. It was like an explosion. I shed a skin that was strangling me and that's when I'd say that I became more creative, because I started not forgetting, but rather bypassing all the clichés that I would have applied before. When I started getting stoned, I could not go back and design a bourgeois little black dress. Impossible. Time had changed.'

Yves had begun his extra-sensory trip. He too started smoking kif, a light-hearted and giggly type of marijuana native to Morocco. It was a means of escape – both from his own ambitions as well Bergé's for him. The peculiarity of Yves and his reaction to both drugs and alcohol is that he needed so little of either for them to take massive effect. 'He would literally have one sip and be roaring drunk or have one puff of a joint and be completely high,' says Thadée, who recalls one memorable lunch a year later when Loulou de la Falaise had joined the gang and was staying with them in Marrakech. 'Loulou bought some hashish in a block a bit smaller than a bar of chocolate and she said to Yves, you know you don't have to smoke it, you can pinch a bit off and eat it, because Yves was always asking us to roll a joint and she was bored silly of doing that. So then we had these ladies coming to lunch at the house – the mother of the Vicomtesse de Ribes, Boule de Breteuil and some other friend of hers – all these extremely chic women, old ladies that Yves had this couture fantasy about. Anyway in the morning Yves got senseless and decided that he had to redecorate the whole house and the garden and he was up on a ladder absolutely frantic that the house was a mess and there were these elegant ladies coming for lunch. And then they arrived and I think the mother of the Vicomtesse de Ribes was like a hippie, she had on this goatskin waistcoat. Anyway, they were terribly dressed and they were hugely disappointing, and Yves took one look at them and completely collapsed, sort of fainted. He disappeared from the lunch table and we discovered that he had eaten the whole block of hashish. He was frightfully sick on top of it.'

In the heat and smoke of Marrakech, Yves' inhibitions peeled away. He wore paisley shirts unbuttoned against tanned skin, faded jeans, crystals tied around his neck. He lay by the ornamental pool writing a diary and sketching, feeling saturated by sleep and a delicious lethargy. Even the look of haunted neurosis that had defined him since adolescence eased, to be replaced by a sensuous grace.

Everyone was letting go, finding and losing themselves. Everyone, that is, but Pierre. 'Pierre never really plunged into it,' says Fernando. 'He remained very much Monsieur La Rochelle. He always had a wider view. Yves and I were gone in our trips. Pierre couldn't get into his trip, because at that time he didn't have one.'

Pierre was not put off by the drugs – he had spent several years close to Jean Cocteau, who was a blatant opium-chaser extolling the delights of the drug with the admission, 'I owe to it my perfect hours'. Rather Bergé was aged thirty-seven and a man intent on self-improvement, not self-discovery. Waiting for Mick Jagger to arrive at the house in Marrakech for lunch one day, Pierre was both thrilled at the prospect of dining with a rock star and furious at Jagger's phenomenal lack of time-keeping. By 2 p.m. there was still no show; Pierre was hopping with fury and turned to Yves and shouted, 'I just hate hippies!'

Yves, on the other hand, did not hate hippies. But for the fact he was born too early, Yves would have loved to be a real hippie. He loved the feeling of liberation that was at long last pulsing through his veins. 'The party had started,' says Fernando. 'It had a lightness, a giggle and an impetuosity to it. Listen, we were free and in our naivety we believed that it was a new world.'

Seated at the table of Régine's nightclub was a young woman, Betty Saint; in her hand was a burning cigarette, on her face was the high gloss of beauty and ennui. She had long, straight, platinum-blonde hair, long black leather boots worn over even longer legs; she was, said Yves Saint Laurent, 'just what I love. Long, long, long.'

Yves was at Régine's that night too. 'At that moment *he* was absolutely divine,' remembers Betty. 'He was all in black leather with shoulders out to here, bleached-blond hair, very shy.' He stood watching Betty in the nightclub, his slender fingers resting on slender hips, leather jacket over convex chest. Betty had the same lithe body as he, the same spare frame, the same lean wrists and the same great height. She had a careless way of folding her limbs about her. 'It was a physical attraction,' says Betty about Yves' reaction to her. 'He liked my physique and he made a parallel with it and his own.' He persuaded a mutual friend to introduce him to Betty that night.

'He wanted me to work for him straight away, he wanted me to do the collection with him. And I said no, that I had already modelled at Chanel.' But Yves wouldn't leave Betty alone. 'He decided that I was for him, he ran after me, he harassed me, he tied me up, he wanted to possess me and I ended up doing one collection with him. I realised that in fact we were very similar.'

Yves met Betty in 1967, the same year he discovered Marrakech, and the encounter was equally significant for his life and career. She was working part-time in an art gallery on the Boulevard Saint-Germain and looked like a deviant schoolgirl with high black socks and short black mini, a tiny plait in the side of her hair, thick belts worn over thin hips. 'She was the best-dressed girl in Paris,' says Jean-Pascal Billaud, who was a friend and shared an apartment with her on the Rue de Verneuil. 'She already had her own defined look and an attitude of provocateur. She was always extremely modern.' She was a debutante with an anti-debutante attitude. She drank crème de menthe and swore she was drunk on the second glass; she flirted with girls and was chased by boys. There was something deliberately ambivalent about Betty.

She went to work as a mannequin at the house of Chanel when she was seventeen. Her mother Carmen Saint played cards with Maggie van Zuylen, society hostess and mother of Marie-Hélène de Rothschild, who was also a great friend of Coco Chanel, and it was Maggie who recommended Betty to Chanel. Betty worked there during the final chapter of the couturier's extraordinary career and Mademoiselle Chanel in her early seventies was as destructive and charismatic as ever. She ran her *cabine* like an emotional harem. 'We were supposed to seduce her, you know, the models. Very funny atmosphere. We were all in love with her . . . in a way,' Betty told *Interview* magazine in 1975. 'Everyone wanted to be her favourite; it was as if she was a man,' reflects Betty over thirty-five years later. Chanel could light up or destroy a body, a face, with her pitiless stare. 'I was just a baby when I went to Chanel,' says Betty, 'I was too young for that kind of vanity.' But the pleasure of pleasing, of seeing and measuring your beauty in the eyes of others was instilled in Betty for life.

From this moment on Betty understood the lore of fashion: 'Divine. You have to be divine. Divine for Chanel but that was just the beginning. Divine for Saint Laurent, but of course, it was, it is, essential to our relationship. These designers are aesthetes; they need someone whom they consider to be divine. You have to make them dream. I understood that from a very young age.'

The year before meeting Betty, Yves had designed his first 'smoking', a dinner jacket with satin reveres and trousers worn with white shirt and satin cummerbund that he had taken from a man's wardrobe and redesigned for women. It was his first step in the exploration of masculine dress within a feminine framework. The idea of girls dressing like boys and the tensions and attraction that could evoke was a daring new concept in fashion after a decade characterised by graphic, doll-like dresses, white tights and bouncing hair.

Betty, who was not related to Clara Saint, had a mixed heritage of Irish father, Italian mother and German grandmother that left her with a Nordic, chiselled bone-structure. 'I know the reason for my success – success, what an idiotic phrase. I don't mean to be vain, but it is quite simply that I don't look like a girl,' says Betty. Linear, longitudinal and different to all those women around her, her body was a shape that would come to represent the fashionable ideal of the 1970s. 'There was this perfect match between what Yves no doubt already wanted to do in fashion and the person he found in Betty,' says François Catroux, Yves' former contemporary at school, who married Betty that same year of 1967. He too met Betty in a nightclub and it was Betty who then reintroduced François to Yves. 'She was for Yves, and I am sure of this, like a drawing. She was a pencil stroke that was *his* pencil stroke. She is what he would have dreamed of being himself, I guess,' says François.

Saint Laurent had known divine before – Victoire and every other *mannequin de cabine* had all been ideals for Yves for a time – but with Betty there was endless fascination in looking at this imagined female incarnation of himself. A year later, when they had become friends, the four of them – Betty, François, Yves and Pierre – were together one afternoon in the garden of the apartment on Place Vauban. Pierre sat on the *terrasse* drinking espresso and discussing De Gaulle with François; meanwhile Betty and Yves danced round the garden to Stevie Wonder, lip-synching for their imaginary band 'les Saints'. 'Let's do crazy things,' whispered Yves to Betty. She was dressed in Saint Laurent and being photographed by *Women's Wear Daily* for an upcoming trip they were about to make together to open a new Rive Gauche boutique in New

York. 'Je l'adore,' he said as he spun her round and round in front of him, tenderly adjusting the silk scarf around her neck, picking a thread from her trousers. 'I want to look like Betty,' he murmured. There was a powerful undertow of narcissism to their mutual attraction – Yves pulled Betty to him and would not let her go.

Betty was the first person to enter the confines of the Saint Laurent set who shared Yves' sense of nihilism and voluntary dislocation from reality. She possessed a wilful separation from others that was similar to that of Yves. 'I suppose I was a bit isolated when I was a child and I like that, being separated from others. Perhaps it comes from being the only child. I feel very little connection with people. I am closed in on myself. I'm a bit like Yves in that way. It is no mystery if we are so close, it is a question of character.'

Up until now the Saint Laurent clique had been defined by a certain high-minded sense of exploration, of cultural pursuit dear to Pierre and Clara; gala nights at the ballet, the after-show suppers with Marie-Hélène de Rothschild. Betty's arrival provoked a seismic shift within the group.

Betty was what Yves was longing for, someone of his own kind, and someone who could play accomplice. She was younger than the rest of the gang. Aged twenty-three, Betty wanted to hang out, go dancing, 'faire des bêtises' as she says, using a parent's expression to describe children's mischief-making. 'We hated everything that was normal, down to earth, real life . . . that seemed so very dull,' says Betty. 'So we were ready to do everything to lose our heads in a way that was totally childish. Ah, we wanted to escape the everyday, to live one thousand and one nights, to be on a permanent high, to try everything in order to escape ennui; yes, that was the root of it.'

Betty's importance as a visual inspiration for Yves and her immediate complicity and intimacy with him provoked envy among some existing members of the set and cold trepidation in the heart of Pierre Bergé. 'He perceived me as dangerous, as a femme fatale,' says Betty. 'He thought I was a bad influence; he was wrong about me. I mounted a charm offensive; it took me a thirty-year seduction trip to convince him I wasn't going to harm Saint Laurent.'

Charm is Betty's strength and her defence. It is a both a highly choreographed and a natural charm, humorous, self-deprecating, at once intimate and detached. It is underpinned by manners and a beau-monde vocabulary that traverses the summits and the depths, so that people are divine, *extraordinaire*, *charmant*, *exceptionnel*, fabulous or very occasionally deadly dull. There is no middle ground. No wonder Yves fell under her spell.

'It is true from the moment that I arrived, things changed a lot. Yves was pretty well behaved when I arrived. Then he started to like other things, another way of life, to misbehave a little,' remembers Betty. 'When you like someone a lot you can have an influence on him or her, but I cannot tell you clearly or specifically how it was. He started to behave as an *enfant terrible* with me and that did change things, certainly. Before me it was very tea party, yes, that was it, and after there was no more tea.'

May in Marrakech and the phone rang through the heavy-lidded still-ness of the garden, across abandoned sketches strewn over tiled floors and international newspapers delivered too late to break any news. It was Paris calling, another world.

Anne-Marie Muñoz's voice sounded more strained than usual as she spoke from the Saint Laurent couture house in Paris, where she was now *directrice* of the studio: 'Yves, I think we should close the house, things are heating up out there.' There was urgency in Anne-Marie's voice and confusion in Yves' ensuing silence. 'We're going to watch the march this afternoon,' she added by way of explanation, using the word *défilé*, which can mean either march or fashion show.

It was 30 May 1968 and Anne-Marie was referring to the pro-President de Gaulle parade on the Champs-Elysées which was due to take place that afternoon as an angry riposte to the thirty thousand rioting students who for the last three weeks had been bearing down the Boulevard Saint-Michel, tearing up roads and the fundamental tenets of French society that lay in their path.

But for Yves Saint Laurent the word *défilé* could have only one meaning. 'Which fashion show?' he asked, his curiosity piqued by the prospect of someone trying to present a couture collection in May, a full two months before the rest of Paris.

In the *quartier latin* of Paris, on the boulevards and dark streets surrounding the Sorbonne, there was violence and euphoria. Youth had kicked a patriarch to the ground. Richelieu's portrait, which hung at the foot of the main staircase of La Sorbonne, had been symbolically slashed at the throat and the head ripped from the body. President de Gaulle, seventy-eight years old, a product of the nineteenth century and unyieldingly autocratic, was the object of fury. War was declared on the bourgeoisie, on their Loden coats and relentless grip on privilege. Those who had been the backbone of France since the revolution were now the symbol of oppression and hypocrisy.

This was a new generation tearing apart the inevitability of its destiny and declaring instead its own desires. Born in the postwar years, they had not physically lived through the Second World War and yet it seemed their whole childhood had been lived in its shadow. 'We weren't allowed to do anything,' remembers photographic agent Xavier Moreau of the physical and moral restrictions on French youth before 1968. 'In the 1960s France was still coming out of the deprivations of the war, families were still traumatised by the uncertainty of the future. We lived little lives. We took our empty bottle to the dairy to collect the milk; we made soup with vegetable peelings. At the same time we grew up with a huge hunger to consume; there was a desire to be someone, to rejoice.'

The first tremors of May '68 began within the concrete confines of the University of Nanterre when a bunch of radical students took to disrupting lectures in the name of Che Guevara. They complained vociferously about the single-sex living quarters and the autocratic functioning of the university. Students at this time in France had no powers of representation within the university executive; they were told what to do and how to live. When one of their leaders, Daniel Cohn-Bendit, was ordered before a disciplinary board in Paris, his friends broke into the dean's office to grab some loudspeakers for a noisier way of demonstrating. The dean locked them in his office, but they escaped by climbing out of the window. The Minister of Education, fearful of an escalation of disorder, then closed down Nanterre, which turned out to be a grave error in judgement, for by doing so he inadvertently moved the arena of protest from the obscure western suburbs of Paris into the heart of the city itself. A week later there were one thousand students hurling pavement missiles in the *quartier latin*. By 13 May the protest had accelerated beyond the realm of students and the major trades unions of

France called for a general strike that mobilised ten million people and brought the country to a standstill.

In Paris there was such urgency and anger to the outburst of May '68 that it felt as if these young students were catching up on a whole lifetime of self-expression. In a matter of weeks inhibitions were blown apart and parental and patriarchal authority was flouted. 'It is strictly forbidden to forbid,' read a notice stuck up by students at the Sorbonne. 'A closed and authoritarian society gave way to a permissive society,' says writer Edmonde Charles-Roux. 'France exploded like a champagne bottle left out in the sun.'

Ultimately the bourgeoisie would be bowed, but never beaten. Charles de Gaulle was forced from office eleven months later, to be replaced by the younger but equally conservative Georges Pompidou. But the turmoil and violence of May '68 freed Paris — at least for a time — from the constraints of classicism and Catholicism and from the country's yet-to-be-digested experience of occupation during the Second World War.

At last Paris was a thrilling place to be. Watching the barricades became an evening's entertainment. Shoe designer Manolo Blahnik, who was living in Paris at the time, remembers, 'In 1967 Paris was still too parochial for me. Then because of the political upheaval the street became exciting. Paris was totally Nanterre, Sorbonne; I used to go many times to this horrible auditorium just to see the students screaming. I couldn't care less what they were talking about. And sometimes with my friends I would go at night and see the piles of cars burning in Saint Germain. It was beyond.'

It seemed that spring '68 held the promise of a new moral utopia. There was a gale-force wind of liberation whipping through the streets and salons of Paris, blowing up skirts and knocking over rules of social convention. All of a sudden your hairdresser wanted to *tutoie* you. Among the younger generation of twenty-somethings there was an extraordinary feeling of release and rapture, among both the students on the Boulevard Saint-Michel and the children of *bonnes familles* on the Boulevard Saint-Germain.

There were only two kilometres between them, but while Boulevard Saint-Michel was deliberating between Trotsky and anarchy, Saint-Germain was choosing between nightclubs Régine's or Castel; not to appear bourgeois was the most tangible their politics ever got. But they shared at least one common belief: the intoxicating illusion that life would never be the same again.

And in a way, it wasn't. Youth now imposed itself as a voice to be heard in France, having called into question the assumed authority of teachers, professors, the president and police, the Fifth Republic itself. Something in society had been severed.

In fashion, a certain way of life that was already dying was rendered *démodé* by 1968. Janie Samet was in Paris working as a young fashion editor: 'At the time we all believed it was the end of haute couture. I remember doing interviews with the major couturiers and they were all desperate; they tried to believe in it still, but May '68 shattered a certain idea of luxury and fashion. All of a sudden one had to liberate the woman. There could be no more restraints.'

As it transpired it was not the end of couture, but it was the end of couture's way of structuring, constricting and disguising the female body. Elsewhere women had already become intimate with their bodies. In London Ossie Clark had given girls sensuality and transparency. Even in France, which was without doubt held back by couture, women had taken off their bikini tops in 1966 and a year later Cacharel made shirts that were close-fitting and sheer enough to show a woman's nipples. This lightness was the antithesis of the haute-couture school with its premise of buttressing and correcting the woman's silhouette.

1968 was also a definitive step in the individual's freedom of choice in what to wear and that inevitably meant the beginning of the end of a couturier's right to dictate fashion. The new generation of potential couture clients were in rebellion themselves – the last thing they wanted was to look like their mothers. Nor did they want to waste precious time in couture fittings, when they could instead swing by a boutique and pick up something funky and young and sexy.

Sexy, people were feeling deliciously ripe and sexy. On the street, in bars, on the bus, they were taking lovers; men, women, married, divorced, homosexual, bi-sexual, *vicomtesse*, just out of school, past the age of retirement, it really didn't seem to matter. Everywhere you went there was someone who wanted to *draguer* you, a word that literally means to chat up, but a word that in France denotes a fine art conducted with teasing glances, nuance and candid desire. Sexual freedom was another new post-68 reality: it had long been practised by the higher strata of French society behind the smokescreen of marriage, but now it was available to all, with or without the alibi of a spouse. As former *Suck* editor Jim Haynes remembers, 'Saying yes to sex in the sixties demanded certain things like a meal or hearing the words "I love you". Then suddenly there were no demands attached to sex. '68 was about kids having fun, talking to each other on the street, getting laid.'

Suddenly existence seemed weightless and for this new generation the most pressing concern was to enjoy, a fact they wanted to express in life as in appearance. 'We couldn't care less about anything; we were the wild, lucky few,' says Diane de Beauvau-Craon, a Patino heiress and daughter of a French duke, who went from being a debutante with a swell ball for six hundred and a couture dress of a thousand ruffles to being an independent single girl who left home, moved in with a boyfriend, wore jeans and looked for kicks. 'It was a time when we woke up just to have fun,' says Betty Catroux. 'It was total futility. I thought only of light things. We woke up and said to ourselves, Where shall we go dancing? Where shall we eat dinner tonight? Who shall we flirt with? What shall we do to amuse ourselves? Day and night; it was the most insouciant period of my life.'

By the time Yves Saint Laurent returned to Paris from Marrakech it was 15 June and four weeks had passed since the city had broken out in violence. The CRS riot police had packed up their truncheons and gone home; students were now installed victorious in the amphitheatre of the Sorbonne, wearing clogs and discussing the relative merits of the orgy as a means of sexual expression. Charles de Gaulle had regained a semblance of control over a country still reeling from the consequences of three weeks of general strikes and bloody violence.

Yves Saint Laurent had not witnessed the upheaval. He had not seen the carcasses of burnt-out cars on the Rue Gay Lussac and he had not heard the battle-cries of the student charges. Yves had spent the last four weeks lying on his back by a pool in Marrakech. And yet, instinctively, he responded to the change.

'Recent political events, the reaction of young people to fashion and the way of life today make the haute couture a relic of the past,' he announced boldly. 'First nights at the theatre, life on a yacht – all things like that belong to a society which no longer means anything . . . a society which is no longer *à la mode*. The Social Ladies are no longer significant.'

It was a fairly punchy statement coming from someone who had staked his career so far on designing for just this stratum of society, for Hélène Rochas who summered on her yacht in Saint-Tropez and Marie-Hélène who called up Yves for something gorgeous to wear to the first night of *Tosca* at the Opéra Garnier.

Faced with what he too perceived to be the potential end of haute couture, Yves' first concern was for himself: 'I do not want to find myself in the past . . . or in a stronghold cut off from everything.' Yves did not relish the thought of being washed up as a piece of flotsam on fashion's forgotten shores, aged thirty-two.

Just six months before, in January of 1968, Saint Laurent had celebrated ten years in couture with an existential questioning of himself and his career. He had complained vociferously of his overbearing responsibilities and workload. He railed against couture for having 'attacked my liberty, my right to live, look around and travel. At my age, I shouldn't take my job so seriously.' And he vowed then, 'One thing you can be sure of, I'll not finish my career doing couture as I'm doing it now.' It was to be a lifelong theme of complaint: no youth because of couture, no fun because of couture, no peace of mind because of couture.

He talked up the pain of fashion, but Yves could not, would not, give it up. 'We will return no more,' vowed Tennyson's lotos-eaters, opting to stay and get stoned instead, but Yves always returned to Paris, always headed back to the lure of couture and its glory. Fashion observers and even those close to Yves assumed it was big, bad Pierre Bergé who forcibly shoehorned him back into the studio every season, shaking the goose to lay another golden egg, and perhaps – much later on in his career in the late 1980s – it was, but not this time.

Yves had always used whatever was within his grasp to propel his creativity, and right now he had so much within his grasp, so much that was new and exhilarating that he needed to express through fashion. He didn't need to hang out by barricades to understand the social change; he was living it himself. Emancipation, sexual freedom, dabbling in drugs; that was Yves' May '68. 'I feel in sympathy with young people today. I feel they are right – the student rebels everywhere, the hippies, the whole youth revolution or whatever you want to call it. They are really changing the world,' he said two years later. 'I envy them their freedom from hypocrisy. Sometimes I feel trapped, a prisoner of success, I suppose. I've never had the time to be young and carefree. Often I rebel.'

Throughout the month of June he worked on the collection. His mind was a kaleidoscope of change. He could close his eyes and imagine Talitha lying on a Turkish carpet under the crescent moon, jasmine in her loose hair. He saw Betty dressed in black, day and night, summoning up all the new ease and austerity of the Saint Germain silhouette.

It was a delicate manoeuvre to pull off: somehow Saint Laurent had to distance himself from the spectre of aging privilege that was couture and yet at the same time continue to pursue his career. The hyperbole machine of the house revved into gear as Pierre Bergé ran round telling the press that Yves was deeply moved by events and this collection was his reaction to May '68. The fact that Yves was on holiday in Marrakech throughout the student revolution went unmentioned. Yves told the press, 'Real fashion today comes from the young people manning the streets,' adding, somewhat obscurely, 'those between thirty and thirty-five.' Even when espousing his revolutionary ideals, Yves never forgot his customer. She was not aged eighteen, nor was she mixing Molotov cocktails. Ironically the press was soon reporting that Yves Saint Laurent had spent every night during the month of May out by the barricades, sketching students.

And then came the day of the collection. In the breathless heat of a July morning ladies in sheer stockings alighted from sprung automobile upholstery. There was a tense crowd around the entrance of the couture house on Rue Spontini, with that strange, uneasy, suppressed aggression that always characterises a fashion show.

To an audience of society ladies and fashion editors, some of whom still wore hats and gloves, Yves showed a collection based around the trouser suit. One journalist wondered aloud if she had stumbled into a menswear collection. The models wore the trousers with attitude and hands on hips; they stood like and looked like Betty Catroux. The silhouette was long and narrow; the colours were black and dark brown in double-faced jersey.

And when an evening dress finally did appear it was black, transparent mousseline and overwhelmingly raunchy for the tame expectations of a couture salon. The model's naked body showed through the floor-length chiffon, there was a circle of black marabou feathers that caressed her hips and a silver belt in the shape of a serpent wrapped around her waist.

The July '68 collection was hailed as a revolution, which it was not, but coming so near to the May '68 revolt it was perhaps an irresistible connection to make. Instead this was the purest, most coherent expression of the Yves Saint Laurent style in his career so far. He had demonstrated it before with the *caban, le smoking*, but here, aged thirty-two, he expressed the concentrated essence of Saint Laurent style with an assurance and sensuality that were astounding. And in doing so he left behind the idea of fashion as trend. Shaking Dior at last from his shoulder, he entered the realm of style. 'I have never done such a disciplined collection,' he said at the time. It was the synthesis of everything he believed for now and for the future. '[It] is based on the idea of the suit – the practical, modern, easy world of the suit,' he said, 'not the suit as we've known it . . . a suit that will look different with a skirt or pants. And pants with coats are part of our life.'

Saint Laurent did not invent trousers. What Saint Laurent did was set them up as the absolute pillar of a modern woman's wardrobe, to be worn every day, all day. He made trousers that could convey power and chic. 'The difference between day and evening clothes is outdated. The new fashion freedom permits people to be as they are or as they want to be . . . to go to dinner, for instance, as they were in the morning in black jersey or anything else.'

Yves had always shown brilliance and invention in fashion but with this collection he entered that exceptional period in every great designer's life, a period that is both finite and glorious, when the designer is in absolute symbiosis with the desires and dreams of women.

Chapter 4

1968–69

No one in Paris knew for certain who Karl Lagerfeld really was. There were many delectable rumours that circulated about him – that his father was a German baron or that his mother was the daughter of a high-ranking German diplomat – and Karl's increasingly mannered appearance and way of speaking lent themselves marvellously to fuelling such rumours.

The one thing everyone knew about Karl was his fabulous wealth. He was heir to a German industrial fortune – was it chocolate, ball-bearings or condensed milk? – the source differed according to who was telling the story, but the private means was an accepted fact. Everyone knew that Karl Lagerfeld was rich and did not have to work, because that is what Karl told them.

And yet he displayed a work ethic that was far from that of a trust-fund dilettante. After four years as an apprentice at the house of Pierre Balmain, he left to take up the position of designer at the house of Jean Patou in 1959. Jean Patou himself had died some twenty years before and by the late 1950s Patou was a second-tier house supplying couture for a principally South American clientele. Even during the house's glory days of the scintillating 1920s, Jean Patou had never cast off the shadow of Mademoiselle Chanel, whose Rue Cambon couture house was on the street parallel to that of Patou.

Karl Lagerfeld's tenure at Jean Patou was brief and unremarkable. There were no rave reviews and no talk of a fashion discovery. He left quietly and by mutual agreement with the owners Madeleine, sister of Jean Patou, and her husband Raymond Barbas in 1962 after designing only a handful of collections. 'It was not deemed a great success,' admits their heir Jean de Mouy. 'They got along very well, there was no clash between them. But Karl was young, at the time he was searching for himself and for a direction.'

The direction he chose was to leave not only Patou but also the world of haute couture and move into ready-to-wear instead. This was a momentous and brave decision for a young man of his generation and education. Up until now his life had been played out to follow a career in haute couture. When Karl entered ready-to-wear in the early 1960s it was still considered the poor relation to haute couture and by definition a ready-to-wear designer possessed none of the grandiose prestige of a couturier. Ready-to-wear clothes at the time were pale, industrial imitations of the real couture thing.

Karl launched himself as a freelance designer for a slew of brands that included Mario Valentino, Repetto and the supermarket chain Monoprix. He worked prolifically, designing not only clothes but shoes and accessories as well. It is hard to reconstruct what Karl's ambitions were at this time; he for one denied that he had any at all. 'I was not ambitious at the time; I didn't care,' he would say about himself twenty years later. 'I came to Paris when I was fourteen and I started working at sixteen. When I was really very, very young, I was very lazy and I was so tacky: I used to like convertible cars, beaches and sunbathing, body-building and nightclubs,' Karl later said. And yet at the same time that he spoke of indolence, he would also insist that the reason he came to Paris alone at such an unfeasibly young age was that he was determined to launch himself in haute couture. 'It was my dream, the only thing I ever really wanted to do was to come and work in a high fashion house in Paris,' he said in 1979.

Fernando Sanchez, who knew Karl from the earliest days at the Ecole Chambre Syndicale, believes Karl made the move out of couture because he understood the future of fashion lay in ready-to-wear. 'He totally grasped the epoch,' says Fernando. 'He knew he wanted to do his own thing and not in some old couture house. Karl is extremely intelligent, he understood the time.'

But perhaps that is the way we see Karl Lagerfeld's reasoning in retrospect, now that we know he went on to be an international fashion success, shaping and defining ready-to-wear, introducing monumental salaries into fashion and conceiving the idea of designing for several major houses simultaneously. But in 1962 Karl Lagerfeld's career path was not so self-assured.

After his early success winning the coat award in the International Wool Secretariat competition, the lacklustre years that followed at Balmain and then Patou must have come as a considerable blow to Karl's design confidence. And all the while he was watching his fellow laureate Yves Saint Laurent leap to the heights of fame and success.

At the time Karl was still a friend of Anne-Marie Muñoz, who had been Anne-Marie Poupard in the Yves-Karl-Victoire 1950s clique, but who had since married and become Yves' right-hand woman in the studio. She has a different view on Karl's career change. 'I think he left couture because he wasn't happy at Patou,' says Anne-Marie. 'And so he became a *styliste* and he was brilliant at that. He was meant to be a *styliste*, not a couturier – that's to say he designed shoes, bags, hair combs, blouses, pens, tables. He drew well and he loved sketching. He loved to cultivate his mind. He knew things. He was always flicking through books, passionate about a subject, interested, surrounded by paper and books. He still is. He was full of great ideas, coming up with models, thinking up fashion shows, always full of ideas.'

The term *styliste* was used to denote any designer working in ready-to-wear for a house that was not his or her own, or to describe someone working for a manufacturer or a design studio. It was a term used to describe a fairly anonymous mass of designers working within Paris fashion at this time.

Except that Karl Lagerfeld was not anonymous. Since his arrival from Hamburg he had gained notoriety for himself as a personality, a prerequisite for success in the *monde*. Already in the 1950s he drove around town in a cream open-top Mercedes, a gift from his father when he won the International Wool Secretariat competition, at a time when the rest of Paris was struggling to find the petrol to run a *deux chevaux*.

Throughout the 1960s he became a highly visible feature of Saint Germain life. He spent his days between the Café de Flore, the Brasserie Lipp and an open-air swimming pool called Piscine Deligny that hung above the Seine from the side of the *quai* near the Assemblée Nationale.

It was a fabulous haunt for picking up and posing. It was the idea of all those oiled and bronzed bodies lying in the sun while others worked nine to five that gave the Deligny its delicious lick of decadence. People would stare open-mouthed as Karl strutted across the watermelon-pink wooden decking, wearing high heels and an all-in-one swimsuit, flaunting the toned physique of a highly motivated body-builder. 'He was incredibly affected,' remembers Jean Eudes, who was a seventeen-year-old student hanging out by the pool at the time, 'with this superb body. Everyone at the swimming pool would laugh at him because he was so sort of extraordinary. But Karl always had this attitude of looking like he couldn't care less that they were laughing.'

Karl liked to be seen as much as he liked to observe. Every morning he shut the door to his garden apartment on the Rue de l'Université and walked the short five-minute stretch to the Café de Flore, drawing looks as he went. He stopped at La Hune to buy a book on the Bauhaus, passed by the newspaper kiosk to buy his foreign fashion magazines and then he called in at Le Drug Store on the corner to buy fifteen or so music cassettes.

Then he sauntered into the Flore opposite, took up position alone at a table on the ground floor, shrugged off his floor-length fur, sat down and proceeded to flick at a relentless pace through the American *Vogue* on the table before him, digesting Diana Vreeland's every fashion dictate. From his corner table he watched all the comings and goings, the new faces and transforming attitudes. He saw it all and he noted every nuance, every change in gesture.

He was an object of fascination at the Flore and, as this was Paris, people stared openly, which did not seem to displease him. They stared at his high-heeled patent-leather ankle boots, at the copper Claude Lalanne bow-tie around his neck, the black hair swept back to his collar, the pouting lips and foppish gestures. 'He was a kind of extraterrestrial for us, a UFO,' says Jean-Pascal Billaud, who was a student at the law faculty near by and one of those who stared. 'He was groomed to death and he already had this kind of discipline about him which was absolutely fascinating for a generation who was in the process of saying that discipline didn't exist. And then of course he was the heir to Nestlé. There was a whole legend surrounding him.'

Gilles Dufour was another well-bred young boy who was watching

Karl and would later work with him for over twenty-five years. 'He looked like an Italian hustler, black curly hair, sexy, always tanned. He did collections in Milan and he was very Milano,' says Dufour. 'It was always too much, the cashmere sweaters, the long camel overcoat, of course you wouldn't think twice of that kind of thing today. He looked like he was the one with the money.'

Karl was already a regular feature of the fashion and style press. He had done his eighteenth-century apartment out in 1960s white futuristic style with a leather and steel table and huge white plastic sphere lamps dotted around the floor. He was immensely proud of the look and it had been photographed by several interiors magazines and hailed for its striking scheme of contemporary furniture set within the classicism of an eighteenth-century *hôtel particulier*.

When Karl's father died in Baden-Baden in 1967 at the age of eighty-six he left him, so Karl told a reporter, many paintings by major artists. Karl took great pains to remain resolutely nonchalant in the face of such Lagerfeld *richesse*. In this case he was adamant that the paintings, however important, would not interfere with his cool, white contemporary décor. 'None of them fit in with my modern furniture,' he said with a shrug. 'Sargent is relegated to the kitchen with Ruysdael – just where they belong.' Although, as the journalist herself noted, at the time of the interview the paintings had not yet arrived from Baden-Baden.

From the start of his career Karl was engaged in the highly effective construction of an image, so that everything about him – his look, his world, his background – was calculated to appear larger than life.

Karl-Otto Lagerfeld was born on the 10 September 1933 in Hamburg. His father was aged fifty-two and his mother thirty-six. They lived in comfort on the banks of the Elbe in Blankenese, a desirable western suburb of Hamburg where residents tended to pink rhododendrons and lived behind leaded window-panes.

Karl's father, Otto Lagerfeld, was a Hamburg-born entrepreneur who began his career at seventeen as an apprentice to a coffee-importing company in Hamburg. Otto spent the first twenty-five years of his career in a state of travel and high adventure, seeking his fortune by dint of ambition, hard work and nerve. He sailed across the world to South

America, New York, San Francisco and Vladivostock, working as a merchant for various import companies, picking up languages, witnessing the San Francisco earthquake and escaping the Russian Revolution on his way before returning to Hamburg and setting up his own import/export company that dealt in general food supplies.

By 1925 business had stagnated and he chose to close down the Otto Lagerfeld Company and work for the American Milk Products Corporation instead. He became managing director of Glücksklee, which was the name of the condensed-milk brand that the American Milk Products Corporation sold in Germany, and worked incessantly to make the company a success. Otto Lagerfeld became a prosperous businessman but his wealth was limited to that of a salaried man.

His first wife died shortly after having given birth to their daughter Thea, and Otto Lagerfeld was a 49-year-old widower when he married Elisabeth Bahlmann in 1930. A year later a daughter was born, Martha Christiane, followed two years later by their son, Karl-Otto. The first year of Karl's life was spent in a house in Baurs Park, a private road set in Blankenese woodland that meanders between detached houses. The Lagerfelds had just moved from the house next door up the hill to number 3, from where they now had a splendid view out on to the silvery eel light on the River Elbe. They watched as the huge passenger liners, barges and freight ships moved in and out of port. The thud of ship engines reverberating through the water was almost constant.

In 1934, when Karl was aged one, Otto Lagerfeld moved his family to Bad Bramstedt, a small town forty kilometres to the north-east of Hamburg. At the time it was a town with a population of 3,500 made up predominantly of tradesmen and farmers. The population grew considerably during the Second World War with the influx of refugees fleeing from the east and prisoners of war put to work in the fields.

A stream runs through Bad Bramstedt and a main road divides the town and its landscape of municipal begonias and marigolds, red-brick bungalows and automatic garage-doors. For much of the year the light is grey, melancholy and overwhelmingly northern. There is a ghostly beauty to the landscape outside the town. The skyline is dominated by silver-birch trees, which stand bare and etched against the endless horizon. Beyond the trees, the countryside reaches out flatly, interrupted only by dips and puddles of water, forming the marshland of Schleswig–Holstein.

Otto Lagerfeld bought a handsome four-bedroom mansion house called Bissenmoor that stood in a clearing and was reached by a long, narrow drive through woodland of beech, oak and fir trees. The house was four kilometres to the south-west of town and stood on what had once been a landed estate, although by the time Otto Lagerfeld bought the house the estate had been split up and the land sold off. Along with the house he owned a couple of fields and a tract of woodland.

The house was spiffing by Bad Bramstedt standards and reflected Lagerfeld's hard-earned middle-class status. It had a columned stone portico, pretty arched windows and large terrace at the front. 'It was a very nice, big house, but not one of those grand, big country manors in Schleswig–Holstein that have thirty or forty rooms,' said the late Kurt Lagerfeld, Karl's cousin and Otto's favourite nephew. 'This was a perfectly normal house, it had pillars at the front and three spacious rooms downstairs.'

Moving to the country was a considerable change in lifestyle for the family, but according to Kurt Lagerfeld it was a premeditated decision on the part of Otto Lagerfeld to get his family out of Hamburg. 'Uncle Otto was someone who thought ahead, war was coming and he realised that the advantage of farm buildings and a farm meant there would be something to eat.' A tenant farmer lived just next door with his family and smallholding of three cows and two horses.

Karl's father was an abstract figure for his children: removed, self-contained, a businessman who was absent and older. He drove back and forth every day between Hamburg and home while the children and their mother stayed put in Bad Bramstedt. It was a punishing commute and he also travelled extensively throughout Germany marketing and selling the milk, which meant he was often away from home. There were also frequent trips to the Glücksklee factory in Neustadt in Holstein, which is a small fishing town thirty-five kilometres north of Lübeck on the Baltic Sea. Hamburg, Lübeck and Neustadt all formed part of the Hanseatic League, a mercantile league of medieval German towns that had been founded in the twelfth century to promote and protect their economic interests. By the twentieth century the league had petered out and the term Hanseatic had come to describe a way of life that had connotations of prosperity, toil and trade.

Karl Lagerfeld as a young schoolboy with fellow pupils of the Jürgen Fuhlendorf-Schule in Bad Bramstedt.

As the children grew older their distinct personalities took shape. Christel, as Martha Christiane was fondly known, was the tomboy. She shimmied up and down the huge beech tree by the side of the house, played hide and seek all over the woods with the next-door children and liked nothing better than to nip across to the farm and help muck out the cows. 'Karl wanted nothing to do with the cows,' remembers their childhood next-door neighbour Karl Wagner. 'He would walk past the cowshed holding his nose.'

Karl preferred to sit on the terrace, legs crossed as he sketched or read. 'From the age of two or three he developed a habit of cutting out pictures of ladies dressed in fancy clothing from magazines,' remembers Kurt Lagerfeld. 'He used a little pair of nail scissors to do it and his father always made sure there was a supply of magazines for him to cut up.'

Karl was sitting outside reading when Karl Wagner and a schoolfriend ambushed him one afternoon in late summer. They had stained their bodies and faces by rubbing them with blueberries and they crawled through the hedge beneath the balustrade whooping like Red Indians. Karl ran screaming with terror into his house.

'We had a French prisoner of war and one from Serbia; we were always trying to push Karl into the cowsheds with them, but Karl kept running away,' remembers Wagner. 'When we went off climbing trees in the woods, playing hide and seek, he held back and went and got his books. He used to read cowboy-and-Indian stories. He always wanted his mother to read to him and she said he needed to learn to read himself.'

Karl was also an outsider at school. His fellow schoolboys of Bad Bramstedt, now its civic elders, remember a boy who was effeminate, bright and not like them in any way. He was nicknamed 'muhle' but no one seems to remember why; the word *muhle* does not mean anything in German. 'He didn't have any real friends. He was always a loner. He really was strange,' says Hans-Joachim Bronisch, who was a fellow pupil at the Jürgen-Fuhlendorf Schule and sat behind Karl in class. He stuck out by the way he dressed, as he was the only one in his class who wore a jacket and tie and three-quarter-length shorts. He was always well turned out, clothes pressed, dressed as if for the office, and this at a time when most schoolboys went barefoot in the summer. The school photo that Bronisch has kept shows a class of ruddy-legged country boys in hand-knitted V-neck tank tops and open-neck shirts, looking as if they've just been called in from playing in the woods. All except Karl, who is pictured in the centre of the front row, legs crossed at a jaunty angle, hands neatly folded in his lap, long black hair swept back and pomaded, dressed in dark jacket and tie.

His hair was a cause for scorn among his fellow pupils, who disliked the length and lushness of it. Even Karl's teacher told him to get himself to the hairdresser and have his hair cut off. He did not. 'It was very brave of him to refuse: at that time if a teacher told you to do something, you obeyed,' points out Bronisch's wife. 'You needed to be strong to be different, after all it was a time when all the boys had the same typical short Hitler haircuts.'

Karl was a clever boy, not top of the class but recognised for his artistic talent and photographic memory. 'He was totally unsporty,' says Bronisch. 'You couldn't play football with him. He wasn't into girls. He played with dolls at home and that completely disqualified him from the boys.' He would not get his hands dirty, he didn't play outside and he spent endless afternoons alone at the cinema. Lagerfeld and Bronisch shared textbooks due to the shortage of supplies during the war and they made the daily swap by meeting on a bridge at 4 p.m. in the afternoon, but it was only necessity that precipitated the contact. 'We both lived to the south of town but we never walked home together.'

Karl, inevitably, was the butt of much teasing. Earlier on in his school life other boys had threatened him and so for a time Karl had to be escorted home by older pupils. 'We didn't understand him as a child. He behaved totally differently to us,' says Karl Wagner as he surveys the land where the Lagerfeld house once stood. Karl clearly lived in exclusion, but what is not so clear-cut is whether that was enforced by those who could not understand him or self-imposed by Karl as a means of protection, or perhaps both. At the same time Karl had an overblown sense of superiority that can only have infuriated his contemporaries even more. In 1952 Karl went with his father to Neustadt in Holstein, to the Glücksklee factory, where celebrations were being held for twenty-five years of business. Neustadt was unprepared for Karl's levels of sophistication. Kurt Lagerfeld remembered: 'Uncle Otto had invited all the farmers and one farmer got talking to Karl and took him to the bar and said, "Let's have a drink together, let's have a beer," and Karl replied, "I only drink champagne." Well, the news of that conversation went round the whole town and there was much laughter. That was on the 1 May 1952 and Karl turned nineteen that September.' There was already a deliberate bid to disassociate himself publicly from his immediate horizon of beer and pickled herrings. In an interview with *Der Stern*, Karl himself admitted, 'As a child, a very young person, I had the feeling: "It doesn't matter what you do – you're compelling!" I thought I was sacrosanct – wasted on dismal postwar Germany. It was quite frightening really. When I compare myself now, I think I'm quite modest and shy.'

It is easy to imagine Karl's solitude and perhaps too the claustro-phobia and disillusion of finding himself stranded among small-town children in Nazi Germany. Here were girls with thick plaits and boys with catapults singing nationalist folk songs, and there was Karl with effeminate mannerisms and racing speech wanting to discuss how to transform the Bissenmoor garden and sketch fashion silhouettes.

His means of defence was isolation. 'He was very hard to needle,' remembers Wagner. 'He was always pretty sanguine. He just pulled back and went off somewhere.' Mostly he escaped into his books or his mind.

In front of the Lagerfelds' house was a little stone grotto guarded by diminutive decorative lions, and although the house has since been pulled down the grotto is still there, overgrown and forgotten. This is where Karl Lagerfeld and Karl Wagner would sometimes sit and spend afternoons together, for as Wagner remembers, 'The only way to play with Karl was to sit down and daydream with him.'

In 1964 Karl went to see Gaby Aghion at the ready-to-wear house of Chloé. He went with a packet of sketches in his hand, looking for a job. She leafed through his drawings and came to a stop at 'a rather charming dress in beige shantung which Karl had drawn with the most ravishing yellow tights. No one thought about doing tights with the outfit at that time,' remembers Gaby, 'so you see already he managed to give a kind of total look to his clothes.' Gaby liked the sketch, although she worried that Karl's taste was too baroque for Chloé, but her business partner Jacques Lenoir found Karl intelligent and encouraged her to take him on.

Gaby Aghion had started Chloé from home twelve years earlier when she was an affluent 1950s wife who had never worked before in her life. 'I said to my husband, "I've got to work, life should be full, it's not enough to eat lunch",' remembers Aghion. She was passionate about fashion and wore couture some of the time. 'You dressed in couture when you had the money and the rest of the time you wore clothes by what we called *les couturières* – dressmakers – because, after all, you needed a lot of clothes, morning, lunch, afternoon, evening,' explains Aghion. 'What these couturières did was to copy the couturier's clothes but adding bits here and there and everything they added was horrible, so you ended up with this kind of half-baked couture.'

It was postwar Paris and, as Gaby saw it, fashion was divided between the perfectly dressed woman in haute couture and the mediocre-dressed woman wearing couture copies and 'grubby, white gloves'. She sensed a need for refined, elegant ready-to-wear or what she calls 'prêt-à-porter de luxe'. She started out by designing six cotton-poplin summer dresses that she had made up by seamstresses. She packed them up in a suit-case and then drove around Paris showing them to the couture houses, who ordered the dresses for their own boutiques to be sold under their own label.

By the time Karl joined, Chloé had evolved into a collection of ready-to-wear produced twice a year and designed by a handful of free-lance *stylistes* under Gaby's direction. Karl started at Chloé in a minor way, coming up with just two designs per season and working along-side the other freelance designers that included Tan Giudicelli, Christiane Bailly and Maxime de la Falaise. The Chloé premises were a modest two-room affair, one room for management and the other jammed with bolts of floral printed silks and creative egos where all the designers gathered to fight it out. Aghion remembers it as 'a Marx Brothers room. The designers would sort of kill each other every season and in the process somehow we came out with a coherent collection.'

Gradually Karl went from two designs per collection to doing ten and then over the years the other designers left. Tan Giudicelli, for instance, launched his own ready-to-wear line and Maxime de la Falaise went to live in New York, so by 1965 there were only two designers left – Karl and an Italian woman called Graziella Fontana, who was good at designing sharp suits. 'Karl is very intelligent and I got on well with him. I've always worked better with men,' admits Aghion. 'He chased them all away.'

Karl still spent his mornings at the Flore, but he started turning up of his own accord at the Chloé studio every day at 2 p.m. to work all afternoon with Gaby. He called her Madame Aghion: she was fifteen years older than him and a powerful mentor at a time when Karl had not yet found his fashion direction. They shared an intensely pedagogical relationship. 'Of all the *stylistes* I have worked with, Karl was the only real intellectual,' says Gaby. 'We had a perfect accord.' She was shrewd and cultivated; Egyptian-born, she was a collector of futuristic painting and tribal art and had been a friend of Picasso and Lawrence Durrell – 'when he was still a poet', she stipulates. It was during Karl's time at Chloé that the rumour began making the rounds of Paris that Gaby Aghion was the inspiration behind Durrell's magnetic heroine Justine. Karl would have loved that added glamour, but it is a rumour that Aghion herself denies.

During these first years of his break from haute couture, Gaby showed Karl that fashion could be something else: lighter, faster and without the frou-frou. It was Gaby who taught him how to simplify his ideas and edit his abundant output. 'There was something between us; I don't know how to explain it. We would say, "What shall we do?" Then Karl would go back home and one or two days later he'd bring in a whole packet of designs and I would look through them one by one and he would watch me.' Gaby had an eye and instinct for what was fashionable and, crucially, what would sell. 'I have always said fashion should be as fresh as a salad,' she explains. 'There would be designs among the sketches that I set aside as right, other sketches that I would put in a different pile. Karl would want to rip up the sketches in the second pile straight away and I would say, "Wait, don't throw them out. We'll keep them to the side for the moment. It's not exactly right for now, but there is an idea in there."'

Karl was listening, watching, learning, assimilating and working with utter tenacity. He was prolific in his output. Gaby admits she only realised just how prolific and consistent Karl was after he had left and she had to wring the sketches from the designers that followed. 'You asked them to do ten sketches and you'd be dead by the time they came up with them,' says Aghion, whereas with Karl there was always a surfeit of ideas, sketches, accessories, words, energy.

This prodigious rate of productivity was to characterise Karl's fashion career, as was his ability to design clothes that sold. He might have eschewed his father's career as a Hanseatic merchant, but he shared his same keen sense of commerce. 'Karl has always made collections that sold well,' says Francine Crescent, who became editor-in-chief of French *Vogue* in 1967. 'He has always had a sharp sense of business and his collections were always impeccable and extremely commercial. Not in a bad way; they were pretty, ravishing and at that time he was helped by Madame Aghion. They made a great team.'

He and Gaby would work together all afternoon and then at 7 p.m. they would drive across Paris in Gaby's car, back to her apartment in the fifth *arrondissement*, talking all the way, discussing fabrics, what women were wanting, would trousers last? She would drop Karl at her house and he would continue home by foot, cutting west across the *quartier latin* back to the Rue de l'Université. 'He was marvellous, Karl. When he came back with me in the car, if he saw students – well, you know, sometimes the students had certain charming ideas on how to dress – Karl would take the students' ideas and then transform them into something beautiful,' says Gaby. 'He had an undeniable art for transposing their vision into fashion.'

Chloé was just one of Karl's jobs as he still kept his multitude of other freelance contracts on the go. By 1965 the first wave of *créateurs* had sprung up in Paris; it was a movement that included Sonia Rykiel, Dorothée Bis and later Emmanuelle Khanh. *Créateurs* was the name given to these young, new designers who were launching their own ready-to-wear lines under their own names and who had nothing to do with the couture world.

Karl could have done the same; he was aged thirty-five in 1968 and at a stage in his career where he had the maturity and experience to go it alone. But he did not. Instead he continued to work freelance for others, forever conjuring up clothes for someone else's house, someone else's brand, someone else's identity. It is a strange contradiction that while Karl was already deeply involved in the creation of a Karl Lagerfeld persona, he did not attempt to create a Karl Lagerfeld style or launch his own label in fashion. It seemed Karl was always happier designing in someone else's skin.

The years passed at Chloé with Karl gaining steadily in confidence and reputation until one day in 1969 Antonio Lopez and Juan Ramos came to call. Antonio was a fashion illustrator, Juan his art director; they were new to Paris from New York and sent by French *Elle* magazine to sketch the Chloé collection. They were bold and brilliant, diminutive matinée idols. Antonio had a rakish black moustache, Cuban heels, a gold earring in one ear and kohl about his eyes. He was a slave to beauty.

'Antonio wanted everybody to be beautiful – himself included,' said Karl thirty-five years later. 'This was in the days before a certain kind of ugliness would become a new form of beauty. And, in fact, in his portraits and in his illustrations everybody did look beautiful. Sometimes *too* beautiful. He didn't want to reproduce his models' imperfections (as is often the case in photography today). Beauty was the only thing he desired. He lived for beauty, his vision of it and his *idée fixe* of it.' Like many men in fashion, the fixed idea reverberated about a fixed point: his mother.

His mother was a seamstress and Antonio a poor boy born in Puerto Rico in 1943. They moved to the Bronx, New York, when Antonio was seven. His artistic talent was profound; he could have been a painter, an artist, but he chose fashion illustration as the way to pay endless homage to the indelible and idealised image that possessed his imagination – his mother's reflection.

'My mother to me was the sexiest woman I have ever met in my life – so far,' said Antonio in 1976. 'My mother could not walk down the street without having four or five men follow her wherever she went. The vibrations and magic she had were incredible . . . I would sit and watch my mother for hours every day because she was really, really narcissistic. I would watch her put on her make-up and fix her hair. This is where I learned the gestures of my drawings – the feminine movement.'

Now it was Antonio following someone beautiful; he could not walk down the street without picking someone up and inviting them to come and sit for him. Back in New York his studio at Carnegie Hall had been a revolving stage of girls and boys, dancing and gossip, Diana Ross blasting on the tape recorder in the corner. And when he sketched he pulled every atom of energy that was in that room to him and channelled it – Diana Ross, tape recorder and all – on to the white page before him. His line had grace, energy and an erotic allure. 'I never saw anyone more gifted at sketching than Antonio,' said Karl.

Even before he left New York for Paris, Antonio had established a reputation. He had revived the art of fashion illustration that had been left for dead by the explosion of fashion photography. When Antonio arrived in Paris in the autumn of 1969, he was only twenty-six years old and he brought with him a new definition of beauty that electrified the city. It was a definition of beauty that began with glamour. 'That is the most important thing to me, that people are sexy and sensual and glamorous.'

His head was whirring with the fractured images and influences of an immigrant life, and his coming-of-age in inner-city New York at the birth of consumerism. What made Antonio's vision radical was that, for him, ethnic, blonde, black, working-class, homosexual, transvestite and transsexual, man or woman could all be glamorous and beautiful. His fantasies were not limited to well-bred white ladies. Paris fashion had never contemplated this possibility before.

There was an intoxicating glow to this glamour of Antonio's – in the way he dressed and drew, in the arch of his line, in the way he danced. He was determined to make what he saw in his head happen in life. This was Antonio's magnetic pull: the potency of his dream.

He came with Juan, whom he had met while studying at the Fashion Institute of Technology in New York. By the time they got to Paris they were no longer lovers, but they worked in intense collaboration. Juan both art-directed and channelled Antonio's volatile creativity. He was the constant presence at the drawing table, hovering behind Antonio's left shoulder. He thought out the graphic construction of each picture, but he also possessed a profound artistic knowledge and taste, providing the painterly references that were fundamental to Antonio's development of line and his rich palette of sources.

They shared a visual and cultural background: Juan was also born in Puerto Rico, the year before Antonio, and had been brought up in Harlem. They worked together in an often strained but always inspirational collaborative process. But, strangely, Juan was rarely credited for his partnership. Antonio referred to him instead using the disposable job description of 'my assistant' and his work was signed in the singular – 'Antonio'.

The root of Antonio's ambition lay not in material success but in his compulsive need to be in the vortex of fashion. In New York he had left behind his status as bright young fashion illustrator, where he was leader of a fashion pack and friend of Andy Warhol and designers such as Halston, Stephen Burrows and the illustrious and fallen couturier Charles James. As soon as they arrived in Paris Antonio and Juan set about constructing a new glamour crowd. Antonio's first priority was a model. He always drew fashion from real models and according to long-term friend, painter Paul Caranicas, 'Both he and Juan believed that the results achieved from having a live sitter could not be matched by any other method.' Antonio needed someone to sit for him straight away so that he could draw the advertising and editorial images for which he had already been commissioned. He called up Donna Jordan, who was an old friend from New York, a skinny girl who had hung out on the Factory edges as an Andy Warhol discovery. She was gap-toothed with brown hair, sexy in a goofy, nineteen-year-old kind of a way. She had left New York to conquer Europe, but pending victory was temporarily waylaid in London and was only too delighted to escape to Paris when Antonio called.

A month later in October 1969 Corey Tippin arrived from New York in a flurry of face powder and the core of Antonio's new crowd was in place. Corey Tippin had met Antonio and Juan during the term he attended Parsons School of Design in New York, shortly before he was asked to leave the premises. He was a bad and beautiful boy from Connecticut who had made his precocious entrance on the under-ground scene by skipping boarding-school, on his mother's instructions, to take a train to Warhol's Factory to audition for one of his movies. He stepped out of the Factory freight elevator, aged sixteen, and into the arms of Warhol's dashing business partner and art dealer, Fred Hughes. By nightfall Corey Tippin was downtown, dancing in a loft for film director Antonioni.

Now eighteen, Corey came to Paris with impossible dreams of glamour, models and provocation. He came expecting the centre of the fashion universe. 'I was expecting fabulous, flamboyant, happening, a culturally developed city,' says Corey, 'but when we got to Paris it was not sophisticated *at all*. We were shocked. You still felt the war: dour, grey and black. There were no telephones, there was no technology; everything shut down early, it was like being in some kind of dead suburb.'

In New York they had danced every night at Max's Kansas City and Yellow Fingers nightclub. Corey had been a go-go dancer at school and he and Antonio were constantly inventing new dances. Billina was a cabaret singer and dancer at the time and remembers them in the clubs of New York as a swirl of fedora hats, scarves and collars. 'I always had my eye on Corey, he was so cute and, God, they all danced so well. It wasn't disco-dancing, it was more like a combination of tango, disco, cabaret, whatever. When Antonio or Corey got on the floor to dance with either Donna or Pat Cleveland it was just fantastic. People would clear off the floor and then sit and watch them throw and pull, up and down over the shoulder, it was like *dramatic* disco-dancing.' This was the energy they brought to Paris in 1969. They had a lightness and freedom that the French had never imagined.

They arrived in Paris to find music-hall ballads, Juliette Gréco, Mistinguett, but nothing to dance to. They found what every foreigner finds on arrival in Paris: behavioural codes unfathomable to the outsider and a set-piece social life that takes place behind closed salon doors. The fashion scene was unrecognisable from the New York hotbed they were used to. Paris fashion had yet to fuse with music or street or any kind of ethnic culture. 'For us it was so retro. The fashion shows were old-fashioned, there was no music, they held numbers, there were girls "working a pocket",' remembers Corey. 'It was crazy.' It was haute couture.

Antonio and Juan found work immediately, travelling to Japan and around Europe working for French and American fashion publications. After their first encounter with Karl Lagerfeld at the Chloé studio, they started seeing him regularly. Karl spoke fluent English and had a multi-cultural attitude that was open to encounters with new and different kinds of people, a characteristic that would stay with him throughout his career. In this way he was poles apart from the French. He was also a foreigner, like the Americans.

Donna and Corey began a lonely year, staying in cheap hotels around Saint-Germain-des-Prés, moving on when the bar ran dry. 'Donna and

I were freaking out because there was this hippie rock-and-roll thing going on and we were looking for dance clubs which didn't exist.' Donna was schlepping across town on the Métro trying to get a modelling job, doing test photos for free with young photographers David Hamilton, Alex Chatelain, Patrick Demarchelier and getting nowhere. They were doing their best to get noticed. In the mornings Corey dared Donna to run across the Boulevard Saint-Germain from the hotel to get coffee wearing nothing but a T-shirt and curlers. They spent whole days together in the Flore, Donna screeching at waiters in brawling English, Corey slipping down a handful of Black Beauty diet pills (a mild form of speed sent by his mother in the post) with a mid-morning kir.

When Corey wasn't at the Flore, he was across the road at the make-up counter of the Monoprix supermarket on Rue de Rennes, buying cosmetics and experimenting on Donna. He was ravenous to make it in fashion and to get close to exquisite physical perfection. 'As far as I was concerned there was nothing else beautiful except a model, that is what defined beauty for me,' says Corey. 'I lived in Paris and I never went to a museum. All I wanted was to devour the fashion business.'

To begin with, Antonio and Juan kept their relationship with Karl closely guarded. 'I don't think they felt comfortable enough yet to introduce Donna and me,' says Corey, but gradually they were introduced into Karl's life and Karl liked what he saw. They were taken round to his apartment and started to be included in the daily schedule. Karl must have seen the potential of this band of cool and highly visible Americans. 'I think Antonio and Juan realised that Karl was eager to provide himself with an entourage,' says Corey, 'make a statement, kind of, about having all these Americans around that had no connection to France.'

Chapter 5

1970

It was early evening and they were running along the platform at the Gare de Lyon, running to get out of the emptiness that is Paris in August. They were late for the train and laden down with luggage. Donna was stumbling to keep up – she had bought her high-heeled shoes one size too small on purpose, to give herself a Monroe sexy wiggle as she walked, but now her feet were killing her. Karl had enough steamer trunks to fill a porter's trolley; he was a vision in flowing jersey and bell-bottomed trousers, with a narrow scarf tied around his neck that streamed out behind him as he ran, clutch bag in hand, towards the carriage. 'Corey, take this,' he shouted, tossing his jewellery box in the direction of Corey, who promptly dropped it on the platform. Corey watched, horrified, as a tonne of art-deco jewellery – black and red Bakelite and star-struck diamanté – bounced all over the platform, and immediately scrabbled on his hands and knees to get them back in the box.

The Americans boarded the Train Bleu with squeals of delight: it was just as they had imagined, a luxury train travelling south through the night, stopping at movie destinations only – Antibes, Nice and Monte Carlo. It had been Karl's idea to come south in the first place. He had rented the large house just off the old port of Saint-Tropez that awaited them. He had paid for them all – Antonio, Juan, Corey and Donna – to take the train and it was perfectly pitched for their jazz-age pose. The original Train Bleu was a steam train, an art-deco marvel of mahogany and rosewood marquetry, with glass panels of sinuous nudes by René Lalique and passengers dancing the Charleston all through the night. By 1970 it was an electrified train, but it still had echoes of another age: panelled night-cabins and bouquets of mimosa on the white linen tablecloths in the candlelit *voiture-restaurant*. There was still a tradition of popping open champagne bottles as the train pulled out of Paris.

They were flushed with the stares of other passengers and high on the excitement that the Côte d'Azur lay at the end of the train tracks or, as the Train Bleu railway poster had always promised, '*Le pays de votre rêve est au bout de votre nuit.*' The land of your dreams is at the end of your night. They were travelling fast through life now, finally living in the Europe they had dreamed of. Late that night Corey and Donna went creeping along the train corridor to spy on Karl, curious to see what kind of strange and blousy attire he might wear in bed. Donna choked her giggles as Corey tried the handle on Karl's cabin door, pushing it as far open as the safety chain would allow. They peered into the dark but were disappointed at what they saw: Karl was fast asleep and dressed in a long white T-shirt.

The Americans found Karl both extraordinary and vaguely ridiculous. He blinded them with heritage. He told stories of his childhood days spent in a castle in the far-flung reaches of northern Germany, of the fleet of servants and the French governess. He had an encyclopaedic knowledge of French culture, literature and the arts, which he was eager to impart. And when he spoke, in French, English or German, his sentences were careering and unstoppable, a race to get out all the information he knew.

'He was so educated he almost spoke in tongues,' says Corey. 'He was all over the place with ideas and he would babble, literally babble. He had this theory about past lives and parallel lives. I remember we were sitting outside a café and Karl was talking about how he had lived as an eighteenth-century gentleman in a past life. Then I started to pay attention, because I started to believe it.'

There was a material dimension to their relationship that started in the guise of presents and would end in a rather more explicit form of maintenance. Indeed material benefit was a dimension that could never be ignored in any relationship with Karl. He had money and he spent lots of it, at times with overbearing generosity.

Money gave Karl both momentum and a vital source of power within fashion. What was perceived as huge inherited wealth was in fact money that Karl earned and accumulated both through his design and from his shrewd collecting and selling of furniture and works of art. Wealth had always been a key feature of his self-created personal image, but from this moment on Karl used his money as a means to pay for both him and others to live out their fantasies. And this is what he did all that summer of 1970 and for several summers to follow in Saint-Tropez.

Saint-Tropez was no longer a fishing village, but it was still a chic holiday resort of Scotch and soda, of the blasé European jet set playing gin rummy on polished teak decks with the odd stray hippie washed up on the port. Then off the train from Paris stepped Antonio, Juan, Corey, Donna and Karl, arch and provocative, picking their way across cobbles and in between the red gingham tablecloths of the port cafés, shiny cigarette-holders poised between fingertips, causing an immediate sensation.

Antonio's every move and gesture was a studied pose for an effortless effect. He used his body to make stylised shapes and arabesques against the blue horizon, one foot tilted against the other, a hand turned to shade his eyes from the glittering sunlight or thrust into a trouser pocket, a chin slanted towards a camera lens.

Every day in the brittle heat of August the boys wore wide-legged herringbone trousers, long-sleeved shirts and fitted waistcoats. They dressed before the mirror, adding spotted silk bow-ties, putting on the red and black Bakelite bracelets, pinning diamanté clips to their waistcoats. Corey covered them all in a landscape of tan foundation. They adjusted their panamas for the off. Corey checked the mirror one more time with a loving glance, pulling at his bow-tie to leave it perfectly undone. They were ready for the beach.

They sauntered out in harmony, Antonio, Juan and Corey, past the decks of topless bathers and stares, past the *mobylettes* and the Hawaiian suntan oil, to the far end of the shore, where they lay down fully clothed to drink gin cocktails in the heat. Karl was there too, draped on a sun lounger beneath the shade of a large parasol, wearing a navy-blue wool 1920s bathing-suit that plunged rather dramatically down his chest to reveal a body that was Popeye-like in proportion after months of weight training. On his feet he wore a pair of black stack-heeled booties.

Antonio pulled out paper and pencils and started sketching Donna. All that summer Donna basked in the focus of Antonio's, and therefore the group's, attention. She had on a striped red-and-white hat with a wide brim that rose in an arc against the sky and underneath her brown hair was bleached so white you could see the pink glow of her scalp beneath. 'Like a rabbit,' said Corey. She kept her pills in a transparent art-deco compact until they melted in the sun and turned into a glossy scarlet pool of barbiturates.

Antonio sketched Donna endlessly, teaching her how to pose, showing her gestures of the old Hollywood stars, Jean Harlow, Mae West. She shone with the euphoria of a newly minted beauty; she threw her head back for Antonio, fingers caressing her throat in an ecstasy of glamour. Antonio drew Donna how he imagined her, sketching her the way he thought she should look and the way, pretty soon, she would look. 'Like a divinely innocent Marilyn Monroe,' said Karl, who was watching.

They were a closed clique riding high on the presumed importance of their youth and restless exhibitionism. It was Antonio who led them, decided who was beautiful. 'We were craving attention, all of us,' remembers Corey. 'It was all about superficial: if you weren't a model, if you weren't famous, if you weren't beautiful, then it was, "Well, who cares about you?"'

Antonio and Juan dressed the Gatsby part, but used their Latino skin and features to skewer the Waspy image. Corey bleached Donna's eyebrows white and smeared them with a cheap white grease crayon so they shimmered in the sunlight against her tanned skin and matched her newly bleached hair. 'It was fun. You do what you're told,' remembers Donna. 'I had all these sculptors around me and they were sculpting me, moulding me and making me who I became – the blonde bombshell! They were creating this image and I was allowing it.'

Soon after their arrival on the Côte d'Azur *Women's Wear Daily*, poised to pick up on every ripple in the fashion millpond, spotted Donna, 'who stops traffic in her short shorts, high-heeled shoes and halo of gold hair'. They failed to get her name right, calling her Diana, but they grasped the essential: in terms of fashion Donna's high-shine camp rendered everyone else passé. 'Established Saint-Tropez celebrities like Bardot and Jacqueline de Ribes get barely a glance in their *démodé* turtlenecks, ballet slippers and miniskirts.'

Karl was in the group, but he was not one of them. He was older, he was German, he was the odd one out. He paid for everything, the dinners and the champagne, the rented *mobylettes* and the motorboat that Juan drove. 'He was scary for me,' says Corey. 'He seemed much older than I was, like a real adult; he seemed from a whole other generation.' He shared their flamboyance in dress, but while the Americans' look suggested high-dandy, Karl's preference for high heels and clutch bags was rather more effeminate and was regarded by the Americans as a strange affectation.

They laughed at him, but at the same time they were intrigued. Karl had packed dumb-bells in his steamer trunks and electronic gadgets to apply to the chest for working on muscle tone. 'He was compulsive about his body,' remembers Corey, who would stand with Donna outside Karl's bedroom every morning, holding their breath and waiting for the sound of the electric shaver to start buzzing. 'He's shaving his chest!' Donna would stage-whisper and they would collapse in giggles. 'That was unheard of at that time, just shocking for us. We were absolutely fascinated and didn't dare talk about it openly,' says Corey. 'It was years and years later that I realised how really ahead of the curve Karl was.'

At night the Americans were off dancing on bar tables, drinking and indulging in sexual encounters, but Karl's behaviour was considerably more inhibited. Perhaps the fact he had his 73-year-old mother Elisabeth staying at the villa in Saint-Tropez was a reason. After his father's death, his mother came to live with him in Paris and even holidayed with him. Or perhaps Karl never had any intention of losing control of his body or mind.

They were always encouraging him to go out and find a boyfriend, loosen up, but Karl never did embrace their lifestyle and he never did loosen up. 'He looked flamboyant, but he didn't act flamboyant,' remembers Billina, a friend from New York who met up with them all that first summer in Saint-Tropez. 'He was fun to sit with at dinner as conversation-wise he was very, very funny. But he would always sit in the corner, sort of as if he was thinking, "Let everyone have fun and let me be".'

Group entertainment was 'dishing, talking about each other,' says Billina, 'or the person who had just left the room.' It seemed every time Karl left the room there was one more hilarious story to recount. 'We were constantly mocking Karl,' admits Corey, 'but I couldn't help it, he was such a character. A lot of times I was making fun of him and we would say funny things; I thought he wouldn't understand, but he *did* understand.'

Karl undoubtedly heard their stifled giggles – after all, hadn't he heard them before throughout his childhood? But for the time being he compromised his pride in favour of his self-interest. He was mesmerised by the Americans, by their sheer talent, modernity and Coca-Cola glamour. He watched as Corey, Antonio and Juan transformed Donna with make-up, peroxide, pose and attitude. They didn't know it, but as they flirted and sketched each other incessantly, plucked at eyebrows or took photos in the tender evening light, they were showing Karl a new way of imagining fashion.

The Americans carried with them a whole new culture of fashion that was underpinned by the visual influences of contemporary American art, Andy Warhol's pop mentality, Hollywood movies and the throbbing beat of soul and dance. Theirs was a new-world culture that was profoundly different from any Parisian notions of elegance set down by Balenciaga or Dior. It was their approach that heralded the future: a careless merging of street, screen, art, irony, music and the individual. Karl saw all that.

They talked of Josephine Baker and Marlene Dietrich, surrealism, Richard Lindner and Rauschenberg; they listened to Antonio's tape of Chicago soul over and over; they pinned art-deco ribbons to their panamas and hung out at the gay Aqua beach club, cross-breeding visual references until they created hybrid trends, ambiance and, therefore, fashion.

That first summer in Saint-Tropez they showed Karl that fashion could be created outside the confines of Paris and therefore away from the influence of the couture salon. It was the Americans who taught Karl Lagerfeld that fashion was no longer a question of hemlines. From now on fashion would be all about attitude.

But if Karl realised how much he had to learn and gain from the Americans, they had not yet got the measure of Karl. They saw only the eccentricity, the highly agile mind and the cash. They did not realise the scale of his ambition and stamina, or the range of his talent, but at that stage so few people in Paris did. For the Americans and for many who knew Karl in 1970 he was, in the words of Corey, 'A kook. I don't think anyone was prepared for the progressive momentum he gained.'

The Saint-Tropez fashion magic was always dependent on an audience and when the summer of 1970 faded, so did the crowds. Karl and the Americans packed their steamer trunks and returned to Paris. Antonio and Juan moved into a guest apartment that Karl kept on the Rue Bonaparte just opposite the Ecole des Beaux Arts, a step away from the Seine.

Their life there was fun and bohemian, sketching and posing all day, showing off and dancing all night. There were constant new arrivals of models and strays who wanted to sleep on the apartment floor, sleep on the chairs, sleep anywhere and with anyone to be a part of the movement and excitement. No one had any cash but it didn't seem to matter: life was thrilling and champagne-coloured and Karl paid.

Most days the Americans passed by his apartment on the Rue de l'Université to hang out and sketch. Karl always had something new to show them, a purchase, a book or a piece of furniture. He had a penchant for high-tech gadgets and there was a Xerox machine and gym installed at home, both of which impressed even the Americans. He worked out several hours a day and had put aside one whole room for physical exertion – unheard of in Paris at this time – equipping it with dumb-bells, weights, hanging bars and electronic scales to chart his progress.

By now Karl had largely disposed of the white futuristic interior of yesterday and in its place was installing a *mise-en-scène* of art-deco furniture and *objets*. The period had infiltrated every aspect of the group's life. Antonio and Juan had presaged the trend in New York when they started collecting Tiffany lamps in the mid-1960s and by the time they got to Paris they were mad for the hedonistic curves and dazzling ornament of art deco.

Since the Second World War art deco and its precursor art nouveau had both languished as a kind of stylistic white elephant, disparaged for their 'superficial' decorative and popular spirit and absence of ideology. But towards the end of the 1960s there was a reaction against the ascetic functionalism of modernism, a reaction that was echoed in fashion by a rejection of the space-age, moon-boot vision of Pierre Cardin and

Courrèges' futurism. What had seemed so modern and had defined Paris fashion in the early 1960s – the bright white short shift dress and matching vinyl helmet, the cut-out shapes and volumes – now seemed out of date and contrived. There was a yearning for romance, for clothes with soul and femininity, for fantasy of the retro kind.

Joan Juliet Buck was working as a stylist for French *Vogue* photographer Guy Bourdin and writing articles for the magazine *20 ans*, moving between London and Paris and hanging out with photographer Berry Berenson and Antonio. 'There was all that dowdiness of our mother's fashion superseded by what we were told were the "youthful" clothes of Courrèges and Ungaro, none of which we – and by we I mean myself, Berry and Marisa Berenson, Angelica [Huston], Jane Gozzett – none of us wanted to wear that stuff. I remember my fantasy, my aspirations, my longing went to this book that was all about the extraordinary, voluptuous charge of that perverse and curved line of Art Nouveau.'

A major exhibition held at the Musée des Arts Décoratifs in Paris in 1966 entitled *Les Années 25: Art Deco/Bauhaus/Stijl/Art Nouveau* was one of the first signs of a revival of this movement. Three years later interest in both art nouveau and art deco was given a phenomenal boost by the publication of Martin Battersby's *The Decorative Twenties,* followed in 1971 by *The Decorative Thirties*, as well as Bevis Hillier's *Art Deco of the 20s and 30s*, and fashionable people snapped up copies of these books.

Art deco and its time line of 1910–39 appealed to a generation filled with nostalgia for the perceived opulence and abandon of their parents' or grandparents' lives. It was a period that, during the austere rule of modernism, had been treated with utmost disdain and viewed in pejorative terms as 'indecent luxury'. Nowhere was the art-deco revival more popular than among the Paris fashion crowd, who yearned for nothing more than that their lives be characterised by just such indecent luxury. 'The '60s rock'n'roll era was replaced by a kind of nostalgia for the cream interior of a Rolls-Royce,' says Joan Juliet Buck, 'yet it was very uneducated. I remember being told that Eileen Gray lived around the corner from me on the Rue du Bac and I didn't know who the hell she was. It was a sort of ebony and ivory cigarette-holder obsession with the '30s.'

It was logical that the trend should be adored in Paris, for the city had been the birthplace of the movement and still held the living memory of the style in its shop fronts and typeface, hotels, ateliers, cabaret and restaurants such as the favourite of this time, La Coupole. Many of the mythic figures were still alive in Paris: Josephine Baker, who symbolised the exoticism and eroticism of 1920s Paris, was aged sixty-four and still performing in her Dunand bangles, a live panther on her arm. The Duke and Duchess of Windsor endured as the epitome of the Paris *monde*. They lived out their exile in a villa on the edge of the Bois de Boulogne, bearing their morbid and impeccable chic around town. Both were already immortal fashion icons. 'I remember I wanted to be the Duchess of Windsor so badly had it been possible I would have killed to be her,' says Joan Juliet Buck.

Karl was introduced to art deco by Andrée Putman, whom he had met in 1968 and with whom he became great friends. She was working at the time as a journalist in design and was a champion of both fashion and design. She had bought a set of eight dining-room chairs designed by Edgar Brandt at auction in New York in 1967, which Karl saw and liked when he was round for dinner one night. As it turned out Andy Warhol had a set of the very same chairs and was in the process of amassing art-deco furniture and jewellery in New York.

Karl picked up early on the trend and began accumulating in a manner that was fast and meticulous. He was attracted to the pure, high-style, Paris art deco and the exquisite craftsmanship of furniture by Ruhlmann and Groult, bronzes by Brandt and lacquer screens by Jean Dunand. He constructed his interior scheme to be thematic and absolute, a period drama down to the finest detail of silver cocktail-shaker and glasses, crystal fruit-press and sleek silver cigarette-holder.

Every day Karl went shopping with Juan to La Hune, where they bought masses of books, mostly on American contemporary artists as Juan was introducing Karl to the art scene of New York. Back at the apartment Karl devoured the books at high speed, while Antonio sketched Karl's designs or at times styles from his own imagination. Juan added ideas and suggested stylistic influences. He ran round gathering design inspiration for Antonio, coming up with movie posters, graphics, objects, exhibition postcards or flea-market finds that were right for the feeling they were striving to conjure. Karl incorporated this magpie-like approach to inspiration into his own design process and it is exactly this concept of 'mood board' that is the starting point for how fashion is created by designers today.

There were trips to the groovy men's tailor, Renoma, where Karl bought Antonio and Juan new three-piece suits, and there were also regular hand-outs of clothes left over from the many collections he designed. These would be bequeathed in a strange ritual whereby Karl stood over a trunk and tossed shoes, dresses and waistcoats over his shoulder. 'Here, my dear, take this!' he would say, as a pair of brogues came flying through the air at high velocity. As always in fashion, there was a pecking order: Antonio came first, then Juan and then Corey. Donna picked up dresses from past Chloé collections that Karl occasionally gave her – 'scraps' she called them. Karl treated her and Corey well, although they both knew they were never the main attraction. 'Karl was fine, he was good, he was funny and I think he was intrigued by us. The real relationship of course was with Antonio and Juan; we were just sidelines,' remembers Donna. 'He obviously admired Antonio *a lot*; Antonio was a big seer of fashion and he was way ahead, ten years ahead of his time, his stuff was ground-breaking.'

At night after work Antonio, Juan, Corey and Donna went home to change, meeting up again with Karl for champagne dinners at La Coupole. As the financial implications to their relationship became more explicit, so the balance of power shifted, imperceptibly at first, until the group came to be seen, at least from the outside, as Karl's group.

This was the first time Karl had had his own group. For most of the 1960s he had existed in fashion on his own, sharing a relationship with actor Gérard Falconetti in his private life. He had of course been part of the Saint Laurent–Victoire gang in the mid-1950s when he started out in fashion, but he had always been limited by Yves' leading role.

Once Saint Laurent found stratospheric success, it was inevitable that Yves and Karl's youthful friendship would fade. One can imagine the immense frustration of being someone's equal in competition at a young age and then watching as that person is swept away from you on a high tide of success and fame, while you are left wading in the cross-current of labour. If Karl was going to make it in fashion, he had to remove himself from the blinding light of Saint Laurent's celebrity and talent. Karl, however, chose to stay on the Paris stage. And in doing so he was perhaps making a tacit decision to take on the challenge of Yves Saint Laurent.

Karl's acquisition of a clique marked a considerable leap forward in his conviction in himself and the path that lay ahead in fashion. Was it rivalry that pushed Karl into constructing his group, his superstar image and the future fleet of houses? They were certainly everything he needed for a power base from which to launch his fashion attack.

The way he bound this first clique to him would serve as the proto-type for the rest of his career. The faces might change – and they did, continually – but the way Karl wielded power over those in his favour remained constant. The memories of those who have been in prox-imity to Karl at some point over the last fifty years bear a strikingly similar theme: gifts, always the gifts. 'I'd come home to find bags full of books from Karl hanging on my front door,' says one fashion editor. 'Karl gave me those pearls,' says another fondly, looking at a yellowing Polaroid of herself taken during the early 1970s. 'Karl dressed me then and he still dresses me now,' says Victoire. 'Karl would buy twenty Turnbull & Asser shirts for himself and ten for me,' remembers Gilles Dufour.

Often Karl's gifts were not simply things that money could buy; they were gifts with history, significance or fame: it was not just a diamond necklace but an heirloom from his mother's family; it was not just a dress but one that he had designed for Marlene Dietrich herself, or that is how Karl described it. The glowing provenance added a layer of signif-icance to whatever the object was, a fine powder of celebrity shimmer that seemed to rub off on your skin, particularly when you came from the Bronx or Brooklyn, were aged twenty, newly arrived and breathless in Paris.

Late in 1970 model Pat Cleveland arrived in Paris with liquorice hair, legs like pipe-cleaners and a Harlem shimmy dance-movement that recalled Josephine Baker and her 'danse sauvage'. Pat came with one fixed idea: 'Living a beautiful life is what I was wanting.' Juan picked her up from the airport and drove her back to the Rue Bonaparte apartment and Antonio started sketching. After several days spent posing for Antonio cooped up in the apartment, Pat went to La Coupole for her first night out in Paris.

'I was wearing a blue gown which Karl had given to me; it had first been worn by Marlene Dietrich, and it was a kind of lingerie that Karl had made for Marlene Dietrich. It was transparent and it had twenty-five yards of fabric and it was pleated and nude. When I had my arms down you couldn't see through the dress, but as soon as I walked into the room I put my arms up and it became transparent. I moved through the room the way Isadora Duncan would have moved, that's how I entered La Coupole for my first drink of champagne in Paris aged twenty-one. I was with Karl Lagerfeld, Antonio, Juan and everyone started applauding and I knew I had arrived in Paris. I felt like a dove released in the world of fashion and I sat down and all the waiters came over and offered me champagne and I ordered a *steak au poivre*. I didn't know which fork to use, but Karl knew which fork to use even though he didn't eat.'

Over thirty years after that dinner, Pat's memories are even now a patter of wonder and reverie at finding herself living this beautiful life that she had always been wanting and that it was in some way thanks to Karl that she was doing so: Karl who knew which fork to hold, Karl who gave her the blue Dietrich dress, who paid for the dinner, who provided the setting in which to shine.

'He kind of swirled you in with all this glamour and fantasy of past and present and future,' says Paloma Picasso, who met and became friends with Karl at this time. 'He's a very good storyteller, but maybe because I was younger I was also less critical in a way, I was taking in whatever was coming.'

Being part of Karl's world, then as now, conferred on you a level of extravagant living and a proximity to wealth and history that was overwhelming, exhilarating and fun. 'There was the thrill of feeling that these people were really living the life they had dreamed about,' says Pat Cleveland. Living your dreams was the sensation Karl Lagerfeld evoked.

The clique was a concept that had long existed in Paris fashion – Paul Poiret, Gabrielle Chanel and Christian Dior had all had one. When a couturier's social status was still that of a tradesperson or *fournisseur*, the clique was a way of infiltrating walks of life that were still *interdit* to the designer. Even after couturiers started receiving invitations to dine out in society, the fashion tradition of a troop of society girls and boys that were linked to a specific couturier continued to cast a glow on the designer's still-sensitive social skin.

Chanel used her clique as both a means of gathering intelligence and prestige by association. As she told Paul Morand, 'Inasmuch as I seldom went out, it was essential that I be informed of everything that went on in the houses where my clothes were worn. I developed the habit, then unprecedented, of surrounding myself with people of quality so as to establish a link between myself and society. The Russian, Italian and French aristocracy, English society women – all came and did service in the Rue Cambon.'

Gabrielle Chanel mixed up her aristocrats with *artistes* – the avant-garde scene of Diaghilev, Les Ballets Russes, Picasso, Morand and Cocteau were all drawn to the immense creativity and charisma of Chanel and they in turn all added to her artistic credibility and inspiration. Hers was the clique that every succeeding designer sought to emulate, not least Yves Saint Laurent and Karl Lagerfeld.

By 1970 any designer, whether ready-to-wear or couturier, with ambitions for success and recognition had a clique which they used as a means of identity, aggrandisement and a weapon for power play. Hubert de Givenchy tapped his handsome patrician looks and noble lineage, positioning himself at the hub of the American society ladies; Marc Bohan at Dior had succeeded in seducing Princess Grace of Monaco, while Pierre Cardin was surrounded by a cluster of fine-boned French boys dressed in Mao suits.

Rivalries and intrigue between the cliques were brutal; they always had been. 'It was a game,' says fashion photographer Guy Marineau, 'a closed and secret world. All of these people from the designers through to their clients and their followers, they all lived in autarchy; they lived with each other and they lived for each other. If they weren't all together, they were lost.' There was subterfuge or at least constant suspicion of subterfuge, accusations of attempts to poach clients, accusations of imita-tion. 'I read that Bohan is going to Marrakech, well now he's even copying Yves' vacation spot,' sniped Pierre Bergé about Marc Bohan when he dared to turn up there on holiday. Bergé blasted off in the press at least once a week about other couturiers and during this period the subjects of his wrath were Marc Bohan and Pierre Cardin.

Other than journalists and fashion editors, who were allowed to flit between groups and socialise with them all, fashion cliques demanded blind loyalty and rare indeed was the person who managed to belong to two groups at the same time. Corey remembers, 'The French were really, really camped out in different groups and they didn't intermingle.' Paloma Picasso would prove a notable exception. Betty Catroux was a great friend of Cardin's business partner André Oliver back in 1966, but once she became Saint Laurent's confidante there was no going back. Jacques Grange, who made his entry on the *monde* at this time, admits he too started Parisian life in the embrace of the Pierre Cardin clique but soon abandoned it for that of Saint Laurent. 'Why? Because I was more in love with Yves Saint Laurent than Cardin. He corresponded more with what I loved profoundly myself, and so I was seduced, I went towards that which attracted me; it was Yves that pleased me, his taste that I loved, Jean-Michel Frank, Christian Bérard, Cocteau, his aesthetic language.'

What Grange doesn't say was that the Yves Saint Laurent clique was the chicest, the most exalted and the hardest to gain entry to and it took every fashion ambition to scale its well-defended ramparts. Yves was rarely seen out, even then – well before the reclusive years. He was never accessible. He was not on display at the Flore. He was between the couture house and his home, with dinners out. Limited access was an integral element to the mystique of Saint Laurent and his remarkable powers of seduction, as well as to the exclusivity of his clique. For how sweet the sensation if you were admitted to his inner sanctum. You stepped with care and spoke in hushed tones of reverence. 'Saint Laurent was undeniably the higher plane for us all,' says Jean-Pascal Billaud, who from time to time would be taken off to visit Yves on the arm of Jacques Grange or Betty. 'When Jacques said, "Do you want to go and see Saint Laurent?" it was considered rather like having an audience with the Messiah. When you were allowed access to Saint Laurent, you knew that you were in contact with a superior quality of life.'

Beyond loyalty, it was devotion that was a principal law of the Saint Laurent set, devotion to Yves, to his talent, his clothes, his taste, his moods and his every whim. Once in the group you stayed. It was close-knit, incestuous, glittering with prestige and hierarchy. It was more than a clique, it was a clan. And there was always a certain hard-edged cruelty to it, although perhaps that wasn't obvious to begin with.

It was from this time on that the Saint Laurent clan began to polarise into two camps of 'adults' and 'children'. The adults were led by Pierre and full of parental responsibility and day-to-day practical administration, while the children were led by Yves and set on self-indulgence, fantasy and escape. It was endlessly amusing to flout the authority of the adults safe in the knowledge that they would always be there to hold you in check, to come to the rescue.

Into the Saint Laurent clan blew a new inspiration causing commotion and delight: Loulou de la Falaise. She met Yves and Pierre in the summer of 1968 on the Place de Furstenberg, a bright clearing of sun and chestnut trees in the middle of Saint Germain where Fernando Sanchez kept an apartment. Fernando lived between New York, Paris and Marrakech and he held a tea party at his Place de Furstenberg apartment every Sunday afternoon when he was in Paris, serving warm brioche from the *boulanger* downstairs and fat joints of marijuana. Fernando hand-picked his tea-time cast of characters, which included what he calls the 'Sanctos Sanctum gang' of Pierre, Yves, Thadée, Clara and Betty Catroux, as well as others who turned up: Mireille d'Arc, Jeanloup Sieff, Talitha Getty and Jack Nicholson. 'All kinds of people came to the house, from models to hookers to famous people,' remembers Fernando, who always had an adventurous approach to his social life.

That afternoon in July 1968 there was a young girl floating around the apartment, giggling madly behind a dandelion puff of hair. She had the face and poise of a Burne-Jones portrait with none of the passive tragic overtones. She was filled with a sort of electric vitality. She was stoned and ravishing in Ossie Clark chiffon tunic and matching satin fly-away trousers, headscarf around her head and beads around her neck.

Loulou de la Falaise came as a shock to Yves' thoroughly French taste. There was a fantasy and colour and daring to her style that was truly original. He took in everything about her — the Bakst-inspired fauna print on chiffon, the way she stood with one arm flung up behind her against the door jamb, the wide-set blue eyes and narrow bone-structure. His eye was drawn to her tiny wrists and a bracelet she was wearing which he could have sworn was one of those metal bands they put on the corner of tables to hold down the tablecloth in the wind. It was; Loulou had taken if off the table at the Bistro Petit Saint Benoît and wore it as a Paris talisman.

Loulou didn't knock through the protective ramparts that surrounded Yves, she didn't need to; she stepped lightly through them, as though they had never existed. They were all in love with her: Yves, Fernando, even Pierre, in love with and in awe of her. She came along bearing both the lineage of the old world so dear to every couturier and, crucially, the cool swing of London.

Her maternal grandfather, Sir Oswald Birley, was a society portraitist who painted the glamour of England's ruling classes: portraits of George V and VI, Churchill, dukes and viscounts, cheeks flushed in the heat of the fireplace at gentleman's club White's. His wife Rhoda Birley was an intimidating Irish eccentric who drove through the Sussex countryside with muslin netting wrapped around her face to counter hay fever. She had a grand passion for gardening and her mid-summer garden and arts festivals at her home of Charleston Manor were full of whimsy and colour. One July day she served up violet cake and violet-coloured ice-cream shakes to accompany a Christopher Lloyd lecture on clematis and violets. Their delightful garden looked out over the Sussex Downs and they entertained a bohemian, smart set which included Harold Nicolson and Rudyard Kipling. But the idyll of the setting could not hide the conflict within their marriage or the emotionally bleak upbringing of the children.

Maxime was Loulou's mother. She was a combination of original mind and English beauty and she married a French count, Alain de la Falaise, and moved to Paris after the war where, as she tells it, she owned one pair of jeans and a push-up bra. They had no money and so Maxime started work at Schiaparelli, in a typical couture role of chic girl used to lure the English clientele. She was pregnant with Loulou when she worked there. After Schiaparelli, she worked at Paquin and Fath and was photographed wearing striped Paquin taffeta by Cecil Beaton for *Vogue* in 1950s hieratic pose. It was about this time that Beaton, sitting halfway up a staircase in Paris, paid Maxine an unlikely compliment, telling her: 'You are the only English woman I know who manages to be really chic in really hideous clothes.' She left the cocktail couture circuit to become a talented ready-to-wear *styliste* in her own right, working freelance for the house of Chloé, where she was known for her chiffon evening dresses. Maxime's brother was Mark Birley, who married Lady Annabel Vane Tempest Stewart, daughter of the 8th Marquess of Londonderry. Birley opened a nightclub in Berkeley Square in 1963, naming it after his wife, and Annabel's became the most fashionable club of 1960s London.

Loulou was just twenty-one when she got to Paris that summer and fashion was her escape route. Her exuberance hid a severely unhappy childhood. Maxime and Alain de la Falaise had divorced in 1950, when their children Loulou and Alexis were aged three and two respectively. 'I knew nothing about the French law and if you allowed yourself to be divorced you became something called "une mère indigne" [an unfit mother]. You lose all your rights as a mother,' explains Maxime. 'Alain said I could have one of the children but not both. But I couldn't do that. I couldn't separate them. I know I shouldn't have married Alain, but I am so glad I did because I've got the kids.' Maxime's mother-in-law sent the children to live in the countryside with foster families. 'First in a very old Catholic family and then a younger Catholic family, who were not perfect,' says Maxime. 'I should have been stronger you see and put my foot down and made a terrible fuss, but I was streaking off with a boyfriend.'

Loulou and her brother stayed in the Seine et Marne with the foster families until Loulou went to boarding-school in England at the age of seven. After that her school holidays were shared between mother, father and the second foster family. 'I know that the kids suffered terribly badly,' says Maxime with regret, 'And a lot of Loulou's strength lies in the fact that she protected her brother and she made herself strong.'

Loulou's force also lay in her ability to cut herself off from reality and escape inside her imagination. She remembers her childhood and the long school holidays spent talking to ghosts and 'sculpting gods to the wind from stumps of wood'. She and her brother Alexis went out hunting truffles under the trees, which they rooted out without the help of a dog and then took to a local market to sell. Eventually, recalls Loulou, posters were put up on the trees prohibiting truffle-hunting, but that did not stop the fearless duo. The posters threatened that anyone taking the truffles would be 'susceptible de poursuite', the word 'poursuite' meaning both prosecuted and pursued. 'Alexis and I thought that meant they'd run after us and we figured we could always outrun them if it came to a chase, so we kept on truffle-hunting.'

In 1966 she made a first, hasty marriage to Desmond FitzGerald, the Knight of Glin, but her role as chatelaine of a looming neo-Gothic castle in County Limerick did not last more than a year. She arrived in Paris after eighteen months spent in New York, where she had lived with photographer Berry Berenson and charmed the New York fashion world, hanging out with designer Halston, Warhol's partner Fred Hughes, Fernando, Elsa Peretti and Antonio and Juan. She had tried modelling, but was more successful designing fabrics for Halston, drawing prints that included small excitable rabbits with erections. She turned up in Paris looking for fun and moved in to share Fernando's flat. 'It was the first time Loulou was free,' says her mother Maxime.

'She was a little hippie girl, she was very pretty and very everything,' remembers Thadée Klossowski, 'but she was a bit shocking too and exciting in the way that she belonged to a very proper world, she was from a good family and all that, which was reassuring, but at the same time she was wild and she thought the French were incredibly square.' 'They were terribly stuffy,' remembers Loulou of the French society scene. 'Everyone thought I was after their husbands and then when I wasn't, they'd be rather insulted. One has a very exaggerated reputation.'

Her dual nationality meant that she slipped through your fingers even as you sought to define her. She spoke English with a distinct, clipped, almost pre-war accent. Pretty and gamine in real life, seen through a camera lens she became a portrait of bone-structure and brittle grace. She faced life with laughter. 'I had this kind of light atmosphere because it was a way of saying, "Let's pretend everything is fine,"' says Loulou now. 'I tend to block things out.'

Yves invited Loulou to Marrakech, where she arrived to stay for a week with a duffle bag out of which she pulled sarong after sarong after scrap of fabric, astonishing everyone with her outfits and imagination. 'It's a sort of rags-to-riches thing. All we had were rags and Loulou could turn them into riches and create a new look,' says Maxime. 'She was the best-dressed woman with a safety pin.'

She was a show-off, fearless, unafraid of Pierre who reminded her of a character from *Tintin*, and even more importantly, unafraid of Yves. 'Everyone was there to tell Saint Laurent he was a genius and Loulou was there to perturb him,' says Hélène de Ludinghausen, who was *direc-*

trice de salon at the house of Saint Laurent for thirty-one years. Loulou was never in awe of the myth that was Yves Saint Laurent. Where others tiptoed around him, she teased him with all the daring of youth.

Back in Paris he wanted Loulou near him, at first just as a friend and then later at work. In 1972 she entered the couture studio. 'I think Yves and Pierre just fell in love with her,' says Maxime. 'This mad little bohemian creature, full of ideas, full of jokes, hopping around. In a way it was Loulou's first holiday from family, from marriage, and she was finally living in the sort of milieu she loved. I don't know whether they defined to themselves what she was going to do. Pierre probably felt she was going to cheer up the atmosphere in the design room.'

Pierre was no doubt impressed by Loulou and wanted her in the Saint Laurent clique, but it was Yves who wanted her by his side and it is interesting to note that when Yves wanted something to happen, it did. Despite her youth, Loulou had highly sophisticated visual references, taste and a precise mind; she also had immense discipline, which appealed to Yves, and yet she was not rigid. She had the same effect on Yves as marijuana did, she liberated him from himself, she exorcised the bourgeois in him, made him less self-conscious.

'Maybe one world was ending and another world was starting which Yves knew less about,' reflects Loulou on why Yves wanted her by his side. 'I mean, the fashion business is a lot about small boys fantasising about either their mothers or a couple of generations before them and therefore fantasising about a way of life which is already more or less extinct by the time they get to be twenty-one. They are always a little bit in a time warp.'

Yves needed objects of fantasy. Fashion for him was like a play, a novel or a film peopled by characters with whom he could fall in love, idealise, be infatuated with and conjure up through clothes. He needed women around him to trigger his imagination and seduce him aesthetically. He had Betty and now Loulou, who was ready and able to play an active role in the couture house. Role-playing was what she was good at: one week she was Desdemona in purple velvet flares and a crown of flowers, the next Marlene with plucked crescent-shaped eyebrows. Loulou remembers with glee her first Saint Laurent couture evening-dress of sky-blue mousseline and the fact that it ended the night with a great hole burnt through it by a drunken Yves. 'She was a wild animal stepping lightly around him,' says Hélène de Ludinghausen. Her invention and irreverence were entirely in synch with the new voice of fashion that was chanting: be yourself, be individual, express yourself, be free.

Girls were breaking away from social roles and husbands' approval. If they were searching for a role now it was one of fantasy: the tragic romantic heroine, the Hollywood movie-star Marlene or Marilyn, the 1940s tart – anything but the perfect bourgeois wife with bouffant hair and the yellow Labrador.

'This was the time when there was the biggest change in fashion ever and the greatest change in attitude,' says Loulou de la Falaise. 'It was the first time there was a breakaway from looking like a lady into looking like something else. I think Yves was very struck by my London attitude when he saw me and he wanted to get his finger into that pie too.'

In October of 1970 Andy Warhol came to town and was greeted as a superstar from the moment he arrived. It was strange, everything he did in Paris was a hit and every time he came he created a frenzy. Parisians found his blazer, wig and blue jeans both ineffably chic and daringly subversive. His portraits fast became the de-rigueur work of art to grace every self-respecting fireplace. They were perfectly suited to the aesthetic of the moment, combining as they did flattery, glamour and narcissism on a large and multiple scale (touched-up, stylised portraits sold by the quadruple). Ironically Warhol managed to make vast inroads into society and contemporary art in Paris at a time when he had not yet attained that level of acceptance in America. His social success was in part due to Fred Hughes, who used his charm and connections to get Warhol into Marie-Hélène de Rothschild's dining room. But it was also due to a mutual fascination between Warhol and the Parisians: they found him inscrutable and exotic, while he marvelled at their ambiguity, *ancien régime* lifestyle and ruthless intrigue.

Warhol came ostensibly to shoot a new movie with his Factory filmmaker Paul Morrissey, although he spent rather more time whipping up portrait commissions with Fred Hughes and chasing down Ruhlmann chairs among the *antiquaires* than he did shooting the movie. He brought with him his own entourage, a handful of his Factory youth including model Pátti d'Arbanville, voluptuous twins Jed and Jay Johnson, and Jane Forth, a strange Edvard Munch beauty with transparent skin and two lonely antennae where her eyebrows had once been (she had plucked them all out at a party one Saturday night and the antennae were all that grew back).

Warhol's previous films had been controversial, combining a provocative content of drugs and genitalia, and *Liberty*, a Warhol film made at the end of the 1960s, was still banned in France at this time. The new Paris movie had a working title of 'Gold Diggers '71', although it would later be released under the rather more romantically inclined title of *L'Amour*. It was a story of two Hicksville American girls turning up in Paris, undergoing physical and sartorial transformation in a bid to find their fortune in the form of a very rich husband.

Donna was cast with Jane Forth to play the Hicksville girls; Corey was to be the Pygmalion character who masterminds their transformation and Karl Lagerfeld picked up a role as one of the parvenu bachelors who was a German aristocrat. He was also lending his apartment for the film to be shot.

There was no script, not much plot, acting ability was thin and there was heavy reliance on improvisation with, at times, disastrous results. Unlike some of the other Warhol movies, *L'Amour* was resolutely obscure, never widely distributed and it is a challenge to find anyone who has seen it, even among those that starred in the film. But all that autumn of 1970 the making of *L'Amour* caused tremors of anticipation within the fashion world.

The high-camp posturing and alien glamour of Antonio and Karl's group merged with the trashy pop vibes of Andy Warhol and formed a kitsch moment that Paris and, most of all, fashion found thrilling. The mood of irreverent fantasy that Antonio and his clique had created in Saint-Tropez took on greater intensity and significance when it was refracted through the camera lens of Andy Warhol in Paris. The Americans were everywhere: ice-skating in front of the Eiffel Tower; gadding about in flea-market dresses and wedge heels; Donna pulling up her T-shirt on the Métro station platform to flash a nipple for the camera. 'They were titillating, they took too many drugs, they puked on your shoes, but they were young and fun and they saw things that you didn't see because you didn't think of looking at them. Their ignorance gave an interesting twist to things,' remembers Thadée Klossowski. The language barrier only added to their attraction.

The very idea of kitsch was a concept totally at odds with the principals of haute couture. Perhaps couturier Elsa Schiaparelli had sailed closest to kitsch in her collaboration with Dalí and her lobster dress in 1936 and shoe hat of the following year. But even so, her pink lobsters were inspired by the high art of surrealism and worn by the then Mrs Wallis Simpson, whereas *le kitsch* of the Americans – its sex, youth and pink tongue-in-cheek antics – blew a great hole through couture.

Their significance can be measured by the speed with which the fashion world now rushed to make them their own. Donna, who up until this time had done one measly Badedas ad during her year in Paris, was suddenly in hot demand. She turned up one day unannounced at the studio of star French photographer Guy Bourdin and by the next she was posing for the front cover and a sixteen-page shoot for French *Vogue* in which she was pictured straddling a motorbike, wearing no knickers and a glazed expression on her face. Corey, who had transformed Donna and Jane for *L'Amour* with arcs of glossy colour, was a wanted man both as a runway model and make-up artist. 'Once we made that movie everyone in Paris really thought we were celebrities,' says Corey, 'and of course we didn't tell them we weren't.'

Karl Lagerfeld's role in *L'Amour* and his encounter with Andy Warhol and his followers were of fundamental importance to his career. It gave Karl an opportunity to observe Warhol close-up, to watch and analyse his masterful manipulation of image, reality and people. 'Karl learned so much from Andy,' says Andrée Putman. A year later, while in Japan for Chloé, Karl picked up a fan and brought it back – it was to be his signature accessory for the next thirty years. He used fans as Warhol did his wig, as both a system of defence and mystique as well as a fetish object to be remembered by. Gaby recalls it was around this time that Karl started turning up thirty minutes late on purpose for meetings with journalists. 'He knew how to portray himself,' says Gaby.

Karl's flirtation with the New York underground boosted his profile by giving him an entrée into the international scene, for Warhol by this time had founded his own highly influential *Interview* magazine and it was from this time on that Karl became a recognised personality within its pages.

During the filming of *L'Amour* Antonio, Juan, Corey and Donna were having dinner one night at La Coupole without Karl. Donna sat between Juan and Corey, imitating the cigarette girl who was doing the rounds of the restaurant by shouting, '*Ceegarette, ceegarette,*' in a deliberately pantomime French accent. Donna had on silver platforms and an ivory satin charmeuse minidress. 'Her hair was freshly white and pin-curled into tight dry curls,' remembers Corey. 'She had on hardly any make-up except for red lips. She looked almost albino.'

Juan looked up to see Yves Saint Laurent step through the revolving glass doors. There was a pause throughout the restaurant as Pierre Bergé led the way to the table, a bristling manager leading his prize boxer into the ring. Only Saint Laurent didn't look like a boxer, he looked like a Parisian Jesus Christ with long hair flowing, a slight beard and a tremulous chihuahua held like a clutch bag under one arm.

Yves and Pierre approached their table, walking closer and closer before stopping short to take their place at the banquette of the table directly opposite. The Americans had been waiting for this to happen ever since they got to Paris, fantasising about finding themselves within touching distance of Yves Saint Laurent. They sensed it was their moment. 'I knew enough not to look at them,' says Corey. 'I assumed they were looking at us.'

And pretty soon they were. For almost immediately Corey reached his hand under the tablecloth and started to touch Donna, who responded with voluble and increasing abandon, writhing about in her satin. A playful, reckless sexiness pulsed beneath the skin of the Americans and they understood instinctively the power that lay in their sexual emancipation. They used sex both to seduce and to destabilise the French. As Corey remembers, 'I knew it was sex that would do it for Yves and Pierre.'

The two tables did not speak that night, but confirmation of their fashion ascension came soon after when they received the phone call.

Yves and Pierre were having a party at Place Vauban. Would they like to come?

Chapter 6

1971

The guest list for the party was select and those selected suitably elated to be there. Andy Warhol sat stroking the tape recorder in his pocket, intent on recording party indiscretions. Fred Hughes accompanied him, dapper in double-breasted blazer and signet ring weighing heavy on his little finger. Betty Catroux sat blonde and motionless before the television. Most of the cast of *L'Amour* – Corey, Donna, Jane, Jay and Jed Johnson – were there, with the exception of Karl, who was not invited.

Corey chased Yves' chihuahua round and round the dining room, threatening her with abduction. A dirty movie flickered on the television and in the library a Portuguese butler padded about wordlessly handing out vodkas.

It was the first time that the two style cliques of Saint Laurent and Warhol had come together, the first time Yves and Andy had met. Both were mutually impressed by the encounter, although tellingly it was artist, not fashion designer, who was star-struck. 'Andy liked stars a lot and Yves was rather pleased to be treated like that, I suspect,' says Loulou de la Falaise, who was responsible for introducing the two groups.

In the library stretched an enormous bus of a sofa, big enough to seat eight, and guests were jostling to get on it and claim the party high ground. Helmut Berger was already ensconced and causing a frisson. Luchino Visconti's lover and favoured actor, Berger was at the height of his seduction and glory. He had just starred in the Italian director's epic of the rise of Nazi Germany, *The Damned*, a movie more interested in

sumptuous, saturated colour and operatic decadence than historic reality.
Berger played the destructive scion of the corrupt and aristocratic industrial Von Essenbeck family, a man possessed by hate, who sings cabaret
in silk stockings and feather boa, has sex with his mother on satin sheets
and later hands her a phial of cyanide with which she dies, wrapped in
a beady-eyed fox fur. Visconti set the macabre and intimate family
tragedy against a backdrop of homoerotic, bleeding massacre – his
version of the routing of the SA and the inexorable rise of the SS. Both
Berger and the movie were a cult success in Paris fashion.

Back in life and sitting on Yves' sofa Helmut Berger never could tear
himself out of character: arrogant and fragile, he personified the mood
of ambiguous gender play that was beginning to sweep through Paris.
His bleached hair was slicked back Weimar-style and he looked as if at
any moment he might don his top hat and boa, jump on the sofa and
growl his Berlin cabaret songs.

Donna and Corey were aching to get close to him and being as
disruptive and precocious as possible, chewing gum all over the sacred
high chic and Casablanca lilies of Yves and Pierre's library. Donna started
making burping noises to attract Helmut's attention. 'I can shit too,'
Helmut snapped at her. 'We all thought that was deliriously funny,'
remembers Loulou, 'and so Donna was very vexed because she was
given the brush-off.'

Next to Helmut on the sofa sat Patti d'Arbanville, cooing in his ear;
she was wearing a belt with two silver sculpted heads as the buckle. It
belonged to Helmut and Patti had been boasting all night that he had
given it to her. Donna, now seething, sat opposite and by her side was
Corey, giddy and manipulative on a cocktail of Mandrax, white wine
and Helmut. 'Look at Patti, she's got Helmut's belt on! She thinks she's
so great,' whispered Corey to Donna. 'She thinks she's got Helmut all
wrapped up.'

Donna needed no more provocation. She leapt across the low,
smoked-glass table, over Yves' Moroccan daggers and obelisks of crystal,
over Pierre's precious first editions, grabbed Patti hard around the neck
and hurled her fist down on the coffee-table, shattering the table and
cutting Patti's knee in the process.

There were shards of glass, blood and screams. Fred Hughes had to
rush Patti off for treatment at the American Hospital and she then

insisted on walking with a stick for weeks after. 'It was a genius fight!' remembers Corey. 'Of course Yves and Pierre were horrified but at the same time secretly thrilled that this should have happened.'

The vying desire, the sexual and gender ambiguity combined with melodramatic squeals of wrestling girls – that party marked a new mood in Paris. As Loulou remembers, 'It was a weird evening, everyone was trying to out-shock everyone else. I mean nobody was really evil, no one was drug-addicted, at least not then in any case; everyone was trying to outdo each other, showing off. Yves and Pierre had never lived that wildness before.'

In a way it was perhaps inevitable that violence should have broken out before the two great passive forces of Yves Saint Laurent and Andy Warhol. Everyone in the Warhol clique knew the way to get more of Andy's attention was through provocation. An extreme reaction is what Andy craved. Andy Warhol, whose every conversation began with a query about the size of your penis, or that of your neighbour's.

There was something about Yves too that incited a certain aggression. Whether it was in the school playground, Victoire grabbing his arm and telling him to get out and greet his audience, Madame Zehnacker bullying him at the Dior studio or Pierre Bergé's apparent domination, somehow Yves was always to be found at the centre of a jostling, vibrating mass of aggression. Yves incited in others an overwhelming desire to claim his attention. 'He had this incredible magnetism. I mean he was really a superstar. When you arrived somewhere with Yves at a party or at someone's house it was always Yves who was the focus, even if there were other stars present,' remembers Clara Saint. 'It was always him right at the centre straight away. It was around Yves that everything happened.'

Being in his presence brought on a dizzy spell of fascination and in and out of his entourage there was always the same desire, the same reflex to impress him, to be approved by him and to be seen by him. 'He was the prince,' says Jacques Grange. 'Yves was the one we all wanted to conquer.'

One reason for his immense power and seduction came from the fact that everything he touched, in that slow, deliberate way of his, became beautiful – a sheet of paper upon which he drew, a woman's body around which he wrapped a length of *grain de poudre*. 'I always look at his hands,' says John Fairchild, who watched him for years of couture fittings. 'When he touches a woman, when he works with the fabric, you can *see* it all in his hands. It's instinct. It's like petting a dog you love, it's like stroking a horse after it has won; there is an animal feeling there of beauty.'

It wasn't only with his hands; he could render beauty with his charm and his attention. '*Comme tu es jolie ce soir,*' he would say on seeing Betty or Loulou as they entered a room. '*Ah, quelle belle robe,*' his voice a caress, part lover, part brother. When Yves was inspired by someone he made that man or woman feel as if their face was turned up to the sun on a balmy day. 'Yves' eye alighting on something, someone, lit up that thing, that person. It is exactly that, it is strange,' says Jacques Grange. He made you hyper-aware of how you looked, of your beauty and your body.

Yves was homosexual and yet, as he himself said, 'I'd like to sleep with everyone I like.' And you could feel that very desire in him; he had a relentless sensuality so that there was an erotic charge of possibility in the way he looked at you and the way he touched your skin. 'Yves Saint Laurent, who can look you straight in the eye while wondering what someone a few feet away looks like naked,' is how one journalist put it. He kept a mass of erotic drawings that he had done with vague thoughts of publishing them. He showed the drawings to Bianca Jagger, who asked Yves if he liked erotic things. He replied with enthusiasm, 'Oh yes, absolutely. It's one of the motors of emotional life in people.' Then she asked if pornography excited him and he let out a sigh: 'Pornography? I don't know what that is. Pornography, eroticism, love, it's all the same to me . . . in love all is possible.'

In the couture house he held both men and women under his sway. 'It was rather like a harem,' says former house-model Nicole Dorier, who like so many of Yves Saint Laurent's faithful women started at the couture house in the early 1970s and was still working there thirty years later as *directrice de mannequins*. 'He could have been the most incredible Don Juan. He had every woman at his feet; the fact that it was all platonic is not really the point. All those women, every one of them in the couture house from floor to ceiling, they all wanted the same thing: a smile, a compliment, *le regard de Saint Laurent.*' It is a phenomenon that François Catroux confirms with a wry smile: 'Women all want to be noticed by him, and they all think that they are the only one.'

It was this same system of fascination that held the Saint Laurent clan entranced. It was Pierre who intimidated them all into submission, Pierre who held the purse strings and the sinecures; it was Clara Saint who manned the doors and scrutinised entry to the clan. But at the centre of the magnetic force field of grace stood Yves Saint Laurent, alone.

One world was fading and another was beginning. Everywhere in Paris it seemed there were the strange and converging cross-currents of these two worlds and their generations. The resignation of Charles de Gaulle in April 1969 was the dramatic finale to a presidential rule that stretched back to the time of the Occupation. He had headed the opposition to the Vichy government from London during the Second World War, led the French liberation forces down the Champs-Elysées on that August day in 1944 and inaugurated the Fifth Republic. He had ruled France for an aggregate total of some twenty-five years when he was finally forced from office after a vote of no confidence. He died in November the following year.

In fashion the illustrious couturier Cristobal Balenciaga retired, closing the doors of his couture house in May of 1968. Balenciaga left with a sigh that there was no one left to dress. It was the same complaint from a host of other smaller couture houses that found themselves unwanted as ready-to-wear took over, French clients fell away and haute couture increasingly became a market of evening clothes, American buyers and licences. In just one year, from 1966 to 1967, the number of couture houses in Paris plummeted from thirty-nine to seventeen. The reality for many houses that closed was that their real estate was now worth more than their business.

Gabrielle Chanel, whose drive and genius had dominated fashion since the 1920s, died on 10 January 1971 at the age of eighty-eight. She had created everything: her persona and borrowed past as well as a radically new way for women to dress in the first half of the twentieth century. She was a fashion myth as only Paris can breed and appropriately she died at the Ritz just days before her couture show.

The Parisian artistic elite of the first half of the twentieth century –

Pablo Picasso, Jean Cocteau, surrealism, the legends and literary salons, the grand patrons of the arts – were living out their final years. Jean Cocteau had died in 1963. Man Ray was seventy-eight and living as a recluse. Salvador Dalí was installed in his wheelchair in a suite at the Hôtel Meurice inviting the clotted cream of Paris youth to tea. Marie-Laure de Noailles, inimitable hostess of the 1930s, descendant of the Marquis de Sade, patron of the surrealists and now in the final months of her life, invited handsome young men Jacques Grange and actor Pierre Clémenti to her Picasso-hung salon. Poet and literary giant Louis Aragon was over seventy and lunching daily at Maxim's with the precocious François-Marie Banier dressed all in white and brimming with the success of his second novel. It was hard to tell who was the more impressed by the encounter.

In December 1971 Marie-Hélène de Rothschild threw a 'Bal Proust' at the Rothschild family château of Ferrières to celebrate the centenary of the birth of the writer. It was a fancy-dress ball in the tradition of the grand *bals costumés* of the 1920s and 30s hosted by Comte Etienne de Beaumont, Princesse Jean-Louis de Faucigny-Lucinge and Marie-Laure de Noailles and it was to be one of the last such balls in Paris. Cecil Beaton was the ball portrait-photographer and he captured the ancestors of Proust's *faubourg* confronting the new blood of society: Elizabeth Taylor and Richard Burton, Serge Gainsbourg and Jane Birkin, Jane Holzer and Andy Warhol. The night was steeped in nostalgia. 'It was a big party in the spirit of an earlier time,' remembers Guy de Rothschild. 'It celebrated the last quarter of the nineteenth century, which was a God-blessed period in France.' Marie-Hélène wore a cream satin evening-dress by Saint Laurent, although she drove the couturier to distraction by her insistence on having the sleeves cut off the dress.

In the same year Luchino Visconti's film of Thomas Mann's hypnotic novella *Death in Venice* was released with extraordinary success, winning an award at the Cannes Film Festival of that year. The movie featured Dirk Bogarde as the repressed German writer Gustav von Aschenbach and Bjørn Andresen as Tadzio, the ravishing schoolboy and object of his obsession. It was a powerful study of longing, old age and the maddening insolence of youth and beauty. It had a strange resonance with the Paris of the beginning of the 1970s, where each age surveyed the other and wondered at what they could have lived. The older generation were nostalgic for a youth they had lost, longing to feel the surge of desire and possibility of youth course through their own veins, while the younger generation yearned for a past they could not recall.

From this strangely thrilling atmosphere of paradise lost and a society in dramatic flux and mutation, a rich seam of creativity revealed itself. At the turn of the new decade in Paris it seemed it was no longer art but fashion that captured the dazzling mood and expressed it. And it was through fashion that the new generation chose to express and invent themselves.

Picasso was still alive but in his late eighties and living in the south of France. Now it was his daughter, Paloma, who enchanted Paris with her red lips and Picasso eyes. Aged twenty-one, she was not yet the heiress she would become, but she was an already intriguing figure and a source of fascination in Paris. She lived with her mother Françoise Gilot and grandmother in a nineteenth-century villa in Neuilly. She had shoulder-length black hair and her face was still that of a young girl, yet to find the dramatic definition of later years.

'I was very shy and having the name meant that I could never just go and be myself. Everybody would always point and say, "There's Paloma Picasso",' she remembers. 'I always felt people were looking at me, just because of the name; people were always interested and that made me even more shy. I decided to start dressing up in a way to shift the attention from the person I was to what I was wearing. It became like a shield. This extravagance also made me a little unapproachable, so some people might have been afraid of me, whereas in fact I was the one who was afraid of others.'

She quickly became a friend of all the different fashion fragments of Paris. She met Yves and Pierre, Clara, Loulou and Fernando and at the same time she became friends with Antonio and Juan, who introduced her to Karl. She was close to Manolo Blahnik and his two great American friends Eric Boman, illustrator and textile designer, and artist Peter Schlesinger, who was David Hockney's lover at the time.

She hid beneath a large orange capeline hat and dressed in a girl's white broderie-anglaise dress. She wore diamond pins on stripy jumpers, black ski-pants, black tights and beige wedge shoes that were so high she fell down the steps of her grandmother's house when Schlesinger was taking her photo and lay giggling on the gravel with a broken foot.

'Oh, she was the most,' says Manolo Blahnik, with whom Paloma was making funny commercials for Twinings tea at the time. 'She wore tweed skirts with no hem and no lining, in a kind of lilac pink, so chic at the time. She had crystal flowers in her hair that came from cemeteries in the south of France. She was very original.' The tweed skirts were made by Tatatita, Paloma's Spanish nanny, who ran them up on the sewing-machine at home; otherwise Paloma went to flea markets to find the clothes to make up her look.

Yves met Paloma at a dinner given by Rive Gauche hostess Charlotte Aillaud in 1970 and not surprisingly he was entranced by her gene pool and daring style. That was the year she started making jewellery and in October Fernando asked her to design some jewellery pieces for his ready-to-wear show. She did, and the night after the show Paloma happened to bump into Yves and Pierre at a restaurant and went over to ask Yves for his advice about pricing the jewellery pieces, as Fernando had said he would sell them for her. 'So, I showed him the jewellery, and then he said, Well why don't you come and see me tomorrow at the house. And the next day I went and instead of answering my question about prices, he offered me a job to do jewellery to sell in his stores.' Yves had no qualms about pinching Fernando's discovery. He always recognised the need to surround himself with the right people who would help realise his vision; that too was an intrinsic part of the Saint Laurent genius and wile.

The studio at Rue Spontini took on a fresh, new, foreign feeling, with Loulou now dropping by every day, Paloma coming in to show her jewellery, belts and shoes that she had designed, and Eric Boman working on textiles. There was also a sixteen-year-old schoolboy, Michel Klein, who was a family friend of Paloma's and worked helping on prints at the house on Thursday afternoons only, because that was the afternoon there was no school. 'It was this incredibly fun epoch, so creative and amusing,' remembers Michel about these early 1970s years in Paris. 'It was the beginning of fashion without constraints.'

In January 1971 Yves presented his couture collection, which was the most controversial of his career so far. Even before the show began Yves was in a state of fever-pitch anxiety, feeling both wildly excited and apprehensive at his own daring. 'He knew it was going to be a disaster,' says Loulou, who had been strategically seated along with Paloma and

Marisa Berenson among the press. Loulou was wearing a Saint Laurent salmon-pink satin jacket, purple shorts and tights, with her hair in ringlets, while Paloma had on a bright red turban and her mother's old black 1940s dress, a hint of what was to come.

In the hothouse of the Rue Spontini couture salon Yves showed a parade of plunging-neckline chiffon dresses, worn with short, fur chubbies in electric green and blue. There were navy sleeveless blazers outlined in white piping with wide lapels, a velvet coat that was covered in lipstick kisses, puffed shoulders and clinging ruched waists, wedge shoes and clumpy heels (after two generations of pumps). The show was styled to shock, with huge great Carmen Miranda velvet turbans, foxy boas, lipstick-stained mouths and a marked absence of underwear. There was a redhead model who was braless and blowzy, 'so that everything jiggled,' remembers Loulou. 'She was very sexy. People were used to couture models who were very spiky; it was a shock to see a big sexual girl like that.' 'It was the first time in haute couture that the model was shown as a woman, rather than as a lady,' remembers Hélène de Ludinghausen, although it was 'tart' not woman that was the word on everyone's lips at the time.

The press did not approve of the look: Eugenia Sheppard told the New York Post it was 'completely hideous' and the Daily Telegraph called it 'nauseating'. Critics accused Saint Laurent of being over-influenced by ready-to-wear while the buyers were furious at the idea that short skirts were back when they had been pushing long. Saint Laurent himself hit back, calling the press 'petty, narrow-minded reactionaries'. 'Fashion is the reflection of our time and if it does not express the atmosphere of its time, it means nothing,' he said, condemning haute couture for being 'bogged down in a boring tradition of so-called good taste and refinement; it has become a museum, a refuge for people who do not dare to look life in the face and who are reassured by tradition.'

Over the years the collection's controversy would come to be interpreted in terms of the 1940s fashion references of its wide, boxy shoulders, turbans and platform shoes that reminded the audience of wartime Paris and the clothes of a nation under occupation. But the outrage in the couture salon that day was to do with not the Second World War, but rather the slutty feel to the collection. 'I think the Occupation aspect of it was some kind of an alibi,' says Gerry Dryansky, Women's Wear Daily bureau chief at the time. 'I think people were really revolted by it because for them it was very vulgar. No one in couture did that deliberately camp flirtation with vulgarity; that was definitely gay taste and I think a lot of people objected to that. I think they weren't ready for it.'

Yves was neither the first nor the only one to explore this period of 1940s fashion at this time, contrary to the way fashion history has since retold it. Ossie Clark had been making gorgeous 1940s yoked, bib-fronted dresses and tough-shouldered Blitz suiting for at least three years, and the London flea markets were already stripped bare of any fabric or accessory that was remotely 1940s.

The collection did not spring original and unaided from Yves' imagination. It was his visual synthesis of everything that was happening in Paris at that moment and his own memories of the past, conscious and subconscious. In the months before the collection he had seen Donna in peroxide satin, Andy Warhol and all his 'kids' running amok in his own salon, Talitha and her Ossie dresses, Paloma dressed in tweed and platforms, and all those other young fashion girls in Paris who lived and dressed in flea-market finds. 'He has an eye that sees everything, nothing escapes him,' says Charlotte Aillaud. 'It wasn't so much that these people were important in fashion,' reasons Michel Klein. 'What was important was Yves' attitude to these people around him, what they brought to him. He was like a sponge.'

Every designer soaks up inspiration but what made Yves stand apart from the rest was what he then did with those influences and vibes, and what he did was to create in the absolute. 'Yves' tremendous talent was for taking what was going on and, by giving it his sign of approval, making it look better, sharper and stronger,' says Loulou. He pushed fashion to that definitive point where it transmutes and emerges as style archetype.

With this collection Saint Laurent made the shoulder of his jackets squarer and more pronounced than before, making it a shoulder to bear a woman's new expectations and confidence, giving it that bold linear hike at its outer edge which made it the 'Saint Laurent shoulder', on which his every jacket would from now on depend.

'These are clothes to be worn sitting on the bidet!' sniped one journalist sitting right behind Loulou at the show, but as it turned out these were clothes that changed the tide of fashion, taking it retro, camp, anecdotal, letting risqué thoughts of a tarty sexiness race all through its imagination. For even if haute couture was on the wane, when Yves Saint Laurent spoke, the world of fashion still listened.

As homosexuality bounded forth with delight from the smoking ruins of an authoritarian society, so there was a new perception of homo-sexuality within fashion. Up until now fashion and homosexuality's interdependence had been conducted on furtive and euphemistic terms. Homosexual couturiers such as Monsieur Dior and Monsieur Balenciaga had 'friends', not lovers. Saint Laurent and Bergé were one of the first homosexual couples in fashion to live and work openly as such. From now on in fashion, as Maxime de la Falaise remem-bers, 'It was the period of homosexual outage. Suddenly *they* were the fabulous ones, *they* were the attractive ones; no straight man was attractive.'

A generation of homosexuals entered the scene that bore none of the trussed-up shame of before. They were open, curious, light-headed in their sexuality and libido, and consequently at ease with their bodies. 'For the first time you could express your desires in the light of day,' says Claude Aurensan, who was working as a barman at the tiny gay club Les Nuages on the Left Bank in 1970.

A host of young and beautiful men appeared in Paris setting pulses awry, bourgeois boys with angel faces who in the heat of the summer packed their Proust and broke their mothers' hearts as they slammed the gate on the lilac-covered villa and set off for Paris to find a protector, write a novel, be a model, make love, whatever happened first.

In 1971 Yves Saint Laurent launched his first men's fragrance and used his naked self as the central star of the advertising campaign. It was a far cry from his former buttoned-up self and shows how radically Yves had been influenced by the storm of sexual liberation. It was French fashion photographer Jeanloup Sieff who took the photograph, but crucially it was Yves, not Sieff, who devised the idea for the image; he wanted to be shown naked. Yves appeared in a black and white portrait, sitting on a pile of black leather cushions with his body shown at the height of its allure – slim, taut and mesmerising in its grace. It was the body type that was considered the homosexual ideal at that moment in time and the image became a pin-up poster for a new generation of teenage gays.

There is something intentionally Christ-like about Yves in the portrait. It is not only the passing resemblance to Jesus – or is it Jesus Christ Superstar? – in the beard and shoulder-length hair, but also the aureole of light that radiates around Yves' head and upper body. Yet it was of course a contrived image intended to sell, an image premeditated by Yves to cause a scandal for the commercial benefit of doing so – and it did – an image that positions Yves Saint Laurent the person as the product. Saint Laurent had an uncanny ability to bathe fashion and commerce in divinity.

All around there was a rapturous delight in bodies and flesh. Antonio was pouring blue dye into the bath and getting Pat Cleveland to hop in naked so that he could photograph her. 'We undressed in a second for Antonio,' says Renata Zatsch, who was a model and posing naked beneath fur coats for Antonio at the time. 'We couldn't care less it was so funny. We were playing, we were not inhibited, we liked our bodies, we looked nice, we felt so natural that we would have taken our clothes off in the middle of the street if he had asked; it was all about freedom.'

As Antonio's fame grew so his group and influence expanded to fill the space around him. He and Juan had moved to a larger apartment that Karl rented for them at 134, Boulevard Saint-Germain and girls were always ringing the doorbell and coming in to be sketched and transformed, idolised and eclipsed, for Antonio's propensity to consume was insatiable.

'Antonio moved from person to person like a bee tasting pollen,' recalls Billina. 'He was always the one that people were attracted to first; he just drew you towards him by his charisma and star appeal and then he would move on, always moving on – he always had other friends to bring in, he was busy, he had to go out and meet this person, that one, but you were still there; once you got into the clique you always stayed in the clique. Antonio had more acquaintances and friends than anyone could imagine, he was the original going-out queen.'

Although you might stay in the clique, the effect of being eclipsed by the new beauty that had just got off the plane was nevertheless painful – particularly as Antonio's relationships with his girls often had a sexual dimension. There was something of the unfulfilled and frustrated to this restless quest for beauty and Antonio later admitted, 'I was looking for a mother and they [the girls] were looking for fathers. It's ridiculous and obvious but that's what people do all their lives. We all carry our pasts around with us on our backs.'

Beyond Antonio's high-voltage energy were black days of depression when he was paralysed before the paper. Then it was Juan who kept Antonio going, jump-starting his imagination with ideas, verbally summoning up the images that could start the Antonio magic and pull him back out of the dark. The doorbell would ring and it would be Pat, Paloma or new discovery Jessica Lange, smiling and velvety, and Antonio would rally. He had bought a Kodak Instamatic camera and was experimenting incessantly with it as well as with a Polaroid camera. He set up fashion narratives of a set of nine photos that ran like a series of moving illustrations for a cartoon. 'I couldn't believe what a wonderful time we were having,' Antonio said some years later, 'and I wanted a record of it. The Polaroids were like a proof of time.'

The pictures were instantaneous and conveyed the exuberance and spontaneity of the moment and Antonio loved their snapshot intimacy. He and Juan invented backdrops and props for the photos and illustrations; he sketched Paloma in her bra and knickers, photographed Manuela Papatakis in her underwear, wrapped in huge frills of plastic sheeting, and girls with a razor-blade hanging from a choker or a shard of broken mirror pressed to their skin. It presaged the S&M obsession that would enter fashion later in the 1970s but without the pain.

Pat Cleveland was eating up the catwalks with her shimmering sexiness and laughter, bringing a movement and dance to fashion that no one had ever seen before. No one could get her to stand still; she was a mass of twirling arms, legs and spins. The first time she modelled in Paris she caused a sensation. She was with Donna Jordan, modelling for Karl at Chloé. She swayed down the marble staircase in slow motion, pouting and posing, teasing and turning the audience on with a mouth drenched in lipgloss and her shake and grind. 'I started to smile, I started to move my legs; I was doing all sorts of poses on the stairs, I was doing every movie star I ever knew, Marilyn, Jane Russell, blowing kisses; I was touching my hair, touching my body and people were screaming and standing up, applauding and trying to touch me.' No one had seen such smiling, such personality and such uninhibited sexiness in a fashion show. 'Karl was so excited,' remembers Pat. 'People kept saying, "Who is that?" and Karl was saying, "Oh that's Pat and that's Donna, they're my models."'

It was a time when Paris runways were peopled by anonymous mannequins who showed the clothes, not themselves, but Pat had other intentions. 'We came to Europe to show off,' she says, 'and we did just that. The point was we came from nowhere. We came out of America like wild, crazy people. We had grown up with movies and movie-star attitude and we were there to be stars, superstars. We wanted to shine day and night.'

As day slid into dark, so the possibilities of the Parisian night unfolded. At the entrance to the Rue Sainte Anne stood a gigolo in cowboy boots and leather chaps with a saucy smile. He stood sentinel on a street lined with lesbian and homosexual bars and clubs with names such as Eve and Pimps. But it was to number 7, Rue Sainte Anne that the Paris fashion world now came to live out its fantasies.

Club Sept was the new nocturnal focus for the city's energy and sexual charge. It opened in 1968 as a small restaurant and nightclub, homosexual in its inclinations and yet radically removed from the clandestine gay clubs of the Rive Gauche. There was no furtive checking of the door to see who was walking in, no fear of being caught in a position of compromise. The sense of freedom was rampant there, in every encounter, every joke shared, every glass of champagne offered. 'T'en veux, chéri,' came a whisper in your ear as an unknown hand held out a pink pill of seduction.

But the greatest innovation of Le Sept was that it was defined by glamour, not homosexuality. Everyone came – gay, straight and the undecided. 'You didn't have to be rich, you didn't have to be famous,' says former Le Sept DJ Guy Cuevas, 'you had to be beautiful.' In this city where clans were divided and intrigue brutal, how fitting that it was only at night they should come together and only beauty that could unite them.

'If it's not a mask we're not going out,' Corey would say as he, Pat,

Antonio, Juan and the rest of them jostled before the mirror, getting ready for Le Sept. 'We had a mirror the size of a matchbox, but we were *all* in it putting on that eye make-up. If we didn't have enough foundation on, Corey would come round with a big sponge and wipe it across all our faces to make sure we were all the same colour. We had to match,' says Pat Cleveland. She had deleted her eyebrows and removed her false eyelashes in homage to Paris.

Pat, Billina, Donna and Corey had moved out of Karl's apartment and were all staying in musty rooms at the Crystal Hôtel, falling asleep under candlewick bedspreads and faded cornfield wallpaper. But not even that reality managed to intrude upon their fantasies. 'The hotels were beautiful because Paris was outside,' says Pat. They spent hours every night transforming themselves with make-up, Lycra bodysuits, lipgloss and stilettos, then they set off walking across the postcard of Paris, dancing over the Pont des Arts, across the Seine and through the dusk and the courtyard of the Louvre, before veering off to the left to head up the Rue Sainte Anne to Le Sept, for, as Pat remembers, 'These were faces that had to be seen.'

Fabrice Emaer, owner of Le Sept, was always hovering somewhere near the door. He was another fugitive from provincial mediocrity. He was the son of a wool merchant from Pas de Calais, a melancholic grey stretch of northern France, and a former beautician and make-up artist and lifelong devotee of Greta Garbo. Baptised Francis, he reinvented himself as the rather more dashing Fabrice and as impresario of the Paris night. Tall and rococo, he dressed in a double-breasted blazer and arranged his hair in a great sweep of platinum blond maintained by a twice-weekly wash and blow at hairdresser Carita.

He had a way with his clients that was both seigneurial and camp, greeting them at the door with kisses and calls of 'Chérie!' and 'mon bébé d'amour'. He instigated a discriminatory policy at the door and a philanthropic one at the bar whereby the rich paid for the poor. 'They never asked for money inside the club; we were never asked to pay for a drink downstairs and it never even occurred to us to do so,' remembers Loulou de la Falaise. Every so often Loulou would ask Fabrice for her bill, he would shoo her away with a wave of his hand and some time in the vague future he would present her with a bill for the paltry sum of 250 francs for six months of drinking every night, all night.

'Kenzo and Yves were the ones who paid,' says Loulou, 'the ones who could foot the bills.'

Fabrice's door and bar policies, combined with the fact that Le Sept was open to members and friends only, encouraged an ambiance of intimacy and voyeurism between old and young, talent and beauty, celebrity and unknown. Inside the club was a small, dark, dining area and when your eyes had adjusted to the light you realised that there, seated before you, was Francis Bacon playing cards, Nureyev who came late having danced at L'Opéra, Roland Barthes or Bianca and Mick Jagger. Some nights Andy Warhol and Fred Hughes dined there on caviar spaghetti.

It was a meeting of *monde* and *demi-monde*. There would be Eric de Rothschild flirting with Susi Wyss, a feline beauty who was known for her hospitality and talent for procuring gorgeous girls. She held dinners at her apartment in the fourteenth *arrondissement* to which she would invite a high-octane mix: Yves, Pierre, Clara, Loulou, Karl, Antonio and the gang. Guests arrived to find Susi's personal 'slave', a German male naked but for a frilly apron and high heels, trotting round the room serving drinks and peanuts. Susi lived in an apartment John Paul Getty had bought for her where she enjoyed an adventurous life of *amour*. She remembers with affection the arrival one night at Le Sept of Bjørn Andresen of *Death in Venice* fame, which caused a near riot. 'I thought he was homosexual,' recalls Susi, 'but he fucked me beautifully.'

Le Sept was a place where all the fashion clans of Paris converged. Kenzo was always there, dressed in a shrunken V-neck and bell-bottomed pinstripe trousers with a beatific white-toothed smile. He had shown his first collection in April 1970, of light and freshly floral mini-kimonos, headscarves, knitted hot pants and aprons in clashing colours, and he was the new favourite of the fashion press with his innovative pattern-cutting and exotic prints. 'I wanted to express youth,' says Kenzo looking back at those first collections. He had arrived in France in 1965, having travelled from Japan by boat, docking at the port of Marseilles after a month aboard. 'From 1963 it was easier to get yourself a passport in Japan, but airplane tickets were still so expensive. So I came by boat with the intention of staying for six months.'

Born in 1939, Kenzo Takada was one of seven children and his father

owned a *machiaï* or teahouse in Himeji, where Kenzo spent his childhood among customers and geisha girls. He studied fashion at the Bunka
College of Tokyo, but, says Kenzo, 'Japan after the war really wasn't much
fun. Work, work, work, work: it lacked joy.' He was inhibited by its
rigidity and found the liberty and sexual freedom of Europe an immense
boost to his creativity. He worked as a freelance *styliste* for four years
in Paris before opening his own boutique in 1970 at the age of thirty-
one. He painted a huge mural of tropical foliage and water lilies in
homage to Douanier Rousseau on the walls, installed his Tokyo friends
upstairs on sewing-machines and called the shop 'Jungle Jap'. It was an
overnight hit.

His clothes were the antithesis of French couture. They were light,
young and fun, innovative and a hybrid of ethnic influences. He used
Japanese techniques of flat cutting and kimono sleeves, he played with
proportions, mixing abbreviated tops with billowing trousers, and he
created bright, complex and gorgeous prints to cover his fabrics. In
contrast to the traditional suiting idea, Kenzo proposed pieces of clothing,
knits and layers – what is called sportswear in fashion terms, which
although already a staple of American fashion was still underdeveloped
in Paris. 'Kenzo was the first competition Yves had in years,' says Loulou
de la Falaise. 'They greatly admired each other. Kenzo really invented
the laid-back look; his stuff was not so proper.'

As well as being close to Yves, Loulou was also hanging out with
Kenzo and his crowd, drinking cocktails at La Closerie de Lilas, turning
up at Le Sept late, dressed as 'a sort of pirate, troubadour and medieval
page' is how she describes it, which meant odd stockings – one fuchsia,
one purple – and a dancer's shirt torn from a costume wardrobe. Her
proximity to Kenzo combined with her funky past meant she was on
a different fashion wavelength to couture Paris. 'I was closer to this very
creative thing of youth and international atmosphere rather than the
very grand scene and I remember that sort of worried the proper
couturiers who were more installed in the Comtesse de Paris,' says
Loulou. She was ten years younger than Yves, single and in demand,
and she went out constantly.

At about 1 a.m. the crowd headed downstairs to dance in an ecstatic
frenzy before the walls of mirrors, watching each other, watching
themselves. Pat jumped up on the bar and stripped for them all, 'just

taking off a little bit of this and a little bit of that'. She lay atop the bar and shimmied naked as Fabrice sprayed her body with champagne.

In 1971 Guy Cuevas arrived as the new DJ at the club, playing joyous sounds of Tamla Motown, Diana Ross and Marilyn Monroe that induced dancing on the tables and dancing through the night. 'But I was a DJ like you used to be, not a technical DJ of today – I had no headphones, nothing. I used to put on a record and then go and dance on the dance floor with Antonio,' remembers Guy. He played music that was 'funky, sexy, always upbeat. It was a crazy mix – just like the club, which was a crazy mix of cultures, race and bank accounts.'

The suspended reality and potent charge of celebrity sent an electric current whipping round the room. There was an incredulity that this could actually be happening, this much flirtation and delight. 'The only reason I left Le Sept was because I knew I could come back the next night,' says Ariel de Ravenel, who was a society child and French *Vogue* accessories editor at the time. And every night they did come back, over and over. There was always this need to be together.

Corey turned up with artist Shirley Goldfarb in tow. She was a Saint Germain institution, a Brooklyn-born painter and close friend of David Hockney. Corey had picked her up at the Flore and made her his fashion pet. He was fascinated by her face, which was like a Pompeian wall fresco, eyes rimmed in liquid black with huge black spidery fake eyelashes. He got her hooked on diet pills and took her to all the fashion parties; she was even a dresser for a fashion show in Venice with Karl. But later Corey tired of her freakish looks, the fashion crush passed and Shirley was summarily dumped.

Karl was there every night. Sitting downstairs by the dance floor, he watched the action from his chair. Yves would arrive much later in the evening, with Betty, François and Pierre. The choreography of Yves' arrival was always identical. Wherever Yves alighted – whether at a nightclub or in his studio – a protective ring formed immediately around him. In social situations it was Pierre, Clara, Loulou and Betty who formed the front line. At the couture house it was Pierre, Loulou and Anne-Marie Muñoz. The chairs were claimed, the banquette occupied and Yves sat cocooned in the centre. An invisible and impenetrable cordon was erected. Everyone knew his or her role.

The few times that Paloma Picasso went out accompanying Yves at night as his date she was surprised to find herself assuming the role of *protectrice*, even though as she points out she was much younger than him, less experienced and a woman. 'He makes you responsible for him,' says Paloma, a fact Fernando Sanchez confirms when questioned about the constant protection around Saint Laurent. 'Yves demands it!' says Fernando. 'He's always demanded it. When he was at school he demanded it; he has always been like that. People would do things for Yves that they wouldn't do for someone else because he demanded it. I mean he demanded not by words, but by a certain attitude. It came with the trip.' So it was Yves that wanted the constant protection, but from what or from whom no one seemed to know.

He came to dance, to watch or to indulge in his latest crush. There was always a crush with Yves and it was always obsessive, tempestuous and short-lived. The object of his crush would be at Le Sept, dancing or perhaps serving, and Loulou or Betty – if she was there – would tell the young man of Yves' imminent arrival in hushed tones.

Drugs were fuelling the energy. Mescaline was still popular, as was a new wave of amphetamines taken with alcohol for a more enhancing high. People were divided between uppers, downers and those that didn't do drugs at all but watched the effect. Those going up took the amphetamines and poppers, those going down opted for Valium, Quaaludes or the most fashionable downer at the time, Mandrax, which was a barbiturate-type sedative commonly prescribed as a sleeping pill in Europe but could be taken with alcohol for guaranteed, sexy, good times. Downer is a misleading name, for in fact these drugs induced a feeling of euphoria and loss of inhibitions. Corey had just discovered Mandrax. 'That was the thing,' he remembers. 'We would take them swilled down with bottles of wine.'

Nights at Le Sept ended in the arms of someone else. There was a freedom and lightness to these encounters. 'It was *sans conséquence*,' says Ariel de Ravenel. 'It was to do with having fun; going home with someone was just a way to prolong the night. It was not that you went out for that, but it could happen. The real motivation for the night was dancing, having a good time.'

Often the male suitors escorted the ladies home at the end of the night only to be found two hours later back out and cruising in a boys-only club elsewhere along the Rue Sainte Anne. In 1971 Fabrice asked Claude Aurensan to manage Le Sept, where, as a 22-year-old French Brando look-alike, he was much admired. Claude remembers, 'You used to say to yourself, "Who am I going to sleep with tonight?" because it was five in the morning and things were winding down and you thought, *Oh merde*, I don't want to be alone tonight. But it was never the point of the night.' The point of the night was the party.

At the same time that Le Sept became hot there was a fascination – teetering on obsession – in the fashion world for cabaret. From the big cabaret shows at L'Alcazar and La Grande Eugène to the quirky little restaurants Chez Michou and Le Boutoc on the backstreets of Montmartre, every night there was a cabaret to be seen. It was an integral part of Parisian night-life, an infatuation that lasted a couple of years before fading.

Thadée Klossowski kept a diary during this time and when he looked back at it, 'I realised that our lives in 1972 and '73 seemed to be, or at least the night-life was, entirely about transvestites.' Thadée, Clara, Yves and Pierre drove all over Paris looking for cabaret, which seemed to consist of endless impersonations of the French pop singer Mireille Mathieu performed by strapping waiters who first served you supper and then reappeared in blond page-boy wig, full make-up and microphone. 'I remember Pierre Bergé started taking us to some really low dumps behind the Gare de Lyon,' recalls Thadée, 'and I have memories of louche bars where the railway people would go and dance together. I remember getting to the place one night and Pierre saying to us, "Wait here in the car for me, I'll go and check," and he came back disappointed, saying, "*Il y a que les hétéros qui mangent les tripes*."' [It's full of heteros eating tripe.] As well as their high culture, Yves and Pierre both shared a taste for the low.

Corey was another fan of cabaret and was going to see shows several times a week. 'It was fascinating,' remembers Corey. 'It was the transgender thing, still being a man but being able to be a woman. It was also a very intimate form of entertainment because you were part of it: you could feel the spotlight on the back of your head and you could see the spittle coming out of their mouths.' The greasepaint and transvestism, spotlight and feathers were all part of the fantasy of transformation that fashion was exploring. It was part of the same search for reinvention that inspired the retro or jazz-age vibe or the glazed afternoons in Marrakech. 'Well,' says a deadpan Thadée, 'I don't think any of us were particularly interested in reality.'

Chapter 7

1972

By now Antonio was drawing the Chloé collections on an almost daily basis, stylising the lines of Karl's clothes as he did so. 'Antonio went far beyond reality in his drawings and it seemed to give Karl a path, it led Karl to the next design,' says Corey. 'It started to really, really, justify this entourage and I think Karl was amazed at what was happening at this combination of talents.'

It was Antonio's vision, at once monolithic and arresting, that was pushing everyone further. On a practical level he taught the girls how to pose: how Pat should hold her chin, lower her shoulder, or how to present her profile. 'He would tell me how to dress to make someone fall in love with me,' says Joan Juliet Buck. 'It was like, "Oh no, oh baby, you shouldn't wear that." And there was also the aesthetic delight of being in the presence of someone who can render those lines.'

Corey spotted a new girl in the audience at La Grande Eugène cabaret one night and invited her back to sit for Antonio. Her name was Eija, she was Finnish and had already been photographed by Helmut Newton. She was rather mysterious in that she didn't talk much and she had the fatale allure of a Hitchcock heroine. Corey introduced her to the Antonio and Karl connection. Day and night she wore 1950s suits with small hats perched upon her head, thick pale foundation, gashes of blusher and black eye-shadow; the effect was punk five years before the phenomenon.

Eija's formal tailoring and eerie way of being inspired Karl to design a whole collection around her, just as Karl's knowledge of European fashion history boosted Antonio and Juan's references. The whole group was a feeding frenzy of inspiration. 'It was a mutual exchange,' says Anna Piaggi, who was a freelance fashion editor working with both Antonio and Karl. 'Antonio was bringing the ethnic new culture and Karl the aristocratic European.' But in Piaggi's view it was 'Karl who was the driving force of the group. He was not so flashy as the others, he was more subdued but doing wonderful fashion that never stopped.'

The girls were modelling in Karl's shows, wearing his clothes out at night, being seen around town. 'Pat was starring in the street, starring everywhere, in make-up and heels, outfits and diamonds,' remembers Billina. When Antonio went out for the first night with Jessica Lange, who, pre-*King Kong* fame, was studying mime with Etienne Decroux in Paris, he pulled out a gold lamé evening-dress by Karl for her to wear.

Yet at the same time that Karl Lagerfeld's working relationship with Antonio and Juan was running at full tilt, their friendship began to buckle beneath them. By 1972 the group was fraught with personal tensions. Karl was the subject of constant impersonations – his accent, his mannerisms, the licking of the lips, the way he carried a clutch bag or the monocle that he now sported. Sitting opposite Karl at the Flore, Juan would wait until Karl was looking the other way and then whip one of the wooden butter-dishes off the table and slot it in his eye as a monocle, or put a book under his arm mimicking Karl's clutch bag. Juan's mocking was both the funniest and the cruellest, because it was of Juan that Karl was fondest. Every evening at the Boulevard Saint-Germain apartment when the time came to telephone Karl with the plans for that night, there was now a clamour of 'You call him!' 'No, you call him,' 'I'm not calling him, you do it.'

The arrival of Paul Caranicas in September 1971 was particularly divisive. He was a young Greek American painter who had come to study in Paris at the Ecole des Beaux Arts. He grew friendly with Juan and eventually became his lover. He was cynical and intelligent, a whisky drinker with wit and an eye for the ridiculous. He picked up the pieces when Antonio's favourites were forgotten and he observed the daily habits of the group with a raised eyebrow and a sardonic smile.

'Karl came over all the time in 1971 and 1972,' remembers Paul. 'They

[Karl, Antonio and Juan] were mutually using each other. They would sketch together and Karl would pick Antonio's brains and you know ideas came out of Antonio like water; he could draw a collection in a minute. Then Karl and Juan would go out and buy scads of books at La Hune and come home and pick through them and that was part of the whole thing, a super-editing process. Karl was going to get there. But Antonio and Juan were the people to get him there fast and he recognised that.'

Quite apart from the freedom and the funkiness by association that Karl enjoyed with the Americans, their true impact was felt in the creative method that they introduced Karl to. 'They changed Karl's mind,' says Tan Giudicelli. 'Antonio's vision was global, Antonio was glamour. Karl wasn't modern at that time; he came from Balmain. Antonio kind of showed the way.' Karl took up a creative path of constant renewal. It was an approach founded on trends and one for which he was ideally suited. Nimble and resourceful as a polo pony, Karl could hit upon a trend, explore it, draw it and then three weeks later eject it ruthlessly from his intellectual system and pass on to the new, the next.

Karl had constructed his persona and now he began to build his career on the superficial. It was pick-and-mix fashion, thinking art deco today, *The Damned* tomorrow, channelling Colette last season and Fernand Léger the next. He visited every theme with huge wit, finesse and rigour. No one could summon up a mood more thoroughly or more accurately than Karl Lagerfeld. His energy was endless; he had a fast and photographic mind and a vast memory bank that he nourished with books and fashion magazines. Even at fashion school, fellow students remember him devouring magazines and being the one who could identify a Poiret or a Vionnet dress down to the very season.

He turbo-charged his knowledge with a massive personal archive system whereby he bought two copies of every book purchased, one to keep and another to tear apart for references and to file as a future visual resource. His was a creative method that necessitated constant feeding and incessant visual stimulation from others. Karl's genius lay in observing, assimilating and recreating as well as a consummate sense of timing in knowing when to move on. It was this process of fashion alchemy that would enable Karl to carry on renewing himself and his fashion while others expired in terms of creativity around him.

And as the decades passed and Karl grew older, his entourage grew ever younger by inverse proportion. In this way Karl could keep himself permanently and artificially hot-wired to the Zeitgeist, even as he himself slipped towards and past the age of retirement.

'Juan and Antonio always said he was the ultimate editor,' remembers Paul Caranicas. Karl had his own word for his fashion method: 'vampirising'. As early as 1975 he admitted, 'I am a sort of vampire, taking the blood of other people.'

It was the summer of 1972 and Karl had booked the house in Saint-Tropez for the month of August as usual. It was a large and attractive villa that was set high up on the hill out of town and looked down over the port. The house was grander than in previous years, fitted out with maids and swimming pool. But unlike the two previous summers there was no fabulous Train Bleu voyage south together, no cortège of steamer trunks, no delirious fashion moment. People arrived in dribs and drabs.

Antonio and Billina caught the train from Paris and Antonio laughed so hard en route that he ended up in hospital for a week with a split appendicitis scar and an intestine infection. Paul Caranicas had gone to Iran on holiday and was due to arrive in the last week. Corey and Juan were installed with Pat. It seemed new boyfriends were turning up every other day, diluting and disturbing the group dynamic.

Karl's mother Elisabeth Lagerfeld was also staying at the house. She had caught the train down with Corey, slipping him a fifty-franc note under the table so he could pay for dinner. Karl called his mother 'wool-mouse' as a pet name, but Pat Cleveland misheard and insisted on calling her 'wool-mouth' throughout the holiday amid much sniggering.

Corey was on a fashion high, feeling infallible. He had recently modelled for Yves Saint Laurent's first menswear collection and had been wrapped in elation ever since. Yves had been there backstage at the show, adjusting Corey's tie before sending him out into the salon of the Rue Spontini with the whispered words, '*Tu es très, très chic.*' Corey memorised those words to play back to himself over and over.

He was modelling for Helmut Newton, working as a make-up artist with Guy Bourdin doing shoots for French *Vogue*, and had become great pals with Thadée Klossowski and Clara Saint, which meant he was flirting illicitly with the Saint Laurent gang. He and accomplice Jay Johnson had even been out to dinner with Yves and Pierre, who took them up to Montmartre to Chez Michou for a night of drag. But by the time they sat down to dinner, Corey remembers, he and Jay 'had had lots of pills to eat – Mandrax, we were swallowing them like candy – and lots to drink. So we were feeling really woozy.' Jay was an object of transatlantic desire and the fact his twin brother Jed Johnson was the long-term boyfriend of Andy Warhol only added to his appeal. 'Suddenly Jay passed out and his head went boom on the table,' says Corey. 'Immediately Pierre and Yves were like, let's take a cab, let's get out of here, and I was furious with Jay because this was our big chance. I guess they were worried about their reputation, aware of the paparazzi; they had enough experience by then.'

Clara Saint was on the Côte d'Azur that summer of 1972, sailing on Hélène Rochas' yacht, and kept calling Corey, telling him to come on board. He knew he shouldn't. Karl was due to arrive the next day from Paris and mixing with the Saint Laurent crowd was not an approved pastime for the Lagerfeld entourage. But the thought of sailing round the Mediterranean with French society's golden hostess was too exciting. Hélène Rochas was the widow of the couturier Marcel Rochas and ran the house of Rochas, which since her husband's death sold only perfume. She was renowned for her elegance and beauty, hence her Offenbach sobriquet of 'La belle Hélène'.

Clara rang again to say they were leaving for Saint-Tropez and would pick him up at the port in an hour. Corey tried hard to persuade Juan to accompany him, but Juan refused and told him he'd have to go it alone. Corey left the house in a clatter of Lagerfeld heels that were several sizes too small but which he insisted on wearing. The yacht was in port to meet him and Madame Rochas was there. She gasped at the sight of Corey's red and blistered feet, whisking him below deck to bathe and dress the wounds. 'But what a monster Monsieur Lagerfeld is to make you wear such shoes!' declared Hélène Rochas. Corey did not tell her it was he who had chosen to wear the shoes. On deck Kim d'Estainville was droll and mischievous and mixing up bull-shot cocktails at 10 a.m. as they set sail for the Countess Brandolini's house in Cap Martin. There was a light breeze across the sea and Hélène lay naked in the netting beneath the bowsprit, sunbathing in the bright morning sun.

It was clear to all that Corey was walking close to the edge, which in fashion, as in society, makes for highly desirable company. He was a court jester. They stopped off at the Countess Brandolini's and Corey and Kim ran through the house, bursting in unannounced on the ladies as they dressed for dinner. By early morning Corey was loaded out of his mind on pills and alcohol, but he knew he had to get back to the house before Karl arrived. 'I was his guest and if he found out that I wasn't there and that I was with Hélène Rochas and Clara and the Saint Laurent people he would have freaked out,' says Corey. 'There was a lot going on that I didn't understand; I could feel the tension but I didn't know what it was about.' Kim ordered him a taxi and Corey got in and passed out as they drove along the Moyenne Corniche, arriving at Saint-Tropez as dawn broke.

Corey stumbled out of the taxi and ran round the back of the house just as he saw Karl's car drawing up the drive. Corey was banging frantically on Juan's bedroom window, shouting, 'He's coming, he's coming, let me in.' Juan opened the door and Corey burst in dressed in his dinner jacket. 'I ran over and I jumped into the bed with my clothes on and I pulled up the cover over my head just as Karl came into the room.'

Karl was not alone. He had a new friend in tow, a young Frenchman who bore the pinkish hue of the king's new favourite. His name was Jacques de Bascher de Beaumarchais.

Fashion is an endless process of elimination: in and out, now and then, new and old, right and wrong. Being among the chosen provides the nervous adrenalin on which fashion runs. It is a highly visible state of grace, for you are seated on the front row of fashion, you are invited to Yves' party, you are the face in every magazine, you are deified. But with the thrill of being chosen comes the fear of the fall from grace. Fashion's compulsion for change means it is only ever a matter of time before you are out, rather than in, you are wrong rather than right. It is the coexistence of these two states – euphoria and fear – which creates the ecstasy and terror of fashion. Anyone who has ever sat in the audience of a fashion show has sensed that terror.

From the moment Jacques turned up in Saint-Tropez, the Americans knew their days were numbered. 'Fashion is so disposable,' says Corey. 'We knew we had a limited run and we were working that as much as Karl.' The very morning of his arrival, Juan and Corey were asked to move out of their bedroom, to make way for Jacques.

He was everything they were not. They were new world, streetwise and fashion-savvy. He was old world, patrician and dressed like a French Sloane. 'He was totally not one of us,' says Corey. 'He was naive and had not yet acclimatised to the fashion world. He came from a privileged, organised family life and he was trying to bring that vision into the world of Karl and fashion. We were interested in being irreverent, having fun, sarcastic, silly. He didn't get the jokes. We looked at each other blinking, who is this guy?'

But Karl's eye had turned. Within twenty-four hours it was Jacques planning the day's activities: it was Jacques deciding which restaurant to go to at night; it was Jacques whom Karl wanted to sketch as they lay out by the pool. 'He always got to drive the boat,' says Corey, 'and he did it terribly. He became the centre of attention and we got kicked to the kerb a little bit.'

They spent long hours sitting around the pool, Karl, Jacques, Juan, Antonio, Corey, Pat and Billina, bickering and boasting, snapping at the remains of power in the stifling afternoon. Jacques talked about his family château, his family vineyards, his ancestry, conversational topics that the Americans found deadly dull and pompous. They didn't realise these were all subjects Karl was longing to explore.

After three years the aesthetic high that once had bound the group together was disintegrating and the void opening up between them was overwhelming. The love affair with the jazz age was over, Scott Fitzgerald thrown to the back of the dressing-up box, the Bakelite jewellery packed away with all the vague distaste for the *démodé*.

Juan and Antonio, at the height of their powers for predicting and making trends, had discovered sportswear and were at this time dressing in tight, old-school sports shirts, Lacoste-look polos and jeans that they picked up on trips back to New York. Pat strutted round wearing nothing but a G-string and diamonds. Karl meanwhile had moved further into the flamboyant, a cause of considerable amusement for the Americans. Corey was hanging out down by the port one afternoon with Karl and Jacques when a bus-load of American tourists drove by, and in a moment of clarity Corey suddenly perceived Karl in the light of reality rather than through the kaleidoscope of fashion: the tourists were staring open-mouthed through the bus window, ice creams held in mid-air, gawping at the apparition that was Karl. Jacques was driving the *mobylette* and Karl sat behind, riding side-saddle dressed in hot pants, long strands of pearls and dark glasses; he was wielding a raw frankfurter straight from the packet in one hand and a bottle of Coca-Cola in the other. 'I remember thinking, I am with this total freak,' says Corey.

When Paul Caranicas turned up from Iran for the end of the holiday, the friction only heightened. Karl was not pleased to see him; he disliked Paul resenting his intimacy with Juan and sensing, no doubt, his unapologetic dissension from the cult of fashion. One evening Karl went out and the boys were all left playing around the pool. Jacques was there, too. The mood was drunken and overexcited and someone threw an aluminium pool chair – that happened to be the one Karl's mother used – into the pool. Paul and Juan dived in to sit on the chair underwater. There was hilarity and shouting and the chair was left to drown in the swimming pool. Karl returned home to find the chair at the bottom of the pool and the garden in a state of post-party wreckage. Jacques swore it was Juan and Paul who had thrown the chair in; they swore it was Jacques.

Karl was livid with Paul. The next morning Juan and Paul were in the bath bitching fiercely about Karl, Jacques and the pool incident, not knowing that their every word was blowing through the open window and out into the corridor where Karl was standing listening. Karl hit the roof. He shouted and screamed, he ordered them out of the house. Paul and Juan packed their bags and left that very day; the others were allowed to stay on in Saint-Tropez for the end of the holiday.

The break-up was violent and bitter. 'Maybe Karl was sick of being made fun of,' admits Paul. 'Or maybe he realised that he had gotten everything he could out of this crowd and it was time to move on.' That would be the reason for many other amputations of friendship that Karl committed over the ensuing years, although not necessarily this one. After all, the American crowd in 1972 were still driving Paris fashion. They were in, not out. Perhaps the mocking and derision had gone too far and, contrary to Karl's persistent claims of Warholian superficiality, he felt the pain. 'He is defensive, Karl, and he hides. But if you touch him he is like an eggshell,' says Anne-Marie Muñoz, alluding to his vulnerability. Karl had huge respect for Juan's intelligence, eye and art direction; he must have been deeply hurt if he threw Juan out of his house. Some even wondered if there wasn't a crush buried beneath the admiration. And yet he sliced Juan, followed years later by Antonio, out of his life. He would never forgive them.

The new favourite was installed. Jacques lay out by the pool and Karl sketched his profile. The Americans were right: this guy knew nothing of fashion's etiquette. But Jacques de Bascher was a fast learner.

'I remember the first time I saw Karl: it was at La Coupole and he arrived, it was something like a birthday party. There were about twenty people including Antonio, Juan, Donna Jordan, Jane Forth, Gérard Falconetti, Amina Warsuma, Pat Cleveland, Eija and Kenzo. I really can tell you that when all of this group was entering La Coupole, in the whole Coupole, there was a divine silence. The only noise was coming from this group winking through the tables to go to this huge table where they were seated. He was a fascinating man to look at. And he still is,' said Jacques de Bascher three years after that encounter.

From his words one can imagine Jacques that night sometime in 1972, aged twenty-one, sitting at a table and looking up to see an orgy of glamour glide through the revolving glass doors. Pat laughing with her great ripe strawberry of a mouth, Antonio parting waiters with his hips, and Karl, diamonds on his cashmere lapel, leading the trail of tinsel to the table.

In that suspended moment Jacques saw a group of people living the life he yearned for. Jacques was a man on the edge of the *monde*, looking in and, most of all, looking for a way in. Is that where Jacques' attraction to Karl began?

Jacques was born in Ho Chi Minh City on 8 July 1951. His father worked there as a government administrator and the family had moved to Vietnam the year before and were living out the last decaying years of French colonial rule of Indo-China. Jacques was the fourth of five children. He had an elder brother Gonzalve, two elder sisters Anne and Elisabeth, and then there was a gap of five years before Jacques arrived. Two years later his youngest brother Xavier was born.

The parents and two youngest sons stayed for five years in Vietnam and then Cambodia before returning to France in 1955. Anne and her elder brother and sister Elisabeth were all at boarding-school in France and hardly knew their two younger brothers. Anne remembers the joy of being reunited with Jacques when her parents returned from living abroad. Anne, Gonzalve and Elisabeth waited all morning for the car to arrive, and when it stopped the doors burst open and out flew a small boy she hardly knew, Jacques, who ran to her and flung himself into her arms, calling out, 'My sisters, my sisters, my sisters.'

The De Bascher family moved to an apartment in Neuilly, a suburb to the west of Paris where schools were Catholic and cardigans Fair Isle. They lived on the Boulevard du Commandant Charcot in a ground-floor apartment. Madame de Bascher did not work and the father Antony had left the government and worked in Shell management. During the months of July and August the De Bascher family holidayed in their château in the Loire Atlantique. Château de la Berrière was built at the beginning of the nineteenth century and the De Bascher family became the owners in 1825. The house inside had the bleak and frugal feel so typical of many French provincial family châteaux. What money there was had to be spent on its upkeep: the courtyard was covered over in tarmac to save on gardening and there was little furniture to go round. The beauty of the house was in the grounds. There was a lovely park to play in, a small moat and at the side of the house a chapel. Inside the chapel it was cool and smelt of plaster and leaves. It was dedicated to Saint Roch and on one side of the altar a simple plaster statue of the saint hung on the whitewashed walls. The five children rode their bicycles down to the river and swam unaccompanied in the turbulent eddies of the Loire.

Back in Neuilly and aged fifteen, Jacques became friends with a young teacher at a Parisian *lycée*. His name was Bertrand and he was French, homosexual and debonair. He taught English and was a fan of Oscar Wilde. He lived in a maid's room at the top of a smart residential building in the sixteenth *arrondissement* and there was a trail of school-boys leading to his door eager to be initiated into another kind of life.

It was a bizarre set-up and one that is perhaps indicative of a time and place: France before the 1968 liberation of its mores.

Jacques was impressed by Bertrand, who was ten years his senior. He was esoteric and a dandy, he wrote letters in Latin and drove a large Jaguar in which he would pick up Jacques from school. In March 1967 Bertrand introduced Jacques to another schoolboy of his age, who was called Renaud de Beaugourdon. He took Jacques and Renaud off to England in the Easter of that year for a cultural tour. They left on the ferry and when they docked Bertrand rented another Jaguar to drive around the south of England, visiting Canterbury, Brighton and later London. They bought clothes for Jacques with the pocket money his parents had given him.

Over the next six months Jacques and Bertrand went on several trips together, including a return visit to England. Renaud keeps three post-cards that he received from them during this time. The messages are sparing, not more than a line or two – 'Off we go', for instance, sent from the ferry terminal at Boulogne-sur-Mer – but the cards are signif-icant for the signatures they bear. To begin with Bertrand and Jacques sign separately, then the two names are gradually reduced and merged until finally the third postcard is signed 'Berjac'. Two men become one.

'He was a kind of mentor to Jacques and he was a determining influence on him in ideas of literature and image,' says Renaud. Before Jacques met Bertrand 'he was a young man of a good family who lived in an extremely conventional bourgeois way,' says Renaud. He wore lambswool V-neck sweaters in conservative colours and a navy-blue Burberry raincoat. It was Bertrand who introduced the idea of dandy to Jacques. Bertrand who was, says Renaud, 'cultivated, mysterious, with a kind of Prince of Wales allure. He impressed us both. He was an elegant man, the only person I knew at the time who wore detach-able collars.' It was through Bertrand's tutelage that Jacques made the first step in his metamorphosis. There was a degree of appropriation to the friendship as, according to Renaud, 'Jacques took what inter-ested him' and was 'somewhat predatory'. And even though Jacques admired Bernard's learning, he also held a certain snobbish disdain for him as a 'petit bourgeois'. The friendship ended the day Bertrand announced his intention to marry, a decision that left both Jacques and Renaud incredulous.

Jacques started studying law at the University of Nanterre in 1969 but he gave it up sometime during the first year. Instead he signed up early for his obligatory military service and was sent on a world tour on the naval training ship, *L'Orage*. This was a plum posting in itself, but Jacques managed to wangle the cushiest job of all, that of librarian on the ship – 'The least tiring post,' points out his sister Anne.

After his military service ended he returned to his parents' home and started making assignations at the Flore and La Coupole, perhaps in the hope of being noticed. He communicated with friends by writing short notes in a style that was formal, a little mannered and deliberately old-fashioned. 'He made a lot of spelling mistakes,' says Renaud, 'but I would have been happy to make all the spelling mistakes he did, if I could have written with his charm.'

Jacques was already planning his illustrious future. Strolling in the Place Saint-Sulpice one day together with Renaud, Jacques, aged nineteen, stopped and looked around him at the sun high over the white fountains and turned to Renaud and said, 'One day, you'll see, I will live here.'

Even though he was still living at home at the time and the address on the back of his envelopes still stated Boulevard Commandant Charcot, it was at this point that Jacques started to remove Neuilly from his life history. 'He considered that part of his life and family bourgeois,' says Renaud, 'and he did not want to hear it.' He wanted to focus on the noble.

In spite of France's protestations of *égalité* and the revolution's attempt to remove them, France's nobles are still alive and they are not all equal. French nobility is ranked by a measure of *ancienneté*, whereby the earlier in history your family was ennobled, the better. The precedence of *ancienneté* is combined with a fiercely defended and highly convoluted system of degrees and types of nobility. The *noblesse d'épée*, for instance, who were granted their nobility on the battlefield from the Capetians in the tenth century onwards, regard the *noblesse de robe*, mostly former *haute bourgeoisie* ennobled late in the day for their loyal book-keeping, tax-collecting, etc., as mere parvenus.

Broadly speaking the nobility is divided between the *haute noblesse* and the *petite noblesse*. It was the *haute noblesse* or grand aristocracy who in the age of kings appeared at court in a throng of intrigue and ambition. They were the first and foremost of the land, the princes and princesses of blood joined by the oldest noble families – the Rohans, Gramonts, Noailles, Polignacs or the great military dynasties of the *noblesse d'épée*, all those who could trace their lineage far back through history. They called the court *ce-pays-ci* (this country here) with the blithe presumption of a people for whom no other country exists. Typically they owned several large châteaux and vast tracts of land around the French countryside, as well as a *patrimoine Parisien* of an *hôtel particulier*.

When there was no more court at which to appear, the grand aristocracy transferred their intrigue and ambition to the new country, the salons of the Faubourg Saint-Germain. Here they lived lavishly and incestuously, whiling away the days plotting marriages and affairs for Proust to write about, and then, as the decades wore on and the fortune wore out, calling up Christie's to come round and value the family collection of eighteenth-century silver.

And then there is the other, the *petite noblesse*, also known by the unflattering name of the *noblesse d'hobereau*. Hobereau is the French name for the hobby, a small falcon that lays its eggs in the abandoned nests of other birds. This is the nobility who in the age of kings lived far from the thrill and treachery of court, tucked away in a remote château somewhere in the provinces. Sometimes they were former *haute bourgeoisie* who had been ennobled in recognition of their job or administrative post. They stretched a living on poor-to-mediocre revenues brought in from their land and vineyards, and while the eldest son could usually make ends meet, the younger sons were caught in a state of miserable penury so acutely observed by Balzac. After the Napoleonic reform of inheritance laws whereby the inheritance is divided equally between all heirs, families were faced with the incessant division of the estate and the dismal phenomenon of what is known as a *château à sec*, a dry château, which means there was no more land to provide revenues and all that was left to cling to was the house. They played bridge among themselves and discussed the cost of mending their roofs, and although they enjoyed the assurance of being squire of their village, they also bore the bitter knowledge that in the grand salons of *ce-pays-ci* they were no one.

Jacques wanted nothing more dearly than to be the issue of a grand noble family. Instead the reality was that his De Bascher ancestor had been ennobled in 1818, during the brief restoration of the monarchy under Louis XVIII, and therefore barely registered in *ancienneté*. Before this time they had been a family of *haute bourgeoisie* from the town of Nantes and loyal royalists fighting in the Vendée for the restoration of the monarchy. They owned a small nineteenth-century château and a modest acreage of Muscadet vineyards tucked away in the village of Barbechat in the western department of the Loire Atlantique.

The *petite noblesse* wasn't the only social disappointment Jacques suffered. 'Our mother's maiden name is Petit,' says Xavier de Bascher. 'You couldn't have a more commonplace surname than this in France. She comes from a rural background in the Limousin and my father's surname is De Bascher, which is unique and comes from the Vendée nobility. Personally I have always been proud of this meeting, this fusion, but Jacques always hated the fact my mother's name was Armelle Petit.'

Jacques' burning trajectory through Paris fashion began from the inconsolable desire to be grander than nature allowed. And in their social frustration Karl Lagerfeld and Jacques de Bascher shared a common bond. Mediocre, normal, middle-class – these are not concepts that fit in fashion. Life should be exceptional, not predictable. Karl Lagerfeld understood this from the start.

But that which nature had thoughtlessly denied Jacques, he sought to create through image. Here nature proved more generous, having provided him with considerable beauty and presence – both attributes that may take you far in Paris and in fashion.

Chapter 8

1972

In November 1972 Yves flew to New York for a holiday where he was welcomed, as always, both as fashion messiah and celebrity in society. There was a party thrown for him, and Bianca and Mick Jagger were there. Yves' hippie days were over. He had cut off his shoulder-length hair, shaved the beard and wore a bow-tie and suit. He stood chatting to Bianca, who was sultry in halterneck white dress with emerald polka-dots and a pillbox hat lashed down with a pheasant feather. She carried an antique black-and-white-tipped walking-cane clamped between upper arm and breast in a pose that hovered somewhere between Berlin cabaret and drum majorette. 'Braless and backless,' noted *Newsweek* about her appearance, for it was a time when braless and backless was still considered a sensation.

Days after the party, Yves and Bianca got together again for a story for *Interview* magazine. Bianca asked the questions and Yves replied, while Andy Warhol sat alongside and recorded the whole conversation on his tape recorder. The transcript was printed in the January 1973 issue of *Interview* magazine, next to a full-page photo of Yves and a fashion shoot of several pages of Bianca.

The conversation between them was a peach-skin celebrity chat of mutual admiration. They talked of Yves' aestheticism and his constant quest for visual perfection, which led Bianca to ask, 'Aren't there qualities you look for in people?' Yves' reply is perhaps the most revealing public statement he has ever made about himself. 'No,' he said, 'because ultimately the qualities I see in people are what I perceive them to be. It is my vision of people that counts. It's all projection. If I am deceived it's my own doing. What interests me is my vision of others.'

Yves carries the world around inside his head and it is a world defined by him. The real world passes before Yves Saint Laurent like a projection screen on to which his ciné-camera of a mind can play whatever he wishes to see. Everything else is shut out, blocked; his voice is the only one he listens to. It is never you that interests Yves, but only his idea of you. Once you do not conform to Yves' idea of you, you cease to exist for him. The withdrawal is as absolute as the vision. 'He is implacable, he forgives nothing,' says Charlotte Aillaud. The wide-eyed delight that you once stirred in his imagination is gone, the face is closed, the impatience tangible; you are lost.

'Like all creators he has an appalling ego and so others don't really count much for him because of that,' admits Pierre Bergé now. 'I am someone generous, Yves is not. I do not mean he is miserly. I mean he is someone who can only live wrapped up in himself. The outside world does not interest him. *Voilà!* You know it is like every artist, every creator; they invent their own solar system just as he has done and the whole world turns around this sun and the sun is him. *Voilà!* And the sun is not there to ask how the satellites are doing. He could not care less. But I do not mean that as a criticism. Yves is someone who will never ask after your news; he will never ask how you are for the simple reason that if you say you're not well, he will be extremely put out. It's not possible for him to have someone ill in front of him, it is out of the question. People who are ill do not interest him. When I first knew him there were many things like that which shocked me about Yves, which upset me even and if he hadn't been the genius he is then I would have left. Because I couldn't have taken for instance the sort of thing he said to Bianca Jagger. But I accepted it because I understood what it meant and that his need to create uses up all his strength and there is *nothing* left for anyone else, for the others.'

Pierre would always maintain that Yves' abnormal talent absolved him from the conventions of normal behaviour. But perhaps this was a way for Pierre to justify to himself the nature of their relationship and that there might be nothing left for him, Pierre. Yves' immense self-absorption was combined with an unflinching personal vision that rendered him impervious to the needs of others. 'There is no compassion,' says Jacques Grange. 'He can say "*Ohh, la pauvre*," but deep down there is a profound egoism to Yves. Profound. Much more so than with Pierre.' His lopsided solar system is both a source of strength and cruelty. 'He is the strongest of them all,' says Betty Catroux. 'He has this kind of detachment from others that means, even if he is wounded, his river keeps on flowing.'

Nowhere was Yves' force more in evidence than at his couture house. For the *mannequins de cabine* who worked with Monsieur Saint Laurent and on whom he modelled and 'built' the couture collection, their day was ritual: filled with pleasing him. Unlike the models used for photography and magazine work, the *mannequins de cabine* worked principally for one house only. Not only were they the models on whom the couturier would fit and create the collection, but it was also they that modelled the haute-couture collection daily throughout the season. For this was a time when each couture house still held a fashion show every afternoon and the clients would come by, watch the show and pick out their wardrobe for the next season.

During the weeks when Yves Saint Laurent was working on the forthcoming collection, the models awaited their summons downstairs in the *cabine de mannequins*. They sat before the lights and mirrors, dressed in white housecoats, plucking at their eyebrows until there was only skin. The new line was sketched where the eyebrow had been. They pinned their hair up in a severe chignon in the way Yves liked. The scarlet lipstick was applied. Then they sat in the languid, empty hours of the harem, each one waiting her turn.

The call came from the studio; Monsieur Saint Laurent was ready for the fitting. There was a final flurry before the mirror and then the model walked up the stairs to the studio to make her entrance and the encounter in which his attention was won or lost.

'*Ah, voilà, Joan Crawford*,' he said as Nicole Dorier walked into the mirrored studio wearing a plunging sheath dress of black silk-satin tied beneath the breasts. All eyes were on her reflection. It was a time when Yves' imagination was caught up in the severe and shiny glamour of the heroines of 1930s cinema: Marlene Dietrich, Greta Garbo, Joan Crawford, all the cinematic icons of his youth. This is where his power lay: he pulled you into his world and into his obsessions. 'He made you enter his game. He gives you this role and you are obliged to follow it. And either you take the role and play with it or you do not stay,' shrugs Nicole. 'I remember one poor girl who arrived as a *mannequin de cabine* and she had long hair down to her waist and so she was told to cut it all off, which she did. Three days later she was told, "Mademoiselle, thank you, you are not needed".'

The models showed the winter collection during the summer and of course they wanted to go off and sunbathe and get a tan. 'We would come back bronzed from Greece and Monsieur Saint Laurent would be furious,' remembers Nicole Dorier. 'He wanted those models with white skin to look white. He was extremely demanding. You really couldn't disappoint him. Sometimes there were models who turned up one day not looking perfect; well, they shouldn't have come in that day. They were finished after that. There is a great severity to him. He is the eye. You cannot make an error. You must always outdo yourself every time. If he sees you one day not looking your best that will shatter the image he has of you.'

Image. By 1972 image was both the word and the idea that gripped Paris fashion and it seemed that no one could bear to destroy the ideal Yves created. To do so was to fail to register on the Saint Laurent radar; to do so was to fall from his grace. Yves was the eye, but he was also the mirror in which they saw themselves. Yves Saint Laurent was at the centre of the narcissism that grew and magnified throughout this time in Paris. And in these glory years of Saint Laurent it seemed there could be no greater joy than pleasing him.

There was an aesthetic responsibility to being within his radar that was unspoken and implicit. If you were a woman entering his studio, you did so in high heels. No woman entered his presence without wearing lipstick; even Loulou de la Falaise, who preferred herself without, gave in to his demands. If your hair was not right that day it was advisable not to go at all. Dominique Deroche, who joined the house in these years as a press assistant, had her own solution to the days when she was obliged to go and see Monsieur Saint Laurent, even though she knew her outfit did not measure up. She exited his studio walking backwards, as if leaving the audience of Louis XIV, that way avoiding any risk of a less-than-perfect rear view. The studio was Yves' Galerie des Glaces, brightly lit with mirrors everywhere that were outsize and watching you. 'There was no obligation, simply we had all understood,' says Jacques Grange. 'He never said anything, but no woman would ever arrive less than impeccable.'

Betty dropped by at the studio from time to time, to laugh and gossip, but mostly she kept herself removed from the couture house and its machinations. She knew better than to bore Yves with her problems. That was something Betty never did. She talked to Yves about *him*, about *les bêtises* that they could get up to that night, about his hair, his boyfriends, and most of all she listened. Of all Yves' satellites it was perhaps Betty who had the best protection to withstand the long-term effects of Yves' ego. She gave nothing away. She hid her intelligence, discipline and loyalty beneath dark glasses. 'Betty did very well by standing still and doing nothing in a pair of trousers,' says one close to the Saint Laurent group. 'Her strength is very simply in not saying anything.'

Betty had given birth to the first of two daughters in late 1970, an experience that she describes as a 'disaster'. 'That was another thing that I tried to run from. I had marvellous children, but it was awful for me having them. I am not the slightest bit maternal. I didn't feel right. I didn't like the contact. I don't like small children at all, I like it more when it starts to be, "Let's have a drink".' Was it post-natal depression she is describing? Who knows with Betty? She has made a fine art of the pose of nihilism. She affected an impassive platinum-blonde exterior and a dandified disinterest in life. 'Ahh, nothing interests me, absolutely nothing at all,' she claims. 'My only passions are my dancing, my white wine, my man *et voilà*.' She possessed a disconnection from others that had an interesting effect on Yves, who for once found himself outmanoeuvred in terms of passivity and forced to give something away. 'The men in my entourage have always treated me as if I was, I don't know, something so precious, that I must be protected, spoilt, put in a cocoon. It is shameful what I am telling you but this has given me a detachment as regards others; I don't need to tire myself with anyone at all.'

While Betty stayed out of the studio, Loulou was there every day. She was by Yves' side night and day. 'I've never been very passive,' says Loulou. 'I've always been someone who contributes or makes the atmosphere.' She did so by giving of herself. And Yves wanted it all: her sense of colour, her lightness, 'my grooviness,' says Loulou, 'to use a word from those years.' 'I think she gave him confidence by being so enthusiastic. She is never negative, Loulou,' says her mother Maxime. 'She wouldn't say, "Oh I don't like this sketch." She'd say, "I like this one better than that."' On a practical level it was invaluable for Yves, as for any male designer dreaming up dresses, to know what a woman really felt.

Loulou was a catalyst in Yves' rediscovery of colour. He had used colour throughout his career but often in serious Parisian combinations. He was highly influenced by Chanel and her palette of navy, black and white. Loulou remembers the collection the season before she joined being 'ghastly, actually it was quite elegant but it had no success at all. It was too pure with sort of jersey cardigans. It was very, very simple and everything was black, navy blue and brown. It bored everyone stiff.'

It was at this time that Loulou gave one of her first interviews to the press, in which she blurted out that she hated black and navy, only to be sharply reprimanded when she returned to Rue Spontini. But the very fact that Loulou dared to say such a thing would have been a shot in the arm for Yves.

'He has a phenomenal sense of colour,' says Loulou, 'but he needed me to jerk it out of his system. He always had it in him because he was brought up in colour, but then there was all that sort of good education and Parisian conformity. Most people think that if they use colour it won't be *comme il faut* and I think I showed him that colour was not vulgar. I think I opened the doors to him. That is what creativity is: you use people to open doors that are your own. You do not copy other people, but they make things accessible within you.'

Yves even used Loulou's friendships as a source of motivation. 'I used to see a lot of Kenzo and I think that was a great driving force for Yves. I think he has always been very competitive and in a way he wanted to impress me too, kind of say to me, I'm as great as your friends are and you can have as good a time dressed by me as you could by so and so', reflects Loulou.

Muse, inspiration, provocation: how does one gauge Loulou's effect on Yves Saint Laurent? 'Loulou arrived and the pastry became light,' says Michel Klein simply. 'I just want to go around and influence people in various things,' said Loulou in 1973. 'She was an influence for us all,' said the late Helmut Newton.

Meanwhile, down a small flight of stairs from the studio sat Pierre Bergé in his businessman's office, angle-poise lamp at the ready, working to secure the success of the house of Saint Laurent. He had grown a beard and wore his hair swept forward across his forehead in a style that gave him a kind of latter-day Napoleonic campaign bluster. He drove around in a chauffeur-driven Rolls-Royce, surveying Haussmann's vistas from the heights of his bouncy leather upholstery.

In the couture house he masterminded significant structural changes. Richard Salomon was approaching retirement and so decided to sell Charles of the Ritz to Squibb Beechnut, which was a large American group producing mainly pharmaceutical products. Unlike the pleasant personal relationship of Bergé and Salomon, the new business marriage was full of conflict as the corporate American thinking of Squibb clashed with Pierre Bergé's highly developed idea of sovereignty. In 1972 Yves and Pierre signed a complex deal, brokered by Salomon, whereby they gained control over the couture house at the same time as ceding control of the perfume business to Squibb, although Pierre and Yves still received royalties on the perfumes.

Ironically that left Yves and Pierre in control of haute couture at a time when couture sales were falling dramatically and the end of haute couture seemed in sight. Yves himself said in 1974, 'It won't last another seven years.' There were still private clients, although increasingly they bought couture for evenings only, preferring to dress in ready-to-wear by day. But the real drop-off at this point came in the American department stores, which for years had paid for the right to see the shows and then paid again for the right to make copies of the couturiers' designs. This had been the mainstay of the couture industry. Now, almost overnight, department stores stopped bothering to pay the $3,000 it cost to attend each couture show. They were too busy over at the Porte de Versailles watching the ready-to-wear shows that everyone was talking about.

It was a crucial moment for both Paris fashion and the house of Saint Laurent, and Pierre Bergé was determined to direct both. The Chambre Syndicale de la Haute Couture had been dragging their feet about recognising and organising the ready-to-wear designers and the ready-to-wear shows. In 1973 Bergé stepped in and formed the Groupement Mode et Création, a new organisation that was part of the Chambre Syndicale, intended to unite the ready-to-wear designers such as Kenzo,

Chloé and Sonia Rykiel with the ready-to-wear of couturiers such as
Saint Laurent and get the calendar and show-time organised and up
and running. The following year Bergé got himself elected as President
of the Chambre Syndicale, a highly significant post which enabled him
to wield considerable influence over the fashion industry, at which point
he promptly dismantled the Groupement Mode et Création of the
previous year.

In their own house Yves and Pierre were not discouraged by the fall-
off in couture sales. Their business strategy had always been clear-cut:
they saw licensing as their route to gold and glory and the agreement
with Squibb gave them the rights to license any product other than
perfume and cosmetics. From this time on Pierre accelerated the licensing
agreements, selling the name to manufacturers of sunglasses, belts, ties
and cigarettes. In 1973 even the ready-to-wear label Yves Saint Laurent
Rive Gauche, which up until then had been a partnership with the
manufacturer Mendes, was transformed into a licence. It was handed
over in its entirety to Mendes and although Yves Saint Laurent continued
to design the collection, it was now Mendes who had total control over
manufacturing, quality and distribution through the franchise stores.
Sales were expanding rapidly – in 1972 Bergé told *Women's Wear Daily*
that worldwide retail sales figures for Rive Gauche ready-to-wear were
$24 million.

This was the beginning of the boom years of fashion-licensing and
blockbuster perfume deals, with the growing realisation that here in the
fabric and glamour of fashion lay a cash cow. Bergé has been roundly
criticised for following the licensing business model. His critics accuse
him of getting rich while contributing to the ultimate depletion of
French manufacturing. But the house of Saint Laurent was not the only
couturier getting rich this way during these years; Pierre Cardin is
another example of a couturier who licensed his name extensively
during the same period. It was so easy to sign licences: you needed no
manufacturing base, no knowledge of production or management and,
in the case of cigarettes and sunglasses and such like, no creative input
was required either. All you needed was the name (houses were not yet
called brands) and a signature on the dotted line and then you waited
for the royalties to come rolling in. It was a house of mirrors, empty
on the inside.

The strategy was indicative of where Pierre's interests really lay. Bergé's business outlook was brilliant but specific in its scope; he was not a manufacturer or an industrialist. Pierre was an inspired promoter and a power broker.

'If you ask me to describe Pierre, I cannot,' says John Fairchild, 'other than to say he is, like so many in the fashion industry, power mad.' How far he could wield his power, how effectively he could impose both his will and that of Yves, became an overriding obsession and one that was exacerbated by Yves' passivity.

'When I don't like something I tell Pierre,' Yves once said. A nod from Yves and Pierre picked up that big cream telephone of his in his shiny black businessman's office and let rip around fashion offices of the world. Journalists at *L'Express*, shoe licensees in Milan, the maître d' at Maxim's who'd failed to secure the right table – was there anyone in these years who didn't receive a punishing, high-decibel blast from Pierre Bergé?

The late Helmut Newton was sitting in French *Vogue* editor Francine Crescent's office on the Place du Palais Bourbon one afternoon when the call came through from the Saint Laurent couture house. It was Bergé who began shouting at Francine about the way Newton had photographed a Saint Laurent dress in a shoot that appeared in that month's issue of French *Vogue*. 'I grabbed the phone from Francine and said, "Listen Pierre, don't tell me how to take pictures and I won't tell you how to make frocks!"' remembered Helmut. 'I was furious. He is a rough customer but I like him very much. He's a Scorpio like me, and I'm just as big an old bastard as he.'

Bergé's astrological sign is frequently cited as justification for his behaviour. So is the tale of the scorpion who kills the frog who is giving him a lift as they cross the river, shruggingly explaining, 'It is in my nature.' Some who worked alongside Bergé insist that he delighted in throwing his weight around and the shouting was nothing more than a power game. It is a theory confirmed by friend Jacques Grange: 'There is a desire in Pierre to be able to say it's me that directs everything, it's me that makes everything happen, it's me that chooses everything. He is someone who loves to control. He gives you everything if you are under his control.'

He ordered those working in the couture house around, not least

Yves. 'Sit up straight', 'Don't talk like that' – there were endless orders in everyday life. Journalist Pat McColl turned up to interview Yves at the apartment in Place Vauban. She watched as Yves wrung his hands beneath the glass table. She had just returned from a ski trip and Yves asked her what it was like to ski. '*Tais-toi!*' ordered Bergé, cutting Yves off mid-sentence.

'Well, he is Scorpio with a Scorpio rising sun,' says Didier Grumbach, who in 1972 was managing Mendes, his family firm and the manufacturer of Rive Gauche. Grumbach worked with Pierre Bergé for over twenty years. 'He always feels guilty and I think when he screams at people it is not that he is furious with people, but rather he's furious with himself.'

Grumbach recalls the time Richard Salomon came to the Rue Spontini offices to sign a licence contract and witnessed a Bergé fit of temper directed against Madame de Peyerimhoff. She was a genteel and elegant lady, who had been the *directrice de maison* since 1962, had known Yves when they worked together at Dior and was the person responsible for introducing Salomon to Bergé and Saint Laurent in the first place.

'So Monsieur Salomon is sitting at Rue Spontini waiting to meet with Monsieur Bergé. He is downstairs and Monsieur Bergé's office is up in the middle of the staircase with just one door,' recalls Grumbach. 'Monsieur Salomon can hear Monsieur Bergé screaming at Madame de Peyerimhoff. Monsieur Bergé is absolutely furious and shouting. Monsieur Salomon hears her answer in a very weak voice. He is green, waiting in embarrassment, and then right in front of him Madame de Peyerimhoff comes running down the stairs in tears and she is crying so much that she runs out and leaves the house. Monsieur Salomon has the meeting with Monsieur Bergé and that evening he calls Madame de Peyerimhoff and he says, "Yvonne, *what* happened? I'm so embarrassed, I feel awful, I don't know how to react, what to say; what is all this drama?" And she says, "What are you talking about?" And he says, "Today, what happened this morning," and she says, "Ohhh, but that is nothing! It happens all the time, don't worry about it. Tomorrow he will send me twenty-four roses and it will all be over." And that is the way it always happened, it has no real significance, it is of the moment and then he is sorry.'

And all the while that Pierre roared, Yves sat mute in his studio, cocooned in thoughts of silk gazar, his long, tapered fingers pressing the pleat of a shoulder between finger and thumb. Yves' artistic talent gave him an innocence that was just that – creative innocence. But for many years and by many, even those close to him, Yves' creative innocence was misconstrued and he was perceived as being without guile.

In 1972 Yves and Pierre moved into a new apartment, a large duplex at 55, Rue de Babylone in the seventh *arrondissement*, which they had bought two years before and had been renovating since. The Rue de Babylone was just a short walk south-east of their former apartment, but the new home marked a significant break with the amateur decorative dramatics of Place Vauban and its faux Louis XVI chairs and cotton velvet sofa, always an endless source of mockery for Karl Lagerfeld and his clique.

Everything about the Rue de Babylone apartment was an aesthetic and symbolic *mise-en-scène* intended to impress and seduce, two interchangeable ideas in Yves' mind. No one understood the power of beauty more than Yves Saint Laurent. 'I'm an aesthete, I'm constantly looking for perfection,' he said in 1974. He used beauty – his own, that of his house, the clothes he designed – to thrill, to dominate, to inspire awe and to sell.

The move marked a new phase in Saint Laurent's life and career. For a start, he and Pierre were now flush with money and spending it in considerable style. They were building the image of the house of Saint Laurent on the cult of the man and the new home was in perfect accord both with this cult and with Yves' chosen social status of couturier. Yves did not use his new wealth to elevate his middle-class roots; on the contrary, he made his colonial bourgeois past – albeit seen through his and Bergé's sepia-tinted memory – a key element of the Saint Laurent legend. Yves' aspirations for himself and his home lay not in joining the patrician elite, but rather in proving himself to be among the mythic taste-makers of Paris. This is where Yves's vanity lay. He wanted to be talked about in the same breath as Marie-Laure de Noailles, Misia Sert and Jacques Doucet, all of whom had ensured their Parisian immortality by their rarefied and assured taste. Marie-Laure had lived in Jean-Michel Frank-designed splendour on the Place des Etats Unis, while

Misia Sert had lived in bohemian luxury entertaining Sergei Diaghilev, Cocteau and Chanel.

Taste is a peculiarly Parisian preoccupation, not least because it is regarded as the ultimate proof of being a successful Parisian. Ideally one's taste should be multi-layered, cultivated and all-encompassing, informing every aspect of a home from bookshelf to the choice of tea-leaf. In this respect, Yves and Pierre's new home was unassailable.

The apartment, although situated in the Faubourg Saint-Germain, was not the house of an aristocrat; it was not an *hôtel particulier*. It was an apartment intended for the *grande bourgeoisie*, built in the 1920s for a wealthy American by Yves' favourite architect, Jean-Michel Frank. It had the plain elegance and monumental proportions characteristic of a Frank interior, with vast stretches of cherry-wood walls. Unfortunately the Wall Street Crash of 1929 meant the American never got to live in his home and it was bought instead by Marie Cuttoli, wife of a Corsican senator and collector of an extraordinary collection of paintings that included works by Picasso, Braque, Matisse and Léger. She lived in the duplex for thirty years and left the Frank design largely untouched.

Yves of course kept and restored the Frank interior and decorated the apartment with voluptuous layers of art-deco furniture and arte-facts, tribal art and his own Léger paintings. These paintings were the beginnings of what would develop into a sumptuous and mainly late nineteenth-century and modern art collection, give or take the odd Goya.

The result was wildly impressive. Entering the apartment felt like stepping into the ripe and grandiose secrets of Yves Saint Laurent's imagination. It had the effect of subjugating visitors and connoisseurs alike into awed admiration. The entrance hall was dark, red and lacquered, and dominated by a striking Senufo bird sculpture, a series of Warhol portraits of Yves and a black Ruhlmann piano. In the salon was a carpet by Boisseau from the 1920s, decorated with a flock of white, woven parakeets with beating wings and outstretched black claws. A sullen mauve African violet was placed upon the lacquer table. Everything was arranged in artful juxtaposition.

Over on one wall of the salon hung five pastel panels by Edward Burne-Jones depicting the adoration of the lamb, and directly opposite were five enormous windows opening out on to the green lawn beyond and splitting Jean-Michel Frank's cherry-wood and chrome-framed walls wide open.

'It was one of the sexiest places I've ever been in,' says writer Marian McEvoy. 'The surfaces were all tactile, the colours were almost edible and the lighting was perfect and so flattering. There wasn't one lamp that if you walked by you didn't feel absolutely beautiful in its light. The fires were always at the right point, there weren't too many logs or too few. It was an overwhelmingly sensual interior.' Every room smelt of lilies and ivy; the yellow light cast a wistful shadow on a chosen face.

It was all great showmanship. Also on the ground floor was the Oriental room, with smoked-mirrored walls and ceiling. There was a mass of 1930s silver lamé cushions arranged on the floor for seating and a huge sixteenth-century Chinese Ming gilt wood Buddha sat in front of the mirrored wall. 'It is the late, late nightspot at the end of a long evening where there is only candlelight and intimacy,' said Yves.

A powerful statement of couturier heritage and provenance under-pinned the house and its decorative scheme. The couture references were everywhere: it was Jean-Michel Frank who had designed Elsa Schiaparelli's apartment and later her Place Vendôme boutique. There was an Eileen Gray serpent chair that once belonged to fashionable 1920s hat-maker Suzanne Talbot and a standard lamp by Rateau that had originally been owned by Jeanne Lanvin. Downstairs in the library there were several prints formerly in the possession of Christian Dior. There were also several important pieces that Yves had bought from the sale of Jacques Doucet's collection.

Indeed much of his artistry in mixing tribal art – or 'art nègre' as it is called in France – and art-deco furniture with modern art was directly inspired by Doucet's own daring decorative mixes, which had characterised both his apartment on Avenue du Bois and his Neuilly studio.

Jacques Doucet, a couturier at the beginning of the twentieth century, spent much of his life amassing an important collection of eighteenth-century furniture and works of art that he then sold at auction in 1912. Doucet then started afresh, shaping his ultimate artistic setting with the building and decoration of a studio in Neuilly on Avenue Saint-James in 1926. Here, under the guidance of André Breton, Doucet created an important example of an exotic art-deco interior, commissioning the leading artisans and furniture-makers of the movement such as Eileen Gray and the great cabinet-maker Legrain. He placed their furniture alongside tribal art and paintings by Picasso, Rousseau and Modigliani.

Unlike Doucet, Yves was not the slightest bit enthusiastic about commissioning or buying contemporary. The Warhol portraits of him were one of the few contemporary works he had in the house and it seemed they were treasured more for reflecting the glory of the sitter than for their art, for when Yves found out Warhol had been commissioned by designers Valentino and Halston to paint their portraits as well, he flew into a white rage of pique and declared he was going to burn his. He never did carry out his threat.

Yves had nothing else from the present but a few grazing-sheep sculptures from François-Xavier Lalanne that writer and critic Philippe Jullian dismissed as looking like 'great big poodles'. From Betty's husband – his friend François Catroux – who was an interior designer with a contemporary style, Yves had bought one table. Even the all-white library downstairs had echoes of the past in that the white slip sofas were modelled on those of Marie-Laure de Noailles and her stylish salon on the Place des Etats Unis. The photographs and postcards propped against the bookcase, featuring pictures of Yves' heroes Ludwig of Bavaria and Marcel Proust, were another Marie-Laure-style mannerism.

The apartment on Rue de Babylone was photographed and exalted in countless magazines, but accessible to a handful of people only. Hidden away from the street behind a huge wooden doorway and beyond a courtyard, guarded by a fleet of impenetrable servants, this was a large and significant step in Yves' retreat from the real world.

At this time only Pierre really knew the depths and extremes of volatility of Yves' mind. To the rest of the world, even those close to him, it was gentle, kind Yves, shy Yves, a sweet and suffering boy. The reality of the man was hidden from view. And the reality of the man was that he was mentally ill. 'He is a manic depressive,' says Bergé over thirty years later. 'That is the exact name of his illness.'

Bergé announces this now with the equanimity of an old man, but that was not the way Bergé talked about Yves back in 1972, when Yves was the world-famous couturier upon whom Bergé and a rapidly expanding business relied. In those days Bergé threw up highly effective screens so that Yves' tantrums, depressions and irrational mood swings were, for the most part, hidden from public view. Sometimes not even Pierre could smokescreen the damage, like the time Yves was so angry that he punched a wall and broke his wrist.

When Yves' health was discussed both Yves and Pierre explained the opaque depressions in the great French romantic tradition of tortured genius. Pierre called on Rimbaud's *A Season in Hell*, while Yves preferred to conjure up the plight of Proust. By now Bergé had committed himself to a lifelong battle to keep Yves on the rails and his dark side under wraps, a battle to which Pierre's own personal fortune and ego were intimately and increasingly bound. The fashion stakes were rising, money and celebrity were pouring in, and Yves was the icon that had to be kept holy.

Pierre had his work cut out: he had to keep Yves stimulated, to allow in enough folly for the creativity to whirl and yet at the same time impose draconian damage-limitation measures. He had to control what was known about him, but keeping the lid on Yves became an increasingly difficult task once he started playing with recreational drugs and alcohol. Yves possessed a will to self-destruct, a wild aggression and a curiosity to explore his own shadows, which together with the addition of drugs and alcohol made for a dangerous liaison.

A series of cartoon stories that Yves wrote and illustrated under the title *La vilaine Lulu* offers a rare, unobstructed view into Yves' mind. The book was published in May 1967 by Tchou in a limited-edition portfolio of large format, loose sheets. Inside is the roly-poly Lulu, a butch little girl drawn in red and black ink who came about back in 1956 when Yves was still an assistant at the house of Dior. At the end of the working day the Dior apprentices used to fool around dressing up in women's clothes, and one night boutique stylist Jean-Pierre Frère tried on a straw boater and a red tulle petticoat, pulled up his trousers to reveal knee-length black socks and paraded round the studio.

From this spectacle, Yves conjured up the strange and vindictive vilaine Lulu (she had no connection to Loulou de la Falaise). Stubby and perverse, she carries a fat white rat for a pet (intended to symbolise her sexual appetite, the rat is pictured on one page emerging from beneath her skirt) and has a penchant for reading *Playgirl*. The book is full of Paris in-jokes about nightclubs and lines reminiscent of a Françoise Sagan novel, and is based around a series of dastardly escapades involving

Lulu committing acts of mass murder, electrocution, poison and the abduction of babies.

She has pronounced pyromaniac tendencies which she indulges again and again, including 'one dull Thursday' when she calls up her school-friends, invites them round, locks them in a shed, douses it in petrol and sets fire to it, using her binoculars for a better view of the children as they burn alive and saying with a jaunty smile, '*Comme c'est amusant, Schmuck Pluck.*'

La vilaine Lulu and its expression of infantile sadism (at Easter she deliberately poisons her whole class by feeding them rotten Easter eggs and then turns up to their funeral to hop all over their graves with glee) is both diabolical and grotesque. Realising of course that every reader would leap to the obvious conclusion that *La vilaine Lulu* was an open window on to his own psyche, Yves pre-empts any such judgement by taking the first page of the book to make the following handwritten declaration:

'The author warns that it is pointless to try and psychoanalyse him through his heroine. Contrary to what Gustave Flaubert thought when he affirmed, "*Madame Bovary, c'est moi!*" the author would like to make clear that it is out of the question that he should declare in turn, "*La vilaine Lulu, c'est moi.*"'

Despite the witty and insistent disclaimer it is hard not to associate Lulu with her creator Yves Saint Laurent. There are so many similari-ties. Lulu suffers from nervous depression. She has a monumental ego and delusions of total power. She is self-obsessed — Yves draws Lulu staring at her reflection in the pond and murmuring, '*Quel bel enfant!*' She has a remarkable appetite for sexual exploits.

But perhaps the greatest parallel between Lulu and her maker is in the predilection for martyrdom and melancholy. In the final pages of the book Lulu lives out a passing and passionate crush for a young student, called JoJo, newly arrived in Paris from the provinces. For a page or two she flirts with bohemian life, drinking cheap Beaujolais and making passionate 'Schmuck Pluck' with JoJo in a maid's room in the *quartier latin*. But bathing her feet in the basin on the corridor and tramping up ten flights of stairs is not the life Lulu had intended; soon 'the lack of luxury destabilises her' and she dumps JoJo. 'La vilaine Lulu,' writes Saint Laurent, 'can't bear this mediocre life any longer.'

She chooses instead a life of wealth and protection in the arms of the aristocratic Gontran Pontchartrin. An old man with a beard shaped not unlike an erect penis, he has paedophile tendencies and has been pursuing Lulu throughout the book. On the final page she runs to his house in the middle of the night and throws herself into his pyjama-clad arms. 'Of course,' thinks Lulu to herself a few days later as she lies in the Saint-Tropez sun with a grimace on her face and Gontran in her midst, 'it is not the dream, but he's so reassuring.' And with a large, melancholic and quintessentially Saint Laurent sigh, Yves finishes the book with the words: 'She understood then she would always be sad.'

La vilaine Lulu meets her fate in Saint-Tropez.

Chapter 9

1973

From the start there was an ambiguity to the role Jacques de Bascher played in Karl's life and indeed how he got there in the first place. Antonio and Juan swore they were the ones who spotted Jacques dancing at Le Sept one night before the summer in Saint-Tropez and told Karl that Jacques had the perfect look to be his boyfriend. But Gilles Dufour remembers a more opportunistic mode of arrival: he recalls meeting Jacques as a young and ambitious buck at a dinner one night and Jacques begging him to introduce him to Karl. Later in the 1970s, Jacques told a friend that he used black magic to gain entry into Karl's life, but by that time Jacques' every word was carefully weighted for its power to shock.

By the return from Saint-Tropez, Jacques was integrated into Karl's life. It was hard to decipher what exactly he was doing there. Was he lover or muse, boyfriend or ideal? Karl consistently denied that he and Jacques were lovers. He protested over and over, year after year, indignantly and repeatedly asserting there was no physical relationship between them. Others close to Karl and Jacques refute this, insisting the relationship began with a physical dimension. But certainly the physical was never the crux or the constant to their union. From the outset Karl was driven not by flesh, but by image.

Jacques had prominent cheekbones that captured light and shadow; his lips were curved; he held a cigarette and the room's attention with aplomb and he knew it. He possessed the sensual allure of the *fin de*

siècle, those delirious final years of the nineteenth century still so tantalising in the imagination of Paris and the homosexual.

And there was something else about Jacques that recalled the nineteenth century: the beauty spot on his jaw, his talent for conjuring an
atmosphere around him, his ability to fascinate men, his infidelity and
his delight in sensation – all these were the attributes and accomplish-
ments of a true Parisian courtesan. It was during the Second Empire
under the rule of Napoleon III that high society rejoiced in the illicit
entertainments of the *demi-mondaine*. Courtesans and actresses – they
were the idols of nineteenth-century Paris and they lit up the parkland
of the Bois de Boulogne, bunches of violets quivering at their breast,
arousing envy and admiration as they passed in their brougham down
the Allée des Acacias.

Jacques was out every night now at Le Sept, glittering beneath the
spotlights, dancing the dance of seven veils to keep Karl in his thrall.
At the same time he was slicing through the young men of Paris like
a hot knife through butter, and not just the men. He was also having
an affair with the teenage Diane de Beauvau-Craon, who was titled,
reckless and, according to her memory, 'in a state of total revolution'.

Diane was seventeen and a daughter of one of the most illustrious
families of the French nobility. The Beauvau-Craons are dukes who can
trace their nobility back to the year 1000. They have ancestors that
fought with Richard the Lionheart and a collective job résumé that
over the centuries reads like a *Who's Who* of France: *maréchal* de France,
war minister, bishops, ambassadors, chamberlain to the king. The family
seat is the Château de Haroué, a so-called 'palace in the countryside'
near Lorraine that was built for the Beauvau-Craons in 1720. Diane's
mother was Maria Cristina Patino y de Borbon, a Patino heir who
divorced when Diane, her second daughter, was three, leaving her ex-
husband to bring up the children.

Diane's father, who carried the title of Prince de Beauvau-Craon,
took a realistic view of his daughter's revolutionary state. She had shaved
her head at the age of fifteen and dressed now in a punchy style of
waiter's black jacket, white shirt and jeans. 'He didn't know what to do
with me any more,' remembers Diane. 'It got to the point where all he
could say was, "My darling, what decision should I take so that nothing
terrible happens to you?"'

Diane left home and lived as a friend with Tan Giudicelli before moving into Jacques' small duplex on the Rue du Dragon, just down from the Flore. At night they danced at Le Sept, legs rammed together and Diane's torso bent so far backwards that her head touched the floor.

Karl maintained a certain sangfroid in the face of Jacques' sexual infidelity. But the affair with Diane annoyed him intensely. So much so he took it upon himself to call Diane's father to complain about the fact that his daughter, still a minor, was living with a man. Down the telephone line came the duke's booming reply: 'I do not take rendezvous with my daughter's *couturiers*.' It was a gigantic social put-down and one that must have been particularly galling for Karl to bear.

The pace and intensity of Jacques' social success – a designer for a protector and a princess for a lover within months of his arrival in Paris – must have catalysed his already burgeoning ambition. He was in the *monde*, he was the new favourite. Now it was a question of remaining there. That was not such a fait accompli: there were eighteen years between Jacques and Karl, and if Jacques held the ace of beauty, Karl held every other – age, experience, power and income. Karl's favour could never be taken for granted.

'The thing that was weird was that Karl had a funny relationship with him; he wasn't all-giving to Jacques at all, and especially in the beginning he rather mistreated Jacques,' remembers Paloma Picasso. 'In the sense that I remember Jacques would moan and say, "Ohhh, I'm not coming to this party because Karl won't take me." Karl didn't want to be the one to call and say, "I am bringing Jacques," because he didn't want to acknowledge that he was with Jacques. I just thought it was weird and so I would say, "Well, come with us then." That I cannot explain.'

Jacques felt the new and treacherous ground underfoot. He was a favourite and in fashion and yet unacknowledged. Will you, won't you, be invited? Are you, are you not, the favourite? And if you aren't a boyfriend, then what exactly are you? A gigolo? It was unnerving, destabilising and compulsive.

In the spring of 1973 Jacques posed before a camera in Karl Lagerfeld's lush and newly rented apartment at number 6, Place Saint-Sulpice. From where he stood, Jacques could see the roof of Saint Sulpice church tied up in buttresses and the canopy of raspberry-pink blossom from the horse-chestnut trees shading the fountains.

He was looking out on the very *place* where, just three years before, he had announced to his friend Renaud that this was where he would one day live. And one day he would, but not yet. For now he was being photographed by *L'Uomo Vogue* to illustrate an article about himself that would be entitled 'Revival of a Dandy'.

He stood with his back against a mirror, facing the photographer. Above his head on a glass shelf was a vase of overblown peonies, and in his hand he held a cigarette. He was dressed in a silk smoking-jacket with shawl collar, which was tied loosely at the waist and worn with silk pyjama trousers; both were decorated in a dancing, fuchsia print of girls tossing garlands of flowers in the air or fluttering through space in the arms of a beau. The outfit and print were the work of Karl Lagerfeld. At Jacques' throat was a boisterously large black bow-tie, which he wore with a wing-collared white dress-shirt.

Jacques by now had grown the moustache that was to be his Paris signature, and his hair was combed so that it swept over on to one side to leave the forehead high and bare. The artifice of his pose is as acute as his studied look of languor. It is not a smile that plays about his lips, but there is something there: a look of detached amusement. Or is it bold complicity between Jacques and the camera, Jacques and his beholder?

It was in his capacity as a new and beautiful young thing in Paris and protégé of Karl Lagerfeld that Jacques was of interest to *L'Uomo Vogue*, and as such his interview was full of suitable hyperbole. He declared that he had abandoned university to 'dedicate his life to beauty in the absolute sense'. At other times Jacques would maintain that he left university because it was simply too dirty for his sensibilities.

And so the new Jacques emerged from his chrysalis. Gone were the lambswool V-neck sweaters and Burberry raincoats of Neuilly. From now on he and Karl honed and polished a look that was increasingly exaggerated in its contrived elegance. He wore wing collars everywhere; the moustache was groomed to a tapered conclusion and trimmed at Carita, where Jacques also went for facials once a month. His appearance was a fusion of 1930s film star and French dandy and he borrowed imagery from all his literary and historical heroes: Huysmans, Montesquiou, Proust, Thomas Mann and Ludwig of Bavaria, as well as the debauched suavity of Helmut Berger. The Wagnerian fantasies of the Bavarian king, the longing and aestheticism of Proust – these were all references that resonated with the fashionable homosexual in Paris at the time, not least Yves Saint Laurent.

Years after the *L'Uomo Vogue* shoot, when Jacques was well established as Karl's favourite, he returned to his family home of La Berrière for an overnight visit, where he collided with his conscience in the form of his sister Anne. She was seven years older than him and the moral and intellectual force of the five De Bascher siblings. Anne was intelligent, beautiful and politically committed. She was out on the barricades in '68 and an active member of the French women's liberation movement. Jacques was her favourite brother; they shared a bond of wit, intellectual ability and homosexuality.

Anne loved her brother and hated his life choices: his dilettantism, his laziness and his role as a kept man in fashion. 'So tell me, Jacquot,' Anne said over lunch that day at La Berrière, fixing him with her unavoidable stare, 'you are fascinated by Karl, OK, but what may I ask fascinates Karl about you?' And Jacques replied, 'Listen, Karl has no *particule* [the "de" before the surname which can denote nobility] and no amount of money can ever buy him that. And no amount of money can ever buy him a social family heritage either.'

'Well, yes,' said a puzzled Anne, 'perhaps I could understand if you were the Polignacs, but what are we but three peanuts on the map of France?' The Polignacs are another illustrious French family of dukes, with *ancienneté*, fortune and a vast and imposing château – they were everything in name and grandeur that the De Bascher family was not. Jacques was furious with his sister's social realism, claiming that their family could trace their blood back to King Louis le Gros (1081–1137), yet at the same time admitting, 'I have played the aristo card to the hilt.'

Unlike most people who come into contact with Karl and accept his accounts of his past and German grandeur, Jacques perhaps sensed from the start the social frustration in Karl since he himself was eaten up by the same longing. Jacques must have realised his own worth in that tableau of desire.

From the moment he began his assault on Paris, Jacques laid on the aristocratic airs with *élan*. He blanked out both the Limousin rural roots of his mother and his own Neuilly childhood. Amplifying his surname to De Bascher de Beaumarchais was something one of Jacques' ancestors had already tried to do in 1890 on the back of a rather tenuous link by marriage, but his request to join the names had been rejected. Perhaps Jacques was hoping to blur the divide between him and the ranks of the grand aristocracy, or that someone might associate him with the illustrious eighteenth-century playwright Caron de Beaumarchais. The name-change certainly impressed for a while, until a member of the De Beaumarchais spoke out and threatened to sue. Later Paris wags would poke fun at Jacques' name, calling him '*de pas cher de bon marché*', which was a wordplay that translates to 'not expensive and cheap', and was also a pun on the Parisian department store called 'Le Bon Marché'.

Fashion has always had a tradesman's fascination with nobility and Jacques used this to his advantage. He elevated the family, the château and Muscadet wines to Versailles-like dimensions. He fused the revved-up family history with seigneurial manners, all of which was deemed deeply exotic and thrilling in the fashion world. He made a great show of the French aristocratic greeting of kissing the hand of a married woman or woman older than oneself rather than kissing her on the cheek. 'You could meet him in the middle of the night and he'd be dead drunk and he'd still have the perfect manners and hand you over a *baise-main*,' remembers journalist Pat McColl.

'He was extremely seductive,' says Christian Dumais-Lvowski, who was introduced to Jacques by his old friend Renaud de Beaugourdon. 'Beauty is entirely subjective so whether or not you found him beautiful was one thing, but I don't think anyone could deny that Jacques was a remarkably intelligent boy. He was very cultivated, someone who read a lot, who loved beautiful things. He always astonished me with his ability to talk on just about any subject in a brilliant manner. In fact the word brilliant is an adjective that suits him well. Jacques was someone brilliant, in his conversation, in the subjects he chose to speak on, the way he spoke, his flamboyance and gestures.'

There was an enigmatic quality to Jacques' intelligence, for it seemed to serve no defined purpose other than to dazzle and impress and, above all, to arrive. Beyond the brittle, shiny surface of the man there was another dimension to Jacques, known by very few. At the age of fifteen Jacques had attempted to declare his homosexuality to his father. Jacques' father was discreet and intransigent, strait-jacketed by the moral code of his generation and upbringing. He was the indisputable reference by which Jacques measured himself and which he never felt close to equalling. Jacques lacked the courage to tell his father himself, so he turned to Anne to inform him. When Anne told her father, the news was met with silence. The father would later accept Anne as a lesbian, but strangely he would not accept the irrefutable fact of his son's homosexuality. He refused to discuss the subject with Anne or with Jacques. His son never dared broach the subject again. According to Anne, his father was the man that Jacques venerated above all else and no amount of worship or adoration from the rest of his family, or anyone else for that matter, could ever make up for the father's refusal to accept his son's sexuality. Indeed Anne believes that their father's disapproval was Jacques' greatest source of hurt and the starting point for his self-destruction.

From 1973 onwards Jacques appeared constantly at Karl's side: turning up at gallery openings, the launch of a magazine or the opening night of a new cabaret show of Brazilian transvestites called Dzizi Croquettes, all the routine appearances that together make up the intrinsic life of the *mondain*. At Maxim's he and Karl made their entrance one night in co-ordinating dark jackets with diamond art-deco brooches clipped to their breast pockets. Jacques wore white bags and wing collar, while Karl wore a floppy black bow at his neck and monocle in his eye.

Karl too had undergone a considerable change of image, emerging from the pop American glamour years and the flamboyance and femininity of Saint-Tropez as something altogether more double-breasted. He had grown a large black beard and had taken to wearing a monocle either attached by a black ribbon or simply suspended in the eye. When the monocle tumbled out Karl made a point of never bothering to pick it up, abandoning it where it lay and pulling another from his pocket.

He wore new, strong-shouldered suits and blazers accessorised with plump polka-dot ties or a silk scarf wrapped at the throat, pin-tucked shirts and a white handkerchief in the breast pocket. It was a level of foppishness that sat uncomfortably on his muscular and stocky frame.

The effect was of a body-builder dressed for the stock exchange; Helmut Newton called it Karl's 'Mafia look'.

As always with Karl, his new image necessitated a new decorative scheme, a setting in which to shine and be photographed. The new apartment was on the second floor of an elegant building that stands on a northern corner of the Place Saint-Sulpice and has the distinction of being the one apartment building on the square to have been designed by the architect of the church, the eighteenth-century Florentine Giovanni Servandoni. The apartment itself was of magnificent proportions, with floor-to-ceiling windows looking out over the church and a four-metre-high ceiling in the bedroom.

In contrast to the Rue de l'Université apartment, which was a thoroughly lived-in and cluttered setting for his life, Karl conceived the new apartment as a backdrop of 1920s and '30s decorative arts in cream, white and black, with high-shine surfaces of chrome, lacquer, satin, glass and mirror. There was a certain graphic precision to the furniture and its positioning. The overall effect was that of a sleek set from a Marcel l'Herbier black-and-white 1920s silent movie, a favourite Lagerfeld reference at the time. The apartment reflected Lagerfeld's burgeoning profile within Paris.

The new interior featured all those characteristics by which Karl's houses would be recognised from this point on, whatever the design period: an immaculate decorative scheme, bountiful bookcases, high-tech gadgetry and tireless historical research. The monochrome colours and the German tradition of hanging net curtains at the huge windows conjured up 1920s Berlin. There was a pair of magnificent Dunand vases, narrow, bronze and iconic, that were mounted on lacquer side-tables. Alongside them sat a pair of shell-shaped armchairs and pouff in ivory duchesse satin and gold lacquer that came from a house decorated by Elsie de Wolfe.

There were also the odd indiscretions of taste, in this case in the loud black-and-cream velour and chrome chairs and matching day bed by Lurçat. Karl's propensity for veering away from accepted good taste may be a characteristic deemed undesirable in French culture, but it reveals an admirable willingness to experiment and dare in both fashion and decoration, even if that meant getting it wrong from time to time. Karl was never tied up by the protocol or restraints of *bon goût*, which

often worked to his advantage when it came to fashion design, particularly later in his career.

The most striking thing about the apartment, however, was not the
furniture, but the fact that Karl's decorative vision was so exhaustive.
The floors, for instance, were covered in rather dramatic specially dyed
black and dark-brown carpets. 'They show off my art-deco pieces like
diamonds in a Cartier showcase,' explained Karl. It was showcase, not
home. With the exception of his bookshelves, Karl kept the apartment
swept clean of the personal. 'That apartment seemed planned as a photo
studio. Karl wasn't taking photographs yet, but he had that sense of
creating something, freezing it into a photographic moment,' says Philippe
Garner. 'Those two Eugène Printz thin console tables, what were they
for but to lean against and be photographed?'

Karl and Yves were both living in an art-deco setting, yet the approach
and result could not have been more different. Yves Saint Laurent was
paying homage to the Parisian interpretation of the movement in his
use of exoticism, colour and sensuality, while Karl's rendering of the
period owed much more to a conceptual ideal of the decorative period,
imagined in stark and polished tones of black and white.

By now, in Paris, Andrée Putman, Hélène Rochas and Tan Giudicelli
were all collecting art deco. Years later Andrée Putman was credited in
print as being one of the first in Paris to champion the rediscovery of
the *époque*. It was a justified claim for which she received an enraged
phone-call from Pierre Bergé, telling her it was he and Yves, not she,
who rediscovered art deco in Paris.

Karl and Yves' mutual interest in the period and their ensuing race
to find exceptional pieces in an increasingly fashionable market place
echoed the growing competition between the two designers. It was not
that Karl was a threat to Yves' spotlight – how could he be when he
was just a ready-to-wear designer working freelance without even a
label bearing his own name? It was rather that, by building an identity,
decorating an apartment in considerable style and having a beautiful
and highly visible entourage, Karl was encroaching on Saint Laurent's
territory of image. And not just that. With Jacques de Bascher, Karl had
something in his possession with which to arouse the curiosity, the envy
even, of Yves Saint Laurent.

Unlike Yves and his Rue de Babylone retreat, there were no limits in access to Karl. Not only was the Saint Sulpice apartment repeatedly lent out for fashion shoots and featured in endless magazines, but Karl kept himself doggedly in the public fashion domain, surrounded by people – models, groupies, journalists, famous offspring, new friends – and never more so than once Jacques de Bascher entered his life.

Patrick Hourcade was a young accessories editor at French *Vogue* and met Karl at precisely this Saint Sulpice art-deco period, when, as Patrick remembers, 'Karl had already developed this marvellous concept of himself as a personality within a setting.' They went on to work together for twenty-five years. 'Karl is one of the most accessible people I know. This is one of his great forces,' says Hourcade. 'If Yves Saint Laurent is the ivory tower, Karl is the Tower of Babel and that is the exact difference.'

Don Tait also became a member of Karl's team at just this period. A Scottish interior-design student straight out of college, he got an appointment with Karl thanks to François Catroux, who called up Karl and then drove Don straight round to Place Saint-Sulpice in his chocolate-brown Rolls-Royce. 'Karl had black hair, black beard, white make-up, very austere. Normally a child would be terrified,' remembers Don. 'I must have been twenty-one years old. I was impressed by his kindness. He looked through my entire portfolio and then he said, "What would you like us to do together? I'm in fashion, you're in interior design. I like your shirt." I told him, "I designed it myself."' And so began a fifteen-year working relationship during which Don worked freelance for Karl, creating his sets and décor for the fashion shows.

It is an anecdote that expresses not only the ease and spontaneity of fashion encounters in this period, but also Karl's brilliant ability to see the potential of talent in others. Even before he had his own label, Karl always maintained his own staff who worked directly for him, designing prints, researching collections, making sets or, in Patrick Hourcade's case, working on Karl's houses. 'When you go to visit Karl's studio there are hundreds of people there; he is never alone, you can go and see him at four in the morning and there are still ten people surrounding him. He is instinctively inviting to others, he is someone who needs that, that is his life; he needs others,' says Hourcade.

But what did Karl need these people for – was it company or comfort, inspiration or renewal? According to Patrick Hourcade, 'Karl is by nature someone who needs to evolve, that is why he is so at ease in fashion, which is a world that is in a constant state of evolution. He doesn't want stability; change is his life-motor. He is not unstable, he is insatiable, hence the need for nourishment all around him.'

But there are others who see the constant entourage as a source of comfort. 'I think that he is someone who has no confidence in himself,' says a long-standing friend. 'There is such a huge fear of being wrong, of missing something, that is the reason that he needs these people so close to him all the time, and yet at the same time, he doesn't even want to have dinner with them, he wants to rid himself of them. He needs them but he doesn't want them around him. That is where the ambiguity and the mad contradiction lie.'

According to many, Karl's multilingual loquacity and his constant sociability belie a solitary nature and a visceral isolation from others. He is alone in a crowd. At the centre of this solitary soul is a denial of intimacy. The bedroom at Saint Sulpice was dominated by a huge, rust-satin tomb of a bed, flat and linear and mounted on a stainless-steel plinth designed by Printz. The result was both impressive and frigid, as Karl was the first to point out. 'Those types of beds were made for lonely persons anyway,' he said in 1975. 'If you see the whole room, you will think about everything except sex, because it's the unsexiest bedroom ever. And I love unsexy bedrooms.'

Karl maintained he was deaf to the hum of sensuality, both in his body and in his surroundings. He was, so he said, immune to love. 'I never fall in love. I am just in love with my job. I think it's much more important to love your work,' he said in 1975. 'I think for a man to be in love with his job, that's the real thing.' Perhaps his job was the only thing Karl allowed himself to be in love with.

It was a stance that positioned him in opposition to Yves Saint Laurent, for Yves had long claimed love and passion as his theme tune. He had put it on his clothes in 1966, with a multicoloured-velvet pop coat decorated with appliquéd graphics running down the side of the coat spelling out 'Love'. He had made it his talisman with a fake-ruby and paste heart pendant he designed in 1962 for Victoire to wear in his first show and that subsequently appeared on the runway at every Saint Laurent show, worn by the model wearing Yves' favourite outfit of that collection. In January of 1970 he sent out a *faire-part*, which is the French equivalent of a Christmas card, but it is sent at New Year with a message of good will and hope for the coming year. Yves drew a card with a pair of embracing serpents wrapped around the word 'love', spelled out in capitals. Every January for the next thirty years, with the exception of 1978, Yves sent out his hand-made cards of collage and graphics, featuring varying images of snakes, sun and seas but most of all hearts and always around the same word every year, 'love'. And so Karl claimed the contra-ground.

He built up the whole Saint Sulpice decorative scheme, had the apartment photographed in the requisite magazines and then what? He sold the lot at auction in November 1975, at the peak of the art-deco fashion, three years after the Doucet sale when the trend for the period had turned mainstream but was still racing. This voluntary and total dismantling of a house and collection was to become a habit of Karl's. More than a habit: a reflex.

By 1973 Karl had risen from being one of a number of freelance stylists at Chloé to becoming indispensable at the ready-to-wear house. Day by day, year by year, he had integrated himself into the structure, working incessantly, listening to Gaby Aghion's direction and imposing his talent until he was now the sole designer at the house.

Graziella Fontana, the Italian designer who had been working alongside Karl since 1965, left the house in 1972; many believe she could no longer take the competition. Twelve years later, when Karl's relationship with Chloé had shattered into mutual recrimination, Jacques Lenoir, the joint owner of the house, described Karl's ousting of Graziella Fontana to *Women's Wear Daily*: 'He [Lagerfeld] learned to mimic Fontana's highly structured style of coat and suit design in a competitive phenomenon Lenoir likens to "white corpuscles eating the red". Karl could do Graziella, but Graziella could not do Karl. She lost confidence and left,' writes the reporter.

Made in the heat of a bitter wrangle, this statement should be treated with some caution, yet it does offer an interesting insight into Karl's approach to competition and his tremendous capacity for endurance. Karl had his own version of events to explain the gradual diminution of designers at Chloé; ten years later he would say; 'I sold more than them. Perhaps I also got rid of them [*fait le vide*].' It was the first sign of Karl's ability to impose himself as the dominant force over a period of time. It was a personality trait that was to characterise his fashion career.

Lenoir's observation of Karl's capacity to imitate someone else's design style calls to mind an episode later on in Karl's career when Italian designer Gianfranco Ferre was about to make his debut for the house of Christian Dior in Paris. Karl was working late at night, sitting at a round table with a group that included Ralph Toledano and Pascal Brault, Karl's right-hand administrative man. Someone asked Karl what he thought Gianfranco's collection for Dior would look like the next day. Karl replied by taking three pages of blank paper and dashing off his version of Ferre's Christian Dior collection. Then someone else said, 'Well, what about Sonia Rykiel's collection, what do you think that will look like?' and so Karl drew the Rykiel collection. Then someone else said what about Ralph Lauren? And on and on Karl went, sketching more and more collections in the style of other designers, faster and faster before a table of disbelief, until by the end Karl had drawn fifty collections, not one of them his own.

At Chloé Karl was making a name for himself as an innovative ready-to-wear designer using lyrical art-deco prints to match his apartment life, removing linings, leaving hems unfinished. He was making money and there was talk of a Chloé fragrance contract in the future. He had moved way beyond the state of anonymous *styliste* to become a fashion personality in his own right. His contract with Chloé was supposed to be exclusive, but in reality he kept his myriad lucrative freelance contracts going. Aghion and Lenoir turned a blind eye; they were delighted to have someone so hard-working and commercial in his approach to fashion design. 'From the beginning, Karl understood that our market had a very wide range and we needed a lot of variety. He was always there working at it,' said Lenoir in retrospect. 'The more successful he became, the more agreeable he got. In the beginning he was dour. He always had a nervous aspect to his character that was calmed by being more VIP than the VIPs.'

The Chloé job gave him his first real flush of money and with it Karl bought himself a château in southern Brittany, in the department of Morbihan. He was nearing his fortieth birthday and this was the realisation of a childhood dream. Approached by a long and sloping drive,

still lined in beech trees at this time, the Château de Penhoët lies lost
among slumbering meadows in the Breton countryside. There has been
a château there since the sixteenth century, although the present one
was built in 1756 – 'the same year Mozart was born,' Karl liked to say.
'It doesn't look anything like a Breton château, it looks like an *hôtel
particulier* on the Faubourg Saint-Germain,' was another of Karl's boasts
of pride.

Penhoët is a fine building with a slate mansard roof and pinkish
granite walls that light up in a blush in the Morbihan midday sun. The
symmetrical façade suggests a closed-square formation, which turns out
to be a *trompe-l'œil* as there is only one wing to the château, the west
wing, which stretches out north to form two sides of a rectangle. The
north and east wings had burnt down years before, leaving the château
exposed and open at the rear.

The château lies about seventeen miles to the north of the town of
Vannes and two miles to the north of a small town called Grand-Champ.
Karl and his entourage referred to the château as Grand-Champ (meaning
large field in English), ignoring its actual name of Penhoët. Later André
Leon Talley, a close friend of Karl, would write that Grand-Champ was
the French translation of Karl's Swedish surname. Lagerfeld, although a
proper name, has no meaning as a word in Swedish. But the name
displacement was imposed to great effect: soon all of Paris fashion and
the fashion press referred to the château as Grand-Champ and marvelled
at the Lagerfeld/Grand-Champ name coincidence.

The purchase of a château was highly significant for Karl and the
development of his personal mythology. The concept of nobility had
always held a fascination for him. According to his mother, by the age
of ten Karl was reading the letters of Liselotte von Pfalz and imitating
the accent and mannered enunciation of the eighteenth-century German
nobility to the point of obsession.

Karl had long indulged in stories of his nobility and family fortune,
but from this time on his memories of his childhood became more
grandiose. Now, when interviewed or among friends, there was talk of
a personal valet as a child and a French governess, and he remembered
his mother dressed in a purple lamé dress by 1920s Paris couturier Paul
Poiret. The villa at Bad Bramstedt metamorphosed into a 'country estate',
a château or a castle dating from the nineteenth century. He moved its

location 150 kilometres further north than it was, placing it 'near to the Danish border'. He insisted his father was Swedish, never German, and Karl was able to recall 'huge luncheons and dinners during the war at our country estate. We had a great many Polish and Russian servants. Germans weren't available. As my father was Swedish, they considered themselves in a foreign land.' A few years later, in 1978, Karl said, 'At five, I started my French lessons with a teacher who was one of fifty-six war refugees that lived in our country castle outside Hamburg after World War II.'

Was it nobility that so obsessed Karl or merely the desire to live and be perceived as exceptional? Everything he came from was grey, flat and colourless, other than the time frame of Nazi Germany, and he could hardly glamorise that. He knew he needed to project to get noticed in fashion. 'There is a grain of truth to everything he says and then it is exaggerated to make himself more interesting,' says someone close to Karl.

Even as late as 2004, at the age of seventy-one, Karl would not give up this tale of childhood splendour. In an American *Vogue* profile on Karl that appeared in September 2004, the journalist Kennedy Fraser writes that Karl often speaks of his mother and 'his early childhood on a huge family estate in Germany near the Danish border'. Karl transforms the next-door-neighbour farmer and his modest three cows, remembering instead a cow barn like a palace with fancy brass nameplates for the pedigree cows. He tells Fraser during the course of the interview that his mother was an aristocrat who had lived the high life in the 1920s and could translate philosophy from Spanish.

Indeed it was Karl's mother who appeared to undergo the most significant transformation in his memories. Kurt Lagerfeld remembered her as working as a salesgirl selling ladies' underwear in Berlin when Karl's father met her. After their marriage she became a dedicated and strict mother and housewife, and is vividly remembered as such by Karl's childhood friends. But Karl recalled her not as a *Hausfrau* but as a liberated and aristocratic *artiste*. Her father, according to Karl, was the governor of the region of Westphalia. However, Karl's late cousin Kurt Lagerfeld remembered him as a more lowly '*Landraht* from Munster', which is a district administrative post and decidedly less grand.

'My mother, a violinist, stopped my lessons as she knew I wasn't gifted for music. She often rehearsed on a rare nineteenth-century German violin for three hours in the morning. And to this day, I hate the screeching of the violin. She used to have quartets with people who came to the house. Funny, one day she put down her violin and never picked it up again. She never liked anything from her past; it didn't interest her. Flying around in her own airplane in 1919, she was very modern, very liberated,' said Karl in 1983. 'I never heard of that,' said Kurt Lagerfeld on being asked about Elisabeth Lagerfeld's hobbies. 'I would have known if she flew a plane. I was there almost every day in their first year of marriage at the house and I would have known that. That's his imagination running away with him.'

What was interesting was that the more the fashion media were captivated by his stories, the more vocal and fanciful his self-promotion became and the more Karl's celebrity grew.

Chapter 10

1973–74

By the early 1970s, fashion photographers were the new visual heroes. Helmut Newton and Guy Bourdin were producing powerful and arresting images at French *Vogue*, each exploring their own highly personal obsessions under the patronage of fashion photography. Newton was transfixed by sex, power and a subversive tension to his narrative compositions, while Bourdin's images were influenced by surrealism and expressed themes of sex, death and a strange and shiny violence, such as a model shown lying on the ground as if murdered with a pool of what looks more like scarlet nail-varnish than blood at her mouth. Newton and Bourdin shared a common denominator in the commerce of their images: they were trading in beauty, sex, clothes and luxury.

Newton's vision of woman coincided almost exactly with that of Yves Saint Laurent. 'I like to photograph a certain kind of woman that seems to have a certain availability, a woman that is probably gonna cost a lot of money to have but that makes it even better,' said the late Helmut Newton. 'Yves made a woman look just like that. A lot of his clothes, *le smoking* for instance, are exactly the way I wished my ideal woman was dressed. It is the glorification of the sixteenth-*arrondissement bourgeoise* woman with too much money, too much free time on her hands, and up to all kinds of tricks.' Newton photographed the 'Saint Laurent' woman in memorable and sexually charged compositions, such as the two models standing in a hotel lobby, one dressed as a man; they embrace by their lit cigarettes. In doing so Newton provided a vital link in the creation of the Saint Laurent visual world; thanks to Newton's imagination you could actually 'see' the Saint Laurent woman in action and witness the decadence and adventure of her life.

Newton, Bourdin and other significant fashion photographers, such as Steve Hiett and Laurence Sackman, were all working extensively at that time with Kodachrome, a film that produced highly saturated pigments of green, blue and lipstick red when developed, so that the colours leapt fantastically from the magazine pages, summoning up and reflecting the heightened reality of Paris life.

It was fashion not art that was the heartbeat of the city now. Painter Shirley Goldfarb stumbled upon that truth when she wondered aloud in *Interview* magazine, 'Did you ever hear of an artist not wanting to come to Paris? To look at the paintings, the Louvre, the Mona Lisa,' she added by way of explanation. Paris, the cradle and nurturer of the avant-garde, where Giacometti, Picasso and Brancusi carried out their greatest work, had desiccated artistically to become a cultural pilgrimage, the ultimate art-historical reference behind glass.

In contrast ready-to-wear designers were experiencing an explosion of creativity and discovery. 'Everything was terribly inspiring,' remembers Loulou. 'The models were great fun, they were very inventive themselves style-wise and designers were very influenced by the way people put together a look. We didn't have money and that made us all more inventive.' Everything designers did seemed new and pioneering and there was tremendous anticipation for their collections. At Kenzo's show in 1972 five hundred people were invited and two thousand turned up to force their way in. Journalist Pat McColl was there and remembers her joy at the sight of 'the outfit I wanted – I can still see it now – a nut tweed pantsuit with a blouson and the model that wore it, Carol Raysse, had a great tweed hat with a feather in it, it was wonderful. The big difference was seeing clothes that you felt that *you* could wear. I would look at things in the couture and they were beautiful but my life did not include a ball gown with a train. But I could wear a pair of tweed pants and a tweed blouson.'

Kenzo was sending out a helter-skelter of looks: Peruvian-style full skirts and smocks, apron dresses or high-waist trousers and tiny bolero jackets worn with berets. There was no stopping him. Karl did a whole collection lined in gold. Yves' ready-to-wear could always be relied on

to clothe you in an eternal mystique. 'Maddeningly sexy in a stand-
offish sort of way,' was how *Queen* magazine described his chemise tops;
it's an accurate description of the Saint Laurent look in general. 'When
you wore trousers by Saint Laurent, they made you sit differently, light
a cigarette differently,' says Maxime de la Falaise. 'You did it with the
confidence of a man.' Such was the power of transformation of Yves
Saint Laurent.

In 1973 Helmut Newton photographed Paloma Picasso, aged twenty-
four at the time and staying with Karl Lagerfeld and Jacques de Bascher
down in Saint-Tropez. Hair wet and slicked back, nails painted and
wrists heavy with gold bangles, Paloma Picasso is pictured wearing a
black Lagerfeld stretch dress pulled down to reveal one breast, which
is visible but teasingly obscured by the light reflected from a glass that
she holds in her right hand. That it should be the daughter of the
twentieth century's greatest artist rather than the artist himself (he had
in fact died several months previously in April 1973), that the photo
should meld glamour, dynastic celebrity and eroticism in one iconic
pose and that it should be a fashion photographer who took the image,
says so much about the growing compulsions of Paris at this moment.
Or as Helmut Newton put it, 'Paloma had the most beautiful breasts
that looked like they were carved from marble. And she had the hands
of her father.'

Antonio and Juan were still in Paris and had succeeded in forging a
life after Karl. They had moved out of Karl's guest apartment and found
their own place on the Rue de Rennes, where Antonio continued to
produce a prolific and exceptional output of illustrations both for editorial and advertising. He was by now a pilgrimage stop for aspiring models
and anyone trying to make it in fashion. Antonio kept his coterie of
girls fresh, and the newest entry on the scene was Jerry Hall. She strode
into Antonio's life as a hillbilly Texan from Mesquite, aged eighteen,
equal parts beauty and ambition. She had used her compensation money
from a car accident she'd been involved in to pay for a plane ticket to
Paris, and within weeks of arrival she was having lunch with Jean-Paul
Sartre and Simone de Beauvoir at the Flore. Jerry and Antonio embarked
on an affair together that seemed to be propelled along by their mutual
thrill at making Jerry famous.

For every new star rising in fashion, there is one falling fast. By 1974

Corey Tippin was skidding all over the place. He was still modelling, still doing make-up, but he was choking on drugs and drink. He was still living in a hotel and had wound up in an ambiguous relationship with an older man that left him paranoid and resentful. Thadée and Clara Saint were concerned for him, sensing his desperation. They would drop round at his hotel and leave notes if he wasn't there. 'Where are you?' 'Don't disappear!' 'Show up.' 'Pick me up at Rue Spontini,' wrote Clara. And from Thadée there were underlined and urgent messages: 'We're worried about you, please call us, come over now!' Corey remembers, 'They were always looking out for me, because they knew I could have passed out, overdosed or disappeared, gotten killed.'

Over thirty years later, Thadée Klossowski sees Corey's vulnerability as revealing of an anxiety shared by other beautiful young things skating around Paris at the time. 'There was this thing of being so insecure – that has to do with youth I suppose – one didn't know what to be, how to make it, what to accept, what to do. I remember poor Corey had this weird adventure with some African prince who set him up in Hôtel l'hôtel and who would walk into his room and drop some money on the bed and leave without even taking off his clothes. Corey was very, very disturbed by that; he didn't understand what was going on, what was expected of him.'

From the start Corey had been fascinated with the idea of image, hence his obsession with fashion, models and Andy Warhol, who not only manipulated people's images but whose very artistic manifesto was to describe the surface of things, be that Chairman Mao or an electric chair. Corey's latest relationship was another dimension of that idea, for the man pursuing him was in love not with Corey, but with his image.

'I didn't really have a job, I wasn't really a model. I wasn't really anything. All I had was me. It was all about that youth and that extreme power of seduction at that moment, that was all I had to work with,' says Corey. Those words describe so many men and women whose image was their living at that time.

Corey had felt the worship of fashion and he had believed in it. 'Fashion feeds you. You are there, it's your moment and fashion starts to feed you this extreme elation, adrenalin and this belief that is like divinity. Then suddenly just as quickly as you have gotten it, after you are used to believing it, you are chewed up and spat out and it's over.

That is the hell of fashion. Then the hard reality of it is knowing that it's all a lie.'

But for Corey and so many others, even the bitter realisation that it is all a lie cannot sever fashion's grip on them. Fashion's powers of idealisation are centred on the three peaks of beauty, youth and everlasting renewal, a combination so potent that even as you are thrown from the summit the illusion lingers, more scintillating than anything else. And so you are stranded, full of longing and regret, in a no man's land.

Corey didn't tell Thadée or Clara he was leaving; he didn't tell Antonio or Juan, Paul or Billina. He just got on a plane back to New York. 'I got out because I was forced out. I didn't want to go, but I just knew I couldn't show up any more. I couldn't do it, I was dying,' says Corey. 'This thing had such a hold on me. This glamour, this fashion thing, I didn't know what else to do. I didn't have another world. I was lost. I was twenty-four and I kept saying again and again: "My life is over."'

When Karl bought the Château de Penhoët, the house, formal gardens and outbuildings were all in a state of ragged disrepair. Here was another house to restore and decorate, another stage on which to dress up in costume and play fantastical games. Patrick Hourcade, who had studied history of art and worked at historic monuments before joining French *Vogue*, told Karl that, before he touched a brick of it, he should get the original documents detailing specifics of the château from plumbing to paint colour. Karl turned to Patrick and said, 'You do it. Find them for me.' So off Patrick went to the Parisian auction house of Drouot to track down the treatise, so that Karl could replicate the decoration and refurbishment as authentically as possible. This was classic Karl, both in seizing the opportunity and in surrounding himself with the right people in the first place. He saw someone who could help him realise his projects, he handed over the cash and said go out and do it.

When Patrick speaks of his collaboration on Karl's houses over the next twenty-five years, one gets an idea of the extraordinary exhilaration of working with Karl Lagerfeld. 'He is bulimic, bulimic with curiosity,' says Patrick. 'His enthusiasm is boundless, he is so enterprising, and when he commits to something it is in the absolute.' Rapidity of thought, extensive knowledge, immense curiosity and dynamism – these are some of Karl's most endearing and enduring traits. 'I want to know everything,' he said in 1998, and there is a charm to the impossibility of such a desire.

With each new housing project, fashion collection or show, Karl finds a true delight in the possibility of what lies ahead, what can be achieved. At Penhoët, Karl commissioned a maquette to be made in Paris of what the château would look like if he undertook a vast building plan to add on the east and north wings so that the house was enclosed. There were plans for extensions, for the formal gardens and for the park. Karl possessed a massive will and desire to create his wonderland, and his surge of energy, buying and rush for perfection propelled all those around him in the direction of his gilded dreams. He already had an interest in the eighteenth century, but with the purchase of Penhoët Karl threw himself into the literature, architecture, painting, porcelain and fashion of the period so that he might know everything.

Penhoët could be reached from Paris by a four-hour train journey to Vannes and then twenty minutes by car to the château. Alternatively, Karl made the four-hour journey by chauffeur-driven car. In those early years Karl went frequently for short, one-night stays. He went to draw and sketch and plan the building works, and in the first year or so he went accompanied by Jacques and a friend of Jacques' called José.

Once he became the king's favourite, Jacques started introducing others to the court while making sure he was never eclipsed. José was one such courtier, a young man also from the Loire Atlantique whose family lived in a château called La Turmelière, less than six miles from La Berrière. José had known Jacques at university, where he had studied law. He was living in Paris, staying at his sister's apartment while looking for a job in a bank. His full name was José de Sarasola and he joined the Lagerfeld entourage sometime in 1973. Karl gave him a role as 'business manager' and José was charged with helping Karl negotiate contracts, although in reality the only person with control over Karl's contracts was Karl himself. He was a business manager in title only, as according to José's sister her brother did not receive a salary but was paid in clothes and such like. Jacques said José was his cousin 'Breton-style', an expression used to describe a habit the Bretons have for calling a friend a cousin, even if there is no blood link. José had been useful at the time of buying Penhoët as his parents helped Karl by introducing him to their local notary, who prepared the necessary legal documents for the sale. Jacques wrote to José's mother afterwards, expressing his delight in the purchase of the château, thanking her for the part she played and suggesting that she come to Paris to be fitted for a Chloé outfit.

Jacques loved the Château de Penhoët, although he too referred to it always as Grand-Champ. It was only a fifty-minute drive west from his own family home and the two departments were linked along with the Vendée by a tide of royalist tradition that had existed since 1793, when southern Brittany, the Vendée and the Loire Atlantique had fought together against the revolution in favour of the king in an uprising called La Chouannerie. Penhoët was grander, larger and older than the De Bascher château of La Berrière and Karl had money to spend on the restoration, which was not the case in Jacques' family.

Here Jacques was free to behave as he liked; he could indulge his whims and fantasies. There was no sister to confront over lunch, no father to face or silence to endure. While Karl came and went, Jacques and José installed themselves at the château in a flurry of exhibitionism. They played the young aristos to the hilt. They drove around the estate and up the hill into the town in an old black Rolls-Royce that Karl had bought for use in the country. Jacques called the town 'le village' with infinite condescension. They dressed all in black to appear at the Sunday mass in the town of Grand-Champ. 'We felt they came to mass to look and laugh at us country hicks,' says the farmer's son who lived next door to Penhoët. 'They came to be seen,' says the farmer, who from the start sensed the urges of Karl and his entourage.

In the mornings the housekeeper removed the empty whisky bottles from under the beds. When the Rolls-Royce broke down, Jacques and José took to driving *mobylettes* round Grand-Champ, and the farmer watched them struggle up the hill with a smile on his face.

Guests were invited to Penhoët on the weekends: Anna Piaggi, a fashion editor for Italian *Vogue* who had been a friend of Karl's since the late 1960s and was becoming increasingly important as a muse, would arrive with Vern Lambert and a trunk of clothes she had found at Portobello Market. Patrick Hourcade came too. Jacques dreamed up evening picnics where they would take the Rolls-Royce and drive thirty minutes to the empty beach of Erdeven. They dressed up for the occasion. Anna Piaggi wore a Zandra Rhodes silk empire-dress trailing beads and pheasant feathers. She stood barefoot in the sand with fronds of seaweed in each hand and Karl sketched her. Jacques laid out his wind-surf and threw a finely embroidered white tablecloth over it, then arranged a picnic of foie gras and wine and crystal and silver candelabra. They sat and ate and laughed. That was what Jacques did best: he could trans-form a moment, conjure up an atmosphere be it light or dark.

He had begun to animate Karl's life. Back in Paris, he organised lunches and dinners regularly at Karl's apartment. Was it Jacques who arranged the dinner to celebrate Karl's birthday on 10 September 1973 at which Paloma, Loulou de la Falaise, Clara Saint, Thadée Klossowski, Pierre Bergé and Yves Saint Laurent were all present? The two groups had started to see each other again. They were captured together in a black and white photograph that was published in French *Vogue* later that same year, when Karl was featured in a story about his interests, friends and inspiration. That the birthday dinner was fraught with tension is evident even in that tiny snapshot. Thadée turns uncomfortably towards the camera, twisting his neck as if caught by surprise; Paloma is looking uncharacteristically prim-faced and disapproving; Pierre Bergé has to strain forwards to get in the shot and even then all you can see is an eye – wary and suspicious – a nose and forehead. Karl is upright and rigid and, behind the beard, watchful. Jacques has on a bow-tie and a vague smirk. Yves is the only one at the dinner who is smiling broadly. He turns his head around to face the camera, relaxed and giggling in that little-boy way of his, as though savouring some secret, high-pitched, Saint Laurent thought.

Late in 1973 the inevitable happened: Yves Saint Laurent and Jacques de Bascher began an affair. Yves' life had always been punctuated by heart-beating infatuations. For as long as the crush lasted, there were bouquets of Casablanca lilies despatched weekly and handwritten letters of rapturous passion. It was a game that involved the whole clan, Yves taking the lead role of captivated man, Loulou and Betty whispering assignations. Even Pierre had his part to play – that of picking up the pieces.

It was through his desire that Yves revealed the extremities of his behaviour. There was the night he spent pursuing a young man at Le Sept, only to emerge into the dawn with the object of his interest still parrying all advances. They argued for an hour on the Avenue de l'Opéra, with Yves growing ever more frustrated until finally he got into his open-top black Beetle and rammed it straight into a taxi-rank sign, right next to where the man was standing. The episode ended the way all Yves' dramas ended, with the telephone call to Pierre Bergé to come and collect him.

He went from consuming passion to merciless boredom in the blink of an eye. It was all, then nothing. The hand passed over the face, the pantomime sigh and the grimace of horror: 'No, no, no, no, I can't bear him any longer. No, no, no, he must go, he must go.' It was said with the inconsolable chagrin of a man staring at yesterday's longing. The delusion was over, the fantasy at an end. So why didn't it happen that way with Jacques de Bascher?

The two clans already saw each other inadvertently, out dancing most nights, but during 1973 they started seeing each other beyond the low-ceilinged, spotlit rapture of Le Sept. Did Karl and Pierre realise where it was all heading? They must have known. Jacques started turning up on Saint Laurent territory. He was there at the Saint Laurent ready-to-wear show in April 1973, applauding and giggling with Loulou. He hung around afterwards, chatting with Thadée and Donna Jordan and the other models, looking like a Cambridge undergraduate in his cream ensemble of cardigan and cravat, shirt and trousers.

And it was in 1973 that the dinners began: there was Karl's birthday dinner and then weeks later a date at the new restaurant Les Années 30, where Pierre and Yves turned up on time and sat together waiting for Karl, Jacques and Clara Saint to arrive. What was Clara, stalwart of the Saint Laurent clan, doing arriving with Karl and Jacques? And when Saint Laurent had an exhibition of his gouaches and watercolours of theatrical costumes held at the Proscenium Gallery in 1974, there they were at the opening night: Karl and Jacques, Jacques wearing a be-ribboned boater and a large bow-tie that was almost identical to the one Yves was wearing.

Jacques was still living on the Rue du Dragon, in the small duplex apartment just down the road from the Flore, when the liaison began. He was aged twenty-three, Yves thirty-seven. There was a physical reality

The prizewinners of the 1954 International Wool Secretariat Competition: Karl
Lagerfeld, left, Yves Saint Laurent, centre, and Colette Bracchi, far right.

Yves Saint Laurent in September 1961,
pictured in the temporary offices of his
new couture house.

Karl Lagerfeld, c.1960, working on a
couture outfit at the house of Jean Patou.

"Je l'adore," Yves said of Betty Catroux, pictured here in the Place Vauban garden in 1968. Seated behind Yves are Pierre Bergé and François Catroux.

Loulou de la Falaise combined
old world lineage with the
cool swing of London.

Marrakech offered Yves respite from his Monsieur Saint Laurent alter ego.

Donna Jordan, Corey Tippin and Antonio Lopez on the beach in Saint-Tropez, 1970.

Pat Cleveland, dressed in Karl Lagerfeld, in a Rive Gauche bar in Paris.

A body beautiful Karl Lagerfeld emerges from the sea in Saint-Tropez, Juan Ramos by his side.

Antonio, pied piper of fashion, posing in the Jardin du Luxembourg, 1971.

The tarty attitude of Yves Saint Laurent's 1940s collection of 1971 did much to boost his notoriety.

Dinner at La Coupole. From left: Gilles Dufour, Susi Wyss, Antonio, Eija, Karl, Amina and new arrival Jacques de Bascher.

David Hockney's drawing of Jacques de Bascher entitled *Jacques, Paris, April 1974.*

Jacques de Bascher in silk smoking jacket and trousers designed by Karl Lagerfeld, as featured in *L'Uomo Vogue*, October 1973.

Throughout the years of 1976–78 Yves Saint Laurent experienced a creative outburst of colour and exoticism. *From left:* three outfits from the Opéra, Opium and Broadway collections of 1976, '77 and '78 respectively.

The frenzy of creativity took its toll: Saint Laurent exhausted after the marathon Carmen ready-to-wear show, October 1976.

Loulou de la Falaise and Thadée Klossowski's wedding celebrations in the summer of 1977 began with a civil ceremony and ended with a night of intoxicated glamour.

Loulou, Yves Saint Laurent and Thadée in the gardens of the Mairie.

Loulou, Thadée's mother Antoinette de Watteville and Thadée.

Rafael López Sánchez and Paloma Picasso in black YSL couture.

Left: Loulou on the dance floor. *Above*: with Karl; behind, just visible with cigarette in hand, is Kenzo.

Fernando Sanchez; behind him is Marina Schiano in YSL.

A demure Bianca Jagger allows Yves Saint Laurent to transform both her and her dress with ferns and poetry at Loulou and Thadée's wedding ball.

Yves and his muses in 1978: to his right Loulou de la Falaise in flame chiffon, to his left Betty Catroux in white tuxedo.

Paloma Picasso and Rafael López Sánchez on their wedding day in May 1978. Paloma wore Yves Saint Laurent by day, Karl Lagerfeld by night.

Left: Inès de la Fressange wearing the most memorable dress from Karl Lagerfeld's first haute couture collection for Chanel in January 1983. *Right:* Supermodel Shalom Harlow in the Chanel ready-to-wear show of spring/summer 1995.

Jacques de Bascher and Karl Lagerfeld, Paris, 1978.

The thrill has gone. Yves Saint Laurent, Loulou de la Falaise and a model in the final stages of preparation for the spring/summer haute couture collection of 2001.

Yves Saint Laurent and Pierre Bergé on the terrace of the Château Gabriel, 1983.

Karl Lagerfeld and Devon Aoki at the Chanel couture show, July 2000.

Fashion and Hollywood embrace: a reconfigured Karl kisses Nicole Kidman at the Chanel spring/summer 2005 ready-to-wear show.

Yves Saint Laurent bids adieu amid tears and adulation at the retrospective fashion show of 2002, held at the Centre Pompidou. On his right is Laetitia Casta, on his left, Catherine Deneuve.

Yves Saint Laurent and Karl Lagerfeld: a shared stage, but a different destiny.
At Le Palace in March 1983.

to the affair, but much more significant, longer-lasting and more damaging was the psychological dimension, as Jacques became an obsession in the mind of Saint Laurent. 'When Yves falls in love it is in a very mad way,' says Thadée Klossowski. 'He falls madly in love and then he gets bored. Well, Jacques had his ways of not letting Yves get bored.' Jacques drove Yves to distraction by his tantalising games and the affair electrified Saint Laurent.

In April 1974 David Hockney drew Jacques de Bascher's portrait. Jacques sat for Hockney at the artist's apartment, on the same lumpy green chair that Celia Birtwell, Kasmin and many of Hockney's other subjects sat upon that year and the next. The artist drew Jacques in his striped blue neckerchief and cream shorts, lips pressed together and hands folded beneath an open book.

Hockney was staying in Paris, concentrating on sketching and etching. He was a star of the Flore with his bleached hair, celebrity and Yorkshire wit. He hung out with Shirley Goldfarb, going off to visit the Louvre, sketching views of the Louvre courtyard and painting Shirley in her studio. He also drew himself in an imaginary context, standing with a portfolio under his arm before a head of Picasso mounted on a plinth. The drawing was entitled *The Student: Homage to Picasso 1973*. Hockney was enjoying considerable recognition in Paris with an important show at the Musée des Arts Décoratifs that opened in October 1974, and his French fame was further amplified by a film about him and his painting called *A Bigger Splash*, by Jack Hazan, which was premiered at the Cannes Film Festival in May 1974 before being shown in Paris.

The following April in 1975 there was another smaller, selling exhibition of Hockney's Paris drawings and etchings at the Galerie Claude Bernard on the Rue des Beaux-Arts. The portrait of Jacques was chosen not only to be included in the show but as the image to be made into the poster for the exhibition. And so in the spring of 1975 Jacques appeared all over town, in kiosks and on the lampposts up and down Boulevard Saint-Germain. Jacques' face, unsmiling, enigmatic, a man's face in a schoolboy's clothes, was everywhere.

How his ego must have swelled with his conquests. For at the same time Jacques' liaison with Saint Laurent continued in a staged and highly secretive manner. Jacques took Saint Laurent off to dark bars and clubs, away from the effervescent fun of Loulou and Betty's unswerving loyalty,

away from the safety of Le Sept. All this went beyond Bergé's possessive control and protective boundaries, exposing Yves not only to the
dangers of Jacques, but also to a threat potentially more harmful –
himself.

Yves bought himself a new penthouse bachelor studio as a place to
where he might escape. Pierre and Yves' relationship had always involved
extracurricular affairs and it was a way of life tolerated by both men.
Yves' new studio was on the Avenue de Breteuil, a green and bourgeois avenue leading down from Les Invalides, and Yves could walk
there from his Rue de Babylone home. He asked Jacques Grange to
decorate it in a spare and modernist fashion, to look like a set from an
Antonioni film. It was here he met with Jacques de Bascher, and also
at Jacques' own apartment on the Rue du Dragon. At some point in
his laboured infatuation, Yves Saint Laurent tried to persuade Jacques
to leave Karl for him. Was it serious or just one more of Yves' pastime
passions? Either way it must have appeared as one more victory Yves
Saint Laurent wanted to score and Karl never forgave him.

According to Diane de Beauvau-Craon, who was no longer living
with Jacques by this time, 'Karl threw himself into a terrifying temper.
Pierre Bergé made a scene in front of Karl, saying he couldn't control
his gigolo and that was it, the scandal was born. At that time all you
needed was a tiny trace of gunpowder to blow up Paris because everything pivoted on this extravagant world. Now it's different. You have the
fashion world, the business world, the literary world, the art world, but
then, you just had the world of extravagance. Full stop. You looked to
the right or the left, nothing, emptiness. There was only that world and
so of course it possessed an absolute power and significance that today
it no longer has at all.'

For the last thirty years, the affair has been so shrouded in taboo,
secrecy, anger and retribution that it is easy to be swept away by hyster-
ical rumour and hard to gain access to any remnant of truth. To understand Yves' attraction to Jacques is perhaps the easiest part. Jacques
represented so much that Yves, the indefatigable aesthete, would find
desirable: the nineteenth-century pose and physical grace, the wit and
social glamour of Jacques de Bascher de Beaumarchais, a name he was
still claiming as his own in the catalogue of the Hockney exhibition in
1975.

'De Bascher had a great strength in this milieu in that he was the absolute opposite of what everyone already knew,' says François Catroux, who is one of the few to assess the affair in the cold light of objectivity. 'He was not just some little gigolo, loved one day and no longer the next. Jacques was a well-brought-up boy, intelligent, extremely subtle with a certain *ton*. He was also quite mad with a huge sense of fantasy, *folie*. He was the anti-bourgeois and at the same time he had this kind of innate confidence in that he wasn't born a nobody and that of course impressed both Karl and Yves.'

And perhaps there was a certain perverse delight for Yves in pinching Jacques from beneath Karl's very nose. 'I don't think it was ever a great love story,' reflects François. 'No doubt it amused Yves enormously, but love? I don't believe it. It was more deviant than that, there was the thrill of stealing him from Karl and then the whole idea that when he [Jacques] wasn't with one of them, he was with the other; that must have excited both Karl and Yves, these two enormous rivals.'

In Saint Laurent and among some of the clique, Jacques found a new audience to shock and titillate with his increasingly fantastical tales. 'I can tell you I was not in the least bit fascinated by him or his stories that he would recount ten times over, exaggerating every time,' says François Catroux dryly. 'He didn't amuse me, not for a second. But there were many who thought that this supposedly refined decadence indulged in by a French aristocrat rather than just some two-bit gigolo made it something incredibly fascinating.'

Yves was one of those attracted to Jacques' decadence. 'Yves can be extremely wicked,' says one in the Saint Laurent clique to explain the Jacques de Bascher obsession. 'If you've read *La vilaine Lulu*, I mean, there is a great similarity, you know, all those pranks and childish things in the book which would amuse him enormously.'

What is harder to comprehend in the motivation of this affair was what Jacques de Bascher was doing messing around with Yves Saint Laurent, the man whom he knew was the absolute fixation of Karl Lagerfeld. Or perhaps that was the point. The affair between them, apparently fleeting, started towards the end of 1973, and therefore occurred early on in the relationship with Karl. As Paloma Picasso points out, Karl's behaviour was inconsistent at this time and Jacques' position far from assured. 'Jacques never held the reins, it was always Karl, but I can understand that a human being might want to give the illusion that he is the one pulling the strings,' says Diane de Beauvau-Craon. 'That is why the hanky-panky between Jacques and Yves, well, I don't think it is completely innocent that Jacques picked Yves because it was kind of a powerful coincidence. I think that Jacques and Yves entertained a little flirt to begin with, like it happened every day in those days, just a little back-room flirt; I think Jacques made it into something much more important just to annoy and to exist. It really gave Jacques an identity.'

But it only gave him an identity after the fact. For a long time the affair was a state secret to which only a few – Betty, Loulou, Clara, Thadée, François – were privy. Even after it became common knowledge, the talk of the town, Jacques de Bascher remained secretive about what happened. His non-fashion friends such as Renaud de Beaugourdon and Christian Lvowski never heard Jacques speak of Yves Saint Laurent. Diane de Beauvau-Craon remembers that, several years later, Jacques did once tell her, 'Yves really loved me.' But perhaps that is what Jacques wanted to believe by then, that someone really loved him.

Could it have been that Jacques was looking for a new role? Thadée Klossowski was invited to the Château de Penhoët during the year of 1974 and remembers arriving at the train station at Vannes to be met by Jacques and a friend. 'It was quite ridiculous because they were both dressed as 1930s fashion plates, but in such an exaggerated way. I remember Grand-Champ being quite beautiful and complimenting Karl on the place and all that, but I remember being very much struck by the appearance of these two boys and, I don't know, there must have been some old Rolls-Royce. The whole thing was really exaggerated and overdone and silly-looking. Maybe Jacques wanted to escape from that dressing-up, being a doll sort of thing.'

But if Jacques was contemplating escape from the personification of an ideal, running into the embrace of Yves Saint Laurent was hardly the answer. On the contrary, Jacques spent long hours formalising his ritual of style, augmenting his wardrobe and the literary references by which he might hone his image. 'I saw him dress in front of me on several occasions and there was something impressive, mysterious about the process,' remembers Christian Lvowski. 'He was like a character from a novel. He had these camisole vests that were piled up high, fifty of them on a shelf, and he wore them attached with buttons to his cotton underpants. There was a precise, almost military feel to the detail of his dress. And there was always this research of distinction in his clothing and a great refinement to everything, to his pyjamas, ties, to his socks. I remember several years later coming into his apartment and he was wearing a great overcoat and I said, "That's a wonderful coat you have on," and Jacques replied, "I'm glad you like it, I have had it made up in twelve different colours.'"

From this time on Jacques' energy was consumed by his appearance, image and the gathering neuroses they engendered. Unlike Antonio and Juan, whose dandy vanities were always counter-balanced by the great force of their creativity, there was no creation involved in Jacques' role within the life of Karl Lagerfeld, at least not the creation of anything tangible or permanent.

But perhaps that was the point and the attraction of Jacques; his power was as a symbol, an ideal. His dedication to image touched a fantasy common to the minds of both fashion and the homosexual, and that can be traced back to the decadent movement of the dying years of the nineteenth century. The fantasy was in the mystery of a life dedicated to elegance and beauty, the envy and desire that one could incite, the power wielded simply by physical grace.

It is the same fascination expressed by Oscar Wilde's Lord Henry when he exclaims to Dorian Gray with a cry of envy, 'I wish I could change places with you, Dorian. The world has cried out against us both, but it has always worshipped you. It always will worship you. You are the type of what the age is searching for, and what it is afraid it has found. I am so glad that you have never done anything, never carved a statue, or painted a picture, or produced anything outside of yourself! Life has been your art. You have set yourself to music. Your days are your sonnets.'

Jacques never carved a statue or painted a picture, and yet for David Hockney to choose to draw him and then use his image as the poster of his exhibition, for Jacques to be the focal point of desire for two designers, he must have represented something for Paris and for fashion of that moment. By 1975 no one ate dinner at La Coupole any more; those days of Josephine Baker bright-eyed wonder were gone. Instead there was an accelerated urgency to night-life and fashion. And Jacques, in his worship of success, his restless vanity and tenebrous compulsions, personified a new mood that was blowing through Paris, a gilt-edged decadence.

Jacques de Bascher was the type that the age was searching for, and what it was afraid it had found.

Chapter 11

1975

In early 1975 Chloé and Karl Lagerfeld signed a lucrative perfume deal with Elizabeth Arden in the US to create the first Chloé fragrance. It was a crucial moment for Karl. For it is with this contract and the media profile and cash it generated that, for the first time in his career, Karl moved beyond being the hired hand at Chloé to receiving some of the profit share. He was forty-one when he got the deal and the real cash started rolling in.

Significantly, Aghion and Lenoir chose not to give him shares in the actual company of Chloé, but instead formed a new company with Karl called Karl Lagerfeld Productions, dividing the share count three ways, with 50 shares for Karl, 25 for Gaby Aghion and 25 for Jacques Lenoir. 'It was supposed to be a company for licences,' says Gaby Aghion, 'for the perfumes and for the Karl Lagerfeld line which was launched in Japan only, not in Europe.' That meant Karl's profit share was on everything except the Chloé ready-to-wear.

The Chloé perfume was to be launched with an April tour of America to include parties and fashion shows, press meetings and store appearances. No one needed to teach Karl how to behave as the star designer; he'd been doing it in Paris for years. Karl understood that the American voice of approval – both press and stores – was vital in the financial making of a designer. He demanded his entourage come with him, Jacques de Bascher and José de Sarasola. The whole American stay from start to finish was an extraordinary *tour de force* in image. They flew to

LA in a whirl of excitement, arriving with thirty-five pieces of luggage between the three of them and incurring fines of $3,500 for surplus baggage at the airport. They started out in Los Angeles with a fashion show and a party afterwards attended by Ryan and Tatum O'Neal and Jack Nicholson. Then they flew on to New York for the launch of the perfume. They were staying at the Plaza, overlooking Central Park, where they had been assigned a suite of rooms that took over an entire floor of the hotel.

Karl's travelling persona was an ingenious hybrid of Madame de Pompadour meets Andy Warhol. He created an atmosphere of high culture, with novels by eighteenth-century French writer Madame de Staël on his bedside table at the Plaza, trunks full of books strewn around the room, talk of the Vienna Secession period and endless careless quotes from Goethe and Voltaire, a habit that would keep journalists in life-long awe of Karl's learning.

The connoisseur chat was amped up by a deliberate post-modern superficiality. There was Karl's mannered appearance, which was now echoed and magnified by that of Jacques and José, and there was his new and special nutritional diet of blanched and boiled food intended to help kick his twenty-year addiction to fifteen bottles of Coca-Cola a day and by which he had already lost thirty pounds. And there was that other great Lagerfeld passion: shopping. The three men shopped by the trunk load: books, clothes, accessories. Jacques was even moved to buy a pair of jeans, so conspicuous did he feel gadding round New York in his white flannels.

André Leon Talley, a young journalist at the Factory, turned up at the Plaza to interview Karl for *Interview* magazine. It was the first time the highly influential style magazine had given Karl a profile to himself. Finally Karl was grabbing some of the international fashion limelight.

Leon Talley was besotted by Karl and Jacques' European glamour: the silk pyjamas with embroidered initials on the breast pocket, the talk of the eighteenth-century château in Brittany and Karl's parting gift to André of two silk crêpe de Chine shirts. 'Karl Lagerfeld, the genius, who pours silk over the body with the same distinction as he poured his new fragrance – Chloé – on America,' eulogised Leon Talley in the *Interview* article.

In the gang of three, José was the odd one out and it was plain for all to see. José was four years older than Jacques. He was a reserved young man from the provinces with none of the knife-edge brilliance of Jacques. He was strangely out of place in the fashion milieu, a fact remarked upon by observers at the time. He dressed in the Lagerfeld livery, wearing the new menswear that Karl had started to design. But clothes that looked dashing on Jacques made José look awkward and only emphasised his incongruity within the entourage.

'Subdued José de Sarasola, the business mind of the team, balanced the bills on downtown shopping junkets,' observed Leon Talley, 'where the *équipe* acquired American bargains such as a limousine full of surplus uniform shirts, cycling shorts, paratrooper suits for weekly country excursions.'

The interview ran under the title 'Karl Lagerfeld in a cloud of Chloé'. It was a discussion dominated by Karl and Jacques in which they talked of Karl's latest Chloé collection based on costumes from the eighteenth-century French countryside and of Karl's great passion for Isadora Duncan as a fashion influence. Jacques tells of the château in Brittany, the restoration plan and the Marie-Antoinette life to be enjoyed there, which prompts André Leon Talley to ask Jacques if one might consider their style decadent.

Jacques replies, 'In this country [USA], decadence means trashy, pornographic, dirty. Cadent comes from the Latin *cadere* which means to fall. Decadent is something very different, it's the beautiful way to fall. It's [a] very slow movement which has lots of beauty, you know. It can be a kind of self-killing in a beautiful way, a tragic way.'

For Jacques it was always beauty that justified the fall. Beauty made even the idea of self-destruction – or 'self-killing' as he calls it – a possibility. He was aged twenty-four and drawn to darkness. He was fascinated by Gilles de Rais, a grotesque figure from the fifteenth century and a Breton noble who veered between exquisite aestheticism and the boundless evil of Satanism and murder. De Rais represents the absolute zenith of sadism and was cast by French decadent writer Joris-Karl Huysmans as the central, historic figure in his novel *Là-Bas*. 'The Marquis de Sade was no more than a timid bourgeois, a wretched little fantasist, in comparison with Gilles!' writes Huysmans. Not surprisingly, given that Jacques was interested in De Rais, he also read and reread *Là-Bas*, a book that takes Satanism as its dominant theme. 'It was his favourite novel, his reference,' says Renaud, who remembers buying Jacques a new copy to replace one he had lost.

Once André Leon Talley had finished the interview Antonio Lopez turned up at the Plaza to photograph and sketch Karl and his travel companions for the story. Just the month before Antonio, Juan and Paul had left Paris to return to New York. Jerry Hall had made it as a famous model and no longer had the same need for Antonio. Paul had fulfilled his ambition of a Paris exhibition of his work and wanted to pursue his career in New York and all three of them were feeling a little homesick. They found a huge loft downtown on Broadway from where Antonio invited the streets of New York into his studio. The absence of their resolutely bohemian lifestyle and unbridled freedom left a hole in Paris.

Antonio, Karl, José and Jacques set off for lunch in a limousine. The three men from Paris all wore a variation on the same outfit. Jacques and José were dressed in identical white crêpe de Chine shirts with the collars turned up. José had on a striped jacket and dark cravat tucked into his shirt, while Jacques wore a dark cardigan. Karl wore one of his silk shirts and a striped cravat at his neck. Both Karl and Jacques had on black sunglasses that concealed their eyes completely. José was wearing spectacles.

The three men sat in the back of the limousine and Antonio sat up front with his Kodak Instamatic camera, taking snaps, shots of them fooling around, playing with a fistful of dollars as they sped through the streets of Manhattan. The Antonio eye took it all in, the dynamic of the threesome and the powerful current of cash running between them. He had, of course, seen it all before, had experienced it himself first hand.

Antonio took a run of pictures, seven in total, which he then juxtaposed on a page with two rows of three photos across and then one last photo on the third row, alone in the middle. Jacques appears in five out of seven photographs, while Karl appears in three, a measure of how important Jacques had become to Karl's image.

In five out of seven of the photos there is money present, either in Karl's or in Jacques' hands. In one photo it looks as if Jacques has just grabbed hold of the notes and he sits in the corner of the limousine, unsmiling, head bowed in concentration as he counts the bills with a frown, oblivious to the camera and ignoring José, who is smiling and jolly, leaning his head in towards Jacques in order to get himself into the frame. José is the only one whose eyes the camera can see and the only one without money in his hands. But the onlooker's eye is drawn not to José but to Jacques and his black aviator glasses and his manic regard for the cash.

Another shot of Jacques shows him grasping the money up, away from the camera, behind his right shoulder in a gesture of possession, as if to say, 'Don't touch, it's mine.' But it is not Jacques' money; it is Karl's money. And the first and last photograph in the series shows who dominates in this gang of three. Karl is photographed alone, the eyes impenetrable behind dark glasses; in his right hand he holds the dollar bills splayed out like a poker-player while his left hand rests lightly on top of the notes and a slim but triumphant smile cuts right through his black beard.

In the August of 1975 the Lagerfeld entourage, like some French aristocratic court of old, escaped from the bleached sunlight of Paris and repaired to the country and to the closed world of the Château de Penhoët.

The house lay some half an hour's drive away from the ocean. The sea wind no longer brisked off the Atlantic, instead the summer air was dazed with pollen and the scent of the honeysuckle in the hedgerows. In late August the days were still and oppressive with the suggestion of storms. Around the château the dairy cows lay helpless in the lush fields. The stillness of the days was deceptive, for being in the Lagerfeld clique entailed being on hand to scintillate and entertain at all times. It was a fight to stay in favour.

The château had taken on a key importance in Karl's fashion design, a place where he went to work and sketch and seek inspiration. He had moved beyond retro – all those old film stars bored him, they were used up, abandoned, a tired trend that was out of his system. Soon he would rid himself of the art-deco from his Saint Sulpice apartment with the sale of furniture scheduled for November of that year.

Instead Karl turned his considerable powers of attention to the French eighteenth century. He took the countryside not court costume as his inspiration and created split skirts over hidden panniers and hand-painted silk dresses inspired by Meissen porcelain. Anna Piaggi was a huge influence on Karl's fashion during this period. She was outstanding in her originality and devotion to creating style. She would travel to Penhoët with several trunks of clothing for a weekend: vintage haute couture, antique jodhpurs from Chelsea Market, Edwardian bloomers that she had dyed jet black and a canvas cape that had begun life as a costume in Les Ballets Russes' first production of Stravinsky's *Firebird*. Days there were spent sketching. Karl drew Anna as she walked along the chicken run, lay on a day bed or as she set forth on an after-dinner promenade in the park, dressed in white cotton Edwardian suit with bustle, white feather pompom in her hair and staff in her hand.

Jacques was deeply excited about the prospect of Karl giving him the small gatekeeper's lodge at the left-hand entrance to the gardens in front of the château. It was set apart from the château and just opposite the tiny chapel, and Jacques talked about the project and how he would decorate it. When he was in New York he told André Leon Talley that the lodge was like '*le petit hameau* of Marie-Antoinette in the forest of Versailles. I am going to decorate that in a combination of neo-Gothic like Viollet-le-Duc and the castle of Louis II.' All the neo-Gothic references were there in Jacques' imagination: Ludwig of Bavaria (Louis II in French) and Eugène Viollet-le-Duc, the French architect and hero of the Second Empire, both men synonymous with the final throes of romanticism and the recalling of a lost golden age.

Jacques told Leon Talley that Karl would be doing the château out entirely in eighteenth-century style, to host 'guests and somebody who has a nervous breakdown to rest there for fifteen days or more, we all want to have a different kind of thing'. 'I am going to be in the château, the pure eighteenth-century one. Nothing neo-Gothic,' said José de Sarasola.

José was found dead on the train tracks, three kilometres outside Vannes, on the morning of Tuesday, 26 August 1975 at 11.30 a.m. The death certificate bears the necessary facts: his date of birth, 25 November 1946, making him twenty-eight at his death, his residential address and his status marked as student. His name is written out in full: José Maria Bazquez-Sarasola. Both his parents were Spanish and they had shortened their name when they came to live in France. The cause of death is not given, which is usual in French death certificates.

The gendarmerie and the Tribunal de Grande Instance of Vannes no longer have the police records or any report on the investigation of the death, as in France all such records may be destroyed after twenty years have passed.

José killed himself. He left a note. He took his life at Pont Silio, a lonely run of train track just outside Vannes station. It is far enough from the station to ensure the train is still going at high speed. It is a twenty-minute drive from the Château de Penhoët. You drive south for fifteen kilometres and then turn off the main road and down a dead-end track, with a few houses strung out on either side. At the end there is a no man's land of tarmac and weeds, desolation and silence. In front runs the train track, which is laid on a bed of stones the colour of creosote. Beyond is a scrubland of trees and bushes, an uninhabited space. The nearest house on the other side of the track is about half a kilometre away, up on the hill.

All that is between you and the train track is a low, concrete fence forming an abstract pattern of arches low enough to step over. And then the fence stops in mid-air, as if someone realised even as they were building it that it wasn't worth continuing as it was never going to stop anyone stepping on to the rails. Where the fence stops, there is a stretch of eighty metres where the rail lies wide open and accessible by foot, without even the need to step over the stone fence.

José's body was found but remained unidentified for thirty-six hours, enough time for a story of the death to run in the regional Brittany newspaper *Ouest France* with a description of the dead man and his clothes, seeking help to identify the body. It was a taxi-driver, used frequently by Karl Lagerfeld and his entourage, who identified the body.

Questions remain unanswered, unproven about his death. There is one local man's memory of José driving off up the hill on the moped, alone, and Karl and Jacques then leaving in a taxi together fifteen minutes later to catch the train from Vannes railway station. The commonly held belief on the Penhoët estate, then and now, is that José threw himself underneath the train Karl and Jacques were travelling on. And yet this rumour does not tally with the fact that José's body was discovered on the track of the train that runs from Paris to Vannes, rather than on the track from Vannes to Paris.

Jacques was shattered by the death. José was his friend, he had brought him into the court, he had needed him there as his companion. Jacques could never be alone in his decadence.

Within three days of José's death, Karl was sketching again at Penhoët. The delusions of their life at Penhoët had reached such extremes of *folie* that not even death would touch them. Anna Piaggi, dressed up in a Chanel 1926 black flapper-dress, held Jacques' binoculars to her eyes while Karl recorded it in a jaunty pastel. There was another portrait the next day of Anna reclining on a bed, dressed in white lace and red neckerchief, legs bare. The sketch is entirely incongruous with its context – the broderie-anglaise lingerie, the red nail-polish on her toes, her languorous pose – and most incongruous of all is Karl's title for the sketch, 'Les Matinées de Grand-Champ' ('Mornings at Grand-Champ'), dated 1 September 1975, just four mornings after that other morning at Grand-Champ when a young man had been found dead on the train tracks.

The death of a 28-year-old man who had been in their midst just five days earlier hung all about them. But it was back to fashion, back to fantasy, back to dressing up and wrapping up in a fine cashmere shawl from the estate of the Duchess of Somerset, back to posing before an eighteenth-century red lacquer Venetian chair as if nothing had changed, nothing had happened.

In Paris a young man's surrender to mortality and the circumstances of his death provoked a pervading sense of horror among the fashion elite. After all those delicious years of dancing and insouciance, of eternity and indulgence, here was death crashing in on the party.

The death was perceived as a cautionary tale and José himself as a victim, but of what and of whom? 'The poor boy, it pained me to see him,' says one who knew José. 'The poor boy from the provinces, he was brought up to Paris, where he was absolutely dazzled by this world. It was all so horribly shocking because he was weak; he was way out of his depth. He needed to be calmed; he needed to be sent home to his family, he should never have been in Paris. He was not strong enough to resist . . .'

Perhaps José's fate resonated with such force because he was the archetype of someone held in fashion's favour. He was paid for, dressed, lodged in Plaza suites, taken on excessive shopping sprees. He was plucked from the ordinary and suspended in the high-rise glamour of Karl's extraordinary life. Now he had plunged in free fall to his death.

The fallout from José's death was strangely pivotal. When Pierre Bergé heard the news he reacted with force. Bergé had long since sensed a dangerous aspect to this group. Now he gathered his flock to him and seized the pretext to drive the wedge between the two factions. The very night they heard the news, Pierre and Yves rushed round to Jacques Grange and François-Marie Banier's apartment in a state of considerable agitation. The apartment was on Rue Servandoni, a street leading south from the Place Saint-Sulpice that was within two minutes' walk of Lagerfeld's apartment. Jacques Grange was a friend of both Jacques de Bascher and Karl. Loulou and Thadée too had been spending time with Jacques de Bascher, hanging out in the empty afternoons.

Pierre burst through the door, followed by Yves. 'That's it. There is to be no more seeing these appalling people again!' ordered Pierre. He stamped the veto on Karl and his clique. He must have felt a rising sense of panic, for it was Pierre who knew the obsession Yves had developed for Jacques; it was Pierre who knew the volatile state of Yves' mind.

'He [Jacques] made him completely mad,' says Thadée Klossowski. 'I guess he was very seductive and all that, he was also quite evil and he was a sadist. He was fascinated with very sick, I mean he was a sick . . .' then he trails off. 'Jacques was a flirt with this sort of evil twist and Yves having this very mad streak sort of fell for it in this big, big way. And then became raving mad.'

During the course of 1975 Yves Saint Laurent's mental state became increasingly uncontrollable, even for Pierre and his vast resources of command. He was drinking whisky now, by the litre bottle like vilaine Lulu. He was taking cocaine. He was dabbling in a level of physical decadence that he had long fantasised about. There was the exquisite tension between the ultimate aestheticism by day, the sublime apartment and the couture house and its rituals of beauty and perfection, and by night the deliberate physical degradation.

Pierre and Yves would fight; Yves would screech off in his car and no one knew where he went. One day he screeched off and did not come back. Pierre Bergé was managing director of the most famous fashion house in the world, responsible for the supreme deity of fashion – 'The reason we get on the plane to come to Paris,' as the American fashion-buyers put it – and this fashion deity was nowhere to be found. Pierre was forced to phone around police stations. He was called twenty-four hours later and told that Yves had been found in a hospital in the north of Paris. The strain for Pierre was relentless, not only that of safe-guarding Yves's life but that of safeguarding the reputation of the designer too.

'Pierre was trying to pick up the pieces,' says Madison Cox, who entered the Yves Saint Laurent arena two years later as a young American student at Parsons School of Design. 'I mean not that there ever was, but had there been a car crash Pierre would have been the one to get the car out of the ditch. That's where with Jacques, all of a sudden it sort of pushed Yves over to another side, a darker side. Yves is not an addict, he is an obsessive individual, so if he's drinking Coca-Cola he'll drink twenty-five of them, or if there is ice cream in front of him he'll have twenty-five gallons of it, not one gallon. He's a man who in that sense sees no limitations, sees no restraints; I think he's relied too much of his life on Pierre to fulfil that role and I think with someone like Jacques it was another form of excess, another form of going to the end.'

Late at night Yves drove round the Place Saint-Sulpice, where Jacques was now installed in Karl's former apartment. Karl had moved out after the art-deco furniture sale and left the empty apartment for him to live in. Yves was drunk and honking his horn, calling out Jacques' name until the neighbours became irate and called the police station on the corner of the square.

Perhaps for Yves there was the thrill of letting his mind slide into obsession, surrendering to the glorious torment of frustrated desire and irresistible passions. Just as eight years before Yves' vilaine Lulu had fallen hard for the penniless student Jojo and had gloried then in her obses-sive desire. 'This Minet from Dijon is driving me mad . . . but what do you want to me to do about it!' she asked her reader before chanting aloud her Jojo fixation: '*Ce Jojo! Eh bien ce Jojo! Ce Jojo-là! Ce vilain Jojo! Ce Jojo vilain! Ce Jo! Ce Jo! Ce joujou! Ce jojo! Ce joujou exquis . . .*'

Yves' infatuation calls to mind another great Parisian affair – that of Swann with Odette in Proust's *Swann's Way*, and indeed Yves Saint Laurent from 1973 onwards was constantly comparing himself and identifying with both Proust and Swann. Odette, a *demi-mondaine* extravagant in her fading bloom, pursues Swann with no success. All this changes dramatically when Odette receives Swann at home. She leans over to look at an engraving and in that instant Swann sees her resemblance to Zipporah, a figure painted in the Sistine frescoes by Botticelli. And in that moment Odette is made exquisite for Swann: she is transfigured before his eyes; she is no longer Odette of fleshy lips, bulging eyes and rather vulgar manner; she is Odette 'a skein of beautiful, delicate lines' whom Botticelli would have adored. That is enough for Swann, who careers off into a manic, overwhelming infatuation, a state of mind that is then exacerbated by Odette's withholding and infidelity, which drives Swann mad with the destructive pain and masochistic delight of jealousy and possession. It is always and only the idea of Odette that thrills and mesmerises Swann, never the reality, and here is the echo of the Jacques and Yves game.

Chapter 12

1976

Yves' increasingly volatile behaviour and wild-eyed pursuit of Jacques struck a lethal blow to his relationship with Pierre Bergé. Their shared life deteriorated into a collision of recrimination and jealousy and on 3 March 1976, after eighteen years together, Pierre moved out of the Rue de Babylone apartment and into a suite at the Hôtel Plaza Athénée, about five minutes' walk from the couture house.

By his own description, Pierre's departure was precipitated by an instinct for self-preservation, and a need to distance himself from Yves' dismal well of self-destruction. 'Perhaps I did leave in order to avoid drowning,' says Bergé looking back nearly thirty years later. 'And I didn't drown. I never was engulfed. I preserved the essential.'

The essential for Pierre comprised 'the destiny of Yves Saint Laurent the man and the destiny of Yves Saint Laurent the house. I decided that I should come after those two things; it was only many years later that I started to take an interest in myself.' It is, however, a somewhat misleading answer, for in reality Pierre Bergé's own destiny was inseparable from that of Saint Laurent the man and the house. Yves and Pierre formed two sides of the same coin; indeed within the couture house they were known as 'l'aigle à deux têtes' (the two-headed eagle), after Cocteau's play, which Pierre Bergé later staged at his Théâtre Athénée. In 1990 Yves himself wrote to Pierre with birthday greetings, acknowledging their inseparable bond by saying, 'Henceforth we are an eagle with two heads.' Other sly wits in Paris preferred to call them by the name of 'les Saint Laurent'.

Strange ties of possession bound them, so that in one instance Yves' former crush became Pierre's boyfriend. And even after 1976 when Pierre moved out and bought a separate apartment on the Rue de Bonaparte, thereby severing the romantic dimension to their relationship, it continued as a partnership that went beyond the realm of work. They were symbiotic in ambition. And it is this astonishing level of complicity that makes their modus operandi as a couple so hard to unravel; it is almost impossible to decipher their own individual actions and desires. It literally was a shared destiny.

Bergé told Yves Saint Laurent biographer Laurence Benaïm in 1993, 'I am the man who is the most important in his life; is that because he loves me or because he needs me? I don't know.' He still doesn't. 'I stand by that as a valid statement now', says Bergé. 'I do not know. But then in life one never completely knows; perhaps I too have an absolute need of him for the same reason.'

True enough, that same unanswered question of love me, need me could so easily have come from the mouth of Yves Saint Laurent, but for the fact that Yves rarely expresses any thoughts on his relationship with Pierre Bergé. Neither one of them could ever separate their love from their need of the other. Perhaps that is why the relationship has proved so enduring.

For Pierre purposefully to submerge himself in Yves' ego and stay put there all his life means that Yves did undoubtedly fulfil a need in Pierre. As every Bergé detractor (of which there are a considerable number) will tell you, the need is obvious: Yves Saint Laurent is the wellspring of Pierre's power, wealth and influence. But theirs was a relationship more binding than simply kingmaker and king.

Pierre was in the thrall of Yves' talent. Bergé is fascinated by the idea of the *artiste*, the creator and the creative spirit which is so at odds with his own. People have mistaken his ardour for creativity as that of the frustrated artist, but Pierre is a self-cultivated man who uses his culture as a shield; he is not an artist. He may have had aspirations for a career in journalism, but by the time he met Bernard Buffet he was already working as a book dealer, trailing the *quais* picking up first editions in the morning, selling them to dealers in Saint Germain in the afternoon. His brilliance lay in peddling the talent of others and he knew that.

On a practical level Yves could do nothing without Pierre: he couldn't write a cheque, he couldn't board an aeroplane, he couldn't book a restaurant. John Fairchild still marvels at the day when he was having lunch in New York with Pierre Bergé and an urgent message came through from Yves, who was in Paris with a water leak and did not have a clue how to find a plumber. Pierre was part Svengali, part house-keeper.

When the invitations piled up, it was Pierre who badgered Yves to get dressed up at night and go out: he dragged Yves along to the Liza Minnelli gala opening given by Baron Alexis de Redé when Yves refused to go. It was Pierre who told the butler not to put the telephone calls through to Yves, so that friends were unable to reach him, Pierre who organised the doctors and the increasingly frequent hospital stays and Pierre who went through Yves' mail.

Pierre's seemingly overriding behaviour was observed by all and provoked universal gasps of horror. The bullying and the control were all sources of considerable bitterness and anger among many friends and family who saw Pierre Bergé as the architect of Yves' isolation and sorrow. 'We thought that Pierre was wrong,' remembers Paloma Picasso, 'that he treated Yves like he didn't know how to take care of himself. We saw Pierre not behaving right to Yves and protecting him too much and we thought that he should let Yves be more open to the world.' It took many years before she reassessed the balance of power between the two men.

Of all the statements made about Pierre Bergé by those who have known him, the heart-felt testaments to his generosity and loyalty, his resolute support of the sick and the impecunious, the equally heart-felt accusations of his roughshod bullying and bilious fury, the one memory that casts a shaft of light on Pierre's motivation in life comes, perhaps not surprisingly, from his mother.

Madame Bergé was interviewed just before Pierre's sixtieth birthday in 1990, for a special edition of *Globe* magazine produced by friends of Pierre to be presented to each guest at his birthday dinner. When asked about her eldest son, his mother's response was savage. 'Unbearable,' is how Madame Bergé described him. 'He needed a lot of looking after. He spent the whole day clinging to me. He would scream when I left the house. And at the age of two he was already constantly asking me, "Maman, do you love me?" And I would reply impatiently, "Yes, of course I adore you." But he was never satisfied with that reply and he would say, "No, you must say 'I love you my little "Peuo" darling.'"'

It is an episode that conjures up both a small boy's craving to be loved and a mother's frustration at her son's need for affection. Perhaps it is as Betty Catroux says at the mention of Bergé's name: '*Voilà*, one who suffers, a thousand times more than the other [Yves Saint Laurent]. A thousand times more.' How strange then that Pierre should choose as his life partner a man who could give him so little emotional reassurance.

From 1976 on there was a dramatic downhill slide in Yves' mental health. 'Alcohol and drugs played a very important role in his life and largely contributed to the deterioration of his health,' says Pierre Bergé. 'They didn't help his periods of manic depression either.' Yves disappeared from public view and that meant few people witnessed at close hand his irrational behaviour, and even those who did came to regard it as entirely normal for Yves. People's expectations of Yves were never the same as for everyone else, neither in what was expected of his talent nor in what was expected of his day-to-day conduct. 'Monsieur Saint Laurent is not well,' was the standard couture-house tight-lipped reply.

There were long periods spent in the psychiatric wing of the American Hospital in Neuilly, but what exactly he was being treated for and what went on there not even his family knew. His younger sister Brigitte refutes that Yves is manic depressive, although she recognises and relates to his periods of depression. She still smokes forty cigarettes a day, as Yves himself used to during this period. 'Yves is like me, but not for the same reasons. Neither of us cares what life has in store for us. Like me there are days where he is self-destructive and for those moments there are passages of depression, "*Merde*, I cannot go on," and then afterwards life is beautiful again. He is not a depressive all the time, that is not true.'

But in these years and in these moments of desperation, the threat of suicide must have seemed very real. Saint Laurent the man and Saint Laurent the house had to continue, and Pierre was going to see to it that both destinies were guaranteed, whatever it took to do that. It was, as Pierre says with understatement, 'a full-time job'. In 1977 Victoire met Bergé for a *rapprochement* lunch at the Plaza after years of no contact. 'He was there with his two dogs, white as death, and I said, "Pierre, whatever is the matter?" He replied, "But it is hell, you cannot imagine what it is like, I can't take it any more.'"

Madison Cox, who is a former boyfriend of Pierre Bergé, reflects on the role Bergé has played and the pressure he has borne supporting Yves' dry-eyed anguish. 'I think it was extremely draining and exhausting for Pierre and it has been all these years, to see someone every morning or now to speak to them on the telephone and hear, "Oh my life's finished, it's over," or, "I can't work any more." "I have no ideas. Please tell Abraham [a fabric manufacturer] I can't see him because I don't know what to do. It's over. It's finished." And to have to constantly row against stream, the enormous amount of energy Pierre has to expend in order to . . . Of course deep down Pierre knows the man is not going to throw himself out of the window tomorrow, but you still have to deal with that on a daily basis. I think Yves has come to terms with a lot of things now, but at the time you didn't know; if you were to call his bluff he would throw a marble statue out of the window, or he would jump in his car and drive off and you would never know where he went; he'd go out and buy zillions of dollars' worth of things, only not to want them or whatever. I think that now he is much more sedate, much calmer, he's gone through a whole period of psychoanalysis. But he was very volatile at this time. He wanted to check into the American Hospital, he wanted to do a sleep cure. I think that Pierre did suffer enormously; it was just an enormous strain and worry constantly, because you never really knew [what he would do]. I think that was one of the fears Pierre always had.'

Frédéric Mitterrand is another long-term friend of Pierre and Yves from these years, who hints at the true power-play within the relationship. 'Pierre supported him in real life, and he [Yves] during his long periods of lucidity was appreciative of that, during these moments of Valium he worked, but during the moments of *folie* and revolt he could have thrown it all out of the window. There is something of the Nijinksy to this, but whereas it was Diaghilev who dominated Nijinksy, here it is Nijinksy who dominates Diaghilev.'

Paris was under the spell of a heatwave. Between the Tuileries gardens and the Place Vendôme beyond, the sky stretched out like a hot tin roof. Beneath that sky on the Rue de Castiglione a large crowd of people jostled outside the InterContinental Hotel. They were queuing to enter the hotel and the Salon Impérial where the Yves Saint Laurent haute-couture show was due to begin in half an hour.

There was a beat of invitations in the clammy air, appraising stares and Saint Laurent safari suits and the churn of gossip as photographers pushed up against glass revolving doors – there it was again, that strange, self-conscious, pent-up excitement, that welt of clandestine aggression that is the nervous tic of fashion. And whatever the levels of excitement and suspense to be found in fashion, they were always at their apogee at the shows of Yves Saint Laurent. For the first time Saint Laurent and Bergé had moved the haute-couture show out of the salons of the couture house, to hold it instead in the vast ballroom of the InterContinental Hotel.

Two years before they had moved the couture house from the Rue Spontini to large and lavish premises in a Napoleon III townhouse on the Avenue Marceau. But despite the size of the new couture house, there was simply not enough space any more to show there. The guest list had multiplied to one thousand people, including photographers, journalists, store buyers and a stack of worldwide licensees clamouring for a trip to Paris to attend the couture and look at pretty girls.

And then, *après tout*, there were the couture clients themselves: legs folded in oblique angles, puffed hair shimmering like crystallised fruit, a dying species of woman intimate with the work of Monsieur Saint Laurent from years spent abiding by the absolutism of his elegance, women such as Charlotte Aillaud: 'When you wear a jacket by Yves you think it is perfectly normal. It is only when you try on a jacket by someone else you realise everything that is wrong with theirs.'

The couture client was fast being obliterated by a new and burgeoning client whose only intimacy with the creativity of Yves Saint Laurent was the sliding, singular typeface of his name spelt out on a bottle of scent her husband had given her last Christmas. It was she who was driving the ever-plumper sales figures and profit margins. Fashion was now an industry and Yves Saint Laurent, with his 111 franchised ready-to-wear Rive Gauche boutiques, 128 YSL-licensed products, sales of which totalled $200 million for the previous year, was a leader. Yet even as 'fashion for all' became a reality, haute couture was still the means by which to spin the dream.

Bergé and Saint Laurent had spent $500,000 on this show, making it then the most expensive fashion show ever staged. High fashion was generating money and that meant money had to be spent generating high fashion. For the first time in a Saint Laurent couture show a raised catwalk had been constructed down the centre of the ballroom for the models to walk on, which required the audience to raise their heads by thirty degrees in order to watch the models go by. That mere tilt of the head was enough to demonstrate the transformation of haute couture as wardrobe provider to haute couture as stage show. For the first time a make-up artist had been hired to come in and do the models' faces. This meant the age of models doing their own hair and make-up was over. But of course, branding was the new buzzword and soon YSL would launch its own line of cosmetics.

Paloma was there on the front row to see the show. Her father's death and the legal inheritance battle that ensued meant Paloma was no longer the penniless daughter of Picasso fighting over the right to bear his name, but a soon-to-be $20 million heiress. Three years before she had met two talented young Argentinean writers, Rafael López Sánchez and Javier Arroyuelo, who were in Paris putting on experimental plays with their theatre group TSE. It had been a month after her father's death and Paloma and Rafael moved in together and had been boyfriend and girlfriend ever since.

The real clamour of expectation that morning was not for the venue or the money spent on the show or the front-row clients; it was, as always, for Yves. For months now there had been strange rumours circulating in offices and newspapers – Women's Wear Daily, Le Point, Paris, Marrakech, New York and back – about Yves and his health, Yves and his smashing of statues against walls, Yves and his fractured wrist, and most of all Yves and Pierre.

By the summer of 1976 Yves was ill, snagged in a turmoil of depression and explosive moods. By that time, according to Pierre Bergé, Yves' life was sustained by cocaine, alcohol and tranquillisers. Six months later in December 1976 Yves announced, 'I am sick, very sick. I was already before the haute-couture collection in July – but no one noticed, even though they were giving me drips. I was in a deep depression.'

Yves reacted badly to Pierre's departure from the shared apartment, construing the move as abandonment and casting himself as the tragic victim of wrongdoing. They had been together for eighteen years and life without Pierre's force and buttressing must have been a terrifying prospect for Yves, who at that stage did not know that their partnership would continue even without the romance. 'Yves saw himself as Callas abandoned by Onassis,' Loulou de la Falaise said in 1993. 'He took his revenge with the brilliance of his talent, with these collections that were more and more beautiful. He used artificial energy. Time passed very quickly. Rather than grow old, he gave in to his vice.'

In June 1976, the month before the couture shows, Yves escaped to Marrakech to work on the forthcoming collection and to stay in the new house that he and Bergé had just finished building. It was a pink, two-storey mansion called Dar es Saada la Zahia, meaning, ironically enough, 'the house of happiness in serenity'. Yves sat for days in his bedroom, sketching, smoking cigarette after cigarette, his mind racing, his right hand tracing his pent-up dreams of beauty. 'I needed a violent explosion of fantasy. This collection was a dream that I have had for a long time. I have always wanted to do a collection that included everything that I love in my life. I have always wanted to do a collection that was a reflection of all my tastes,' he said at the time.

Usually when he sketched a collection Saint Laurent produced black line-drawings. These were the essence of the collection, the form and silhouette that would then be constructed in three dimensions back at the couture house. The colour, fabric and decorative detail would emerge gradually as Yves picked from the suppliers' new season's fabrics and finishes and as he studied the toiles, the plain cream calicos with which his atelier began the process of making a *modèle*.

But this time Saint Laurent abandoned black on white, for the first time feeling the need and desire to express himself in colour – 'Like a painter,' he said. He opened the box of felt-tips beside him and began to draw, sketching every outfit and every detail of jewellery and belts, print, ribbons and shawl exactly as it should be on the finished piece of clothing.

'For several months now I have been exploding with ideas. I am assaulted by them,' Yves told *Le Point*. There was a kaleidoscope of images that ricocheted about his head and on to the page before him: Visconti,

Flaubert, Madame Bovary, Georges de la Tour and Delacroix. He had seen Vermeer's portrait of *Girl with a Pearl Earring* – or *La jeune fille au turban* as it is known in French – earlier that year in Amsterdam and Yves could not get it out of his head: the translucence of her skin, the erotic charge of her parted lips, hair hidden beneath the satin folds of a turban and the pearl drop of an earring ready to fall.

In his bedroom in Marrakech, sketching alone, he was burning himself up from the inside, 'spinning with ideas', and he needed nothing but his felt-tips and his Lucky Strike cigarettes. On the paper before him there appeared a convergence of fantasy and memory, imagined and seen, subconscious and original. The sketches were not about the modern woman, her needs and wardrobe, but rather the exaltation of beauty and extravagance. 'The clothes incorporated all my dreams – all my heroines in the novels, the operas, the paintings – it was my heart – everything I love that I gave to this collection,' said Saint Laurent.

And when he had finished the last drawing all that was left was emptiness. He suffered a nervous breakdown. He was checked into the American Hospital at Neuilly by Pierre Bergé and treated for severe depression. He was in a state of nervous collapse. He stayed at the clinic for three weeks and was allowed out in the late afternoons. A car slid up to the entrance of the clinic and Yves emerged through the glass doors into the white suburban sunlight. He was driven through the poplar trees and gated apartment-buildings of Neuilly and on to number 5, Avenue Marceau where the couture house awaited him.

The heads of the ateliers had been shown the sketches of the collection three weeks before, without him. They picked the outfits they would be responsible for making up in silence. 'It was terrifying in a way,' says Jean-Pierre Derbord, who was head of the Saint Laurent tailoring atelier at the time. 'I remember Madame Muñoz laid the sketches out on the floor of the grand salon. There were a thousand of them all over the floor, you felt like you were drowning in them; it was agonising, each sketch more beautiful than the other. You could feel the *folie*, a mad beauty, a state of madness. Everything had been thought out in his head, in his imagination, every detail, it was superhuman and for us it was frightening: how would we do it justice?'

For weeks they had been working to interpret his sketches, preparing the toiles and yet all the time suspended in a strange paralysis, waiting for his eye and his approval. The couture house was empty without him, it was a building filled with people waiting for his return. It was incapacitating, this cult they devoted themselves to, demanding loyalty, devotion, faith and worship. And always the same whispered lines between press officer and journalist, seamstress and mannequin – 'He is not well', 'He's in Marrakech' – until at last, 'He is here, downstairs.' Yves Saint Laurent climbed the sweep of stairs up to his studio and with every step taken the cast of the couture house returned to life.

In the studio they stepped with infinite care around the pulse of Saint Laurent's anxiety. Each mannequin entered the studio for her fitting wearing the *modèle* made up in cotton calico and accompanied by the head of the atelier responsible for the making of the piece of clothing. Monsieur Jean-Pierre entered first. He had known Saint Laurent since the house of Dior in 1957 and it was in his hands that the secret of the Saint Laurent shoulder lay. It was Jean-Pierre Derbord who could work the shoulder with an iron, with seaming, with padding that was itself then seamed and worked with an iron, to create the innate ease and angle that makes it the Saint Laurent shoulder. Between them there were few words. Saint Laurent watched the reflection of the mannequin and the toile in silence and then said simply, 'But Jean Pierre, what you have done for me is divine.'

Next Madame Felisa chaperoned in the model and her taffeta gown. She was flustered, new to the house. She had spent thirty-eight years in couture, first at the house of Balenciaga then at Givenchy, but she had never seen the likes of Saint Laurent and his creative excesses. He made her nervous and flighty as a girl. 'It is as if I am drunk,' she said. 'This man has an orgy of ideas in his head. He is exploding.'

Days later Saint Laurent discharged himself from hospital against his doctor's orders, to be present for the couture show. For the first time he could watch his own show happening as there was a door to the side of the stage which he could peak through. He stood propped up against a pillar and watched the banks of upturned faces in the audience as the first notes of Verdi played.

'It was the first show where I remember having goose bumps as I walked out,' says Nicole Dorier, who modelled in the show. 'People were standing throughout. It was the first time that we had opera music playing during the show. It was extremely moving. Monsieur Saint

Laurent had been very, very ill, very absent, and so things had been done with him late at night, towards the end. We saw him far less. And when everything was put together and we were on stage it felt like you were some kind of conquistador. The collection was so incredible, so rich, and the music carried you away with such emotion and the audience were there open-mouthed. I think for me it was the first time I had this feeling of power as I walked out; it was as if you were a queen. Before there was something much softer to his shows; this was the beginning of the spectacular. There was a ceremony to it. The music built to a crescendo and there was a kind of madness that swept people away with it. It was quite extraordinary.'

The models appeared through an arch of lilies, clouds of taffeta billowing from bound waists, acres of skirt flailing several cameramen as they passed them on the catwalk. There was an overpowering beauty to the clothes: gold lamé boots, Cossack fur hats, capes of jade satin that looked as if they had been ripped from the curtain rails of a winter palace, glittering turbans and jewelled head-dresses and hips wrapped in black silk velvet. His use of colour was original and, above all, painterly. One model wore an emerald-green waistcoat edged with zibeline over an orange and gold lamé mousseline blouse, which was set against a crimson-red skirt of satin. He had imagined daring and extravagant combinations, so that a dress bodice was in black velvet, the sleeves in tomato-orange satin and the skirt in pale, duck-egg blue satin edged in red and finished with a pink ribbon at the waist. Yves was pulling Paris and fashion into a rip tide of wealth and theatre, colour and voluptuous indulgence.

Anna Pavlowski glided out to finish the show as the bride. She was an exotic Mongolian model and she held her mouth in a bow like a Russian doll. She looked like a strange hybrid of medieval, Marrakech and madonna statue, the sort found in the Virgin chapel of a church somewhere in the sixteenth *arrondissement*. She wore a North African-inspired tunic and skirt of cream, gold-braiding and tassels; on her head was a cream veil and crown of gold flowers; in her hand was a bouquet of lilies sprayed gold. It was the most ravishing collection Yves had ever shown. It was also highly erotic in its proportions of slender, corseted waist, swelling bosom and voluminous skirts, as well as in the rapturous sensuality of the fabrics and textures. The audience was on its feet, screaming, shouting, weeping, a deluge of hysteria. Yves Saint Laurent walked down the catwalk to acknowledge the applause and the tears and even he seemed dazed by the intoxication of his vision.

Tears at a fashion show – perhaps this is the crux of Yves Saint Laurent's genius. He has an ability to touch people and arouse emotion through clothes. This is what makes his clothes memorable: not their newness or innovation, not their femininity or colour, but their power to stir and evoke emotion.

'That is one of Yves' big talents, making people cry,' says Loulou de la Falaise, 'because I think when you hit moments of perfection, it's got nothing to do with fashion at all. I think it's like when you listen to a piece of music, or stand before a painting. I've cried in museums. When you see total perfection, when that note is hit, every sensitive person will be moved to tears.'

Fashion is not an art; it is, as Yves Saint Laurent himself has always acknowledged, an 'art appliqué'. But Yves is able to make clothes that resonate with the emotional register of the onlooker or wearer. It is the same for his sketches. His drawings for theatre costume or for fashion vibrate with a force, so that their line goes beyond a fashion drawing, to touch you. He is well aware of his power. On the night before the show in July when this 'Opéra' collection was finished, and the dresses were hung in huge cotton bags in the grand salon of the Avenue Marceau and the whole staff of the ateliers and studio were gathered together, 'Everyone started to cry,' remembered Yves.

The American press and buyers in particular threw themselves into a kind of ecstatic frenzy about the Opéra collection, pronouncing it a revolution. 'It is as stunning in its impact as the collection Christian Dior showed in 1947, the one that came to be known as the New Look and affected the way women dressed everywhere,' declared Bernadine Morris on the front page of the *New York Times* the next day, under the headline 'A Revolutionary Saint Laurent Showing'.

It was not a revolution: the silhouette was grand and courtly, the skirts eighteenth-century in their volume; these were clothes to be worn by fabulously wealthy women off to a first night at the opera. As Saint Laurent himself admitted, 'These are not clothes for women who take the Métro.' Indeed Loulou de la Falaise remembers the collection as 'a slight return to conventionality', and her mother Maxime de la Falaise was disappointed by the 'Madameness' of it when she came to pick out an outfit for her daughter's wedding.

Its real novelty lay in its lush timbre, so different to his previous seasons. It was as if Yves finally let rip on his whole colour-palette and indulged headlong in his considerable sensuality. The collection was also significant as heralding the first intimation of what was to come – the 1980s. Yves, his nerve-endings still raw to the passing whims and obsessions of society, sensed the decadence of his own life and that of others, sensed the surge of new money and opulence that was to consume Paris.

The French press were not so effusive. They found something strangely disturbing about the intensity and richness of the clothes, particularly coming from Monsieur Black Trouser Suit himself. For them it was like turning up at a restaurant expecting to eat a well-bred steak and being asked to gorge yourself instead on a *moelleux au chocolat*. 'Whatever has happened to Yves Saint Laurent?' they asked in their show reviews. Three days after the collection, Yves flew to Marrakech. He turned forty on 1 August and he spent the day asleep in his house of Dar es Saada la Zaria.

By that October Yves Saint Laurent was dead. Yves Saint Laurent was dying. Yves Saint Laurent was in a state of mental collapse from which he would never recover. Yves Saint Laurent was drinking two litres of whisky a day. Paris fashion was in the thrall of these rumours of Saint Laurent's death throes and could talk of nothing else. The reaction was multifaceted: grief, scandal, titillation, horror. But there was something else too, as Joan Juliet Buck recalls nearly thirty years later with a slight blush of embarrassment: 'I remember we were all saying, "Oh my God, how will I dress if Yves dies!"' This was the level of steely grip Yves had on the female fashion psyche. He was the last designer who would ever impose his will and his look so adamantly on women. There truly was a Saint Laurent woman; you could recognise her by her scent, her red nail-polish, dark lipstick, severe sex appeal, stilettos, trouser suit, her confidence, her choice of lover.

This monogamous dressing no longer exists. Today a woman dresses as she pleases, mixing high street, designers, brands and styles. There is no bond of worship or deification. And the woman is no longer in awe of a designer. Fashion now is about the designer proposing not imposing clothes and a woman making her pick. There is admittedly a cult of accessories, but even that is different for it is adoration of a brand, not a couturier. 'This was the *époque* when we talked only of clothes,' says Christophe Girard, who was working for Yves Saint Laurent at the time and is now director of strategy for the LVMH fashion group. Marian McEvoy, then fashion editor of *Women's Wear Daily* in Paris, agrees: 'There was no Saint Laurent bag, no Kenzo bag, no Chloé bag. Ready-to-wear was a fledgling thing. We are not talking about billions of dollars, we are talking millions and in some cases not even millions; it was a form of self-expression and I guess in a funny way it was more of an artistic experience then.'

The Yves Saint Laurent death rumour would surge and ebb over the next ten years, at one point in 1977 reaching such a point of conviction that one particularly bull-faced reporter barged into the couture house on Avenue Marceau and refused to move until she was shown the face of Yves Saint Laurent (dead or alive?). She kept her vigil until Bergé turned up at his office and threw her out.

If the rumour was intended to damage, it had the opposite effect. It reinforced the Christ-like imagery already swirling round Yves' head: the suffering martyr, fashion's crown of thorns upon his head, and yet each time he rose from the ashes to save fashion and dress women.

Yves was holed up in the American Hospital again in the run-up to the ready-to-wear show of October 1976. 'The collection was done in the three weeks I was in the American Hospital for a rest,' he said. 'I didn't get much rest. I sketched in the morning from my bed. The sketches were sent to the design studio and things were made up for me to see in the evening. It was a terrible way to work. Awful. After I got out of the hospital, I went straight to the workrooms and then straight to the Palais de Congrès for the show. I did not sleep for two nights.'

It was known as the Carmen collection and it opened with Grace Jones striding down the stage, black and chiselled, a disco Amazon, red silk turban around her head, funky black-and-red cotton top and harem pants caught below the knee and espadrilles on her feet. Yves showed 281 outfits and the show lasted a phenomenal two hours and thirty minutes. Festive and carefree, it finished with finale after finale – jangling beads, sexy bustiers and taffeta skirts pulled up around the girls' heads. The colour and energy of the show was overwhelming: Thadée Klossowski remembers it as the best of all the Saint Laurent collections he has ever seen. 'It went on and on and on and ended twice and then started again. I thought this was absolutely the most fantastic show I'd ever seen, the only fashion show actually for me that went beyond fashion and was really exciting. But it's true that he was completely mad at this time.'

It was deliciously vibrant, casual, sexy and joyful, another break from the androgynous Saint Laurent years. 'I wanted to show there is not just one way to dress and above all I felt that the masculine side which had represented the avant-garde, emancipation and liberty, was entering into a bourgeois cycle. I had to get out of that. I find that the serious is a little dated. And then I'm sick of being constantly copied: I wanted to play a little trick on my colleagues . . . the American couturiers are furious,' said Yves, relishing every moment of controversy he had stirred up.

'It is a personal explosion,' he said after the show. 'All of a sudden I felt suffocated, *démodé*, me myself, not my fashion. Before, the only way to amuse myself was by doing costume for theatre. But for the last three seasons I am enjoying myself madly again in my actual *métier*.'

Backstage at the show there was a doctor standing by for Yves. By the end of the show when Yves came out on the runway to acknowledge the applause, the audience was shocked to see his 'face haggard, undone'. 'Saint Laurent was in such an exhausted state that he was literally held up by the mannequins as he took his bows at the end of the show,' wrote *Women's Wear Daily* the following day. 'Backstage amid all the confusion, he received his admirers, brushing tears from his face. He looks pale and weak. A man with a black case was at his side.' There was a car waiting to take Yves back to the American Hospital.

What had started out as a case of Saint Laurent bad behaviour culminated in the shattering of self and the end of an era. In the Saint Laurent clique it was Jacques de Bascher who was to blame. 'After Jacques, Yves went so overboard he had to cut himself off from fun and drugs, then he would function on pills, which is not the same thing,' says Thadée

Klossowski, 'and I guess it was this cutting himself off from fun in a way that was a significant turn in all our lives, everybody's, because Yves was the funniest person really, we would laugh and laugh and laugh endlessly with Yves.'

'In Pierre's mind De Bascher was the cause,' says one of the Saint Laurent group. 'Pierre hated him. God forbid they should ever meet.' Bergé hated Jacques for ending his relationship, for, as he perceived it, leading Yves astray and having the potency to do so. But he must also have hated the fact he could not control the situation. Jacques held in his hands debris from the affair – letters from Saint Laurent – and these he subsequently handed over to Karl Lagerfeld.

Some years later, in 1983, Karl Lagerfeld accused Pierre Bergé openly in the press of having fallen in love with Jacques himself. Questioned today on Lagerfeld's theory, Pierre's voice jumps several octaves and decibels in reply: 'That is a profound and serious error. Yves Saint Laurent certainly, but definitely not me. Definitely not. Ah no. I do not have bad taste. I do not fall into that trap. Jacques de Bascher was a little hooligan and I understood that from the first day, the very first day. I was never interested in him.'

But Karl's accusation is indicative of the body blows that were thrown between the two cliques. For if there had been mutual suspicion and envy between them before, from now on they were at war. 'It was almost terrifying, there was such a degree of hate and extremity between them,' remembers one person who observed the crossfire. 'There was a moment when everyone was crazy.' If you worked for one, you couldn't work for the other. If you hung out with one group, you were disbarred from the other. Somehow Paloma retained her go-between status for several more years, but it was a source of considerable tension even for her.

The affair with Jacques was but the pretext for the schism that had been bound to happen ever since Yves and Karl had stood together on stage in 1954. They had surveyed Paris fashion coyly from behind their inhibitions and had vowed to conquer it. And Yves did conquer it at the age of twenty-one, with the early and indisputable success that could only drive a rival to obsession. Yves and Karl were two huge, vying talents who would never be content sharing the stage of Paris fashion. There were too many similarities between their ambitions to abide this level of proximity. Life in rampant opposition was to be their solution to a shared fate.

Casting Jacques and his no doubt considerable powers of seduction and perversion as the master of Yves' descent is to ignore the complexity and contradictions of the circumstances. It seems unlikely that a young man of twenty-four could really lead a man aged thirty-nine anywhere that he doesn't already want to go. Particularly when that man is Yves Saint Laurent, the man who Anne-Marie Muñoz tells you is like concrete ('stronger than him does not exist'), the man who Charlotte Aillaud describes as a 'rock'. Could it be that Yves' mental anguish was also the source of inspiration and renewal he so relished and craved? What if he sought out these dangers, if he chose self-destruction as his destiny, as his deliberate route to greater creative glory?

For this was a time when Yves Saint Laurent experienced an undeniable outburst of astounding creativity. The July 1976 Opéra couture collection, together with the ready-to-wear collection of Les Ballets Russes that preceded it in March of the same year, marked the beginning of a three-year cycle during which Yves designed a series of highly dramatic and iconic collections. 'We are talking about this explosion in creativity,' remembers Fernando Sanchez. 'Yves has always been extremely creative and suddenly there was this firework explosion that happened for x amount of seasons; there was the Ballets Russes, the Opéra, the Orientaliste, the Chinese collections, one after the other of extraordinary, flamboyant collections.'

The approach of middle age was hard for Yves to contemplate. He admitted as much himself in 1975, saying, 'I am in the middle of my life. It's not easy to accept the passage from adolescence to maturity – either in one's private life or at work.' It is revealing that he was aged thirty-nine when he talked of leaving adolescence behind. In his work he was searching for a way of escaping his own rigours and inhibitions, the constricts of his perfectionism, so that he could provoke the emotional release needed to create, so that he could escape the stultifying effects of monotony and regain the lost passion of youth. 'God, when I first started I could work day and night, without stopping for food or rest. It was pure excitement,' he said with longing in the 1980s.

He was, like any artistic mind, always looking for something to jump-start his creativity. Sometimes he chose people, other times it was artificial stimulants. He told a highly sceptical Anthony Burgess as much in an interview that took place in Paris the year after the Opéra collection for the *New York Times* magazine. 'We talked of the agonies of art while his chihuahua, Hazel, slept on my knees,' Burgess wrote. 'Artists, who get no end of a kick out of the trade they practise, are always eager to say what hell it is. "Art," said Yves, "is a poison." It's well known that he's had his depressions, his *cafards*, and made his escape from reality into alcohol and drugs. But drugs are more than an escape, he says: they can open new imaginative vistas for the artist. I'd heard all that before, especially from the junkie students of creative writing, and was pretty sour.'

Over the years Yves has talked up a storm over his drug abuse, so that one has the impression he has spent the last thirty years between a puff of opium and a line of coke. But even his drug-taking is a subject on which no one in the Saint Laurent group can agree. There are those close to Yves who entirely refute his self-publicised drug consumption. François Catroux raises his eyes to heaven at the mere mention of the subject. 'Look, there is a huge amount of exaggeration in what Yves and Betty said they got up to. They imagine that they took lots of drugs but I can tell you that, compared to people and friends I knew who took a lot of drugs well, they took very few, very badly. I remember in Marrakech the time they took a bit one night and they talked about nothing else for four days after.' For François there is the practical impossibility for Yves of paying for a major drug habit: 'It's very simple really. Yves has no money, he cannot have money; Yves is entirely controlled by Pierre. If you want to take a lot of drugs you need to spend, I don't know, say back then five thousand francs a night. At the end of the three nights Pierre would have seen that in the chequebooks. It just couldn't have happened and if someone gave Yves five thousand francs then straight away Pierre would have been informed. It is just not possible.'

Anne-Marie Muñoz is another one who does not believe his tales of drug abuse. 'He was taking some stuff then, a little, but never that much. Don't believe it. He will never take danger to its conclusion.' Pierre Bergé, on the other hand, when questioned about the possible exaggeration, denies this and insists that the drug and alcohol abuse were considerable and long-term.

A year after the Opéra collection, during the preparation of another memorable couture collection in July 1977, Yves was complaining loudly of his depression, his professional obligations and his artistic torture in melodramatic terms. 'Designing fashion for fixed deadlines and dates doesn't amuse me. All these dresses that will die in one year and at the same time all those that I still have to design ... I feel myself torn between life and death, between the past and the future. Each time you must call everything into question. You can never make a mistake in fashion. You cannot afford the luxury of being right in three or four years' time. You must always be in direct synchronisation with the outside world. A couturier must feel everything that is happening, everything that will happen, and then translate it. I have made the rope with which to hang myself. I would like to make fashion only when I desire to do so, but I am bound to my commercial empire.'

The martyrdom was absolute, yet in the very next breath Saint Laurent went on to boast how, with this collection, once again he has far too many ideas and he reflects with a certain beatific wonder: 'For the last two years I have been working in a state of grace.'

During this period of blockbuster collections Yves experienced the state of grace that every creative mind yearns for, that moment when the dead weight of fear of failure and mediocrity, of striving for recognition, falls away and the subconscious surges forth. For a limited and charmed time the mind dislocates and, in Yves Saint Laurent's case, the creative impulse planes along, conjuring up dresses of sheer poetry and leaving yards of mousseline flying in its wake.

It is a state of grace that Yves would do anything to attain. Now aged forty, he chose to burn himself up and the results were suitably stupendous. 'His self-destruction was an essential source of his creativity,' says Jean-Pierre Derbord. 'It allowed him to discover things, he used it to take him to heights of creativity. He would go through terrifying periods and yet there was always an exit; it was he who possessed the key to exit this hell. And then he would re-emerge triumphant.'

Even the theory that Karl set Jacques up to destabilise Yves Saint Laurent, a theory that reared its head later in the chronology of the affair, is hard to credit. Not because Karl Lagerfeld would not have been capable of doing so, but rather because it sounds like one more tale in the engulfing myth of Yves Saint Laurent as a marshmallow of helplessness. All such theories acknowledge the child, but never the core of will that was also Yves Saint Laurent. Yves chose his own destiny just as surely as La vilaine Lulu chose hers.

'We all carry demons inside us — are they demons, are they dreams, are they fantasies, whatever, we don't manage to assume them,' says a witness to these years. 'Perhaps there is a moment when they rise to the surface. Yves started this gigantic affair with Bergé when he was young; Pierre is a very demanding person, controlling, possessive. All of a sudden Yves was living this kind of explosion in order to rid himself of everything that was choking him. Sometimes everything starts to erupt and it is beautiful when that happens, marvellous; these are moments that are highly creative, for nothing is harder for creativity than the constant of having to do the same thing. Jacques de Bascher was a path by which Yves could exorcise certain of his demons. Yves nearly burnt himself alive — as in all exorcisms. But it is not Jacques who took him there. It is the profound nature of Yves. Jacques was only the instrument.'

And indeed long after the affair was over, the idea of Jacques continued to be a source of pain that Yves could exploit. 'I saw Jacques today,' he would say for years afterwards, inventing the lie with which to torment Pierre Bergé.

Chapter 13

1976

The salon of the Saint Sulpice apartment was bare but for a large black Harley-Davidson motorbike parked in the middle of the parquet floor. Its wing mirrors were outstretched and turned upwards to face the ceiling and on each mirror was laid a generous and heaped offering of cocaine. Beside each pile a straw and razor-blade were thoughtfully provided so that one might help oneself. Jacques de Bascher was having a party.

'In honour of the Képi Blanc,' read the party invitation, a reference to the French Foreign Legion and its signature white kepi hat. The party was being held to fête one of Jacques' more marginal friends, a man who went by the name of Sergeant Poulet. Ex-French Foreign Legionnaire, active member of the French National Front, his real name was Jean-Claude Poulet-Dachary and he was to end his life in 1995 lying at the bottom of the staircase in his apartment block in Toulon, his head and face crushed by hammer blows, in a strange tale of suspected National Front internecine killing. But for now he was alive and hanging out with Jacques, who was throwing him a party.

When it wasn't the coke-charged Harley in the centre of the salon, there was some other installation – human or inanimate – contrived to provoke a reaction. Designer Lucien Pellat-Finet remembers turning up at Jacques' apartment one day and finding a gynaecologist's chair positioned centre stage: 'I turned around and fled.' Another afternoon in the early 1980s Jacques invited Patrick McCarthy over for a drink and Patrick arrived to find the salon full of thrusting young firemen in uniform. 'The whole local *pompier* station was there having a party; they were all drunk, it was the funniest scene. Jacques had met them and said come on over. They were having a great time, they didn't have a clue who Jacques de Bascher was; there was a whole bunch of Paris social people and then these guys from the fire station.'

The guests for the Képi Blanc soirée were a mix more usually found at Jacques' parties. Jacques' old friend Renaud was there along with friend Christian Lvowski, aged twenty-one, and there was also a young fifteen-year-old boy called Marc Rioufol, a friend from home in the Loire Atlantique whose mother played bridge with Jacques' mother and whom Jacques had newly recruited to Paris night-life. There was a crowd of fashion people and *demi-mondains*, and lastly there was Jacques' other splinter set of friends with whom his principal source of affinity was cocaine.

When the party ran out at around 5 a.m. Jacques told Christian it was too late to bother going home and he could stay and sleep in his bedroom while Jacques took another bed elsewhere in the apartment. 'About an hour and a half later I heard the door to my bedroom open,' remembers Christian. 'It must have been around 7 a.m. – there was a very pale light in the room – and I saw Jacques coming in to get something. He was freshly shaved, dressed from head to toe in an Austrian outfit, with a Loden coat, waistcoat, tie, a wonderful jacket, breeches, a hat with a plume of badger sticking up and his moustache fragrant and perfumed. I was completely staggered, he looked like he'd had ten hours' sleep whereas in fact he'd been up all night partying.'

'Where on earth are you going?' Christian asked Jacques. 'I've got to go and catch a helicopter at Le Bourget, I'm having lunch with the Princess of Liechtenstein at the Palace of Liechtenstein,' said Jacques casually. 'Just slam the door when you leave.' 'That was Jacques de Bascher for me, he lived like that every day, when you tell it now it sounds as if it is a scene in a novel or a film.'

The impression that Jacques gave of being a character in a novel was in large part due to his insistence on presenting his life in one dimension only: appearance. There was no context of reality in which you could place Jacques; there was no job, therefore no working life, and his personality was increasingly crystallised by cocaine.

But it was also a reflection of the role he played within Karl Lagerfeld's life. Perhaps Jacques, with his elegant silhouette and noble bearing, represented Karl's aesthetic ideal? 'But of course,' says Andrée Putman. 'Everything, but everything: the manner, the voice, the style, *le ton*.' Perhaps Jacques was the incarnation of what Karl would have longed to be himself.

Karl had a peculiarly harsh and critical view of his own body. He was self-conscious about the length of his arms and legs, but it was his hands that were the cause of greatest chagrin. He had been made to hate his hands by his mother, who had told Karl ever since he was a boy that she disliked them. Karl's cousin Kurt Lagerfeld remembers that she used to call them 'farmer's hands' or, worse still, 'peasant's hands'. They were in fact Lagerfeld hands, like those of his father: strong and thick-fingered. But his mother's criticism marked Karl and his hands became a source of considerable anguish.

Throughout his career Karl's body weight fluctuated dramatically. During his thirties Karl worked out at least four times a week for three hours at a stretch and his body was highly muscular. Then one day at the beginning of the 1970s, Karl remembers, 'I was at the gym and I realised I was bored to death by it.' He stopped the obsessive gym routine and immediately started to put on weight. He designed what he calls an 'over-blouse', which was a kind of artist's smock that he wore to disguise his changing silhouette. From time to time during his mid-thirties and forties he inflicted extreme dieting upon himself – such as the acupuncture diet, the boiled and blanched food diet – before falling back again into his compulsive twenty bottles of Coca-Cola per day diet. Later in the 1980s Karl would resume his gym fanaticism. Yet still his body did not metamorphose into his ideal. For a period of ten years during the 1990s Karl weighed more than 120 kilos (over 18.5 stone). As he told a journalist in 1983, 'It [my body] does not correspond to my own criteria.' It was only in his late sixties that Karl regained control of his body with a draconian diet that rid him of 40 kilos (over 6 stone).

Jacques, on the other hand, had the same silhouette as that of the Berlin dandy who dashed through the pages of the *Garderoben Gesetze*, a small volume of German sartorial etiquette published in 1923 and illustrated by Kretschmann. The book was republished in 2003 and Karl must have admired it considerably because he wrote a foreword to the new edition. It is filled with engravings demonstrating how a Weimar gentleman should dress for every occasion, be that picnic, bobsleigh, flying or funeral. Kretschmann drew for himself a society of German rakes with graphic slashes of limbs, angled waists, wing collars, silk cravats and cut-away frock-coats, dangling papery cigarettes below moustaches, life viewed through the affectation of a monocle. They wore kid gloves to fit tapered hands. By 1976 Jacques' physical and sartorial resemblance to one of these Weimar figures was uncanny.

Behind the easy charm, Jacques was secretive and kept his life strictly compartmentalised. There were many aspects of his life that even an old friend like Renaud de Beaugourdon did not know or understand. Did anyone really know the nature of his relationship with Karl Lagerfeld, how it worked, how Jacques was funded, what was expected of him, what sort of access he had to Karl? Throughout Renaud and Jacques' years of friendship, Renaud met Karl only once and that was quite by chance, at the auction rooms of the Salon d'Orsay for a viewing of the Paul Morand sale. 'There were so many mysteries to Jacques,' reflects Renaud. On one occasion when they were together Jacques said as they prepared to go out somewhere, 'I have to drop by and see Karl.' They took the car and stopped at the Rue de l'Université; Renaud waited in the car while Jacques went in to see Karl for ten minutes, then he came out again and they continued on for the night without Karl.

The setting of Jacques' life added to the sensation of film set, not because of its grandeur – there were many in Paris living in far greater pomp – but because of the pose of it. The salon was fairly bare, while the bedroom featured a collection of late nineteenth-century portraits and paintings. The bathroom was dominated by an enormous green marble bath and there were black and white portraits of Nijinksy by Baron Adolf de Meyer hanging from the walls, as well as the speakers for a mega-sound system that pumped Jacques' beloved Diana Ross albums all around.

'I remember saying to him one day, "Jacques, your bathroom is amazing," and he said to me, "Ah, you must try it, have a bath in it." So I did and I lay in the marble bath surrounded by the music and his shelves of vests and the shelves of underpants. There was five years' difference in age between us and I think it amused him in a way to see someone who wasn't living in this world step into it. There was a childish side to Jacques,' says Christian Lvowski.

Were these the possessions of his real life, indications of his true character, or were they merely props to sustain his stage character in its progress through Paris? 'He was living in a décor,' says Christian flatly. The apartment was not his; Karl rented it. The paintings, including the large portrait by Pompier at the foot of his bed, were all paid for with Karl's money, so did that make them Jacques' or were they in fact Karl's?

Jacques had no private income of his own. Karl's money was always there, the third force in their *ménage à trois*, sitting at the table of every restaurant, there at the Austrian boutique of Lanz in Salzburg when the lederhosen and Tyrol jackets were tried on and chosen, there at the antique shop on the Rue du Bac as Jacques bought himself a charming and expensive nineteenth-century painting of a fencing scene. The financial dimension to their relationship gave rise to the question of ownership and provoked in Jacques all the insecurities of the kept man.

Less than two months after the suicide of José de Sarasola, Jacques' father died of cancer, on 14 October 1975. He died at La Berrière, where he and Jacques' mother had retired. From this time onwards, Jacques became more compulsive in all of his pastimes. 'I liked Jacques. At first I knew him well; after he scared me. He changed, there was no doubt a social ambition to begin with and then he became extremely destructive of himself,' says Jacques Grange. 'After, I didn't see him again, all his world, those people, it was very hard; he went from a *gentil provocateur* to this destruction.' 'He scared me,' says Frédéric Mitterrand. 'There was something morbid about him.' The darker Jacques' image became, it seemed, the more he contrived to live up to it, to fulfil other people's worst fantasies of him.

But there was another Jacques too, although it was a Jacques known only to a few: members of his family, Renaud and Christian, Diane de Beauvau-Craon, Xavier de Castella, later Patrick McCarthy, American lover Alan Cornelius and, of course, Karl Lagerfeld. He was able to inspire long-term loyalty among those close to him. 'For me he was someone very touching,' says Christian. 'I heard all the things people said about him, that he was insufferable; I heard all about his caprices and bad behaviour, and I think that made up a part of his personality although I cannot speak about that because it was a side I never saw and I did not know. I had a friendship with Jacques that was very different. He was thoughtful, he loved to laugh and in a small group with Renaud and me he could be extremely kind.' Christian was aged twenty when he met Jacques and impressed at the time by the flair of the man, although he was under no illusions. Renaud's friendship was different and based on a realism that is perhaps indicative of an old friend who had known Jacques before his blazing entrance into society. Renaud knew Jacques' propensity for charm; he liked Jacques for their shared history and the fact they laughed together. And although Jacques saw Renaud only a few times a year, it seems the friendship and Renaud's uncompromising reality were important to Jacques as he kept up with Renaud through calls and correspondence over the years.

Marc Rioufol was a self-confessed adolescent 'wild dog' when Jacques introduced him to Paris, Le Sept and all that went with it. Although Marc was not himself homosexual, he was close to Jacques. 'He was extremely protective of me as homosexuals can be. He wanted me to do my studies, pass my exams. I was still at school, aged thirteen or fourteen when I first started going out on Rue Sainte Anne, catching the train back to Nantes to go to school the next morning,' he remembers. 'Yet at the same time it was Jacques who introduced me as his *cousin de Bretagne*, dressed me from head to toe, took me to parties that were more and more unbelievable, *les soirées Parisiennes*. It was a pretty heavy milieu he initiated me into. There was too much coke, too much money. It was destabilising.'

'Ah,' sighs Manolo Blahnik at the mention of Jacques' name, 'divine or the Devil, it depends on how you look at it.' The divided self existed in Jacques long before he found fashion or cocaine, but both had their part to play in exaggerating the division within. Cocaine seemed to exaggerate his powers of charm, entertainment and glamour, and Jacques took large and incessant amounts of the stuff. 'He consumed cocaine in a manner that was extremely consistent,' says Lvowski. 'He seemed to have a remarkable resistance to the drug, and he took lots and all the time. While I have seen the drug have effects on some that rather spoils the personality, with Jacques it was that effect of effervescence, exactly the cliché of cocaine bestowing one with great acuteness of the senses and comprehension.'

The coke was an intrinsic part of the aesthetic pose. 'Jacques could have had a mirror and a straw like everyone else but he didn't,' says Lvowski. 'He had a small, gold, precious cocaine box that he told me used to belong to the Brazilian aviator Albert Santos Dumont, made for him by Cartier. Of course straight away that created an effect – sniffing cocaine from this jewel of a box rather than using a mirror like anyone else.'

Jacques was not alone with his cocaine habit; the drug was now fuelling the pace and exhilaration of so many lives. It burst on to the scene in Paris a few years later than in New York, for example, where it had already featured at every Halston party for several years. It started doing the rounds at night, people were taking it on the dance floor at Le Sept. And then it seemed that every pocket, every handbag had a gram or two to see the night through. It became the *de rigueur* guest at every chic table, more reliable than the person sitting next to you for providing scintillation. Debonair socialite Jimmy Douglas remembers holding one of his buffet dinners to which the Saint Laurent gang turned up and asked for some coke. Jimmy was not a coke man himself and therefore had none, but he was, however, a host who aimed to please. He walked coolly to his bathroom medicine cabinet, pulled out a packet of KH3 – a fashionable miracle drug of the time, much vaunted for its supposed abilities to prevent wrinkling, old age, arthritic knees, etc. – popped open several pink capsules and set the powder down before them on a small mirror. The KH3 seemed to do the trick, for there were no complaints among the takers.

Cocaine seemed to both mirror and shape the hopes and obsessions of these years in Paris. 'The only drug I didn't understand so I gave up extremely quickly is heroin – which brings us back to image and beauty,' says Diane de Beauvau-Craon. 'I tried it, but I dropped it immediately because I found that people were ugly with it; heroin makes you drowsy, makes you vomit, and that is not very sexy. So we were very conscious of our image. Cocaine makes you feel very intelligent but then we thought that we *were* very superior people. We were thrown off balance by the image projected on to us, cultivated by us.'

Karl did not go to the Harley Davidson party at Jacques' apartment. Where was he that night? Off on a trip somewhere to promote Chloé, at home perhaps, reading on his damask-covered *lit de parade* or sketching a collection for one of the twenty freelance lines that he was by now designing anonymously for the German market.

Karl did not take cocaine, Karl did not take drugs; he did not drink or smoke, though he did occasionally drink a small glass of white wine before taking a plane because he was scared of flying.

What Karl did was work – incessantly, consistently, tirelessly. He worked to fulfil an ambition and a vision. Unlike many fashion designers, Karl's vision was never a vision of a certain woman that he wished to impose on the world, but rather a vision of himself that he wished to impose on the world. Karl worked to fulfil a dream of a lifestyle he had seen and wanted and aspired to, and if necessary he would work for a lifetime to make that vision come true.

'As a child I lived in the north of Germany, on the Danish border, in a very cultivated family but in a cadre of German austerity and rigour,' he wrote in the Christie's catalogue for the sale of his collection of eighteenth-century furniture and paintings in 2000. 'From the age of five, at my request, my parents gave me a French teacher who initiated me into the French language and culture. At the age of seven I had a total *coup de foudre* before a reproduction of a painting by Menzel representing Frederick the Great surrounded by friends, one of whom was Voltaire, and receiving them at Sans Souci. I immediately decided that this elegant and refined scene represented the life that was worth living, a sort of ideal that I have since endeavoured to achieve.'

The picture Karl refers to is *La Salle Ronde*, a view on to a dining room lit by a pair of chandeliers and curved into a round by Corinthian columns. A gilded door opens out on to a corridor beyond and liveried footmen stand behind the table. There are nine gentlemen seated at the table, bewigged and ribboned, animated and enraptured by the dinner-table conversation. They lean forward to share one anothers' gossip, theories and witticisms, discussing Voltaire's latest work perhaps or basking in his Enlightenment. Their costume is rich and velvet; before them is a table of fine wines and crystal that serves as a backdrop to their conversation.

The epiphany of the young child seeing before him the possibility of another life is a key construct in Karl Lagerfeld's life story, as recounted by him frequently over the last fifty years. There are slight variables to

the way he tells the story – in some versions he buys himself the reproduction, in others he asks his parents to buy it and they do so at considerable expense, in others they must persuade the antique dealer to open
his shop on Christmas Eve so that the young boy might have his wish
– but the message remains the same: Karl saw, he wanted, he was going
to get it. As he said in 1988, 'This is the purpose of life, to get what
you want.'

The Menzel reproduction revealed to Karl a world of wit and erudite
conversation, a world of light and luxury, choreographed manners and
costume, a world of curiosity and a possibility of the superlative. As he
said in 1979, 'All that has followed [the eighteenth century] is petit bourgeois.' And all that Karl wanted to escape was the small-time, small-
town.

By 1977 Karl's dream world was emerging. There was the Château
de Penhoët, where he had embarked on substantial renovation of the
body of the house and was restoring the garden, its fountains and circular
ornamental pond. Karl had installed his eighty-year-old mother in the
château and the housekeeper looked after her. He still took friends for
weekends there, although locals noticed a change in the behaviour of
the Lagerfeld clique following José's death. Before, Jacques and Karl,
Anna and Vern and other Penhoët guests were to be found occasionally wandering about town. Anna would turn up to buy a baguette at
the *boulanger* dressed in a 1920s purple velvet tea-gown; Jacques would
sweep in and out of the local café leaving a trail of open mouths behind
him. But after the death Lagerfeld and his guests lived life confined to
the château and the environs of the park only; they did not appear in
the couple of streets and the bar that make up the town of Grand-
Champ again. Later Karl constructed a high wall around the south side
of the château grounds, so whereas before the château could be seen
from outside it was now hidden from view.

In Paris Karl had moved into a wing of the magnificent *hôtel particulier* of Hôtel Soyecourt, at number 50, Rue de l'Université. One of
the most illustrious eighteenth-century town houses of the Faubourg
Saint-Germain, it was owned by the Comtesse Liliane de Compiègne.
The house was behind a high and monumental gate and the apartments
inside were grand and lined in original eighteenth-century wood
panelling. Karl was building up a considerable collection of furniture so

that he might live in the manner that historically matched his surroundings. He bought beds for every room, including *lits de parade*, day beds, huge great Louis XVI beds decked and draped with silk faille and topped with ostrich plumes, and he spent much time patiently explaining to those less knowledgeable than he that eighteenth-century life was largely conducted from the bed. He insisted the rooms should be lit by candlelight only, making an exception for Anna Piaggi's guest-room, where one electric light was allowed.

It was 1977, a time of crippling unemployment and recession in France, when the Euro-rich were paralysed by rabid terrorist threats, and here was Karl Lagerfeld, a freelance fashion designer living like a Habsburg prince; no wonder even Paris was duly impressed. There was always a queue of journalists being invited round to take tea with Karl and report on the life of, as André Leon Talley described him, 'a real German baron'. Jacques would be there too, playing his part as a real French aristocrat, handing out his *baise-main* and generally being a wonder of grace. Jacques organised lunches for Karl in the Sans Souci fashion, deviating only by his introduction of that twentieth-century innovation, women. Seated at a circular table beneath the *boiseries* and candlelight, Karl, Jacques, Marian McEvoy, Vern Lambert, Anna Piaggi and Manuela Papatakis, Anouk Aimée's partying daughter, sat and engaged in conversation as servants handed out truffle-flavoured pasta on porcelain and chilled bottles of La Berrière Muscadet were served.

The change in Karl's interiors was marked by another radical change of personal look. What Helmut Newton called the 'Mafia look' and the Hamburg bank-manager suits that went with it were gone, replaced by something altogether more historic and eccentric.

Studying photographs of Karl and his variety of looks through the ages, you are struck not just by his commitment to exhibitionism and disguise, but more significantly by his absolute mastery of image and self-communication whereby with each new image he imposes upon himself he succeeds in blotting out the one that preceded it. For fifteen years Karl was photographed in every magazine, made every media appearance, ended every fashion show ponytailed, with powdered jowls, overweight, black glasses, black, tent-like Yohji Yamamoto suits, fan in hand. But close your eyes now and you see only one Karl – the grated-carrot silhouette, the corset-straight back, chiselled cheek-bones, skinny

Diesel jeans, Prussian high white collars, rings on every finger, foundation on every pore – yet this is a Karl who only came into existence
in the year 2000. What kind of wizardry is this that Karl manages to
exist only as now?

By 1977 Karl was becoming a character from his Menzel reproduction. He was growing his hair to be tied back in a 'catogan' in the
manner of an eighteenth-century gentleman. He received guests at home
dressed in an eighteenth-century floor-length coral and green silk Chinese
coat edged in white ermine with a flouncy bow and stiff wing collar
at his neck. Gaby Aghion sat and watched it all unfold before her. 'He
created himself, he became a character, he had the intelligence to do
that,' she reflects. 'He realised that one can sell oneself as a personality.'

From the late 1970s onwards Karl's childhood was conjured up with
gripping images of wunderkind eccentricity. 'When I was four, I asked
my mother for a valet for my birthday,' he would say, or, 'My mother
made me read a page of the dictionary every day.' He told a *New Yorker*
reporter in 1994 that he taught himself to read in order to follow the
text of his favourite picture book, *Das Nibelungenlied* by Nabokov. There
was an insistence that he never played with other children but stayed
reading, sketching alone, in his atelier in his attic.

And then there was the confusing question of siblings: sometimes he
acknowledged them (in reality one half-sister, one full sister, both older),
other times he did not, referring to himself in a vague manner as an
only child. On one recorded occasion he changed their status by making
them both half-sisters and added a former husband to his mother. 'Was
I an only child? No! Much worse! I had half-sisters from my parents'
earlier marriages. But I was treated like an only child. Everything existed
only for me. I could do whatever I wanted. I couldn't do wrong! I was
the worst, the most spoiled child in the world.'

Reports insisted that he was aged fourteen on arrival in Paris, and
hardly a journalist has ever bothered to ask how a boy of fourteen could
be allowed to leave the country without finishing his elementary
schooling. In this way he became aged sixteen when he won the coat
category of the International Wool Secretariat Competition in 1954,
making him a gratifying two years younger than Yves at the time of
the competition and heightening the impression of the extraordinary.
The idea of Karl as child Mozart was established retrospectively.

In the same breath with which Karl described the child prodigy, when he spoke about his work in the present tense he placed the emphasis firmly on his straightforward work ethic. It was left to you, the journalist, the reader, the viewer, to make the genius link. He never, ever expressed pretensions to being an artist; instead he insisted on his status as a professional, working designer. In 1978 he barked, 'When I hear I am called "an intellectual designer", I hate that. What is the worst is a fashion designer who talks all the time of his or her creativity, what they are, how they evolve. Just do it and shut up.'

There was this same magnificent interplay of contradiction between the preconceptions that his appearance and the Madame de Pompadour life-setting provoked and then the delight of Karl's personality up close. It never failed to unnerve, to charm. His public persona then was perceived as 'antipathique', a French word meaning unpleasant; this was particularly so once the impenetrable sunglasses arrived and, from the late 1970s onwards, combined with the increasingly sliced-tongue treatment of others.

And yet when a journalist or chosen one was invited into the Lagerfeld home they found themselves disarmed by the immense wit, knowledge and modesty of the man they found there. 'His considerate manners are nothing short of royal. Unlike other non-stop talkers I have known – and they include Chanel herself, whom I interviewed (or, rather, was talked at by, many years ago) – he has to be prodded to bring the conversation round to himself and his activities. Never is there a word about his phenomenal success . . . There is no attempt to charm, no hint of ingratiation,' wrote journalist Rosamond Bernier in American *Vogue* in 1992. She went to have lunch with Karl at the Hôtel Soyecourt. Together they ate scrambled eggs with truffles, toured the house, admired the restored gold-leaf ceiling of the grand salon and she left his presence several hours later, smitten. 'I walked out, gasping. It was drizzling slightly. I didn't have a car waiting. "Mine will take you to wherever you are staying," he said. And he walked me in the rain across the courtyard to put me into the car . . . Remembering how in the memoirs of Saint-Simon an earlier owner of this same house was famous for his wit, his intelligence, and good manners, I said to myself, nothing has changed. As in Saint-Simon's day, this irresistible house has found an equally irresistible owner.'

Karl has never lost this element of seduction and surprise in his handling of the media. He understood from the start how to use the media to communicate the story. 'I think Karl's biggest, biggest triumph is his playing of the press to the hilt,' says press and fashion veteran John Fairchild, 'to the hilt. I mean he plays them beautifully, it's like a symphony orchestra.'

He was every journalist's dream – garrulous, controversial, opinion-ated, quotable, intensely humorous and available. 'He was devastatingly funny and very wicked,' remembers journalist Judith Fayard. 'There was never a moment when Karl wasn't one of the most entertaining people you would *ever* have lunch with. In his conversation he was very, very sure of himself; whether he actually was or not is a different matter, but he was very funny, very quick and brusque right from the start.'

He had gossip, sensational rumours, overwhelming personality, was prepared to dish and burn, and he always had something new to show you, some fascinating historical titbit to impart. 'As a human being he was far more interesting than a lot of them,' says writer Gerry Dryanksy. 'He reads enormously, he has other interests outside fashion and this made him fascinating to the editors.' His often barbed observations about others were right on target and made you laugh out loud, both at the wit of the remark and the relief that it wasn't you who was under fire.

Relationships were cultivated. This was not new in fashion, where the relationship between editor and designer has always been one of incest, but Karl performed to a new level. He personalised the rela-tionship to an incredible degree. This was a very busy man and yet it was Karl who ordered the bouquet, not the PR; he chose which flowers to send and wrote the note to go with it. One editor from the early 1970s remembers, 'He was very good with the editors, he was nice with them. I think he gave them gifts and he became personally liked and I think this went a long way with his clothes.' Where many see playing of the press, others see a genuine kindness. 'I have known a lot of jour-nalists who leave their job somewhere and Karl is one of the few people that calls them, that tries to keep up with them and all that,' says Patrick McCarthy. 'Karl is extremely generous.' Art director Donald Schneider remembers attending a Karl Lagerfeld show in the late 1990s and sitting next to an older German lady who told him that she had written the first-ever article on Karl for a German trade magazine years back and since then he had invited her to his every show.

Karl's willingness to allow journalists such proximity and access to him was yet another way in which he differentiated himself from Saint Laurent. And of course journalists were then, and are now, flattered. Even now that he is a household star he still hands out his bedroom fax number to chosen journalists, faxing them back by hand to answer their queries in the dead of night in order to meet their deadlines.

And Karl did all this single-handedly. Karl had no Pierre Bergé to promulgate his personal legend and genius, he did it all himself. And unlike Yves and Bergé, Kenzo and Gilles Raysse, Valentino and Giancarlo Giacometti, Dior and Rouët, Karl never hid behind the bad-guy partner. 'It's always the way with these designers, they always have the front man who comes out as being the nasty one,' says John Fairchild. 'Yves says, "Do this, do that," and Pierre does it.' Not so with Karl; he took his own falls, did all the bad-guy stuff himself.

Beneath the absurd – the ermine-edged gown, the powder and pout and the little finger that leapt into the air as he sipped his Coca-Cola – there was the steel-trap mind, hard work and stamina of a German industrialist. And anyone who has worked with Karl speaks of his absolute professionalism and overwhelming self-exigency. It was as Billina spotted back in Saint-Tropez: 'He dressed flamboyant, but he didn't act flamboyant.' The eccentricity in dress and mannerisms belie the rigidity of his nature, as Gaby Aghion describes: 'He has the most enormous will. Someone like Galliano at Dior has a kind of folly in him, but with Karl there is no folly.'

No folly, but a seemingly limitless capacity and need to work. By 1977 he was designing for Chloé in Paris and Fendi in Rome, had thirty Karl Lagerfeld licences in Japan, plus an Eve Stillmann lingerie line in the US, licences for sunglasses and a porcelain china collection for Hutschenreuter. He was also responsible for a stack of collections that he designed anonymously, including the multiple fashion lines in Germany. These were just the collections Karl was prepared to talk about; there has always been a large amount of secrecy and unknown concerning the exact nature of Karl's employment commitments and their financial reward.

His collections were a supreme balance of new and fresh ambiance and the all-important buyer-pleasing clothes. In every collection Karl always conjured up the right amount of trend for daughter, flattery for mother and appropriateness for grandmother, and he still does. He was someone who understood the fashion game, and was there to make money and succeed. 'Karl had a very friendly relationship with Marvin Traub, who was president of Bloomingdale's,' says Ralph Toledano, former managing director of Karl Lagerfeld. 'Every time he came to Paris they would have tea at the Crillon, so to me they were good friends, and when I made a decision of dropping Bloomingdale's [as retailer of the Karl Lagerfeld line] I was scared of Karl's reaction. I went to him and said, "Karl, I have to tell you that I have decided to drop Bloomingdale's," and he looked at me and said, "Who's going to replace them?" He was intelligent enough to say, If I rely on him I must trust him – that's how he can handle so many things, he has the right people. He didn't ask why, he didn't waste time asking how. He knew all this friendship was just bullshit, business friendship with nothing real behind it. Karl was very realistic, practical; he never thought for a second that if you were having tea with Mr Traub it was because he was in love with you, but just so that he could have you do a personal appearance at one of his stores.'

To achieve the extraordinary volume of design Karl produced every season he relied on fastidious self-discipline and an assimilative approach to his creative process. With Karl there was never any visible angst; there was no flailing around on the studio floor, gnashing of teeth and sobbing, 'I can't do it any more.' There was no thrashing of the breast for inspir- ation, no burnt offerings to conjure up the favours of the muses, no 'Monsieur Lagerfeld cannot talk now, he is in a fitting'. On the contrary, Monsieur Lagerfeld was often to be found talking to a journalist, fitting a dress, composing a press release in verse and negotiating a contract simultaneously. Monsieur Lagerfeld was multi-tasking before the term was invented.

His Chloé shows were held at nine o'clock on a Monday morning and Karl's collection was always ready well in advance, never late. Members of his Chloé team called him Dr Lagerfeld because his professionalism and 9 a.m. start made them think of a surgeon's consultation.

Karl expressed his approach to design in *Top Ten Designers in Paris*, a television documentary made in 1979 during the ready-to-wear collections that featured Karl. 'It's not very modern any more, I think, to talk about the new silhouette. The mood is more important than the line in a way because we are not in the '50s any more when there was the A-line and the H-line and the I don't know what, you know, so it's more a spirit and atmosphere. The only thing you can say is the shoulders are still broad, the waist is not as slim as it was last year and a little shorter, but this to me sounds like old-fashioned talk of the '50s.' Later he adds, 'The whole statement is made with accessories and all the different things I add. The clothes are in fact quite simple and I wouldn't say basic but, in fact, very easy.'

This was a radical thought to have at the time, 1979. Karl in these few sentences sums up the direction that designers would take over the next thirty years, as fashion increasingly became a story of atmosphere and accessories. Did he know then that he was predicting fashion's future?

Karl already placed great emphasis on accessories, although not yet in a branded way but for the spirit they evoked in the show. And when you look back at these collections around 1979 and 1980, it is true that what makes the head turn are the zany accessories set against easy separates and exciting prints. There are belts made from plastic bubbles wrapped around swimming costumes or spouting out from the head like a foam of washing-up liquid. Karl put flying-saucer hats with shiny crêpe de Chine disco skirts, a live parrot on a shoulder and silk fans on the runway. He made the show atmosphere exciting: Jacques was sent off to New York to pick up the latest Donna Summer 'Love to Love You' track, which he brought back and played at the show.

Most of all Karl observed: he saw Anna Piaggi's habit of wearing precious and vintage lingerie to feed the chickens at Penhoët and then he translated her habit into one of his most forceful ideas from this period, which was the use of fine lace as daywear. He surrounded himself with a hyperactivity of visual stimulation, ideas and talent to replenish his mind's eye. The result was fashion that was pleasing, highly wearable and yet not iconic. Looking back it is hard to pinpoint a style or silhouette that Karl created during these years. He did favour a fresh femininity, an ethereal way of dressing – a sort of long, chiffon romanticism that was fashionable at this time and that Karl designed some of the very best of – but he did not construct a Karl Lagerfeld style. It is not like with Kenzo, for example, where you say the name and the style springs back at you fully formed: floral, effusive print, colour, cotton, youth, kimono sleeve, separates, ethnic, casual in the city. No one sentence can conjure up the Lagerfeld style.

Even those who were close to him during these years seem at a loss to describe what it is that Karl Lagerfeld stood for at that time. His friend Florentine Pabst-Schober casts around for a moment before saying, 'He was the first to put tennis shoes on girls, that was a revolution; I tell you it was like people couldn't believe it, it was the oddest thing to do and it was so cool, the whole show was in tennis shoes.' Gaby Aghion talks of the beautiful clothes he designed, the white cotton piqué bustier beneath a suit, jackets and coats and baby-doll dresses ending without a hem. In 1978 André Leon Talley judged his influence as considerable, saying that through his freelance work for Fendi over a period of twelve years, 'Lagerfeld has turned furs inside out, upside down and the fur industry around with his innovations.' Leon Talley also cited other Lagerfeld triumphs: 'He started his kind of layering in '69, unconstructed silk dresses in '72, unfinished hemlines in '74 and in '77 a return to the use of lace on cotton tulle.'

But although these were all innovations, they did not invent a style. They were, however, in perfect synch with the feelings of the time, and that is what Karl Lagerfeld did and still does with unabashed brilliance. He did not want to be tied down to a look, a style or an identity, not in life, not in fashion. 'My style is more: Another Spring, Another Love,' he said in 1979, referring to the Dietrich song and his own decorative style, although he could just as easily have been describing his fashion approach.

Karl resolutely refused to stand for anything; the only thing he accepted as his style constant was the new, the next. 'I have no opinion whatsoever about my influence; who cares?' he said in 1978. 'What is important is what I will do, not what I did in the past.'

Chapter 14

1977–78

In May 1977 Loulou de la Falaise and Thadée Klossowski flew to Venice for the weekend. They returned engaged to be married. The wedding took place on 11 June at the mayor's office of the fourteenth *arrondissement* in Paris. The bride arrived in Pierre Bergé's black Rolls-Royce, the door of which swung open to reveal one golden-toed sandal worn over a white sock. The rest of Loulou appeared in a puff of silk and plume, like a figure from Aubrey Beardsley. She wore huge white bouffant harem pants caught beneath the knee, white organza wrap, a mass of beads, a white turban stabbed with an apricot feather and large diamond brooch and carried a bouquet of red roses in her hands. Even with her wedding nerves Loulou didn't forget her Saint Laurent loyalty: 'It's all from Saint Laurent Rive Gauche,' she told a reporter, describing her look as 'very Poiret'. Her groom awaited dressed in white.

Inside the *mairie* was quite a social line-up: Bianca Jagger, Saint Laurent, Bergé, Marisa Berenson, Paloma Picasso, Marie-Hélène de Rothschild, Loulou's mother Maxime de la Falaise and Thadée's formidable mother Madame Antoinette de Watteville all sat contemplating the allegorical paintings portraying the republican ideal of love. The ceremony lasted just four minutes and by the end of those four minutes Loulou and Thadée had transmogrified into Paris' golden couple.

They emerged ecstatic into the *mairie* gardens and Loulou's girlish excitement prompted Saint Laurent to comment with wonder: 'I've never seen her like this before. She looks so girlish, so cute. You know, normally she's so, so *haute*, so stylised, so arch. She's a little different now, *n'est-ce pas*? But I'm sure she will return to her former self in about five minutes.'

The marriage came as a surprise to Paris, for Thadée had been together with Clara Saint since 1965, although they had long since ceased to be a monogamous item. They shared a life and a little apartment on the Rue Jacob, where Thadée lay about during the day contemplating what he describes as 'smoky considerations of image and reality'. Clara would return after a day at the press office and lie on her bed, telephone in hand, waiting for the call from Pierre and then ringing round the Saint Laurent clan organising the night's itinerary and its cast.

There was an inevitability to Thadée and Loulou falling in love: they shared a similar heritage that merged bohemian rhapsody, society and pain. Being the second son of Balthus cannot have been an easy ride, however much of an object of fascination you might be within Paris. Thadée remembers at the time that he was 'aware that I was good-looking, but I was much too preoccupied with what I perceived as a lack of talent'. As granddaughter of a painter, Loulou had an innate understanding of the potentially devastating effects of artistic talent and ego on offspring. Twenty-three years into their marriage she would comment, 'I think to be the son of a great painter is a little crippling. But Thadée had a remarkable childhood. It was all worth it.'

Thadée had the most devastating effect on men and women at this time in Paris. He was regarded as a mysterious, enigmatic, handsome force. The fact that he said very little only added to his allure. 'Thadée is one of those whom people talked about non-stop at this time in Paris,' says Michel Klein. 'There were others – Jacques, Joël, Xavier de Castella – they were people who made you dream by their culture, their intelligence, their physique or allure or just the way they lit a candle. Thadée is someone who has innate elegance, but not only that; he has a culture and knowledge that are unbelievable. He has led a totally artistic life.' But what did he *do*? people ask. Perhaps the question itself reveals the chasm in thinking between that age and now, between a generation when you didn't have to *do* anything to be someone, when simply to scintillate was enough, before life was about pension plans.

After he married Loulou, Bergé gave him his own office at the Saint Laurent couture house where together with Joël Le Bon he started writing a book on the acting/directing love-match of Madeleine Renaud and Jean-Louis Barrault, paid for by Pierre. He wrote – beautifully, according to Maxime de la Falaise – he read, he contemplated and he divulged nothing. 'I am frightfully lazy, that is one of the main traits of my character, so I've always managed to prevent people from expecting too much. I've always let them know that they can be very nice to me, but I am not going to be terribly nice to them. I'll be pleasant and all that, but they shouldn't expect too much from me. And it has sort of worked. I'm sure people are disappointed in me. It takes a long while for them to [work it out]. I mean I can go a very long way on just a smile.'

The emerging love story had a painful edge, for not only had Thadée and Clara been together for years, but Loulou and Clara were great friends and worked together every day at the house of Saint Laurent. 'I saw it coming from a long way off. Friends falling in love with each other's boyfriends is a story that happens every day, it is almost banal,' says Clara Saint now with dignity.

But perhaps less banal was Yves Saint Laurent and Pierre Bergé's decision to throw the wedding ball for the newly married couple. Clara was after all one of their oldest friends, predating both Thadée and Loulou in friendship. It was Clara who had made those early and vital connections for Yves, introducing the couturier to Nureyev, Margot Fonteyn, Thadée, Fred Hughes, Paloma Picasso. It was Clara who had played a part in choreographing the Saint Laurent set early on in the 1960s, as well as showing Yves a world of dance that helped him step beyond the Dior culture to establish his own mythology.

But Loulou was now the shining muse and Thadée the white knight of chic, and there is no doubt that both Saint Laurent and Bergé were enamoured of this glamorous match and the heat it would cast on the house of Saint Laurent.

'It must have been extremely difficult to take,' says one close witness of events. 'It was supported by Saint Laurent, paid for by Saint Laurent and that was like a slap. That was the aspect that was extremely unpleasant. It was not done in a very kind way, it seemed to say, Now they are the beautiful couple so we'll throw their wedding ball; that is the way it was not very elegant.'

Clara, however, remained forever faithful to the cause. She did not attend the ball but was back in her office the next day as press officer, where she continued working until her retirement in 1999. When questioned about the sensitivity of Yves and Pierre's decision to throw the wedding ball she is quick to justify their actions. 'But that was normal too. It was, how can I put it, not a particularly amusing night for me; I went to the cinema with friends. But Loulou was the muse and so I find it normal that they should throw a party for her when she gets married. What else could he do?'

Clara Saint knew even then she had no other option than to take the wedding ball on the chin; she knew that if she gave any other reaction the doors to the Saint Laurent clan would close. When you join the family of Saint Laurent it is with the understanding that you put aside your own hopes and desires for those of Yves. His talent and career and desires are greater than your needs. His suffering is greater than yours: this is the refrain chanted by the Greek chorus that surrounds him, led by Pierre Bergé. Yves does not want to see your pain; the only pain that interests Yves Saint Laurent is his own. 'He was always completely self-centred and not terribly interested in other people's problems except to make fun of them,' says Thadée.

There can be no conflict with Saint Laurent, no accusation or anger, he would not tolerate it. 'Oh, you can never be anything but light, it bores him to death. He cannot stand it, no never,' says Jacques Grange. 'A reproach, a confrontation, he cannot stand it. But sometimes life goes wrong and one has a desire to go deeper, but you cannot, you must always remain superficial.'

Betty Catroux has devoted nearly forty years of friendship to being light and effervescent for him, whatever ups and downs her own life has taken. 'I am never complicated with him, with them. I try to be like a glass of champagne. I never speak of heavy things. He calls me every day and if I can hear he's feeling down, I tell him funny stories, I play *le bébé*, the clown.'

François Catroux has observed the dynamics of their friendship throughout this time while purposefully staying on the sidelines, for, as he puts it, although he admires Yves and his talent immensely, he is not under the spell of Saint Laurent. 'She listens, she is there. I think she is his best friend. The fact he calls her non-stop three times a day means she must reassure him somehow,' says François. 'They have a complicity, they are certainly intimate, but it is always for a life that is a little superficial. They don't go out together at eleven in the morning. I've never heard them say, "Let's go and see an exhibition together." It is always at night, always dinners, their intimacy is from seven o'clock onwards; I think that already says a good deal about the nature of it. It is not one of those neurosis-free, let's-travel-the-world-together kind of friendships, but on the other hand it is not a façade either. It is a way of life.'

Throughout these years Yves was surrounded by women – Betty, Loulou, Clara, Paloma, Marina Schiano and all his mannequins – they were an integral part of his galaxy. Paloma's friendship with Yves consisted of few words; she can count on one hand the number of long conversations she has had with him over the years. She says she is not chatty and so it suited her well. 'In a way it's more of a feeling between us, meeting on certain ideas, falling in the same place at the same time with the same point of view, a real aesthetic connection and bond, but not so much something expressed by words.'

Paloma went to the fashion shows and sat and watched the mannequins walk down the runway and saw the outfits and the different styles before her and she would say to herself, 'Oh look, that's a Betty, that's a Clara, that's a Loulou, that's a Paloma.' 'You could almost see his friends stepping up on stage,' she remarks. 'and we are all very different which is what is so great; you look at Betty, Loulou, Clara and me and you know we have completely different shapes of bodies, colouring, we each correspond to one facet of his personality, or one of his fantasies.'

But fulfilling the role of female fantasy for Yves naturally prescribed a limitation on the friendship between you and him. A fantasy must never become familiar. Michel Klein remembers dropping Loulou back at her apartment after a late night of clubbing and she was giggling, saying, 'Hurry, hurry, I've got to get to bed. I've got to be beautiful tomorrow for the boss.' The level of superficiality imposed by Yves gradually suffused the whole Saint Laurent family and their everyday interaction. Levels of disinterest were high, at times extreme. Several years later Joan Juliet Buck wrote her second novel in Paris and went out at night, every night, with the Saint Laurent group. Unlike the usual barrage of polite questions ('How is the writing going?' 'When will it be finished?'), no one ever mentioned Joan's novel, which she admits came as rather a relief. But one night Joan went out feeling elated, having just sold the paperback rights that day, and at the end of the

dinner she announced her news and that the dinner was on her.
'Everyone looked at me like, "Oh really". Fabulous indifference,' remembers Joan Juliet Buck. 'The conversation with them was always more
about "Oh, that bracelet is pretty," or, "Should you really be wearing
such big glasses? Don't they magnify the bags under your eyes?"'

Thadée and Loulou's wedding ball was held on a small man-made island
in the Bois de Boulogne, that strange and suburban sylvan escape just
to the west of Paris. What could be more Parisian for Paris' newly
anointed couple than to celebrate here, in the Bois with its connotations of Proustian trysts and Manet's pale-skinned *belle* stripped and
naked in *Le Déjeuner sur l'Herbe*.

There were small boats to take guests the short journey across to the
restaurant of the Chalet des Iles and with the ferry trip came the suggestion that one might lose oneself on this fantasy island just metres from
the shores of reality. The boats were strung with garlands of white gardenia
and red lanterns and the guests waited on the shore in a state of high
excitement. It was July and dusk was falling, people were dying to get
across and into the heat and flesh of the party. Guests stepped aboard
gingerly, giggling nervously and trying not to let any of their couture
satin drag in the water before they even got to the party.

The scene seemed like a pastoral idyll, with swans gliding idly behind
chugging boats and weeping-willow trailing low in the water. The ball
had every ingredient to make it a legend: there were the bride and
groom themselves, the fact Yves Saint Laurent was throwing the party
– Yves who for the last year had all but disappeared from the Paris social
horizon – and the highly flammable guest list. 'I invited my English life,
my New York life, Thadée had a Roman life, we had a Parisian life; we
also invited people we'd love to meet and everybody said yes. We invited
people we didn't really know and everyone came, that struck people a
lot. It was the first time in Paris there was such a mixture of age, class,
activities, a jumble of characters and everyone adored meeting each
other, looking at each other. There were some French punks and they
were quite social in a way, they longed to meet grand people. It was a
bit like at the zoo, everyone was frightfully interested by one another,'
remembers Loulou.

They invited three hundred people and five hundred turned up. The invitation stipulated black-tie, but in the 1977 mood for exoticism it was fantasy and Yves Saint Laurent that prevailed for the women. Alexandre Iolas, playboy art dealer over from New York, looked as if he had escaped from the rodeo in a red cowboy suit stitched with swirls of silver, tight pants tucked into red cowboy boots. Guy Cuevas, the DJ from Le Sept, came as Minerva, gliding round in a Moroccan floor-length tobacco-coloured tunic Yves had given him, his bald head dusted with gold powder. He looked more like a high-glamour monk on the run. Marina Schiano, who ran YSL in New York, was there in Saint Laurent purple satin while Paloma Picasso was majestic in a long black velvet dress, hair scraped back and hands on hips, a Velázquez infanta in Saint Laurent.

Loulou and Thadée were waiting on shore to greet their guests from the boats. Loulou had told friends she wanted to look like a summer's night sky in Marrakech. She was ravishing, like a figure from an Indian miniature, wrapped in an acre of midnight-blue chiffon shot with gold, bangles up and down her arms, teetering in a pair of high silver heels. She had a large glittering crescent moon pinned to her head and a huge star on her ear. She had made the star and moon herself that afternoon from cardboard, glue and diamanté. Thadée was her Gatsby hero, dressed in white shoes, white double-breasted suit, white satin tie with a small pink plucked from the table and placed in his buttonhole. They were standing amid white hydrangeas, palm trees and candlelight.

'They were an incredibly glamorous couple,' says Madison Cox, who met them in New York a few months after their wedding. 'Not as in our day now, when you are probably extremely glamorous once fifty people have taken care of you for the picture. These are people who were glamorous inherently, intuitively and incredibly so.'

What was it they personified at that moment that Paris found so thrilling? Just about every Parisian fantasy of the late 1970s – artistic, aristocratic, fashion and elegance, beauty, youth and excess – all distilled in one couple.

Yves had decorated the marquee himself with green and white ribbons, black mannequin heads wearing huge white paper-doily head-dresses, and it was he who had conceived the tables' flower arrangements of white sweet-peas and red roses. He was looking more relaxed than he had for months, in dinner jacket and tennis shoes, a red cummerbund around his waist and a Marrakech shawl thrown round his neck.

Karl Lagerfeld was invited, but not Jacques, who was by now thoroughly banished from Saint Laurent society. How interesting that even in the atmosphere of highly charged animosity between the clans, Karl should not only be invited but should choose to attend. He came in his signature white-powdered face, dark glasses and a sardonic smile, greeting Paloma and her Saint Laurent butterfly sleeves with the comment, 'What lovely lampshades.' Bianca Jagger was the obsession of the night and caused a sensation by the fact that she was one of the few women not wearing Saint Laurent. She was dressed in a sugar-pink puff of tulle by Marc Bohan for Dior. Late in the evening she stood chatting with Yves when it suddenly came to him how that Dior dress of hers could be improved. He led her by the hand upstairs and into the chalet restaurant, sat her down by a mirror and proceeded to dismantle a nearby flower arrangement and very precisely and tenderly place ferns in and all around her dress and hair. It was both fashion and poetry. She had looked a little debutante before, but now Bianca re-emerged as an ethereal woodland nymph. It was also a piece of pure Saint Laurent upstaging, taking Marc Bohan's dress and showing him and everyone else how it should really be done. 'He was totally taken with Bianca, as she was with him,' says Marian McEvoy, who watched the fern scene play out. 'And I think in a funny way he wanted to take possession of that dress *and* Bianca.'

The party swept along in a rapturous euphoria. It was sexy, provocative and voyeuristic, people making out in bushes, others watching the bacchanalian scene pass before them. The social grandees sat at tables outside: art patron and socialite Sao Schlumberger dressed in white Saint Laurent, feathers in her hair and a diamond the size of a quail's egg on her finger; alongside her was baron Guy de Rothschild with his wife Marie-Hélène. Bianca's brother stripped naked and jumped from one of the little ferryboats, dived into the two feet of grimy pond water and swam to shore. There was Bollinger all night, but what really set the pace of the party was the large amount of coke and heroin in circulation. One guest turned up with a wedding present of a large bag of cocaine with a diamond ring buried inside.

'I remember that night offering smack to Mick Jagger, who was horrified,' says Thadée, relishing the memory of shocking a Rolling Stone. 'He went to see my elder brother and he said, "Look, you have to do something about your younger brother, he's just offered me smack and it's terrible." But the truth is we did it very little really, but for some reason we had our pockets full of drugs; well, it was a party so all the kids came with a gram of this or that as a present.'

At that time Thadée liked to mix up a line of coke and a line of heroin and take them together. 'It's very nice; what's nice about it is you don't have to drink, you are in such a good mood you don't actually take anything else for the rest of the evening. So it's quite economical and healthy in a way.'

He remembers the months before the wedding ball and the months that followed as a period of heavy heroin use, but points out that both he and Loulou were always protected by their ability to stop and drop it. 'What I mean to say is, Loulou and I, if we did drugs for more than two days running we'd feel sick and we'd stop. Normally people who feel sick take more. We had very non-addictive natures so we could play with drugs, play with danger without being very conscious of that. I mean we weren't fools, we knew that people were getting very deep into it and pretty unpleasant because of that, but we weren't courting danger. Unless you were somebody who would jump into a bar, then sprawl in the gutter and be spat on and revel in this destitution and whatever – it never crossed our minds that this would be enjoyable, this sort of masochism or whatever the word is.'

In the summer of 1977 the nights still appeared endless. 'Yves had this fantasy that we used to laugh at, about ending up as Marguerite Duras and Jeanne Moreau and we would live in this room together with bottles of red wine under the bed, like three tramps getting drunk together and dreaming up plays,' says Thadée. 'Anyway I think we used to laugh a lot. But we were desperate, all of us.'

During the years 1977–83 Jacques threw several parties that were to prove significant in establishing Karl Lagerfeld as a celebrity in the fashion world. These parties, and in one instance a ball, were held either in Karl's honour or in his name. The first party Jacques organised in 1977 was also the most notorious. It was called the 'Soirée Moratoire

Noire' and held, as the invitation read, in honour of Karl Lagerfeld on 24 October 1977. The invitation bore the names of both Jacques and Xavier de Castella, Jacques' newest partner in night-time adventure. Xavier too was a Neuilly-born provincial aristocrat. He was from Belgium and his parents had died in a car crash when he was one year old. He was homosexual, an aesthete with glowing charm, damaged and looking for ways to forget. But unlike Jacques, Xavier had his own money.

He and Jacques introduced themselves as cousins or brothers, depending on the night and the person. They even looked alike. They turned up to half a dozen dinners a night, arrived late, sat down, ate two mouthfuls, charmed the lady to their left, eyed the boy to their right and left for the next venue. 'They were like two gay musketeers running round Paris,' says Patrick McCarthy. 'To see the pair of them together playing at being brothers was staggering, it was as if they were angels and demons,' says designer Michel Klein.

The Moratoire Noire party was the night of the Chloé show and marked the end of ready-to-wear fashion week. It was held at La Main Bleue, a new club in the south-eastern suburbs of Paris in Montreuil, a run-down area miles from town that was not a habitual destination for the fashion party crowd. La Main Bleue was huge and concrete, a former cinema in a shopping mall and one of Philippe Starck's first design projects, although it bore little resemblance to his later surreal and polished hotels. This was a bleak hangar of a club with blue laser lights leading down the concrete staircase into darkness. '*Tenue tragique noire absolument obligatoire*', read the invitation in a grandiose curlicue of typeface, stipulating that costume for the night was to be tragic and black.

Even before it started the party was a scandal, as word spread that Jacques had planned the night as an homage to Andreas Baader, ringleader of the Baader–Meinhof Group of West German terrorists, who had allegedly killed himself in his prison cell six days previously on the night of 18 October 1977.

There was dry ice gushing along the floor, enveloping bodies and clouding the eerie electric-blue laser-beams. There were people coughing on the stairs. Everywhere people, four thousand people, were dressed in black, wearing strange clothes of mourning – and this in 1977, before black was the livery of fashion. 'It was not a joyful party,' remembers

Kenzo, who that year began a relationship with Xavier de Castella, 'everyone in black, black leather, *très hard*.'

Down below on the dance floor, in among the fashion silhouettes, there were men wearing an assortment of leather chaps, fetishist biker and military gear: strapped and butch and booted. It was a scene torn from gay illustrator Tom of Finland's homoerotic imagination. Later that night there was on-stage entertainment as Jacques and Xavier had organised a floorshow that was worthy of the Anvil, the infamous S&M gay bar in New York. Activities usually practised in specialised clubs were now exposed on stage: fisting, unlikely tricks with lengths of chain, contrived humiliation and subjugation to the sounds of 'Le Port d'Amsterdam' by Jacques Brel. 'Oh goodness,' says Parisian socialite Jimmy Douglas, remembering the night, 'you were gassed with poppers and a kind of mustard gas as you came down the stairs, it was a mixture of gases that would make anyone pass out, it was absolutely terrible. And then the most unbelievable, unspeakable things taking place on the stage with motorcycles and all that, and huge jugs of cold cream, and every kind of perversion going on.'

Many were deeply shocked by the hard-core nature of what they saw on stage that night. But it is worth remembering there were four thousand fashionable people at that party and that those four thousand fashionable people did not walk out. Fashion being a mirror of society's obsessions and desires, there was a fascination to the night in a distinctly voyeuristic way, as images were registered, minds instinctively seeking to extricate some salient image, some mood, some vibration that could be reinterpreted in fashion. As fashion editor Florentine Pabst-Schober reflects on the party and its strange ambiance, 'It's always nice to flirt with something when you are out there in nice and comfortable land.' Fashion flirts with deviancy to assimilate it, or, Pabst-Schober suggests, 'to superficialise it'.

In the audience of La Main Bleue that night was Claude Montana, the French fashion designer who had caused a visual shock wave himself in Paris that week with his show for Spanish clothing manufacturer Ferrer y Sentis. Bomber-jacketed and cowboy-booted, butch of body and breathy of voice, Montana was already known for his new silhouette of enormous, overwhelming shoulders teetering above a narrow waist. It was not the silhouette that caused the controversy, although it was to prove pivotal to the direction of fashion, but rather the black motorbike caps, leather waistcoats hung with chains, black leather coats and leather gauntlets shown in group formations of models and to the sounds of a medley of Wagnerian marches.

Montana and La Main Bleue were both part of a new deviancy and darkness to be found in fashion. It was a mood that had been presaged throughout the 1970s by the photographic fashion images of both Helmut Newton and Guy Bourdin. Bourdin was obsessed with mortality and pre-pubescent girls, while Helmut possessed a pantheon of fetish fantasies of maids and mistresses, Weimar Berlin, *The Story of O* and all its highly strung ritual of sadism and restraining attire. 'The boot of my car used to be full of chains, ropes and manacles,' said Newton, fondly reminiscing at the age of eighty-three.

But while Newton and Bourdin's stylised images were heterosexual and born of a pre-war generation, the new tide of fantasies washing over fashion was more post-modern, deriving from two conflicting cultures, gay and punk. Both possessed their own highly specific iconography of deviancy, although interestingly there were significant overlaps.

The summer of 1976 marked the eruption of punk in Britain and by 1977 it had emerged in a transmuted form in Paris, where it was rather less about spitting at the Queen, there being no queen to spit at, and more about spitting on 1968. There was youthful disdain for the lingering remains of the hippie generation and an outright rejection of the earnest freedom-fighters of the student revolution. 'Younger, more cynical, less utopian than their elder-brother '68 generation, they took a perverse pleasure in taking the exact opposite of the ideals of a generation who (according to them) had totally failed,' say Alexis Bernier and François Buot in their book *L'Esprit de Seventies*. 'In this way their cult of stardom was without doubt the biggest kick in the face to all those who had wanted an egalitarian society.'

Rather than fighting for a political alternative, punk in Paris was about getting dressed up, drugged up and dancing all night long, preferably alongside somebody famous. 'The people from '68/'70/'72 were already old for us, they were the opposite of us, they were baba-cool, hippie, we were much more modern, more urbane,' says Anouschka, who in 1977 was aged sixteen, wearing 1950s vintage, sly-eyed kohl and soon to be christened queen of the Paris night. 'We were not peace and love, sitting on the beach, dressed in afghans and things in goats' hair. We were all about going out at night to party, going to the Palace, being in the capital. If we were punk it was only in clothes and fashion. I don't think it was a very strong intellectual ideology.'

It was inevitable that in Paris punk's real success should be as an aesthetic pose, one of unflinching superficiality and deliberate visual subversion. Punks appeared in Paris with the same desire to destabilise and subvert through their sartorial stance that *les Incroyables* and *les Merveilleuses* had used in Paris at the beginning of the Directoire period in 1795. 'There was this kind of cynicism that was ushered in, a disillusion that came with punk,' says Marc Rioufol, 'and the drugs too, they arrived with punk.' The Main Bleue soirée, whether Jacques intended so or not, was a pitch-perfect expression of the dark malaise, violent imagery and indulgence of this time, amplifying all these sensations in the ephemeral moments of a party. Just turned twenty-six, Jacques spent the night dressed as some sort of Turkish warrior, bearded, with a white turban draped in black netting and a huge stick held in his hand, a look of bloody provocation on his face.

La Moratoire Noire was a party organised jointly by Jacques and Xavier in honour of Karl Lagerfeld, but it was Karl who paid the bill for the night and its entertainments. Later he would boast of it as an 'unbelievable' party, revelling in the controversy of it and the renown it brought him, but at the same time quick to insist that he had seen nothing, knew nothing of the goings-on. Instead it was Jacques de Bascher who became synonymous with the tenebrous extremes of the night, Jacques who had long since taken on the mantle of black prince at the court of Karl Lagerfeld.

Hippie nirvana had ceded to rampant consumerism. By 1977 cash was beginning to pound in people's ears; it was Monopoly money to be spent accordingly. And with the arrival of money, the portcullis of bourgeoisie fell on Paris fashion. 'People suddenly got very rich, all this fashion world suddenly made masses of money,' remembers Thadée Klossowski. 'Not just in the fashion world either. The Saint Laurent clan always used to be invited by Marie-Hélène de Rothschild, and Hélène Rochas was a good friend and she was also a rich woman. But then suddenly everyone was, well, not as rich as the Rothschilds, but every-body had, you know, grand houses; this seemed to happen so quickly in the space of less than ten years. Someone like Andy Warhol was earning huge amounts of money.'

The rich spent their time endlessly discussing the possibility that the socialists would win the legislative elections in March 1978 and deci-mate their hard-earned or hereditary fortunes. Karl talked non-stop about it for months before. 'I must say, I feel like people must have felt before 14 July in France in 1789, sitting on this bed and dressed this way,' he told André Leon Talley, as he lay on his *passementerie* antique bedspread dressed in silk and ermine. 'The day we begin to pay 90 per cent income taxes, life will not be very glamorous. I will then rent rooms here because all I have is beautiful beds. And instead of spending $200 a night for dinner with friends in bistros, it will be spaghetti at home.'

In the end the conservative party won by a narrow majority, but the threat of socialism seemed only postponed, rather than beaten. When they weren't discussing offshore bank accounts, it was the prospect of terrorism that now haunted the elite. The wave of violent kidnappings that had kicked off in Italy reached Paris in January 1978 with the abduc-tion of wealthy Belgian industrialist Baron Edouard-Jean Empain, who was held for sixty-three days before being rescued in a police shoot-out.

The clash of money, paranoia and the not-so-distant thud of socialism lent Paris a last-days-of-Rome feeling of indulgence and egoism. 'After the free-thinking of 1968, cash regained its footing,' says Frédéric Mitterrand, who happened to be the nephew of the failed presidential candidate of 1974, François Mitterrand. 'We had lived this new utopia for several years and it was supposed to make us all more free; in fact all it did was make us all more egotistical. Those that had money now reverted to the reflexes of class: they had one desire and one desire only and that was to live in a socking great eighteenth-century apartment and have grand dinners.' Mitterrand warms to his theme: 'Yes, the dream dinner party of the late 1970s would be a dinner at Karl's house with a guest list of Helmut Berger, Warhol, Alain Pacadis and two transvest-ites. Everyone would be wearing Saint Laurent and saying nasty things about Pierre Bergé.'

Yves Saint Laurent, Pierre Bergé and Squibb, the long-suffering owners of the YSL perfume division, hit the cash jackpot in 1977 with the new Saint Laurent scent Opium, which launched in Europe in October of that year and in the US the following September. It was unveiled with a *tour de force* of marketing, promotion and hype that had not yet been seen in the fashion industry but was a sure indication of where it was heading.

There was something infinitely knowing and premeditated about Opium and its blockbuster success. Rather than start by creating the juice, as was usual in Paris, they picked the name first (the long-held rumour being that it was writer François-Marie Banier who came up with the name and secured himself a percentage on sales for doing so), then the scent was formulated to match the image and provocative name. The perfume was a brilliant evocation of the late 1970s in Paris: opulent, heady, with a strident artifice that you could literally taste in your mouth. In concept, therefore, more coke than Opium.

Yves presaged the autumn perfume-launch with an haute-couture collection in July 1977 of chinoiserie, showing burnished brocades, lacquered red coolie-hats, purple satin trousers wrapped up in tassels and a lamé jacket with jutting pagoda shoulders and armfuls of mink. It was a glorious evocation of Imperial China but also a sensory attack deliberately designed to arouse the market for the arrival of Opium. Surely this was the first time a fashion collection had been conceived around a scent.

Then came the advertising image, which was as highly charged and controversial as the name of the scent. Helmut Newton shot the photograph in the musky and mirrored Buddha room of Yves' apartment on the Rue de Babylone, while Yves stood around and arranged model Jerry Hall's bangles. In a rapture of lamé and white orchids tumbling from a bronze urn, Jerry sat, back towards the onlooker, face turned with a look of wanton seduction. The image was one of darkness and iridescence, Jerry smouldering on command, her mass of curls hairsprayed into a river of static, while before her on the low table and in the foreground of the picture was an oversized bottle of Opium.

As a model Jerry epitomised these last years of the 1970s in fashion, and how characteristic of Yves to sense that. For in the five years since she had arrived in Paris, Jerry had metamorphosed into the creature Antonio Lopez had always seen in his mind's eye. She was a kind of golden panther, pacing down the fashion runways, eating up the crowds with her fame and exultant yellow beauty, her legs stretching up to the ceiling. Jerry from Mesquite, Texas, who had cooked french fries and mashed potato as supper for Antonio, Juan and Paul, was now Jerry Hall, a wondrous thing of blonde ambition, a headlight of glamour, who was offered full-length mink and diamonds by the Shah of Persia and chased all over the world with bouquets of roses proffered on bended knee by Mick Jagger.

Above Jerry's head in the advertisement there was a line that read, 'Opium. Pour celles qui s'adonnent à Yves Saint Laurent.' The word 's'adonner' stretches an octave of nuance in the French language so that the line might imply, 'Opium. For those who abandon themselves to the worship of Yves Saint Laurent', or, in juxtaposition to the name Opium, it could also mean, 'For those who are addicted to Yves Saint Laurent.'

The perfume was an instant hit in Europe, selling more in the run-up to Christmas 1977 than the immortal Chanel N° 5 had throughout the year. The following year Yves and Pierre persuaded Squibb to sink $250,000 into paying for a massive launch party for the perfume in New York, to take place on *The Peking*, a beautiful four-masted barque and one of the last generation of windjammers to sail around Cape Horn, that was docked at a pier within the South Street Seaport Museum in Lower Manhattan. The party preparation – a catalogue of hysteria, Parisian neurosis and delirious manipulation – was utterly emblematic of both the house of Saint Laurent and the fashion world. Marina Schiano was in charge of pulling the party off and it was she who organised the ship, vetoed the overzealous party decorator who was insisting on gold lamé sails, agreed to five thousand cattleya orchids, sent out eight hundred invitations, had a thousand-pound Buddha hoisted on board and arranged for $30,000 worth of fireworks to be set off during the night. Then, two weeks before the party happened, a fight broke out between Schiano, representing YSL, and Squibb.

No one quite knew what started the fight, but everyone knew about it because Schiano kept telling Squibb, over and over again, that if it was not settled she would resort to the house of Saint Laurent's deadly weapon: the Yves Saint Laurent no-show. Yves' presence, always a precious commodity, was becoming increasingly so, augmenting in direct proportion to his ever-diminishing public appearances. By 1977 he was in a state of semi-recluse, hidden between Rue de Babylone and his studio at Avenue Marceau. The mere sighting of Yves in his car being whisked home by the driver for lunch at Rue de Babylone warranted a write-up in the press during these years. The eternal 'will he, won't he' be there was a source of endless power and control for Yves, and for Pierre too, on the occasions when he was able to resolve that question himself.

The threat of Yves not turning up to launch his own perfume in New York was, not surprisingly, enough to bring a grown executive to his knees, and Squibb rushed to acquiesce to all the Saint Laurent demands and Yves flew to New York for the party. Significantly the New York launch of Opium was the first party of these years where the primary intention was to throw a party to sell and promote, rather than a party to celebrate. It was a huge and irreversible step: Tupperware socialising – give or take the decorative detail of five thousand cattleya orchids – had arrived in fashion.

The name Opium provoked significant fighting and protest in the US among both anti-drug-abuse campaign groups and the Chinese American population. The controversy and free publicity had Pierre and Yves crying all the way to the bank as the sales roared, reaching $100 million a year, while their personal royalties on the fragrance were believed to be earning them around $2.5 million per year.

It seemed that fashion and designers were basking in endless amounts of cash. By this time even Kenzo, he of the free spirit, ethnic knits and toothy grin, was making considerable amounts of money, with an overall sales volume of $10 million in 1977. Perhaps that was not so surprising; it is after all an unspoken understanding of aspiring fashion designers that they will one day be rich and famous. They do not make fashion to remain unknown, penniless and having to sleep on the floor under the pattern-cutting table. Kenzo was no exception to that rule. When Maxime de la Falaise had asked him a few years before in *Interview* magazine if he wanted to be a millionaire, or indeed was he one already, Kenzo giggled. 'I like money very much,' he admitted, 'but to spend it, not to look at it.' In Paris the accumulation process had begun.

French ready-to-wear looked to the USA as the new promised land for making money. It was to New York that the models and photographers went to earn serious fees. In 1977 there was an exodus of young European photographers leaving Paris to go and work there, led by Patrick Demarchelier and Tony Richardson and followed by photographer's agent Xavier Moreau and model agent John Casablancas later that year. They went to avoid the climbing income-tax rate in France and the stifling social charges. 'We all went because Patrick told us we were going to earn lots of money,' says Xavier Moreau. 'Life in the US then for Europeans was magic, like walking out of a cartoon from the 1950s with a huge car, house in Long Island, studios in Carnegie Hall. The market was so open there, we could do great business, straight away.'

New York's own home-grown fashion designers Calvin Klein, Halston and Donna Karan were all making headlines and money with their thoroughly modern and refreshingly casual design vision and their increasingly varied roster of licences. There was a host of 'bridge lines' – affordable, accessible fashion – springing up in the USA to satisfy the demands of a burgeoning fashion middle-market.

Even more significant to the future of Paris was the fact that Milan was breeding a new generation of fashion designers. During 1977 there were several articles in the French fashion press praising the considerable design talent and innovation of new young names such as Giorgio Armani, Walter Albini and Gianni Versace. The Milan designers benefitted from the support and infrastructure of brilliant as well as highly competitive textile producers based in Prato and a manufacturing industry that were to prove vital to their development as fashion brands. Many of the licensed lines that the French fashion houses had contracted out were now being manufactured in Italy.

The licensing and perfume bonanza continued, but all the signs were there that the hegemony of Paris as fashion capital was about to be challenged, although at this moment there were very few who heeded the warnings. John Fairchild returned from Milan one season and sat down to lunch in Paris with Pierre Bergé. He told Bergé of the Italians' accelerating prowess and warned him of their ambitions in fashion. Pierre snorted with derision and replied, 'Italians don't make fashion, Italians make spaghetti!'

★

It was not only in fashion but also at night that Paris claimed it still held the edge. In March 1978 Fabrice Emaer, owner of Le Sept, opened Le Palace nightclub and Parisian parties took on a new dimension. Housed in a theatre built in 1923, Le Palace was located just off the *grands boulevards*, amid the hot dogs and sunken grime of the Faubourg Montmartre. It was the Parisian answer to Studio 54, which had opened the year before in New York, although Fabrice insisted that Le Palace was to be everything Studio 54 was not.

Fabrice found New York's vortex of disco hedonism magical but overly sanitised for his tastes. 'It is completely sterilised, a ghetto for model agencies and Régine's emirs,' he said, referring to Parisian night-club owner Régine's rich Arab clients and describing the clientele as 'totally clean, beautiful, they look like they are fed on best quality corn'. 'If that is elegance,' he said with a tart smile, 'then it's obvious the Palace cannot and does not want to rival that.' Fabrice knew the excitement at the Palace lay, as in the Pigalle dancehalls of old, in the mix.

He hired a team of party organisers and press relations to run the gigantic club and spent over fifteen million francs on refurbishing it. Claude Aurensan from Le Sept was the man on the floor, Guy Cuevas was to be DJ, with strict instructions to play anything as long as it was disco, and Elie Schulman was in charge of pulling off the strong pop and rock cultural thrust that Fabrice envisaged for Le Palace. He succeeded: over the years the club would feature a line-up of live perform-ances by Prince, The Clash, Talking Heads, Blondie, Garry Numan, UB40 and OMD.

The Palace opened in March, and on that first night Grace Jones stepped up on stage at 4 a.m. and sang 'La Vie en Rose', an appropriate song for a time when life seemed so rosy-hued that even the coke had turned a shade of pale pink. They called it Bolivian officers' coke – it was more expensive, more delicious, more of it, more effective. Mix it up with cocktails of Chivas Royal, add mescaline to taste.

By now the need to party was insatiable. 'I went out every night from 1975 to 1980, seven nights a week,' remembers Christian Lvowksi, 'and if I didn't go out on the Sunday night someone would ring me to ask me if I was ill.' Throughout 1978 and 1979 there were a host of huge, themed, fancy-dress balls, all of which were linked in some way to fashion, including Karl Lagerfeld's Venetian Ball. For, more than anything in this great communal orgy of desire and narcissism, it was fashion that excited the fantasies of this micro-society, fashion that promised to fill the void.

Fashion designers, models and muses – they were all stars now. Yves, Kenzo, Karl, Jerry, Pat, Loulou, Betty, Jacques, these were the names that made a Paris night happen. Designers were entertaining on a grand scale, hosting dinners and weddings and parties at their homes or paying for parties for the masses in the clubs. Fashion shows had become social entertainment events that people clamoured to attend. Thierry Mugler, Claude Montana and Jean Paul Gaultier were the three young designers of a new Palace generation that everyone was talking about. Their shows were spectacles of lasers, music, choreography and spotlight on a star, an extension of the party from the night before. Photographers now staked out every inch of the fashion runway.

Fabrice had long recognised the power of fashion to excite and in April of 1978 he asked Loulou and Thadée Klossowski to officially open Le Palace with a masked ball. They chose *Anges et Démons* as their theme and Fabrice spent $50,000 on the night. Before the ball Marie-Hélène de Rothschild threw Loulou and Thadée an intimate dinner for fifty guests at her new home, Hôtel Lambert on the Ile Saint Louis. Built by Le Vau in 1640, bought by the Baron de Rothschild in 1975, the Hôtel Lambert is perhaps the most magnificent *hôtel particulier* in Paris. Perched at a divide of the Seine, like the prow of a ship, it is a gracious house of rotundas and golden stone.

The dinner was high-spirited and took place in the Galerie d'Hercule, beneath Le Brun's ceiling depicting the labours undertaken by Hercules. Marie-Hélène insisted guests come to the dinner in full fancy dress and so Loulou darted round the room dressed as a fallen angel in her black and red flame-printed mousseline, with eyes covered in stage make-up and a pair of huge red-feathered wings clanging around on her back. Thadée was her heavenly angel in white trouser suit, wrapped in gold cord, head encircled with lilies and wearing feathered wings to match those of Loulou. Betty and François arrived in dinner jackets – twin black *smokings* and Irish beau Patrick O'Higgins flew in from New York to make a late entry into dinner dressed in a cardinal's full scarlet regalia, gown unbuttoned to reveal black stilettos, fishnet stockings and suspenders with a copy of *Playboy* magazine sticking out of the top of one of his stockings. 'It was all done so lightly, and to be having this wild, hilarious time at the Hôtel Lambert, that was the insouciant side of these last years,' remembers François Catroux with pleasure.

At around midnight they left in a fleet of cars and taxis to plunge into the guts of Paris and slum it on the *faubourgs* of Parisian life. On the Faubourg Montmartre the street was heaving with the crowd waiting to get into Le Palace. First you had to get past Paquita Paquin and Edwige, who stood at the doors every night and decided whether they would let you enter this fragile paradise. Their decision was dependent on whether you were beautiful enough, rich enough, weird enough, punk enough, whether you could cut it as a star.

Inside there was the beat of disco throbbing against red velvet, backstreet and baron, the collision of wealth and sweat that was a source of mutual exhilaration. 'Le Sept was for the happy few,' says Guy Cuevas. 'It was very gay. You could get in as long as you were beautiful in some way; you didn't have to be famous or rich, you had to be *beau*. So that meant some young unknown gigolo could get in because you knew Claudia Cardinale was going to like the look of him. At the tables you might find an old guy playing cards, the King of Sweden in a corner, Francis Bacon in another, Helmut Berger or Karl Lagerfeld. But then at Le Palace all of a sudden you had to fill it up and so it turned into a party of humanity, everyone was there. It became larger than life. I remember one night they didn't even recognise the King of Sweden and they turned him away. Eventually he got in and he was alongside Régine and Maurice Béjart on the dance floor and then there was a bunch of naked drag queens with huge Dolly Parton silicone breasts. There was a drag-queen fight and someone smashed a glass in one of the breasts and it exploded and there was water and blood everywhere.'

There was something disorientating about Le Palace, something vertiginous. Le Sept was the size of an apartment; there was room for 150 people at most to cram inside and only about 40 of those could make it on to the carpet-sized dance floor. Le Palace could hold thousands, and some nights there were up to four thousand people; the dance floor, the converted orchestra pit, was so big you could roller-skate round it. There were streams of people milling around in the corridors, tiered boxes and the stage and you had to queue for hours to get upstairs and down.

'Le Palace has only one fault and that is it is not a sexual place,' said Fabrice Emaer in 1980. 'At Le Sept when you fancy a boy you can always find each other again during the night. At Le Palace you lose sight of him, he disappears.' Fabrice was wrong: it wasn't that Le Palace wasn't sexual – there was sex going on all over the place and at all times of the night. What was different was the boundless anonymity of the place. Who were these people? Who was that guy you fancied, had sex with and walked away from? No one knew.

By the time Marie-Hélène's select party turned up at Le Palace, Karl and his entourage of Jacques, Anna and Vern Lambert were already there, inside the club and in position. Karl was dressed as Merlin the Magician: he had pinned a Josephine Baker beaded dress to his black suit to look like a long, shimmering beard; he wore a black wizard's hat, black gloves, black sunglasses and a large diamond brooch at his neck. Kenzo was screaming round in white tights and white bodysuit covered in feathers, as a bird of paradise. Yves arrived late, having reneged on the Rothschild dinner. He was dressed in demure black tie and sat drinking champagne with his mother. Since Yves' illness Lucienne had reappeared as his chaperone at night and she had already accompanied him to Loulou's wedding party at the Bois de Boulogne. Later Yves did put on his costume, which consisted of a strange mask fit for a pagan ritual that he had designed himself of feathers, twigs and wood bark that covered his head entirely.

Jacques too wore a mask; beaked and feathered, it obscured his eyes but not his beard, so that he was still recognisable. He had on a mini-feathered costume from which his bare arms and legs protruded. He had feathered cuffs at his wrists and Robin Hood suede boots on his feet. He chose to be Icarus from the *Metamorphoses*, the son of Daedalus who recklessly ignored his father's advice and flew too close to the sun whilst flying to escape imprisonment on the island of Crete.

And Loulou the muse was running at full speed. She was drinking and dancing, wild and giddy, carrying the party and the whole great fantasy of Paris fashion on her slight frame. As Thadée said at this time, 'I wouldn't be at all surprised if her name suddenly appeared in lights on the Eiffel Tower.' She ended the night at 7.30 a.m., after the crowds had gone home, dancing among a handful of friends in a mad, whirling, Isadora Duncan spin to the sounds of *The Damnation of Faust*.

Her role at the house of Saint Laurent and in Paris had entered a new phase. She had gone from being the hippie chick stoned out of her mind in her crushed purple velvet flares to something more significant. The fact that Marie-Hélène de Rothschild, who really was the apex of Paris society, threw a dinner for her was indicative of her social importance.

As Yves disappeared from public view, Loulou came increasingly to represent Yves Saint Laurent in the eyes of Paris and the rest of the social and fashion world. In terms of image she was the living embodiment of his collections: one season she was Ballets Russes in Cossack hat and boots, the next Opium in gold tassels and pagoda shoulders, and by 1978 she had emerged as the incarnation of Saint Laurent's absolute chic Broadway collection.

As well as reflecting his image, Loulou was counted on to perform the role of animating Yves' ever more solitary life. 'Loulou and Betty were really the only two doors he had to the outside world,' says Michel Klein. 'Loulou would put herself out there, while Betty was much more reserved,' explains Madison Cox. 'Loulou is very fragile but she pushes everything.'

Loulou was up high and swinging from the trapeze for all to see and wonder at. 'I've always been fairly fearless,' says Loulou now, 'and at the same time fairly shy because I'm quite a private sort of person. I'm quite good at giving but I'm not so good at taking. When you give it's quite easy to be brave and outgoing; it's harder to accept gifts.'

She was giving her all to Yves and fashion. Yves breathed the outside world from Loulou, her stories of the escapades of the night before, her dress and poise, her friends – Bruce Chatwin, Kenzo, Berry Berenson, Halston and Robert Mapplethorpe. 'I think that Yves lived vicariously through Loulou,' says Madison, 'because she really personified the it girl; she was not just a party girl, it was more than that. I will never forget the first time that I met her in this loft in downtown NY in about 1977. She had on gold lamé boots with gold tassels going up them and the fur trim, the Russian top from the Ballets Russes collection. She was like something out of *Scheherazade*, she was mesmerising. For me she had the same effect as Les Ballets Russes must have had on Paris when they first arrived, she was unlike anything else. She had an incredible fantasy and fairy-tale-like quality to her. I can remember when they were making the costumes for that Le Palace party in the Saint Laurent studio and seeing them all there, making things up, it was truly like children putting on a home musical.'

Every so often she had to get out of town, go to Zurich for what was described as 'a rest' to get over a liver infection. She was there in February 1980 and met for lunch with Andy Warhol, who was staying at the Dolder Grand Hotel overlooking the lake. He was in town to paint portraits for private commissions. Warhol recorded the meeting and their conversation in his diary: 'Loulou told us that YSL really was such a genius that he just can't take it, he has to take a million pills and the whole office gets so depressed when he's depressed except for her. She said she acts happy no matter what. That's why she gets sick, because she's always trying to act happy and it's really a lot of stress on her liver. She hasn't had a drink in a year and a quarter but she doesn't think cocaine is bad.'

And then after two weeks away, Loulou would run back up the stairs of the couture house and into the studio, dressed with steely panache, sharp black leather jacket, waist cinched in a man's belt, man's white shirt, tartan scarf and diamond and jade earrings, lipstick carefully applied, something shiny on her brow-bone, a brave smile, bringing inspiration. 'She was like a little elf, English, charismatic. She wasn't going to be tamed. She could always be an inspiration and a challenge,' says Hélène de Ludinghausen, former director of the couture salon. 'She walked so easily around him, in that English way, she had the courage of being tactless, the lightness of de-dramatising things with humour and cattiness. And that combination made it all bubbly.'

She was more resilient than her appearance might suggest. As Pierre Bergé remarked in 1978, 'I don't know how Yves and Loulou do it, going out night after night until seven in the morning. I have good health, and I couldn't do it. Yves does not have good health, but he drinks and can go on like that and still function the next day. I would have to sleep for days to recuperate. But Yves and Loulou are deceptive. They look wan and frail, but they have cores of metal inside.'

Loulou was protected by her own instinct for self-preservation: 'I've never liked people who pull me down to sinister things which I don't understand. I lived through it as a child so I've always kept way out of that. I've always been more of a dancing, fun-time person with very great friendships.'

According to both Loulou and Thadée, it was the couture house and its structure of working life and being part of a team and the workings and discipline of the studio that sustained her as Paris slid into excess. 'I always went to work every day of my life, which probably saved me too. I've always had this thing whereby however little sleep I got, and sometimes it was none at all, I had to get to work, so whatever state I was in I would turn up. I've always been fairly conscientious, oddly enough. I've never wanted to be kept by a man. I've always wanted to be independent and look after myself, so I think that makes one quite resilient in a way and you sort of bounce back without quite knowing how.'

Chapter 15

1978—81

A year after Loulou and Thadée's wedding it was Paloma's turn to be bride. She became engaged to Rafael López Sánchez and Karl offered to host the wedding party at his house on the Rue de l'Université in May 1978. The Picasso inheritance had finally been settled in September of 1977 and Paloma had received her $20 million as well as the two hundred works by Picasso that she chose when the family drew lots to divide the mass of paintings, drawings and ceramics her father left. She was still designing jewellery, while Rafael was writing plays. His optimistically titled *Success* opened in Paris that year to less than optimistic reviews. Rafael was not universally welcomed by Paloma's friends, who disliked his domineering ways. She was aged twenty-nine and Rafael thirty.

There was another fast civic service followed by a full-blown wedding banquet. There was more dressing up and high fantasy. Karl turned up to the *mairie* in the seventh *arrondissement* in swashbuckling mode. He had on a chalk pinstriped three-piece suit, a big black bow at his neck and he wore large dark glasses — his newest style mannerism. His trousers were tucked into a pair of knee-high riding boots with a wide cuff folded over, highwayman style. Anna Piaggi wore a suit that was borrowed from a Visconti film set, with tiny puffed shoulders, violets in her pockets, a cane in her hand and on her head a purple silk hat with gold lace veil; she was channelling Proust for all she was worth. Loulou and Thadée meanwhile were channelling chic. Thadée wore Prince of Wales check with open shirt and one hand tucked in his jacket pocket. His wife was his perfect visual foil and dashing in hound's-tooth jacket, glazed straw boater, white skirt with vertical black edge, black narrow belt, both hands thrust carelessly into pockets for effect. They paused on the *mairie* steps before the crowd of photographers. Inside they found the mayor's assistant, who, perhaps not wanting to be outshone, had painted on two arched and exaggerated eyebrows and was wearing a rather fetching wig.

The bride, ever the diplomat, chose Saint Laurent by day and Karl Lagerfeld by night. Saint Laurent had made her a ruffled blush-red satin shirt with a bow that trailed down her skirt, an ivory jacket which she wore with a spotted black handkerchief in her pocket, and a crown of leaves and flowers around her head. She was glowing and delighted.

At the end of the ceremony, as the guests filed out of the room, Pierre Bergé and Karl stayed on, sitting next to each other, deep in conversation. 'What is this love affair?' asked an incredulous Loulou. André Leon Talley, who was a wedding guest and reporting for *W* magazine, commented that Bergé and Lagerfeld 'haven't been on intimate terms for years' and 'until the wedding day, would rather have been sealed in separate coffins than been seen sitting in the same room'.

There was a strained pretence of *politesse* between Yves, Pierre and Karl throughout the day. 'We all used to see each other for great periods, then everyone would split due to the strong personalities,' said Loulou that day. 'This marriage is not only a union of Paloma and Rafael but it brings together good friends. I only hope it will last. Basically, their friendships are irrevocable because Yves and Karl spent their youth in Paris together.'

Afterwards at the wedding banquet Yves and Karl stepped around each other in a show of courtly consideration. 'And what I love is that Paloma chose a Saint Laurent suit for the day. It was perfection for the situation, and she looked exquisite,' Karl told *W* magazine. Yves returned the compliment. 'Karl is someone I've known for over twenty years. And I think his look with the boots he wore at the mayor's today was one of the chicest things I've seen for a man in years. I find his dress for Paloma ravishing, sublime. We did parallels in red for her but with sharp, contrasting points of view, which is only normal. And this dinner is a dream,' he said, sitting in Karl's huge candlelit salon.

It was the first time Karl had opened up his home for such a large party and guests were mighty impressed by what they saw, both the size of the apartment and the luxury of the furnishings. The main table seating forty guests was in the Four Seasons room and there was a huge centrepiece of fruits and honeysuckle that spread out in banks across the table. Cascades of ivy hung from every chandelier. Guests ate roast pigeon, followed by a strawberry mousse-cake. 'We are not bourgeois, so there is no wedding cake,' said Lagerfeld. Serge Lifar gave the wedding speech – an exceptional dancer of the Ballets Russes, once protégé of Diaghilev, choreographer and former *maître de danse* of the Opéra, the dashing Lifar was also a great friend of Paloma's father and had known Paloma since she was a baby.

Paloma's dress was made of lipstick-red satin. 'I made a dress which looks like two hearts, but I actually wanted something that was a cross between a Greek vase and a Brancusi sculpture, something timeless,' explained Karl. The dress had a puffy crinoline effect beneath the skirt. Yves was curious to see how it was constructed and so Paloma lifted her skirt so that he could take a look underneath.

Jacques was there, of course. He had grown a beard and on his lapel he wore a cascade of amber-coloured cattleya orchids, his own Proustian reference. He was wearing a stiff and impossibly high detachable collar, just like the ones Karl wore.

Anna Piaggi reappeared at night as a kind of dancehall Boudicca, with a dress of silver lamé and red ostrich feathers and a metal helmet on her head bearing three ostrich feathers. Brushing past a mantelpiece charged with silver candelabra, the feathers in her helmet caught fire, provoking screams all around her. Anna, however, kept her fashion sang-froid.

Karl looked around him and was, at last, content. 'This whole scene reminds me of a painting my mother gave me at five by Menzel. It was a scene at the court of Frederick the Great at Sans Souci,' he said in a familiar refrain, this time allowing a reproduction to be taken for the original.

After the dinner, next stop was Le Palace, where Fabrice had laid on the obligatory after-wedding party with a special flamenco theme. To start the night he had organised female wrestlers who, somewhat incongruously, got up on stage and wrestled to the sounds of *Carmen*. They must have had a giddy effect on both Karl and Yves, for the next moment the two rivals stood up and danced flamenco together. The party ended at dawn, and with it the cease-fire.

1978 was a pivotal year in Karl Lagerfeld's personal life and career. It was a huge social coup to host Paloma Picasso's wedding and his personal notoriety and image received a tremendous boost. But it was also the year his mother died.

Elisabeth Lagerfeld died at the Château de Penhoët in September at the age of eighty-one. All those who have known Karl for any length of time insist on the importance of this woman to Karl's life and person, but few can pinpoint or agree exactly what her role or influence was. The personality of Elisabeth Lagerfeld as witnessed in Paris was much obscured by the past that her son bestowed on her. She was, according to various close Lagerfeld sources (past and present), and in no particular order, a woman from a *grand bourgeois* diplomatic background, an actress, an aristocrat, a divorcee, a believer in clairvoyants, a woman of couture and private wealth.

Karl portrayed her as veering hazardously between doting on him as her only son and driving him mercilessly with her ambitions and harsh and acerbic judgements. Karl has often explained his habit of speaking so fast as a result of his mother's lack of patience with her son: 'I talked a lot and my mother started to leave the room when I began a story, so I had to learn to finish the story by the time she got to the door,' he said. It is impossible to know where the reality of Elisabeth Lagerfeld lay. Karl's childhood next-door neighbour Karl Wagner remembers her as 'strict, very correct, very straight, but not arrogant' and as a housewife who looked after the husband, children and home. 'She was nice to everyone, the staff and the POWs. She had her demands and she stuck to them.'

However, the late Kurt Lagerfeld, Karl's cousin and favourite nephew of Karl's father, who knew Elisabeth Lagerfeld over a period of more than forty years, paints a rather less favourable picture. 'Strong,' he said between tight silences. 'I didn't like her much. There are lots of memories that she evokes.' According to Kurt Lagerfeld there was considerable tension between this second wife and Otto Lagerfeld's own family, who found her controlling and money-seeking. In Kurt's eyes she was domineering towards her husband, children and, where she could, the rest of the family. 'She was very bossy, a very overbearing woman. She was keen he [Karl] should make a career for himself.'

Kurt Lagerfeld remembered going to visit Karl's father shortly before his death in Baden-Baden at a time when Karl happened to be visiting too. Kurt and the father sat in one room and Karl and his mother went off to sit in another room. 'They were crazy about fashion. My uncle Otto was basically a commercial man, a businessman, he thought nothing of fashion, so the two who weren't interested in fashion sat together and the two who were could go and talk elsewhere.'

After Otto Lagerfeld's death in 1968 Karl's mother came to live with him in Paris, where Karl gave her a set of rooms in his various apartments, until eventually she moved to live in Brittany at the Château de Penhoët when she became ill. Elisabeth Lagerfeld appears in witness accounts of these years in Paris as a ubiquitous if indefinable presence. She was always at Rue de l'Université when models turned up for fittings, drinking tea, sitting in an armchair, surrounded by piles of books, watching the goings-on.

'She was so cold, that is one thing that I could sense when I met her, and very rigid,' says Paloma Picasso. 'She must have been extremely hard on him, very demanding, very stern.' 'She was the epitome of the castrating mother,' says another close friend of the time. The mother's rigidity and Karl's devotion to her seem to be the two constants in descriptions of the relationship between Elisabeth Lagerfeld and her son. 'He was fascinated, in awe of her. I never saw anyone look at their mother like that with adoration in their eyes,' says Diane de Beauvau-Craon.

And then she died, three days after Karl's forty-fifth birthday. He did not go to the funeral, just as he had not gone to the funeral of his father. Later, much later, Karl would tell American *Vogue* that it was his mother who made sure he did not attend her funeral, just as she had made sure he did not attend his father's funeral. In the article Karl's mother is described as being 'an aristocrat whose salad days had been in the 1920s' and Karl told the journalist that after her death, 'I never saw her. She left a paper to say I was not allowed to see her dead. Or go to her funeral.' In the same interview Karl also says that when his father died his mother didn't tell him of the death for weeks, so that by the time she did it was too late and the funeral was over. Karl recalls his mother saying to him, 'You don't like funerals. Why should I tell you?' Whatever the reason, Karl's absence at the funeral of his father and beloved mother is a striking reaction of denial in the face of death and calls to mind something a former colleague says of Karl: 'If you want to understand Karl, you have to understand his fear of death. He cannot bear sickness. If he has a cold it is this huge drama. He cannot stand the idea of someone sitting next to him with germs. He talks about the future non-stop because when he looks at the past he realises that life is behind him and there is only a small portion ahead. This is what makes him work so hard. He hates the idea of being confronted with himself.' Karl himself, when asked by a German newspaper what scared him, replied, 'Illness – I don't like anything I can't dominate.'

Elisabeth Lagerfeld must have held her son in check in some way; perhaps her authoritarian grip was even a source of reassurance for him, for he suffered acutely now from her absence. Her death unleashed in him a vein of angst and self-loathing. He started eating again, putting on considerable amounts of weight; he could not stop his consumption of Coca-Cola and chocolates. There was a permanent cheese-mountain on his desk in the Chloé studio, slices of Gruyère between cellophane kept within a fingertip's reach.

Gaby Aghion noticed a significant change in his behaviour and identifies this time as the beginning of the breakdown in their working relationship. 'All of a sudden he became very difficult. If I wasn't there for the fittings, he held it against me. I was very busy at the time too. And so there was a kind of small separation even then between us.'

It was from this time on that Karl began to gain a reputation for venting his jealousy and spleen in public. It was the beginning of his tirades against haute couture, which would be repeated throughout these years, telling people that couture was irrelevant, dried up and démodé. He frequently declared his disinterest in having a fashion house of his own, telling the press that he simply did not have the pretension to put his name above the door of his own house.

In the documentary Top Ten Designers in Paris, which was made a year later, Lagerfeld insists upon his aversion to haute couture in a frenzied monologue that he delivers in a breathless fifteen seconds. 'I don't want to design for one special type of client. I want to design for an idea of a woman, more than for a typical client what [sic] I don't like. It's too commercial an idea. You must not flatter your clientele, you must design what you feel and not what you think will please your clientele, so I think it's quite dangerous; that's even one of the reasons I don't want to have a fashion house, because then you have to design for private clients. What I like to do is for private persons, for actresses or people I know, do dresses for fun but to make a collection for a special clientele; that is not a very creative and a very modern fashion idea.'

Often his fashion pronouncements seemed to be criticisms of Yves Saint Laurent and they were certainly interpreted as such. He was deeply aware of Saint Laurent's fashion triumphs, but then it was hard not to be: Yves was still unassailable. In December 1976 Karl wrote to Anna Piaggi enclosing a gift of a pretty orange corset, explaining that he had withdrawn it from his Chloé collection after Saint Laurent had designed corsets for his own couture collection. When Saint Laurent showed a spencer jacket (a short open jacket with lapels) in his Broadway couture collection of January 1978, Karl let it be known among the press that he himself had done spencer jackets for Chloé the season before.

But that was the thing about Saint Laurent. Even when he was not the first to have the idea, when he turned his eye and hand to it he made it non-negotiable, a blockbuster, made it Saint Laurent lore. The spencer jacket is a fine example of this: both Lagerfeld and Claude Montana had indeed featured a spencer jacket in their collections the season before Yves, but Yves Saint Laurent's Broadway collection effectively obliterated theirs. He threw a curve at the lapel that was ease and elegance, chopped the trouser at the ankle to balance the silhouette, made it a black woman's collection of Southern colours and elegance, played the *Porgy and Bess* soundtrack, put his dog on the stage, had the crowds foot-stomping and roaring, so that by the end of the couture collection only Saint Laurent's vision remained.

In 1978 Pierre Bergé staged a production of *L'Aigle à deux têtes* at his Théâtre de l'Athénée. Buying the theatre was the first step in Pierre's exploration of his own interests beyond fashion and beyond Yves. He organised weekly musical nights there on Mondays, where he was to be seen manning the ticket box in flamboyant style. Yves designed the costumes and the set for the Cocteau play, which, together with the production, were harshly reviewed by the French press.

Victoire went to see the play and during the interval she went backstage to find Yves, whom she had not seen for several years. 'I knocked on the door and pushed it open. There he was, sitting all alone at a table, head in his hands. He was a broken man. He looked up and said, "Is that you, *chérie*?" and then we hugged each other. But then immediately the door opened and Pierre came in, followed by Anne-Marie Muñoz, and they came between us.'

Yves, aged forty-two, had entered the tunnel of excess. He was drinking vast amounts – later he confessed to Victoire that at his worst he was drinking four litres of pastis a day. He smoked 120 cigarettes a day. 'He never did anything by halves,' Victoire told *Paris Match*. 'When he drank it was in the manner of Modigliani. It wasn't depression that made him ill, but it was this self-destructive urge.'

He was absent from the couture house for longer and longer periods of time. When he came back there were bad days that stretched into bad weeks, with Saint Laurent sitting in a crumple at his desk, immobile, crushing all around him with his silence and despondency. The whole studio was entangled in the impossible wrangling of Pierre and Yves, a relationship that now played out like a kind of bad Jacobean drama. They worked together but lived apart. They each had their own lovers, but they argued and bickered and bullied as a couple still linked by love and possession. 'In the end, the trouble was the very exhausting atmosphere of anguish, the psychological problems of someone invading your own life to that extent. I would get fed up with him and Pierre,' said Loulou after it was all over. 'I couldn't stand them because they were very heavy people to live with and I'd come home exhausted, emotionally and nervously rather than because I'd been working hard.'

The stories of Yves' attention-seeking theatrics are legion. The days when he sat head buried in his desk, not talking, inconsolable until finally Loulou or Madame Muñoz would search out technical director Jean-Pierre Derbord in the office next door and say, 'Please, Jean-Pierre, you try, we've tried everything.' 'And then,' says Derbord, 'I would go in and say, "Bonjour, Monsieur Saint Laurent," and he would be sitting there, head up, smiling, all bright and cheery.'

There was his unnerving habit of pretending to fall asleep halfway through your sentence. Hélène de Ludinghausen remembers it happening to her both at dinners and in the studio. 'He'd be sitting there looking at me and suddenly he would go like that,' she says, pretending to drop off, 'and I would understand: oh, I see the story has ended, so either I must tiptoe off or I must try to salvage a vestige of pride by quickly coming up with something to say that that would lift his eye. Neurotic people are fantastic actors because it's the only way to minimise or maximise a situation. Nothing bores these people more than something normal, so it either has to be kind of nothing or something fantastic, but if it is just this . . . then it is boring. "*Quel ennui*," that's about the worst thing Yves can say about someone. "Ah, what a bore he is, oh la, la,"' she says, imitating Yves' horror.

In the run-up to the collection the anxiety for every one of them, from Loulou and Anne-Marie in the studio to the ladies in the ateliers physically making the clothes, was at breaking point. There were silences before the mirror as the model and the premier of the atelier came into the studio for the fitting. Madame Felisa and model Mounia tiptoed in and Yves would be slumped at his desk with a look of dismal emptiness in his eyes, cigarette burning in an endless silence that no one dared to break before the master had spoken. Ten minutes went by in silence, the pain of his displeasure everywhere, to be relieved finally by Saint Laurent himself saying with infinite politeness, 'Thank you, we will look at that later.'

That was the dismissal. You left with the excruciating pain that you had disappointed him. He idealised you to such an extent that it was unbearable to break that spell. It was terrifying how much you wanted to please him. 'We accepted everything from him,' says Jean-Pierre Derbord. 'We marvelled at him throughout, we were under his domination and above all we didn't want to disappoint him, we had entered into his game. Why did we accept that? For love and our own masochism, I suppose. We were his accomplices.' Derbord worked for Yves Saint Laurent for thirty-seven and a half years. He has retired now from the house, and Derbord's apartment, like those of so many who have been close to Yves, is a shrine to the man and his iconography. In his salon a replica of Saint Laurent's good-luck charm of faux-ruby and paste heart hangs from a bust, piled on the coffee-table are all the Saint Laurent books and tributes, behind the sofa are the sketches by Cocteau, in the hall the fashion sketches by Saint Laurent and there is, always burning, a heart-shaped 'Love' candle of the house of Yves Saint Laurent.

For there was not only the anxiety of working with Saint Laurent, there was also the overwhelming thrill, which goes a long way to explaining why at the end of his career over half of his 125 staff had been working for him for over twenty years. 'It was a bit like having a living god among us,' says Derbord. 'There was a huge power to his work, to his drawings and sketches and this incredible precision. He already knew what he was going to do, he could see it all in his head and then he communicated that to you, often without words. You sort of felt what he wanted.' All those around him learned his language, his vocabulary, they knew instinctively what a line on a sketch stood for and which silhouette, shoulder or sleeve Saint Laurent was searching for.

At the beginning of each couture collection the *premiers d'ateliers* would be invited into the studio by Madame Muñoz to look at Saint Laurent's sketches, they would pick several depending on their area of expertise, be that tailoring or *flou*, which means anything floaty or draped, like a mousseline dress or a silk blouse. Then they would carefully roll up the chosen sketches and take them back upstairs to the ateliers and start dividing them up among the *petites mains*, the ladies. 'We were so nervous. He would show us these beautiful sketches with such a light touch and I would think to myself, "Oh please, let me be able to make the outfit as he has drawn it, so I don't disappoint him," because he even idealised his sketches,' says Jean-Pierre Derbord. 'I used to lay out the toiles to be cut out on the first day, and then that night I would lie awake in bed thinking about it. It was totally obsessive. And then if you did manage to make the outfit in the way that you thought was close to expressing his original idea you felt this joy that was beyond all definition; it was as if you'd been handed the Château of Versailles. Working for Saint Laurent was like entering a religion, you gave of yourself completely; you shared his doubts, his pain, his joy.'

Downstairs in the salon it was Hélène de Ludinghausen who looked after the couture clients, greeting them, preparing each season's wardrobe, taking their orders and following every fitting and stage of the making of their outfits. Ludinghausen describes the compelling nature of being part of the Saint Laurent world: 'You felt that you were on top of the world when you were working for Yves Saint Laurent. There was no other house I would have wanted to work for and no other clothes I would have wanted to wear. There was this calm confidence of perfection.'

There were even days when flashes of Yves' humour would return and the studio became a place of laughter as before. 'Ohh, that looks a bit *prison de Melun*,' he would say, referring to a prison in the outskirts of Paris to describe one rather gloomy outfit subsequently ditched from the collection, or, 'But Madame Felisa, I asked for a *saucisson* and you have given me a dream.' Sometimes he would be stuck as to what to do and then he would come in with a drawing of a rather overblown outfit and say, 'Ahh, isn't this wonderful!' 'Then as the collection would go on he'd be more and more doubtful over the great idea he had had and then finally we'd see this very serious model coming in, frightfully proud with this absurd-looking outfit, and we would all get a fit of giggles and then the whole thing would be chucked away and off with this silly idea,' says Loulou de la Falaise.

'There were times when you were sick of it, you said to yourself that is enough, I've had it,' says Nicole Dorier, 'And then all of a sudden he is there, he comes to you and he says, "*Bonjour, ma Nicole.*" *Bon*, that was it, you were there for another year.' '*Bonjour, ma Nicole*': three words and his dusky, caressing tone; three words and the suggestion of intimacy, the hint of possession; Saint Laurent's seduction was for all sexes. 'There was a tenderness, a smile, a look, do you see what I mean? He was the big brother, the son, the boyfriend; he was all of those things in one. He never had that homosexual attitude that certain designers have with women, never him. Because in a way you could think he was completely open to women. He was never closed to women, he was open to their world.' He held that fascination in all their imaginations. Yves knew that. In 1991 he was talking about the relationship with his house models when he said, 'I speak very little with them but I really love them; they are all in love with me.'

It wasn't only the women: Yves' games of seduction kept all those around him dancing like motes of dust in his sunlight. The ceaseless crescendo of victory and depression made hostages of all those around him. Every collection was billed as the last. 'Every time, every single time, it was, Will he pull it off? Will he do it?' remembers Jacques Grange. 'We knew things were difficult. Will he do the collection? No! He's not well. Those of us close to him were privy to it all – the rumours, the whispers of the difficulties. And then every time it was POUM, POUM, POUM, on and on and on, magnificent and spectacular collections produced with such ease.'

The Saint Laurent entourage was now more than ever subject to his whims. Madison Cox recalls the hours of suspense in the aftermath of the Saint Laurent fashion shows, waiting for the dinner instructions. 'No one ever knew where it was going to be or what time it was going to happen, if *he* would be there. It was always a question of "whether Yves was up to it or not"! I remember one time being in Marina Schiano's hotel room at the Plaza Athénée. We were both completely dressed up in evening clothes, lying down on the bed, not daring to move for fear of wrinkling anything, waiting for the phone to ring and for Pierre to say, "Be at Maxim's in twenty minutes!"'

Yves' retreat from view during these years was in part practical: there were many times when he simply could not be seen in public, when the slurring of speech, stumbling and drunken state confined him to Rue de Babylone. There were years when even trying to get him from the car to the kerb was a challenge for Pierre Bergé. No doubt Pierre had his motives in not wanting Yves to be seen for reasons of press image, but there was also something self-inflicted about Yves' isolation.

There was the deliberate severing of the outside world: no reading of newspapers, no listening to the radio, no opening of post, no watching of news, just Me, Myself, I and Moujik, the bulldog, snoring on a cushion near by. John Fairchild recalls a conversation he had with Yves where he tried to pull him out of this solitary confinement. 'When he had a nervous breakdown I kept saying to him, "Yves, your problem is, you know, you are very much into yourself but you gotta live with life. You gotta go out and get your baguette and get your newspaper," I said, "and by the way, you'll enjoy it." He never did it of course.'

He never did it because Yves never did want to be dogged by a life of reality. Perhaps it was something in his upbringing. Certainly it is a sentiment his sister Brigitte Bastian not only understands but relates to: 'I am like Yves but in a different context. I don't want to be bored by day-to-day problems and I have my husband who is there to look after that side of life. I don't want to have to worry about booking an airplane ticket. Maman was just like us. It was Papa who did everything and she was thoroughly spoiled. Ask Yves if he knows how to use a computer. He doesn't. He's just like me. I've got a digital camera, an iPod, and I don't even know how to work them. We are idiots in that respect. We need people to look after us. It's not an easy life we want, it's a life without worries.'

Surely it was Yves who decided to allow Pierre to play his possessor and controller. He surrendered his life's franchise and in return he gained a life without the ennui of every day, a life in which he could explore his ambitions and creativity without ever a thought of having to pay a parking ticket. As Yves said with an extravagant sigh in 1991, 'You know what Proust said, nothing can interest a creator other than a work which is his own.'

And as the years wore on, so the entourage came to realise that all was not actually as they had seen. 'Finally came the realisation that actually Yves doesn't want to look after himself and that in fact it was Yves that created the situation and not Pierre,' says Paloma Picasso. 'Then also realising that when Pierre was not around, whoever was next to him had to take on Pierre's role. Yves makes you responsible for him. He's always been afraid of the world and always needed to be in his ivory tower.'

And that was not the only revelation that Paloma and others witnessed during these years of affliction. Paloma remembers: 'It took me a few years to go from believing that Yves was a total angel to realising that he was not, that he had a lot of strengths in him and also a lot of aggression that was not very often expressed in the everyday world, but in certain incidents and in very secluded environments you could actually even see his violence directly.

'Finally I started seeing that whatever violence was around him was very often created by him, but never directly. So it was never Yves that was perceived as aggressive, always those around him, and obviously Pierre was number one as the aggressive person. But he's often triggered to be aggressive because he gets the message – however he gets it – from Yves and *l'appel du vide*.' If Yves and his propensity to be a kind of emotional black hole did trigger Pierre's aggression, there seemed to be an endless reserve of aggression to exploit.

After forty years of observing the relationship, the members of the Saint Laurent inner clan are now seemingly unanimous in their analysis of the division of power between these two men. 'No, Yves is not dominated,' says Betty Catroux, 'these are roles that have suited them both entirely.' 'Yves allows himself to be dominated on material subjects by Pierre, on life's organisation,' says Jacques Grange, 'but Pierre only executes Yves' orders, the unpleasant chores, all the disagreeable things in life that need to be done. Yves was not abused by Pierre, not at all. He is not dominated. He is sometimes a masochist, because he wanted it like that, he wanted it.'

Charlotte Aillaud shakes her head and smiles: 'Everything that has happened to Yves is a choice. That he has used Pierre to get where he wants is certain, that he has chosen to be dependent, it is all a choice. In every couple it is never the one that you believe imposes things in such an obvious way that does. The wilier of the two leads and with wile one can lead another even to do harm to you, if you so desire. So people look at them and repeat the old cliché over and over, "Oh, there was the baddie and the poor victim." No, no, that does not exist, not with these two figures. Yves is a rock, it is Pierre the tender one.'

Interestingly Pierre never tried to alter the outside world's view of his role. On and on in every journalist interview, every encounter, every day, he allowed himself to play and be portrayed in the role of baddie. Only in 2005, at the end of his career, will Bergé speak out when questioned on the truth behind the legend of the poor little prince locked away in the Rue de Babylone tower: 'I think that we can say it is the exact opposite of what people assume. I am not saying Saint Laurent is nasty, he is not. But I'm saying he was someone who wanted to be protected, who has always asked me to protect him, who has always said that he doesn't want to see anyone and that I must go before to tell them that he won't see anyone. I played the role that he wanted me to play and moreover he chose me to play that exact role. Yes, the one who was most imprisoned was me, but I was a voluntary prisoner. *Voilà!* But I will say one more thing and that is that I couldn't give a damn what people think.'

★

The enmity between the two clans was by now rigidly established. They hated each other and yet they could not live without each other. They saw each other at every major social event and party of these years and at Le Palace several nights a week. When Pierre ran into Jacques at night it was the opportunity for camp-edged drama and rage. 'Get that gigolo out of here!' Bergé shouted on finding Jacques installed on a banquette at Le Sept. A few years later at Le Palace Bergé turned to Diane de Beauvau-Craon, who had moved back to Paris, and said, 'So, I see you are still with that wax doll of Karl's.' Diane responded by throwing a glass of champagne in his face.

Jacques organised a birthday party for Kenzo in 1978, requesting guests to come dressed in drag. He sent out mauve and white engraved invitations covered with tiny violets wrapped in tissue-paper that read: 'Men like women and vices [sic] versa. A few days before the great anxiety, today's permissivity [sic] still allows us to give a den supper where we beg you to shine through your appropriate eccentricity or exquisite travesty . . .' The strangely worded invitation caused an outcry among the Saint Laurent group, who denounced Jacques' provocation. 'It's too disgusting and insulting to have received such a silly invitation,' said Thadée. Clara Saint tore up her invitation on receiving it. The Saint Laurent set vowed they would never attend. Although late at night at Le Palace, Loulou and Thadée did turn up to dance.

It was all unreasonably incestuous. Kenzo was great friends with Loulou, who was by now anti-Jacques, but Kenzo was also the boyfriend of Xavier de Castella, who was Jacques' best friend. Madison Cox went to a party at Jacques' house soon after his arrival in Paris in 1977. He happened to tell Clara and Pierre that he had been and they were appalled and told him never to go again, never to talk about it.

You were drawn into taking sides whether or not you had anything directly to do with the source of dispute in the first place. Anne-Marie Muñoz and Karl fell out bitterly, despite decades of friendship and the fact Karl was godfather to Anne-Marie's son. Andrée Putman had become an interior designer and was still a close friend of Karl and working on several projects for him, including a library at Penhoët. She was also designing the Saint Laurent ready-to-wear boutiques in America with considerable success and was a great friend of Didier Grumbach, who had left his family firm of Mendes to become president of Yves Saint

Laurent in America. One day Didier received an unexpected telex from Pierre Bergé: 'I leave your friend Andrée Putman in the arms of her friend Monsieur Lagerfeld, considering she has had the bad taste to work for him.'

Bergé came increasingly to inspire fear and awe. He was president of the Chambre Syndicale de la Couture for nine years until 1983 and he used it as a means to further not only the interests of Paris fashion but also his own and that of the house of Saint Laurent. With his substantial revenue assured (he signed the 190th licensing agreement in 1980) and Yves Saint Laurent as the source of enthralment, he was a mammoth power-broker both within fashion and, following his friendship with François Mitterrand in the 1980s, within the salons of the establishment.

'For me fashion is a reflection of power,' says Didier Grumbach, now himself president of the Chambre Syndicale de la Couture, 'so as Saint Laurent became weak, Pierre Bergé had to go out and fight for him, fight to increase the power of the brand. He did it by constantly bringing more and more people into the *famiglia*, he brought them into the Saint Laurent network and ultimately even the president of the republic became a servant of his cause.'

Karl Lagerfeld was one of the few in Paris who had the tenacity and bold-faced daring to stand up to Bergé; he was neither daunted nor bulldozed by him. Victoire believes that even in the late 1950s, when Bergé and Lagerfeld first met, there was a tension between the two men as, in her opinion, Bergé was unnerved by Karl's culture and knowledge and his highly developed sense of autonomy. 'Pierre knew that he wouldn't be able to make Karl into what he wanted and that didn't suit Pierre. He likes to dominate, but you cannot dominate Karl. *Ah non, ah non.*'

Designers have long had a problem with the concept of co-existence. Chanel and Schiaparelli sustained an enmity of vitriolic proportions for years. Chanel referred to Schiaparelli through gritted teeth as 'that Italian who makes clothes' and never once pronounced her name. Although interestingly Edmonde Charles-Roux, Chanel's biographer, identifies their antagonism as limited to the personal. 'They hated each other, but it remained very much a kind of society game,' she says, citing the arrival of men, financial backers and huge capital after the Second World War as introducing the real source of competition in fashion. Joan Juliet Buck describes Bergé and Lagerfeld's aggression in gender terms: 'Guys like to fight, you know, Pierre likes to fight, Karl likes to fight. It's very red in tooth and claw. It's all about aggression and testosterone, and where does that all go in a frilly context?' But surely all these fashion rivalries – whatever the gender – conceal the same unspoken dread: that by accepting another designer's vision of dressing as credible you obliterate your own.

From 1978 onwards Yves Saint Laurent's collections resounded with a different pitch and register from the previous years of hyper-creativity. In 1980 André Leon Talley questioned him about the glory days of the 1970s when he was out every night with his fabulous entourage and Saint Laurent cut him short with the words: 'That is all in the past and I don't want to repeat it. It was a marvellous period in my life. My evolution began in those days in the late '60s and early '70s. The whole world changed and so did we. I loved the change when customs, styles of dress, habits were being questioned and turned upside down.'

Over the next twenty years he stepped further and further away from fashion in its ceaseless appetite for the new, to cocoon himself instead in haute couture and the pursuit of his own perfection. 'I think the base of clothes for men and for women is definitively fixed for the twentieth century,' he said the following year. 'I believe this base will not change. There will be fashions that arrive, but they will be like fireworks; they will glow brightly in a burst and then sputter out.' He said this with the unerring confidence of a man who knew that it was he who was responsible for fixing so many of those abiding foundations of a woman's twentieth-century wardrobe.

He had given confidence to a generation of women finding their freedom. He had shown them how to dress to succeed in a man's world: shoulders and chic by day, seduction by night. But twelve years had passed since the student revolution and by 1980 women were experimenting with a whole new set of gender semantics: ideas of domination, deconstruction of clothing, even playing with the possibility of ugliness in faces and clothes.

These were not Saint Laurent's concerns. This new generation was not his and he made no secret of his disdain for its fashion. 'Today, the street is negative, dirty and dumb and, above all, senseless. I don't go out much, but if I see one or two punks, that's enough to understand,' he said in 1983, sounding like an old man with his pipe and slippers rather than the 47-year-old he in fact was. He went from *enfant terrible* to grandee couturier in the blink of an eye.

'I've always hated eccentricity and that's what most fashion is today. The gaiety and excitement of the early '70s was spontaneous and unpretentious. Today it is forced. Then there was a true revolution; today there is nothing but repetition.'

And so in the place of innovation there began a series of homage collections with tributes both to himself and to the work of the Parisian greats. There was a collection celebrating Sergei Diaghilev and his collaboration with Picasso, others dedicated to Braque, Matisse and Léger, Van Gogh and his paintings *Sunflowers* and *Iris*. There was the homage to Shakespeare in 1980 and to Cocteau and Aragon, as well as to Schiaparelli and her extraordinary Zodiac collection of 1938. These collections were feats of beauty and couture craft to be met by 'oohs' and 'aahs' rather than the cracked intake of breath that once greeted his luminous invention. He talked increasingly in a vocabulary of basics, classics and being committed to refining the 'pure YSL' style. From 1979 onwards he began to reference his own illustrious career, revisiting what he had already done to rework, rethink and refine. The Mondrian dress of 1965 reappeared as a jacket in the 1979 collection, a blouse and full skirt from the Opéra collection reappeared in 1980, there was the endless reworking of *le smoking*, *le blazer*, the trouser suit, safari jacket, *le trench* and the peacoat. And although these pieces lost the acme of timely appeal that they had possessed in their first incarnation, they never lost the power of their absolute line.

Yves, in the midst of his alcoholism, sought out new refuges for escape. Together Pierre and Yves bought another larger and more beautiful house in Marrakech, called Villa Oasis, which was surrounded by sumptuous gardens that they eventually opened to the public. And in 1979 they bought a nineteenth-century house in Normandy for a reported $5 million, which they then spent three years renovating. It was called Château Gabriel and Yves and Pierre both referred to it as such, although in reality it was a large and grand seaside villa with gabled roofs which looked out over the grey and opaque skies of Normandy. It was built by Ernest Saintin for an American in 1874, four years after the end of the Second Empire, and was architecturally indicative of all the over-stuffed ornamentation and aspirations for which that *époque* had stood.

Most enticing for Yves and Pierre, it was just behind the small town of Bénerville-sur-Mer and a couple of miles east of Cabourg, the town where Proust holidayed from 1907 to 1914. This stretch of coast was the inspiration and setting for much of Proust's *Within a Budding Grove*, in which the narrator and his grandmother board the 'little train' and set forth for a summer to be spent at the fictitious sea-side town of Balbec. Saint Laurent decided the house was to be his Proustian folly and asked Jacques Grange to 'recreate the ambiance of the country houses where his characters spent their summers'. Rather maddeningly, Proust had never actually stayed at the Château Gabriel, but his publisher Gaston Gallimard's mother used to live next door – as Yves and Pierre never tired of recounting. And by the time Jacques Grange finished with the decoration, getting through several kilometres of draped silk taffeta in the process, it was hard to believe Swann himself wasn't going to whip through the front door at any moment, dressed in white tie and tails. There was a stage-set feel to the house as everything in it had some sort of Proustian symbolism or Second Empire provenance. The *jardin d'hiver*, for instance, was modelled after that of Princess Mathilde Bonaparte, whose salon was frequented by Proust.

It was a villa and décor intended for large weekend house-parties of the Saint Laurent clan, grand dinners for twenty, although it would never be used as such. Perhaps it was the emptiness of the house, or the contrived references that gave it such a sorrowful atmosphere. There were nine bedrooms named after and decorated in the manner of Proust's characters, such as the Duchess of Guermantes, Madame Verdurin and Albertine, as well as Madeleine Lemaire, who was not a character but a salon hostess and real-life friend of the author – presumably included as a little trick question to sort the men from the boys in the *A la recherche du temps perdu* trivia test. The theme-park décor went as far as name-plates bearing the character's name on each of the bedroom doors. Most of these characters were assigned to the most appropriate person, depending on the guest list for the weekend. But the two main roles were set and typecast: Yves was of course Swann and Pierre the Baron de Charlus.

It was at Château Gabriel more than anywhere else that Yves could luxuriate in his overwhelming aestheticism, ordering up vast bouquets of garden roses to be transported from Paris by the van load for his solitary contemplation. The *jardin d'hiver*, a dimpled chintz conservatory that ran all the way along the back of the house, was Yves' favourite room, where he sat, dressed in bow-tie and cashmere, amid the lush and overwhelming profusion of white hortensias, amaralysis, ferns and mighty palms, staring for hours on end through the drizzle to the town of Deauville and the sea beyond. It seemed there was no future to Saint Laurent's life any more, only nostalgia and homage.

And yet there was exaltation to his loneliness and a deep seam of self-indulgence to the extravagance and artifice of his surroundings. Three years later Saint Laurent described his fascination for decadence in words that strangely echo those of Jacques de Bascher nine years before: 'People think decadence is debauched. Decadence is simply something very beautiful that is dying. It's a beautiful flower that is dying and sometimes you have to wait a very long time for another flower to come along.'

It is a beautiful flower that is dying, but woe betide the person who puts the wrong beautiful flower in front of Yves Saint Laurent. The couturier's taste when he was at Château Gabriel was for huge bouquets of one type of flower, and one former housekeeper there made the error of arranging a bouquet of Arum lilies – rather than the Proustian Casablanca lilies – in a vase. Saint Laurent said nothing of his displeasure; instead the housekeeper returned later to find that he had taken a pair of scissors and cut the white flowers from every stem in her bouquet. The stems still stood, humiliated and beheaded. Such was Saint Laurent's rage when reality imposed upon his visual ideal.

Pierre arrived from Paris in his own brand-new, all-white heli-copter that he piloted himself. Although Yves and Pierre lived apart in Paris, they shared houses elsewhere and still functioned in tandem in life. There never was a clear-cut divorce. As Pierre said in 2003, 'We never separated, we chose to live separately. And *chez* Yves I am *chez moi*. I have the keys.' Pierre had lots of hobbies, which he pursued with all the heated enthusiasm of an amateur. As well as flying, he learned how to drive a carriage and so he now toured the property, surveying the fences and park in a pony and trap, either with Madison

Cox at his side or sometimes Yves sporting a country tweed cap.

The house was as indicative of their social fantasies as of their literary tastes, with its opulent spread of chef, staff, gardeners, groom, beds made up for fictitious duchesses, helipad, three race-horses and herd of Normandy cattle bought, as Pierre admitted, because 'they look great with the house'.

'Yves was living the life of a Hollywood movie star,' says Patrick McCarthy, who arrived in Paris as *Women's Wear Daily* bureau chief in 1981. 'I can remember my first dinner at Saint Laurent's apartment and looking over and seeing this painting on an easel and I said to myself, "That looks like a Gainsborough." I didn't think anybody *owned* a Gainsborough! I thought they were all in museums or in some grand castle somewhere and to be sitting in the Rue de Babylone and seeing a Gainsborough next to a Picasso next to a Miro, it was just sort of awe-inspiring and you realised the amount of money that there was to be made in fashion.'

Patrick decided to write a story for the paper about designers' fortunes, which in itself was an indication that personal profit in fashion had boomed. 'They had so much money! Now a lot of it wasn't declared in taxes and all that sort of thing. There was a very 1920s Hollywood element to the whole scene, because they were mostly people of very modest backgrounds who suddenly had a lot of money, so what did they do? They bought boats, they bought châteaux, they had entourages, they had grand apartments, they bought art,' says McCarthy.

The article, which appeared under the title 'RICH RICH RICH RICH RICH RICH RICH' in early 1982, surveyed the wealth of all the major couturiers including Yves Saint Laurent and Bergé, Valentino, Pierre Cardin, Hubert de Givenchy, Marc Bohan and a handful of the ready-to-wear designers, including Karl Lagerfeld. Of course no one was willing to tell McCarthy how much they were making, indeed many insisted they simply had no idea, but McCarthy had his ways and means and a calculator.

His findings were sensational, particularly when set against the general atmosphere of acute recession that dogged France at the time. The figures were based on earnings for the year 1981. Pierre Cardin was the designer earning the most, thanks to his highly developed system of licences, the revenue of which reportedly totalled around $35 million for that year. This enabled Cardin to take home an estimated personal income of $8–9 million a year, while Yves Saint Laurent was pocketing around $4 million a year. Bergé, who was president of the company, owned slightly less than 50 per cent of the shares, leaving Yves the majority shareholder, so therefore his estimated income was just less than the $4 million mark. Hubert de Givenchy was estimated to be making $4.2 million personal profit a year, an impressive sum that explained his life of Euro-elegance with Paris town house, country château and Megève ski lodge.

And what of Karl Lagerfeld? 'Determining Karl Lagerfeld's income is like counting snowflakes in a blizzard,' said McCarthy at the time. This was partly because of Karl's secrecy and partly because revenues were fairly invisible, as Karl didn't actually have a fashion house; he worked freelance and by contract, commanding his own fees. 'I'm like Mr Gulbenkian,' he said, 'I own nothing; I get a percentage of every-thing.'

'Besides a rumoured personal fortune of considerable size, the designer has a staggering number of freelance fashion contracts, some of which, like Chloé and Fendi, the world knows about, and some of which Lagerfeld (now officially a resident of Monaco) keeps deftly hidden,' wrote McCarthy. He was still designing the shoe collection for Mario Valentino, although interestingly neither he nor the manu-facturer would acknowledge it, as well as a mid-market ready-to-wear collection for Italian manufacturer Alma. Lagerfeld was demanding rumoured fees of $250,000 and $500,000 a year respectively from these Italian companies for his services. He was also earning $800,000 per year in fees and royalties from the Fendi sisters, an estimated $1.6 from Chloé and several hundred thousand dollars more from contracts with Germany and Japan.

These were phenomenally large fees for a freelance fashion-stylist to be commanding in 1981. It is a mark of Karl's ferocious business savvy and guaranteed commercial results – he had been working for Chloé, Fendi and Mario Valentino for over twenty years by now – that he was able to introduce this scale of fee and royalty option into fashion. Lagerfeld's income totted up to be in the region of $3.5 million, putting him just a half million behind Saint Laurent.

And in the midst of this slot-machine pay-out – just as Yves was arranging his newly acquired Burne-Jones portrait on an easel in the dining room of the Château Gabriel and just as Karl finalised negotiations on another pretty country house outside Paris – François Mitterrand, the first socialist president of the Fifth Republic, took power.

Chapter 16

1981–83

François Mitterrand finally won the presidential election on 10 May 1981 after a lifetime spent getting there. His victory was a black day of mourning for France's millionaires, who feared not only the reality of the first socialist president in twenty-three years but also his election promise to impose a 'wealth tax' aimed at narrowing the gap between rich and poor. For them the whooping victory celebrations held over in the Place de la Bastille that May night summoned up the terror of the mob rapping at the windows of Versailles. 'The French live in history,' says Guy de Rothschild. 'One always thinks, hopes or fears that a certain event of the last hundred years is going to be resuscitated. At this time one was reminded of the Popular Front government of 1936. I know for a time I felt that it was going to be a mini-French Revolution or that we were heading towards a "dictature du plombier" – a plumber's dictatorship. We did not.'

But such were the fears at the time. The day after the election the Paris stock exchange went into meltdown as the French franc plummeted to the floor. Many of the old moneyed families packed their bags and left town, afraid of the savage decimation socialism would inflict on their fortunes. The 65-year-old Mitterrand never dared to hit the rich hard in terms of taxation, although he did set about a process of nationalisation of most private banks and several major industrial groups. He nationalised the hundred-year-old Rothschild family bank, provoking Guy de Rothschild to move to New York, come out of retirement and set up business there. His wife Marie-Hélène followed him and transferred her *ancien régime* socialising from the Hôtel Lambert to Lexington Avenue instead, leaving a vacuum in Paris high society.

Mitterrand's arrival coincided with Karl Lagerfeld's migration south to the financial escapism of Monaco. The new high-rise apartment he kept there was his principal place of residence, although he still kept his apartment in Paris and spent just enough time in the tax-free principality to fulfil residential criteria.

There was a stabbing paranoia to the summer months of 1981. Marie-Hélène had yet to move to New York but she wasn't seen out on the circuit for months after the election and droll wags were already referring to both Marie-Hélène and her band as 'the dinosaurs'. The debonair Kim d'Estainville spoke for all the beau monde when he said, 'The old order is long gone.'

Fabrice Emaer had plugged the vote for Mitterrand just days before the election, standing up on stage at Le Palace and urging the crowd to vote socialist. It was a major error of judgement of the political temperature of Paris society. Sylvie Grumbach, who was the indefatigable Palace PR, remembers the reaction: 'He was up on stage and I saw the looks of disgust, people just walked out, left in anger. It was the beginning of the end of Le Palace.'

Fabrice had every right to express his personal political leanings, but unfortunately for him his blunder as impresario of the night was not forgiven. Marie-Hélène and her band of social elite were lost from the Palace. But perhaps they were going anyway. Had the apparent opening-up of society ever really been anything more than a passing curiosity? 'It was different groups that mixed in certain places,' stipulates society hostess Sao Schlumberger, 'but they did not mix like that all the time.' They had mixed at night, but the thrill of partying with the masses was always dependent on feeling secure in your kingdom, and when the chill wind of socialism hit town, class closed ranks.

The ceaseless party nights were heading to a dead end. Everyone was older and feeling it – after all, they had been partying now without respite for at least twelve years; how long could you keep up the pace? How long could you bear the constant repetition of themed parties, fantasy and escape? Every month Le Palace published a calendar for the forthcoming month, promising night after night of 'delirium'. The year before, a party for Bastille Day had featured a show of 'Louis XVI and the *Autrichienne*', meaning Marie-Antoinette, being 'maltreated on stage by the people of Paris (four black dancers)'. It was a rather appropriate choice of stage-show considering the following year's political fate.

And for those reliant on drugs, how much longer could you bear the constant repetition of getting high and coming down? There was the agony of coming down badly, trying to live through the crash of daylight until you could get back to the party. Music journalist Alain Pacadis was a regular of Le Palace, ending so many of his nights there unconscious and drugged up on heroin. In 1978 in his *Libération* newspaper column, Pacadis wrote of the void his life had become in prose that resounds with numb desperation. 'Empty landscape, empty sky, empty head: but why does it hurt so much? One morning you find yourself with nails banged into the stomach and needles in the heart. Bland music that means nothing. Rhythmic music in the corridors of Le Palace; every night I go back there because there is nowhere else to go. Empty. I am empty like the foam of night, empty as the eyes of the blind, empty as the sky without stars. My head hurts and nothing can calm me, please Doctor Burroughs give me another injection. Music for my head, I see nothing at all. Nothing at all.'

In January 1981 Fabrice opened Le Privilège, which was a private section downstairs at Le Palace with a restaurant and salon dance-floor that was restricted to members only. Members of Le Privilège could wander up and around in Le Palace, but the crowds of the Palace were not allowed down into the new VIP club – a system that was an outright contradiction of the original concept of Le Palace. It was a vain attempt by Fabrice to recapture some of the intimate joy and *folie* of Le Sept, but it never did inspire the alchemy he was looking for. The space, which Fabrice billed as a 'totally European scene, unimaginable elsewhere, inspired by the spirit of Cocteau and Christian Bérard' dedicated to 'real luxury', became principally a place in which to take heroin in private.

Fabrice's grip on the desires of the Paris night was slipping. He was unwell and in debt; he was laying off staff at Le Palace, yet spending hand over fist to keep up the constant programme of parties and concerts as, for the first time, he was experiencing real competition. In 1979 *Les Bains Douches* opened, a smaller club in a former public baths that was more smack and Joy Division than Palace disco and was popular from the moment it opened its doors. Then, about a year later, gay bars exploded in Paris, opening up one after another in a horizontal stretch that began at Les Halles and ran through to the Marais *quartier*. These small, dark bars with their crystalline powders and brotherhood rituals began to dominate night-life, offering possibilities for intense and multiple backroom sexual encounters.

The flamboyant delight that characterised the liberation of homosexuals in the early 1970s had gone. Those years of flirtation and teasing – of men getting a 'brushing' once a week at Carita and dressing up in diamanté and kohl at night – were supplanted by a new desire for butch, 'le pédé dur' or tough gay as DJ Guy Cuevas describes it.

This new exploration of the homosexual identity involved the suppression of femininity, both in the physical prohibition of women and the eradication of all that was deemed feminine within the man himself. New gay bars such as Le Broad were out of bounds to women and stated as much on the door. Fabrice organised train trips to Normandy with overnight parties that turned to S&M and he introduced tea dances at Le Palace every Sunday at 5 p.m. that were advertised as '*Totalement interdit aux femmes*'.

The fantastic posturing and camp idyll of Le Sept, when girls were there as the dancing partners to dress up and idealise, girls were there to personify your dreams and illusions of glamour, girls were there to dance and cavort untouched on bars, all this was over. Girls and femininity had no place in the new gay order.

'Gays had begun their body-building to be more and more muscular, more muscular than the heteros. And then everything collided,' says Guy Cuevas. 'It was the time of *Closing*, the Hollywood movie by William Friedkin. It was the tough gay, hard, the leather gay, not funny, not optimistic, not happy, not giggling. Everything became so horrible. It was the black-leather aggressor, the black-leather murderer.' 'It was the New Yorkisation of Paris,' says a less emotive Patrick McCarthy, or, as Tan Giudicelli describes it, 'We were living sex like a sport without sentiment.'

Naturally this shift found expression in fashion and in particular within the work of Claude Montana, who by 1982 represented the hottest designer influence in fashion, prompting *People* magazine to remark, 'He just might be the Yves Saint Laurent of the '80s.' Unlike Yves Saint Laurent, who worshipped woman and dressed her as a 'goddess' with all the impossible idealisation that involved, Montana's dynamic with women was darker and more tormented. 'When you went for fittings it was total torture,' remembers Pat Cleveland. 'He was chiselling away at you like you were a block of wood, he wouldn't let you go until he squeezed out every bit that was you and replaced you with himself. You could not be *anything* but Claude. He'd turn and walk away from you and he'd turn and look at you, very angry and irate; he would scare you to death and then he'd come over and push at your body, like he was sculpting you. It was a powerful experience. It was like he hated you for being yourself, but he wanted to be you.'

At the time Montana's shows provoked fashion hysteria. New York female buyers sat on the front row and wept at the assertive clothes for a new generation. Montana introduced his own original form of choreography using a group formation of up to eight models abreast who paced slowly down the mile-long runway, unsmiling, hands held in pockets or on hips. It was Montana who instructed the models on their every step and pose; he took away their spontaneity and made them move only as he wanted them to. He even reduced Pat Cleveland and her Betty Boop leaps and turns to a synchronised robot walk. The music at his shows was a surge of Verdi's *Requiem Mass* and the death march of *Aida*. Irene Silvagni was a fashion editor at French *Vogue* at the time and remembers, 'When I sat in Saint Laurent's shows they felt like a love letter he had written to you. There was so much emotion. Montana was exactly the contrary. They brought out total panic in me, to see this woman that was so mean, pointed; it felt like he hated us.'

To watch video footage of Montana's shows some twenty years later provokes an uncomfortable reaction. The cut of his clothes is indeed beautiful, the finish and leather exquisite, the tailoring masterful, but there is an overwhelming sensation of the obliteration of femininity. It is not so much misogyny as the female eunuch. There is never any sense of Montana's wonder of women, instead there are disturbing connotations of fascism – not just in the eagle imagery, the floor-length leather coats, the wide military leather belts, but in the glacial chilling beauty of Montana's vision as a whole.

Claude Montana's style and the rapturous reception it received were indicative of how radically the fashion direction had changed. There were other new and bold fashion stars jostling for exposure. Thierry Mugler had landed with his diva space-suits and enormous padded shoulders, and in 1981 Azzedine Alaïa launched his label and his first collection, inventing that consummate piece of 1980s clothing, 'the body'. Alaïa's style reflected the new concerns of the new decade – a gym-toned body and large expense account – with uplifting bustiers, raunchy knits and black leather panelled skirts. Meanwhile Jean Paul Gaultier was attracting enormous attention and media coverage for his comic-book sense of warped wit and sampling of punk culture.

One of the first casualties of this new mood was Kenzo. He had split with his business partner Gilles Raysse in a highly acrimonious way in 1980 and had hired business manager François Baufumé to replace him. Baufumé was one of the first trained business and managerial graduates to enter the fashion industry. 'I was the only one of my class at HEC to go into fashion and doing so meant I was considered the failure of the year,' says Baufumé. HEC is one of France's top business schools and one of the country's highly prestigious *grandes écoles*. It is indicative of just how fledgling an industry fashion still was in 1980 that it was not taken seriously by business graduates. That was to change radically and explosively over the next ten years, so that today many would argue that it is business strategy, spreadsheets and people in suits who hold sway over design and creativity.

Baufumé brought the Kenzo business into order, clearing up tax issues, production and distribution, restructuring the brand and launching a perfume, raising turnover from 20 million francs a year to 240 million. But despite the moneymaking, by 1983 Kenzo was floundering creatively.

In 1982 the Japanese designers Comme des Garçons and Yohji Yamamoto arrived on the scene. Their aesthetic of deconstruction and their uncompromising palette of black was so radically new that they immediately rendered *démodé* that other 'Japanese' designer, Kenzo. 'Comme [des Garçons] and Yohji were a big shock to the system but in a way I am closer to them, at least I understood their construction of the garment,' says Kenzo. 'But what really threw me were Mugler and Montana and then Azzedine. They were doing clothes that were beautiful, sublime, but they were clothes that I really *cannot* do, clothes that were so highly structured. For me someone like Montana was the polar opposite of what I was doing. Fashion had changed completely.'

Kenzo was scared and disorientated, intimidated by the infrastructure around him of accelerating production, distribution and employees, and cast adrift by the cash that he was earning. Kenzo admits that, for a period of five or six years, 'I was lost. It wasn't working, I had to follow trends and I wasn't happy. Around 1985 the company got bigger, bigger and bigger, the reviews weren't so good, the collections weren't so good and I had this huge responsibility that the collection must sell, it had to be great, it was a heavy burden to bear.' In one year the turnover dropped from 240 million francs to 180 million. It was a traumatic period for Kenzo in creative terms, for he forced himself to go against his own style, heart and instinct and to follow trends in an attempt to stay fashionable.

It is a grim moment for the designer when he or she finds himself or herself totally out of fashion, left behind, out of synch as time moves on. A new generation is born and the designer's vision or creative expression no longer describes or evokes the time around them. This is a creative pain unique to fashion. Of course there are trends and moods in every art form, the recent domination of conceptual art being an obvious example. But a painting, even if it is not 'fashionable', can still possess its own intrinsic artistic and creative merit. Whereas one of the defining qualities of fashion is that it should describe its epoch and the desires of that moment.

And in an industry based on making money from trying to harness the moment, everyone – designer, fashion editor, member of the clique, model and manager – is consumed by the dread that the moment is slipping through their fingers, that it will be gone and they will be unwanted or, in the case of the business manager, they will be left with three thousand stone-cold spencer jackets to shift.

Being left behind is the inexorable fate of a designer and it is a dread that not only drives them but also generates the aggression that characterises fashion. It calls to mind something Eric Wright, former long-term associate of Karl Lagerfeld, says about Karl: 'His greatest fear was not being part of the moment.'

As an eight-year-old boy Jacques de Bascher watched one endless after-noon as his younger brother Xavier played with his electric train-set. As the two brothers lay on the floor with the dark-green engines whizzing past their ears in their Neuilly bedroom, Jacques thought how pretty it might be if one were to spray the mountains of the train-set landscape with fake snow for a wintry, magical effect.

Rather than do it himself, however, Jacques preferred to draft a letter that he then handed over to Xavier to sign. It was a contract, or at least an eight-year-old child's version of a contract, comprising two possible options and it read: 'I, the undersigned Xavier, agree to pay two francs for the idea to put spray snow on the mountains decorating my Merklin. I undertake to pay Jacques the said amount to have the right to use his idea. Or no, I pay nothing and therefore I do not have the right to use the idea.' Xavier chose the first option, signed the contract and paid the two francs to Jacques, then snow-painted the mountains himself as agreed.

Xavier still has the contract, which he keeps in an album along with photos and pictures and memories. Reading the paper now, over forty years later, with Jacques' proposition to sell his brother his vision of loveliness written out in careful handwriting, Xavier recognises, 'This is something, this is part of it.'

Was it that Jacques was born to be a muse, a man who could create ambiance, provoke ideas, but who could make nothing himself? Was that his destiny or was that his choice? 'I rove, drift, float,' says Mr Gabriel Nash in Henry James' novel *The Tragic Muse*, 'my feelings direct me – if such a life as mine may be said to have a direction. Where there's anything to feel I try to be there!' It is a sentence that summons up Jacques' state of mind by the age of thirty in 1981.

For several years he had been casting around in a rather aimless way for something to do with his days. He often used to suggest to Paloma that they launch a perfume together, proposing his services as a busi-ness manager, but she shrugged him off. Then in 1983 she did launch a perfume with her husband, with phenomenal global success. Jacques had plans to write: one week a novel, the next a biography of James Dean. He talked of writing a biography of Karl and kept a hoard of hundreds of press cuttings on him, a detail that hints at the degree of fascination Karl held for Jacques. But Karl would not contemplate any discussion of his past and the biography came to nothing. Jacques wrote nothing.

Jacques was going to write films, direct films. But his film career amounted to *Views-interviews* – a promotional film for the launch of a Lagerfeld men's fragrance – in 1978 and later a short film of a fashion garden-party held in Karl's back garden. Jacques was going to launch himself in music in some way and he had all the latest equipment, including an enormous turntable system in his apartment at Saint Sulpice. In 1979 he mixed together a stream of Austrian marches for the Chloé show which, when combined with the show setting of the marble block of the Théâtre Chaillot at the Trocadéro, brought the American fashion buyers out in a cold sweat.

Jacques was without the anchor of a tangible role or talent and seemingly possessed by an increasing and overwhelming reflex to shock and provoke. He would insist on speaking German to Helmut Newton, a habit that, combined with Jacques' Tyrolean outfits, enraged the usually politically unflappable photographer. Jacques' anger flared frequently over these years; his mood swings were becoming increasingly exaggerated and one wonders if the change in temperament was linked to his long-term cocaine abuse. Nobody seems to know for sure how much he was taking, but according to friends it was an all-day and everyday habit and had been going on for around nine years.

There was also the alcohol consumption that had been remarked upon since the early 1970s and was an integral part of his life. It is common for cocaine abusers to use alcohol as a means of taking the edge off the cocaine, modulating the high and making the drug more pleasurable to use. There were occasions when Jacques turned up drunk and belligerent at Karl's studio and a time when he drove back from La Berrière to Paris at 150 kilometres an hour with a bottle of Chivas by his side.

The memories and testaments to Jacques' personality were always conflicting and describe a character etched in dramatic chiaroscuro. As Jacques' friend Christian Lvowski says, 'He was a boy that provoked intense reactions. There were people who loved Jacques; there were people who hated Jacques. There was nothing in between.' But the accounts of Jacques during the 1980s are increasingly desolate and almost unanimously describe a man being consumed by rage and bitterness. The concurrence of his prolonged and grandiose substance abuse with his extreme and erratic behaviour raises the question of whether Jacques was suffering from some kind of personality disorder.

By July 1980 American artist Shirley Goldfarb was suffering from cancer, although few people knew she was dying. She had always had a dream to perform, so she concocted a show with a series of monologues, making songs out of Paris restaurant menus with Judy Garland-style dancing, and she asked Pierre Bergé if she could put on a performance at his Théâtre Athénée. He agreed and she did her show for a hundred people with a dinner following it. All this time she was undergoing chemotherapy and radiation with its physical side-effects. She kept going out to the Flore and the Lipp, defiant in her battle against her illness. She was at Brasserie Lipp a few days before her performance when Jacques de Bascher walked in and sat down at her table. A conversation ensued between them. Madison Cox arrived soon after, around 10 p.m., to have coffee with her and found Shirley alone and crying at her table. 'She was in such a state of hysteria,' remembers Madison. 'She told me Jacques had come by and said, "You know, you look just awful, you look like death itself; let me just give you a revolver, so you can get it over with. We don't want to look at you when you are in this state, so why don't you just end your life now?"'

Of course those close to Jacques find it impossible to equate these horrifying words with the affectionate, loving man they knew. 'Jacques was not a cruel man,' says Patrick McCarthy. 'Jacques' diabolic side was more theatrical than anything else,' argues Patrick Hourcade. But there were those in Paris for whom this was the very Jacques they knew.

Madison says when he told people of the dreadful nature of that conversation between Shirley and Jacques, no one seemed surprised; rather they shrugged and said, 'Oh yes, that's Jacques.' 'There was something so odd about the reaction. I mean, there was no, "Oh that's terrible", or, "Let's go run him down or something"; it was as if he was almost protected, you know – yes, he's the evil one in the group and so, yes, that's what we would expect from him.'

The memory of this unhappy encounter prompts Madison to reflect further on the pitiless laws of appearance inherent to Parisian life. 'I mean it's true she looked like death, and it was interesting because it was the first time I had witnessed someone in a state like that, and you know Paris is really so much about *apparence* and for someone to be sitting there obviously in a really poor state, and in a way flaunting it, she was angry, she was bitter, but she was fighting it, she fought it to the very, very end.'

It was at this time that Jacques' former lover, Diane de Beauvau-Craon, walked back into his life. She had spent several highly tempestuous years in New York, hanging out with Halston, Timothy Leary, Robert Mapplethorpe, John Lennon and Andy Warhol. 'I was known as being a totally wild princess,' says Diane now. 'In those days being a French princess and granddaughter of Patino in New York, Jesus, that really hit hard. I didn't do anything special in the sense that I took drugs just like everybody else did, but I took more than anyone else did.' At the age of twenty she was taking experimental drugs with Timothy Leary and writing about her experiences. Later she lived with photographer Robert Mapplethorpe, just after he had split with Patti Smith. She and Mapplethorpe used to go twice a week to a hospital in Long Island to help with young adolescents who were caught up in addiction.

Eventually she left New York and moved to Tangier, where she married (her second marriage), gave birth to her son, converted to Islam, learned to speak Arabic and studied calligraphy. It was an unhappy marriage that held her captive in Morocco. When she escaped the marriage and the country she had to leave her child behind. 'It took five years to get my son back,' she says. 'So when you go all the way on your trek, you have beautiful experiences but tough things happen as well. But I don't complain, it's part of the deal. Life isn't just a big smile – thank God, it would be extremely boring if it was.'

Diane returned to Paris and moved in with Jacques again, this time living at Place Saint-Sulpice. Her black hair was cropped short and she combined an androgynous look with a generous bosom to dramatic effect. Diane's most remarkable attribute was her voice or more accurately her *ton* – she spoke with a kind of throaty, seductive yet deeply authoritative tone. There was something of the Nancy Cunard to Diane with her mannish clothes, butch allure and rebel attitude, although Diane had none of Cunard's political activism. Diane and Jacques went out at night together, Diane picking up men and handing them over to Jacques. They attended a ball at the Opéra in 1980 dressed alike, wearing dinner jackets, black ties and black sashes wrapped pirate-like over one eye.

'I had this feverish thing that quite a few of us had,' says Diane. 'We were running, running, running after time, not wanting to miss *anything* and I think a lot of us were a bit like that, not wanting to miss fun, not wanting to miss joy, not wanting to miss love, basically not wanting to miss everything that we had missed during our real youths – our childhood. I do believe we were the last generation where our parents did not express their love. They didn't hug and kiss us and say I love you my little one. And when I think of my homosexual friends they all had an awful emotional problem with their parents, they never heard those three words and it destabilised them terribly.'

Coked up, mind numb, coked up to forget the loneliness, coked up to forget the emptiness. 'We never had the time to understand people, we were too busy rushing around after illusions,' says Diane. And between every high was the coming-down: life the morning after, empty and shattered, littered in last night's ecstasy, hung-over and hands shaking, the void beyond the illusion.

Karl had objected strongly to Diane's relationship with Jacques back in 1972, but now he was delighted at her return. 'He didn't see me as this horrible image of a woman wanting to take Jacques away from him any more; on the contrary I was fun, I started to inspire Karl and so I was an ideal daughter-in-law to have, because at that point in their relationship I think he saw Jacques much more as his son.'

In January 1981 Jacques asked Diane to marry him, Diane accepted and they held a grand religious ceremony celebrating the engagement at the church of Santissima Trinita in Rome. The Pope blessed the engagement ring and a French magazine pronounced it a marriage 'très distingay'. Was the engagement merely fulfilling another childhood fantasy of Jacques? Anne de Bascher remembers Jacques disappearing into the loo at home in Neuilly as a teenager and reappearing with a copy of the *Bottin Mondain* (a *Who's Who* of the French nobility) in his hand. 'I will marry the girl on whom my finger falls,' Jacques declared, ever the showman, even aged fifteen. He opened the book and placed his finger on the page and according to Anne it fell on the name of Diane de Beauvau-Craon.

One cannot help wondering if Jacques might have already identified his dream bride and her whereabouts on the page before the finger-falling ceremony in front of his brothers and sisters. His finger could so easily have landed on the toothless widow of a poor aristo in the neighbouring county. But no, Jacques' finger happened to land on the youngest daughter of the Prince de Beauvau-Craon.

Within weeks of their return to Paris the relationship began to disintegrate. 'We had a big, big row; it wasn't our first row; but it was the extra row,' says Diane, and the engagement was broken off. Diane returned the ring. Anne de Bascher believes from later conversations with her brother that he planned the wedding to shock his entourage, while most of his entourage is convinced that he did it to marry a princess. There is also the thought that Karl pushed the match. And yet was it only an engagement of purely cynical motives? In a postcard that Renaud received from Jacques in Rome, Jacques writes of his engagement to Diane and the forthcoming ceremony at Santissima Trinita, ending with the sincere and hopeful line, 'Will you spare a little thought for us?'

Today Diane still guards precious memories of Jacques, their time together and his goodness to her. 'I do believe that I was the only woman he loved and he was certainly the only homosexual I ever loved,' says Diane. 'He was a lovely person, he was a generous person, he was an attentive person who happened to think he was someone truly marvellous; so what, haven't we all thought that we were vastly important at some point in our lives? Jacques was absolutely amazing for me, he went over to Morocco to try and get my child out. Yes, you see that's the sort of thing people don't know about him: in a period when we were all running round madly insouciant, Jacques was the only person I knew that risked putting himself in the wolf's mouth so to speak to try and get my child back. Well, Jacques came back with a broken arm, but unfortunately not my child.'

If there was one man who didn't lose his footing in the sweeping tidal change in fashion in the 1980s, it was Karl Lagerfeld. Unlike some of the stars of the 1970s who were fading, Karl was, on the contrary, looking increasingly confident and making more and more noise in the media. By now ready-to-wear was recognised as the dominant force of fashion, both in terms of trend-setting and profit-making, and Karl Lagerfeld was perfectly positioned as a long-established member of the ready-to-wear industry to seize power.

He was moving up in the world, making a host of new high-society connections. The man who had hung out in Boulevard Saint-Germain bohemia with Donna, Corey, Antonio and Juan in the early 1970s was by the end of the decade throwing a sit-down dinner for one hundred of the Paris society power-pack following the premiere of the New York City ballet at the Théâtre des Champs-Elysées. It was a considerable milestone for Karl and a not inconsiderable coup to have seated before him at his dining-room table the three haute-couture graces, Marie-Hélène de Rothschild, Jacqueline de Ribes and Hélène de Rochas, as well as his new fashion patron Ira von Furstenberg and his new next-door neighbour, Princess Caroline of Monaco.

As the 1980s dawned Karl was intricately involved with ambitious moves and career manoeuvrings. There was the new apartment down in Monte Carlo, but even more mysteriously there was another new apartment on the Rue de Rivoli, the first time in nearly thirty years in Paris that Karl had ever possessed a property across the river on the Right Bank. He was determinedly vague about the purpose of renting the apartment and was still living in the Rue de l'Université apartment. And then there was Kitty d'Alessio. She was the American president of the house of Chanel and throughout 1982 Karl was seen often with Kitty in both New York and Paris, taking her out to dine and dance.

On 15 September 1982, after six months of seething gossip and stealth, the announcement came: Karl Lagerfeld was going to design for Chanel. Twenty-eight years after he had stood for that one precious moment on a level with Yves Mathieu-Saint-Laurent and his shining destiny, Karl had finally caught up. He was forty-nine years old.

To take on Yves meant stepping into a dead woman's shoes: Chanel had died eleven years before. Chanel was the job that would bring him excessive wealth and worldwide fame. But most of all Chanel was the house which meant Karl could compete with the prestige, the renown, the haute couture, the ateliers and the legend of Yves, for was there any greater legend in fashion than that of Chanel?

In 1982, when the announcement came, the house of Chanel described Karl Lagerfeld's future role there in downbeat and euphemistic terms. He was to provide 'artistic orientation' for the haute couture, starting with the upcoming couture collection of January 1983. Karl specifically and repeatedly denied having anything to do with the Chanel ready-to-wear, but the denials rang hollow, particularly since Philippe Guibourgé, who had been designing the ready-to-wear since 1977, had not had his contract renewed when it ended in the spring of 1982.

It was in fact a game of dainty subterfuge, kept up because Karl's contract with Chloé, due to end in December 1983, precluded him from designing the ready-to-wear for another house in France. Karl's former assistant Hervé Léger was installed at Chanel, as head of the ready-to-wear studio. The newly rented apartment on the Rue de Rivoli was right around the corner from Rue Cambon. Although Karl denied visiting the Rue Cambon premises, their proximity fuelled speculation that he was working with Hervé and the Chanel team and neatly side-stepping his exclusivity contract.

The reaction in Paris and world fashion to the announcement was one of outright shock, not least at the house of Saint Laurent where, says Madison Cox, 'It was a black day.' Chanel, even more so than Dior, was the couturier with whom Yves had long expressed the greatest affinity. It was Chanel after all who had first felt the quickening pulse of androgyny, who had understood the sensuality and mystery of black, and who had hailed style over fashion, all those principles that Yves adhered to.

Karl knew how much Chanel meant to Yves. 'It's quite obvious that for Karl it was not just a very big jump,' says Paloma Picasso, 'but also a knife into Yves.' Certainly Karl wasted no time in using Chanel as a battlement from which to take shots at Yves. 'Poor Yves didn't need to go to Chanel to make Chanel-style clothing. He's been making Chanels and selling them as Saint Laurents for years,' he said in 1983.

Chanel herself had declared Yves as her rightful heir on a television programme shortly before her death. Perhaps couturier at the house of Chanel was a job that Yves himself might have dreamed of. And yet in 1982 the concept of the split-personality couturier, a designer able to turn his hand to several high-profile fashion houses at the same time, had not yet been established. It was Karl who was about to establish it as a blueprint for the fashion industry, demonstrating that he could change his creative persona as others might change their suit. But how could Yves be anything else but Yves Saint Laurent? He already had his own house, his own identity, his own style.

To the rest of the fashion world the shocking dimension of Karl's appointment derived principally from the fact that he was a *styliste* not a couturier, and there was a marked difference between the two even as late as 1982. Karl himself had long insisted on the distinction: he had spent the last twenty years loudly criticising haute couture, insisting that it was tacky, outdated, a dusty relic from the 1950s and *pas du tout moderne*. And now he was standing at the top of the dusty, mirrored staircase of Mademoiselle, bumping up against her couture ghost eleven years after her death. The irony of Karl's volte-face was lost on no one.

There was also the question of Karl's nationality. Could a German designer really understand the finesse and uncompromising elegance of this quintessentially French couture house? It may have been an Englishman, Charles Frederick Worth, who founded the concept of haute couture in Paris in 1858, but nevertheless the couture sensibility was regarded as intrinsically French – at a push perhaps a little Italian around the edges, with Schiaparelli from the 1930s and couturiers such as Emanuel Ungaro, who was half-Italian, and Valentino, who worked from Rome. But the idea of a Teutonic, Nordic sensibility tackling the romance of couture was one that fashion commentators – particularly French ones – found hard to contemplate.

Added to the doubts surrounding Karl's suitability for the job was incredulity at the amount of money he was to be paid for doing it. Karl negotiated himself a rumoured $1 million contract to be paid by USA Chanel. One million dollars a year in 1982 for a hired designer to design two collections a year for a couture house that was not his own was a spectacular amount of money. People talked of nothing else for weeks.

Behind the deal, the money, the controversy, there was the business vision of Alain Wertheimer, just as behind the legendary success of Gabrielle Chanel there had been the business vision of Pierre Wertheimer,

Alain's grandfather. It was Pierre Wertheimer who had struck a deal with Chanel in 1924 to produce and manufacture her perfumes and who by the end of the 1950s was outright owner of her name worldwide. He was the man who put forward the financial backing to make her the legend she became. But from the moment she signed the deal with Wertheimer to the day she died, Chanel was consumed with resentment at this bond of ownership.

In 1974, three years after Chanel's death, Alain took over the company, replacing his father and his lacklustre tenure of the company. The 24-year-old young man, supported by his divorced mother Lilianne Heilbronn, who also happened to be a formidable lawyer, persuaded the Chanel trustees to declare his own father incompetent. It is worth remembering Alain Wertheimer's ruthless business objectivity when assessing Karl's role and longevity at the house of Chanel.

The fashion business that Alain Wertheimer took over in 1974 amounted to one boutique on the Rue Cambon, plus working couture ateliers, stagnant perfume sales of Chanel N° 5 and a system of over-exposed perfume distribution in the USA. Alain Wertheimer moved swiftly to reinstate the aura of exclusivity to Chanel Parfums by dramatically reducing the number of US stockists and taking Chanel N° 5 out of every corner drugstore around the country.

In 1977 he made a licensing deal with Mendes, the French clothing manufacturers, who were charged with producing and distributing Chanel ready-to-wear designed by Philippe Guibourgé for the American market. But after only three years Wertheimer ended this licensing deal, choosing to bring the manufacturing and distribution of ready-to-wear back in house. This was a hugely significant and strategic move, particularly when put in the context of the trend for licensing ready-to-wear in France that was still raging in 1980. Historically the Wertheimer family were manufacturers (of perfumes and cosmetics), and Alain realised the potential for Chanel ready-to-wear was huge, but he saw that the key to success lay in controlling every stage, from drawing-board to cash register and shopping bag.

Another significant strategic move that pre-empted the market was the hiring by Wertheimer of Kitty d'Alessio in 1980 to run Chanel's fashion operations in the US. She had spent twenty years working on the Chanel advertising at New York ad agency Norman, Craig &

Kummel, and she understood the power of the brand. It was Kitty who found Karl. D'Alessio was very impressed with Karl's talent and his high profile within the industry and in the US. 'I'd been studying him and his successes,' says Kitty d'Alessio. 'He was brilliant and he had never tried to emulate Chanel. He was such a scholar. At the time he was working for so many people, not just Chloé and Fendi; he was working all over Italy and there wasn't a fur coat on Fifth Avenue that he hadn't designed in some way.'

Kitty was dazzled by Karl's clientele and loved what she and many others perceived as his innate patrician background. 'He had the inherent love of elegance and had grown up in the presence of wonderful things,' she enthused in 1985. The more famous Karl became, the more he insisted on his gilt-edged pedigree; in 1981 he told *Le Palace* magazine that he inherited the Château de Penhoët from his mother.

There is a certain dramatic symmetry between Chanel and Karl. Gabrielle Chanel was a woman who spent a lifetime in denial of her past. She denied her peasant family, her innkeeping ancestors and illegitimacy. Chanel's father was a womaniser and itinerant tinker working the markets of local towns around Clermont Ferrand. Her mother was an unfortunate woman who eventually died aged thirty-two, the mother of five children, one of whom died in infancy. Her father abandoned the children, driving Gabrielle, aged twelve, and her elder sister Julia to an orphanage and leaving them there. Gabrielle spent a dismal adolescence as a charity ward at the orphanage that was run by nuns.

Later Chanel reworked the brutal reality of her life. Using real characters and real events, she wrapped them in a skein of make-believe and alias so vivid that she almost believed it herself. She would say her father was a successful horse dealer or a wealthy wine merchant who spoke fluent English. She hid her barrow-boy brothers and turned the orphanage into cruel and loveless aunts. She made up different versions of the same event, contradicting herself, surpassing herself while taking care never to tell the truth. According to her biographer Edmonde Charles-Roux, 'The most arresting feature of this remarkable life . . . is the art she lavished upon rendering herself *unintelligible*, and, having done that, the persistence with which she perpetuated her disguise, remaining confined within it as in the most hermetically sealed prison.' It was a fitting co-incidence that she should have as her heir a man with a similar talent for reinvention.

Chapter 17

1983—84

Mirrored staircases and faded beige carpets, bony chairs and labels written out by hand, la Baronne de Rothschild, Mademoiselle Adjani, Madame Picasso, Madame Pompidou: Karl was back in the world of haute couture, the one he had left over twenty years before. It was January 1983 in the couture salon of the Rue Cambon and the fashion guard was there to pass judgement on his take on Chanel. There were jealously guarded front-row seats and a pack of photographers poised on the winding staircase above the first-floor salon where Chanel herself used to hide to watch her own shows before photographers had breached the secret world of couture. Slivers of gossip were passed around like petits fours between fashion editors: 'Karl says he came with his mother to see Chanel's comeback show in 1954' and 'I hear he's lost twenty-two pounds through acupuncture'.

And then music played for the first time in the couture salon of Chanel and out came Inès de la Fressange wearing a navy-blue suit with a round white collar; it was the height of ladylike sobriety. Karl had chosen to ignore the 1950s revival suits and instead focus on Chanel's work from the 1920s and '30s, with long straight skirts finishing at the top of the shin, worn with cropped jackets and strings of pearls. After so much controversy, the first couture collection was, perhaps inevitably, an anticlimax. How do you take on a legend? Karl did it by submerging himself in the Chanel archives, re-emerging with a homage collection that failed to ignite the audience. 'Lagerfeld sputters,' announced *Women's*

Wear Daily. 'No one can replace Coco Chanel – not even Kaiser Karl – nor should anyone – not even KK – make the attempt.'

The audience and press compared every detail of his clothes to Chanel, and Karl came off badly every time. The proportions were thought bulky, there was too much volume and pockets on the hips, the orange tweeds were too heavy for the summer, tailoring, said *Women's Wear Daily*, 'grabs at the body instead of fitting it', and the conclusion was that 'KK committed too many Chanel Don'ts and not enough Dos'. Whether it was from lack of time or lack of experience in working with the ateliers, many of the day suits were not properly finished; there were threads left hanging down, pins visible between pleats and tags left on necklaces.

Perhaps most significant of all, the armhole was wrong. The armhole was Chanel's most famous personal obsession; she believed the whole fit and ease of her jacket relied upon it. She used to fit and refit the armhole on the model herself with a pair of scissors and pins in a brutal, blood-letting approach, hacking away at the underarm and often the woman until she achieved perfection. Karl's armholes were deemed too low and baggy.

Marie-Hélène de Rothschild, who as a young girl had been fitted for her first Chanel suit by Chanel herself and who was credited as prompting Chanel to make her comeback at the age of seventy-one, walked out at the end of the show to a waiting chauffeur. She patted her trim tweed hips and said, 'He's got a feeling for Chanel, but it's not yet complete. Someone has to tell him more about her. She had such perfect proportions. But no one could have done it on the first try. It will come.'

Marie-Hélène was both right and wrong. Karl's feeling was incomplete, but no one needed to tell Karl Lagerfeld more about Chanel. No one could surpass Karl on knowledge, both the desire for it and the determined mastery of it. He had been reading about Chanel and her collections for years before he got the job. Billina remembers Chanel fascinated him even in the early 1970s, when he would often recount Chanel anecdotes. In the three months since he had been hired he had visually devoured the house archives, as well as his own considerable historic Chanel sources (it would become a point of pride for Karl that he owned more Chanel archives than the house itself). Within a short time of being at Chanel he would know every reference, every collection, every line of her history, invented and real.

It wasn't more Chanel knowledge he needed, but an entirely different approach. The homage technique was never going to work: there were already racks of look-alike Chanel suits being sold in every other store on the Rue du Faubourg Saint-Honoré. Being the couturier making 'suits in the manner of' would mean that Karl would forever face the criticism that they simply 'weren't Coco' or, more damning, that he did not possess the touch of Chanel.

But even more significantly this was not where the future of fashion lay and, after sixteen years of success in ready-to-wear, Karl knew that. The 1950s couturier in him might still seek Marie-Hélène's approval, but Karl the 1980s ready-to-wear realist knew that it was not Marie-Hélène and the couture client who was the future profit of fashion. He saw the crowds of thousands outside the fashion shows of Gaultier and Mugler, pushing, shoving and screaming to get in like it was a nightclub or a rock concert. He saw the PRs standing like bouncers on the door amid a sea of invitations flailing in the air, shouting, 'You, yes! You, no!' He saw the power of advertising turn to dictatorship as brands began calling the shots with the magazines: 'You want our advertising? You give us editorial'; 'We didn't like the coverage last month, and we're pulling the ad this month.' He saw the budgets for fashion shoots roar, photographers' fees quadrupling within a year. He saw model agencies booking hotel suites for models, demanding chauffeurs and cars where once minibuses had sufficed. He saw the models signing fragrance contracts, earning dollars and celebrity, as Jerry Hall and Mick Jagger became a media obsession.

He saw the power of image; he already knew the power of hype. 'I like to work only for big companies with big advertising power. I don't like anything small,' Karl said days before his first collection for Chanel. He saw the video cameras jostling at the end of every catwalk, photographers fighting to get the shot. He saw movie stars turning up to watch the shows, the blast of paparazzi flashes burning up their faces. He saw the designer as worldwide celebrity, known and recognised from Tokyo to Chicago. He saw the power of fashion to incite desire. He had negotiated a rumoured $100,000 worth of clothes at Chanel so that he could dress editors and friends. Karl knew the fashion industry was changing right there and then, transmuting into some-thing global.

And Karl's masterful response to the tomorrow of fashion was there even in that first collection. For amongst the clumsy Chanel-look suits there was one evening dress that pointed the way ahead for both Karl and Chanel. It was a long, black, utterly simple, beautifully fitting evening dress that was embroidered in a trompe-l'œil of costume jewellery. There were huge ropes of fake pearls and rubies worn long and choker-short around the neck, multiple strands of gilt and pearls at the waist and wide cuffs of fake jewels around the wrists, all of which were in fact embroidered on to the fabric.

Crucial to the success and desirability of the dress was the star model that wore it, and this would be a guiding rule at Chanel under Karl. For now it was Inès de la Fressange, another French aristocrat who was Karl's new muse at Chanel. She was black-haired and boyish, with a strong jaw-line and wide, crooked smile that evoked the look of Gabrielle Chanel herself. Karl sent Inès down the runway with cigarette in hand, looking part Gabrielle, part nightclubber. It was a witty pastiche on both Chanel's personal style and Chanel's couturier style that Karl reinter-preted and made relevant for now, now being 1983.

This was to be Karl's magic formula for the house: exploiting the existing iconography of *le look Chanel* and combining that with elements of the moment that Karl anticipates and identifies with unfailing and extraordinary accuracy, so that his fashion resonates with the feeling of the Zeitgeist. 'Fashion is also an attempt to make certain invisible aspects of the reality of the moment visible,' wrote Karl in the catalogue accom-panying the Chanel exhibition at the Metropolitan Museum in 2005; this was also to be Karl's role in the equation. It sounds so obvious now, over twenty years later, now that so many designers rely on a similar formula for success. But it was not obvious in 1983. Karl created the blueprint for this post-modern process of fashion design and for breathing new life into an existing but moribund fashion house.

Karl's method hinges on the ultimate strength of what Chanel designed, the fact that her style was enduring and iconic enough to survive both time and plunder. More than any other designer of her period, Chanel had created a 'look', recognisable even to the untrained eye: the suit, the tweed, black and white, the faux pearls and jersey fabric, the ease and camellias, the chain belts strung with leather and of course the branded and interlocking double 'C's. There was a visual code of Chanel and it was monumental, indelible.

For a designer who relied on his so-called powers of 'vampirisation' to create, Karl had before him now the most wonderful, inexhaustible supply of energy to consume; here was a life, a woman, a supreme body of work, a style.

He turned fifty in the year of 1983, although that was not publicly known, and at last it seemed that, after all the years of grind, the glory had arrived. Eric Wright, who joined Karl's design team as an assistant in 1983, recalls, 'That was the year everything popped for Karl.' He bounced straight back from his lacklustre debut at Chanel, taking on the ready-to-wear collections as predicted. KL, his third perfume licence with Elizabeth Arden, was launched in Europe at the end of 1982 with a huge party held at Versailles, followed in May 1983 by the US launch and a two-week promotional tour. And by the end of the year Karl had signed a deal with American manufacturer Bidermann Industries to launch a line of ready-to-wear under his own name. Bidermann had grand plans to make Lagerfeld the Ralph Lauren of France, producing a less expensive, sportswear line, while Lagerfeld had plans for a higher-priced designer line. The contrast in ambition was perhaps indicative of the miscommunication between the two sides from the outset. Bidermann formed two companies, one in America for the sportswear and a house in Paris for the high-fashion line. But from the start the Karl Lagerfeld line was overshadowed by the greater might, wealth and glamour of the house of Chanel.

Karl was now showing ready-to-wear for Chanel as well as for his own line in Paris twice a year. As soon as those shows were over, he then flew to New York and three weeks later presented another sports-wear line. Add to that his commitments at Fendi and by 1984 Karl was designing eight ready-to-wear collections a year plus two haute-couture collections, and this did not include his other freelance commitments or promotional work for his perfumes.

The more his workload grew, the more it seemed Karl's energy levels expanded to fulfil these enormous commitments. He slept only four or five hours a night, taking micro-naps during the day. He recharged by dropping off for ten minutes' sleep here and there, in a car, on a plane, as described by Inès, who travelled with Karl to America for the two-week launch of a perfume. When they got to Chicago they had a full day of promotion followed by a gala dinner that they escaped from in a stretch limousine to go and find a hamburger joint. They ate hot dogs then jumped back in the car; a few minutes later Inès turned to find Karl fast asleep with his hands curled up like a baby.

'We were working like maniacs,' says Eric Wright, 'doing nineteen-hour days, moving all over the place, different studios, New York, Monte Carlo, Rue Cambon, Rome, shooting the ad campaigns, and throughout the years Karl kept up this incredibly intense work-pace.' 'He is extremely professional,' says Ralph Toledano, who became president of Karl Lagerfeld in 1985 and stayed for ten years. 'I have seen Karl have three dinners in a row just to be able to accommodate as many press people as possible.'

Toledano remembers a trip to Singapore for the Karl Lagerfeld line in the 1980s. It started disastrously when Toledano and Lagerfeld got out of the plane to thirty-eight-degree heat. 'Karl was wearing a cash-mere blazer and sweater and the minute we got out of the plane both our glasses steamed up. Then, instead of having a Bentley or a Rolls as usual to meet us, they sent a Peugeot. We got to the hotel and instead of a suite and twenty-five bottles of champagne, it was a room and half a bottle of sweet white wine,' says Toledano to evoke the unspectacular start to their trip.

'Karl wants to leave and we say, please Karl, so he agrees to stay and he finally falls asleep. We go downstairs to prepare the show and there is the star of Singapore journalism, who has been granted an interview with Mr Lagerfeld, demanding to see him. And I say, I'm sorry you can't have the interview; there will be no interview. And Karl's driver at the time was Bryam and Bryam says to me, "I'm going to wake him up," and I said, "Are you crazy?" Bryam took himself off upstairs and banged on the door and kept banging until Karl came out in a bathrobe, hair totally undone, and Bryam tells him Mr Singapore wants to see him, and Karl says, "Bryam, you are an idiot." Ten minutes later the journalist is still waiting and I see coming towards us a perfectly dressed gentleman: Karl. He gave a ninety-minute interview with a guy who did not have a clue about fashion. Finally the Singapore business partner comes up and interrupts to say Mr Lagerfeld has to finish the inter-view now and Karl looks up and says, "I'm sorry but the journalist has not finished his work yet." This was really impressive and this level of dedication is one of Karl's strengths, one of his very many strengths.'

Karl immediately made wide-sweeping changes at the house of Chanel, which had not changed much since her death. 'I'm working like the Communist Party,' he said in 1983, 'bringing in my own people and placing them everywhere.' He kept the 'Mademoiselle' sign on the studio door, but inside Karl operated it more like a newsroom than a conventional couture studio. He arrived always armed with piles of magazines, exhibition catalogues and information, people he had picked up, a computer magazine, tapes he had bought in quadruplicate, records that he bought by the hundred – later on CDs, eventually iPods – and talk of the film, or more likely films, he had seen the night before. 'An ideal evening out is to go to five different movies, just twenty minutes or so of each. Then eat in a little restaurant near the Champs-Elysées – the Maison de Caviar, or the Brasserie Lowenbrau – then go buy records at the all-night record store. What a thrill,' he said in 1983.

Karl's new job provoked new superstar behaviour: his arrival at the studio came later and later. He was due to arrive at midday; at two in the afternoon there was a phone call through to the studio, 'He's coming,' then ten minutes later, 'He's not coming, he's gone to La Hune.' It carried on like this until finally, at four o'clock in the afternoon, the doorman at Chanel rang up to the studio and announced, 'Karl is here,' so that when he did eventually walk through the door five minutes later, bearing new sketches, news and action, he was greeted by a hot rush of gratitude. It was a means of wielding power, establishing control of the studio. He made his entourage wait too.

He liked the studio packed with people, the more the better, and in a state of constant flux, chatter and distraction. 'He's got the shortest attention span of anyone I know in the business,' says Patrick McCarthy. 'That's what makes him so right for fashion.' To begin with at Chanel he surrounded himself with well-bred French aristos, just as Chanel herself had once done and for much the same reason. The members of his shifting entourage were there to provide information, energy, laughter, ideas and, significantly, youth, and they were replaced when they no longer fulfilled these criteria. 'I have my spies . . . my sneaks and antennae who are out there picking up information for me, but who themselves don't know how to give concrete expression to that information,' said

Karl Lagerfeld in 1984. Jacques was one of those antennae, at this point probably still the most vital, and how it must have hurt to read Karl's words in the press and see his limitations expressed in print. Jacques was often at the Chanel studio, telling jokes, advising on the choice of models, bringing in music and dropping by to get the atelier to make up his black leather stitched blankets. Gilles Dufour, who had been working with Karl since 1971, was now by his side in the studio, where he would stay for fifteen years. 'I brought him sensuality,' says Gilles. 'He has no sensuality, but he is a genius with black and white. He can get something out of nothing; give him a little black dress and he can trans-form it.' Gilles had introduced Karl to his seventeen-year-old niece Victoire de Castellane, a pin-up blonde and the great-great-niece of belle-époque dandy Boni de Castellane. She favoured micro-miniskirts and joined Chanel to design the costume jewellery. Inès de la Fressange was a day-to-day fixture and key to Karl's beginnings at Chanel. Karl persuaded Kitty d'Alessio to hire her under an exclusive contract that paid her a million francs a year. This was a huge amount of money for a model to be paid. Inès was employed to be a house mannequin, which by 1983 was a rare thing to find in the couture houses of Paris. She was the face of all the advertising campaigns, both perfume and fashion, and a spokeswoman for the brand. Inès was less compulsive but aesthetically similar to Jacques, with whom she was a great friend. He called her by the nickname of 'brunette'. She had an androgynous, long-limbed allure as well as taking a childish delight in practical jokes. 'They called me the muse, but I was more of an "amusement",' wrote Inès in her auto-biography. 'I was the king's fool.' Karl wanted her around him all the time, in Paris and abroad, and for a time she seemed to reassure him with her gags and grin. 'In the beginning I thought that I was lucky and that I had to be on my toes to be up to it; then I got the feeling that Karl was sure about me. I felt secure.'

Karl sat behind his desk and watched the studio in motion. The fittings began to a backdrop of noise and incessant conversation. The model appeared with the *premier d'atelier*, Karl made some suggestions and asked all those around him – the model, Jacques, Inès, Victoire, a PR, a journalist – 'What do you think?' 'Nice, *non?*' 'Chic, *non?*' '*Très Chanel, non?*' Karl listened to their replies, their opinions; he listened to their tales of the night before, to what André Leon Talley had seen in

Milan last week. He looked at what they were wearing; the fabulous leggings and Pucci shirt on the stylist from *Elle*, Inès' new black ballet-pumps from Repetto, Victoire's Mini Mouse headset worn with kinky black boots, the PR's white frayed jeans worn with Karl's new cashmere for Chanel. 'All this information was like food to him,' says Eric Wright, 'but Karl himself was generous with his own information, he never hoarded knowledge. He was always putting it out there, eager to hear your opinion. 'It was so vital and invigorating being around him,' says Natasha Fraser-Cavassoni, who joined the Chanel studio as an assistant in the late 1980s. 'He has an extraordinary energy that is very specific to fashion – new fashion. It was all about the next and being the first.' He had a cerebral approach to design – there was no touching of bodies, or fitting or hanging of fabric on a model; it was all done by speech and sketches. He had considerable technical expertise, gained from his years of experience on the front line of fashion. Contrary to the first season's blip of baggy armholes, Karl displayed excellent knowledge of cut, fit and fashion craft and an ability to communicate his desires to the Chanel ateliers.

Beneath the strident creativity and high spirits of the studio, levels of paranoia were high. 'Karl liked the tension of putting the cat among the pigeons; it was his way of controlling,' says one who worked there. There was jealousy, rivalry and the fear of being eclipsed. There was always the favourite of the moment, the one Karl wanted to photograph. And there were always those relegated to the sidelines, or on their way out of the door; they were the ones Karl sketched in unflattering caricature when their backs were turned.

Anna Piaggi was sliding out of his life. She had been crucial for the Chloé years, but she was not part of the inspirational team at Chanel. Karl had abandoned his highwayman outfits for a business suit and ponytail and it was only a matter of time before Anna's fancy dress would be expelled from court. Tellingly, Karl only ever removed someone when the new favourite was already found and in place. In this way Karl was never alone.

He finally broke with Chloé at the end of 1983 after a highly acrimonious wrangle. Jacques Lenoir had been heavy-handed in his treatment of Karl in the past, and it looked as if Karl was relishing his revenge with a series of public verbal assaults against Chloé. He accused them of tampering with his designs ('altering horrible dresses behind my back to sell them – notably to women in the Gulf countries'), compared them to 'some poor East German outfit . . . the management is nothing but a bunch of empty shells', and claimed they were jealous of his financial situation at the house, saying his profit share was twice theirs.

It was an ugly schism and one in which Karl tossed his twenty-year friendship and tutelage with Gaby Aghion on to the pyre. Gaby had exerted a huge influence over Karl; she was no pushover – forceful, maternal and domineering – but she loved him: they had worked together, travelled together, existed together for twenty years; she had helped him grow and take shape. Perhaps he needed to express his independence, but it seemed the only way Karl progressed in a friendship was by severing it completely.

Jacques went home to La Berrière for a weekend, bearing gifts of Chanel tweed suits and padded Chanel leather bags. His mother opened her arms to him, while his sister Anne chose instead to confront him with reality. That weekend Anne told him to get a job, get out of his life of financial dependence, use his talent for languages in some way. She kept pushing him further, determined to provoke a reaction, until at last he cried out, 'I know. I know. But what am I going to do? Work like any other fool?' Jacques knew he was dependent but, desperate as he was, he could not imagine life any other way. Since his adolescence he had sought out older men to educate him or keep him financially and it seemed that now, even though he was over thirty, he was unwilling to take responsibility and unable to grow up, to break with the adolescent in him. He was caught up in his own inner contradictions and seemed powerless to do anything about it.

In Paris Jacques was regarded by so many as 'just a gigolo', and he was angry and increasingly frustrated and humiliated by his role. 'I think at some point no one likes to be in the shadows and Jacques was,' says Patrick McCarthy. 'Jacques was a wonderful, smart man but he was never able to translate it into anything and here were all these people being hugely successful and he wasn't. I think that was a source of unhappiness in him.'

He met up with old friend Renaud for lunch and accused him in a cold and critical way of 'not creating anything'. Renaud was rather taken aback by the accusation as he was working at the time as a teacher in geopolitics and therefore had no pretensions or aspirations to create. It was of course Jacques himself who had created nothing and he knew that. The eight-year-old boy who had preferred to sell his younger brother the idea of spraying his train set with fake snow rather than do it himself had grown into a man who inspired others but who had no *œuvre* of his own. Instead all he had was a box full of press cuttings, photographs of himself with momentary celebrities (he had taken to going out at night escorted by a personal photographer) and a handful of parties that he had organised. 'The Venetian Ball,' says Christian Lvowski, 'that was Jacques' apogee.' Perhaps, but what kind of apogee was that? Just another costume ball at Le Palace in 1978, another party, another two thousand people dressed up in masks and crinoline, paid for by Karl, in honour of Karl.

'*De la Cité des Doges à la Cité des Dieux*,' read the invitation that was in the shape of a black Venetian domino. People had loved it at the time: the Venetian theme of chandeliers and candlelight, the bartenders dressed up as liveried footmen in wigs and satin, Jacques arriving as the Bridge of Sighs, Anna Piaggi dressed as a Venetian fisherman's wife in vintage black velvet Fortuny with a basket of spider crabs and a couple of dead pigeons on her head. But all that was left now were a pile of yellowing press cuttings and memories. Since then even the parties Jacques got involved with had lost their grandeur. He put his name to the opening of a gay bar, Duplex, in 1980 and a party at La Scala, a cheap nightclub on Rue de Rivoli the following year.

'I think he doubted himself terribly, Jacques. He had an overwhelming need to be recognised. Jacques, poor darling, his position was feeble, he did not have the will or power. He was dependent, dependent on everything; the fear that the next day he could be thrown aside by Karl and that would be the beginning of the end of Jacques de Bascher,' says Diane. 'To live in that perpetual anxiety is not very pleasant. Nobody can live up to that without making mistakes.'

'I think that at one point Jacques faced a personal dilemna of choosing between Jacques the person and Jacques the personage,' reflects Christian Lvowski. 'He chose the personage.' Did he choose it, or was it simply that Jacques had nowhere else to go now? 'He could not disassociate himself from his image; he was devoured by his image of a dandy and he would only be himself; he would only relax with those people that he could trust and love,' says Diane de Beauvau-Craon. 'Jacques could not be this image of glamour, of beauty, of the dandy with Karl and then suddenly decide to drop everything and go to the dogs if he had to. It changed his life. He got into it and then he couldn't get out. He had an extremely difficult choice to make. On the one hand he had these luxury voyages, the high life and image and on the other he had what? The anonymous life of a poor gentleman farmer in a small château in the provinces.'

He would go and see his brother Xavier, who was working as a graphic designer for Kenzo and doing photography in his own time, and end up criticising his apartment and his modest belongings. 'Jacques was horrified by mediocrity. He used to say to me, "Look how you live!" and I would reply, "Well, what's the problem? I'm working, I don't care if I haven't got a car. I know this work is going to allow me to do what I want to do and to make something of my talent; all the rest – where I'm living – is not important. There is no mediocrity in that." Of course he knew I was right but at the same time he was living the dream; he had access to all these extreme things and that allowed him to live in a way that was much more intense and far less mediocre.'

From around 1980 onwards Jacques' personal image began to focus on the theme of the Vendée royalist. The Vendée is a department to the west of France that looks out on the Atlantic Ocean and was fiercely pro-monarchy during the revolution. Although the family home of La Berrière is situated in the Loire Atlantique, not the Vendée, both departments were highly active in their support for Louis XVI and were of paramount importance to the restoration of the monarchy in 1814. Indeed several of Jacques' ancestors were champions of the cause and fought on the battlegrounds for Louis XVIII's restoration.

Jacques took the Vendée royalist as his personal mythology. He had already had the fleur-de-lys of the French monarchy tattooed on to his bottom years before, but now he developed a fetish for the period. He had a black leather jacket made that was studded across the back with the slogan *Vive le Roi!* He took the Vendée emblem of red heart atop a red cross as his personal symbol, wearing a badge of it on his lapel, and he talked up a storm to all those around him about his royalist sympathies. It was all vaguely ridiculous, even in the eyes of his close friends, and for many French people Jacques' attitude came with the

rather uncomfortable connotations of the far right with which the
royalist cause was often associated.

All this time Karl's fortune and success were growing immeasurably.
The job at Chanel put him on the world stage as a designer for the
first time and made him a household celebrity, which he had never
been before. He had been a big name within Paris, within the fashion
elite, but Chanel exposed him to a whole other level of fame. He was
constantly travelling, promoting, preparing collections. 'He took aero-
planes like they were buses,' remembers Kitty d'Alessio. He was under
incredible pressure to perform and succeed – Alain Wertheimer was
paying him $1 million a year on the understanding that he would get
results – although some of that pressure was self-induced: in 1985 when
Karl's contract was up for renewal he demanded that Wertheimer up
his salary to $1 million per collection. Wertheimer initially baulked at
the sum, but when Karl refused to come out at the end of a ready-to-
wear show to take his bow, rumours flew that he would leave the house.
Chanel issued a denial and Karl got his money. He also got rid of Kitty
d'Alessio, against whom he had been fighting a bitter war of attrition.
'They say she's director of special projects,' said Karl to a journalist in
1990, 'but we have no special projects.'

Jacques saw less and less of Karl and he spent more and more time
down in Monaco, staying in the apartment Karl kept there. 'A house
without a past' is how Karl described the apartment. How apt. It was
in fact two flats that were interconnected by a private landing on the
twenty-first floor of a high-rise block that overlooked the sea. Jacques
had one apartment, Karl the other; Jacques never shared a living space
with Karl.

Karl's private apartment was decorated with the furniture of the
Memphis group that was fashionable at that moment in 1983. Karl had
the whole place fitted out with the group's rather bizarre contemporary furniture of primary colours that he himself wittily described as
looking like 'Frankfurt hotel concierge furniture'. There was a large
boxing-ring by Japanese designer Masanori Umeda stuck bang in the
middle of the salon.

Like much of Monaco's population, Jacques was bored and restless.
He invited friends down to entertain him and relieve the sky-blue ennui.
He would call up Marc Rioufol and they would arrive together from

Nice airport by helicopter, Marc dressed in a scruffy T-shirt and a pair of jeans. 'I'd have to be completely overhauled. Jacques would take me off for a manicure, a haircut, to be redressed from A to Z, beautiful jackets from Caraceni, so that I was presentable,' remembers Marc. 'We weren't supposed to draw attention to ourselves in Monaco. Karl wanted us to wear dark glasses always; he didn't want any scandal. We had to be chic; we had to be clean.' Jacques wanted to hang out, take drugs, do nothing, sit on the *terrasses* and watch and be watched. 'But after two or three days it would always end in a row with Jacques,' says Rioufol. 'I came by helicopter and I left on the cheapest train out of there. The rows were always about money and power. I left not because I was virtuous but because I was allergic to power. I've always had a strong instinct for survival. I left and it saved my life, because it was all a huge trap; it was like Pinocchio at the fair, it wasn't my money, it wasn't my house. It was all so unbelievable, it was too Memphis, it was like something out of a cartoon.'

It wasn't Jacques' house or money either and that was a source of conflict and utter powerlessness. Karl never gave Jacques an apartment or a house; everything was rented. According to those close to Jacques, there was no independent source of income or capital set up for him. The money was on tap and could therefore be turned on and off depending on Jacques' behaviour. There was no autonomy. Instead there were endless suits and shirts, outfits of lederhosen from Lanz in Vienna, and there were presents, all of which only emphasised the role of courtesan. 'He was spoilt rotten,' says Gilles Dufour.

Christian and Renaud met up with Jacques one night at the Hôtel Saint Albany for a drink and Jacques appeared wearing an enormous brooch of a gold fleur-de-lys and a diamond daffodil on his lapel. After half an hour's suspense Christian could resist it no longer and asked him about the brooch. 'Oh that,' said Jacques carelessly, 'it's a little token because my birthday present is late. My real present will be Grand-Champ but the works are running late and so Karl has given me this in the meantime.' The gift of the Château de Penhoët never came to fruition and one wonders if it was ever promised or if this was one more of Jacques' wishful exaggerations.

In 1983 Jacques moved out of Place Saint-Sulpice and into the fifth-floor apartment Karl had rented at 202, Rue de Rivoli. It was no longer

needed as a studio for Karl, now that he was officially installed at Rue
Cambon. The apartment overlooked the austere and formal beauty of
Les Tuileries. Inside the décor was cold, graphic and functional and the
walls were painted in grey and white. Anne visited him there: 'You walked
down a corridor and there were photographs of naked men everywhere.
There was no place for women in there; it was black, white, frigid.'

There is a photograph of Jacques taken by Roxanne Lowit at a party
held at Radio City in New York in 1983 to celebrate the launch in
America of Karl's new fragrance for women, called KL. Jacques was
thirty-two. It is an image of infinite sadness. All the insolence and
laughter of youth have gone. His once-supple features have hardened
into disillusion. The bone-structure and beauty that Hockney expressed
with the ease and subtlety of pencil have taken on the brittleness of a
copper-plate etching. His face is more gaunt than before, not ill so much
as older, older than his age. His eyes have retreated into his eyelids
slightly, pulling back from the outside world and looking out in sorrow.
He holds up his right hand vertically in front of his chest in a strange
gesture that recalls a martyr's blessing or an entreaty for solitude.

When did Jacques realise he was ill? Did he sense that something
was wrong even before he realised he was HIV positive? No one seems
to be able to say for sure. His sister Anne believes Jacques knew of his
condition only later, around 1987. As early as 1981 the first cases of an
unexplained immune deficiency syndrome were being identified in the
US and referred to by a number of names including GRID (gay-related
immune deficiency), gay syndrome and gay cancer, due to its apparent
link with homosexuals. But it was not until May 1983 that Professor
Luc Montagnier of the Institut Pasteur together with a team of international researchers identified the virus causing AIDS, although the
cause-and-effect relation between the virus and AIDS the illness was
still unresolved at this stage.

The first years of the disease were a period of terrifying unknown.
Paris, despite being central to research, lagged behind America in general
awareness and understanding of the virus. There was talk of a strange
illness brought over from America, then it was said to be Africa. There
were surreal rumours of the disease being spread by monkeys, then later
aeroplane air-conditioning. There was so little real information. And to
begin with AIDS was associated almost entirely with the homosexual

community. It was an appalling blow for a community that had literally only just broken free from the presumed guilt of their sexuality –
now nature was apparently 'linking' homosexual physical pleasure to
mortality. It was an association that was catastrophic and monstrous in
all its perceived connotations of retribution. 'Everybody started getting
sick, nobody knew what it was – the ugly splotches,' says Pat Cleveland,
who remembers getting into the lift one day with the beautiful male
model Joe MacDonald. 'I said, "How are you? What's wrong?" and he
said, "I don't know. Don't touch me."' Don't touch me, said the generation that had freed touch from every taboo.

In June 1983 Fabrice Emaer died and even now the cause of his death
is not agreed upon. He had been ill for some time, confined increasingly to his apartment on the Rue de Rivoli, although he appeared at
Le Palace for a fifth-birthday celebration of the club with the aid of
morphine and a walking-stick. A likely cause of death was AIDS,
although at the time many insisted and still do insist that it was cancer
of the liver. Whatever the actual cause, the rumours, speculation and
suspected hushing-up are all indicative of the panic that now entered
the fashionable world. The funeral took place at the church of Saint
Roch, on Rue Saint Honoré, just behind the Tuileries. It is a dark and
baroque parish church that is the church of *artistes* in Paris and the place
where Molière's funeral mass was celebrated. It was to be the venue for
so many funerals of Paris fashion and night people who were to die of
AIDS in the years that followed.

Two thousand people attended Fabrice's funeral, and as his coffin left
the church and descended the steps, the Palace and Le Sept crowd began
to cheer and applaud him. Fabrice's death signified the end of an era.
He had been the magician who had conjured up the pleasure, the dance
and eroticism, the oblivion of the night.

In retrospect so many identify AIDS as the black hole into which
their world of glamour and laughter now plunged, but the end had
been among them for years. It was there in the coke and heroin that
covered fashion in a film of dust. It was there in the telephone calls
through to the dealer before the night could begin. It was there in the
junkie suicides and deaths, there in the track marks showing blue beneath
the cover-up foundation on the model's inner arm. There in the death
of Emmanuelle, once a favourite model of Helmut Newton, who had

got involved with heroin and was found dead in a Paris apartment in a sordid, macabre tale of overdose, torture and suspected murder.

No doubt the quantity of drugs being consumed numbed not only the senses but also people's perception of the danger they were putting themselves in. Paris had yet to digest the peril of heroin; indeed, according to writer Fran Lebowitz, the major difference between Paris and New York at this time was that in Paris you could take heroin openly and in public.

'In '69 the drugs began. It was just easy joints, then it was cocaine and that became devastating for people,' says Renata Zatsch, who had started as Antonio's model in Paris and by the end of the 1970s lived with a photographer who had developed a drug habit. 'I travelled a lot and I remember I came home one day and there was this brown stuff lying on the table; you know, coke I'd seen before, but this was a strange colour and I said what is this and he laughed and said, "It's smack." I said, "What are you doing? You're going to kill yourself." "Not me," he said, "I can handle it, I can handle it." I would come home and they would all be sitting there with their eyes rolled back. It was such an ugly time.'

Heroin ravaged Paris fashion. 'Coke was bad enough,' says Patrick McCarthy, 'but the heroin was deadly, it instantly ruins your life and people were really getting into heroin in a big way. That is what caused the downfall of people like Claude [Montana]. That all started to happen at this time, people were finding needles in the bathrooms in magazine companies. Drugs took their toll.' But perhaps it wasn't only the drugs but fashion itself that played a role in the litany of casualties from these years. 'Fashion eats people up,' says McCarthy, 'and you know what? It attracts people that are willing to be eaten up. It is a very self-destructive industry, which is probably what keeps it alive. It eats its young.'

'Self-destruction,' echoes Pat Cleveland. 'We started surrounding ourselves with blackness, dark, negative; I'm talking about dark things we were doing, too much sex, too much promiscuity, too much drugs, too much night.'

The end had been there among them for years, but fashion's ability to staunch reality, its endless dance across the mirrored surface of the ideal, meant that it could hold off the fall and sustain the illusion for one more fashion season, one more fabulous party, one more magazine shoot, always one more fashion moment.

'We all knew that somewhere it had to have an end,' says Diane de Beauvau-Craon. 'I think that those people that went all the way through, pushing themselves to a wilder and wilder extent, were totally conscious of that. We would mention the end, we'd live up to the end, we weren't damn fools, we knew it would end. But I'm not sure that we thought the end would hit us individually, because we had always been a group.'

Chapter 18

1983–85

Yves Saint Laurent might have renounced all responsibility to capturing the fashion moment, but he did not rescind his claim to fashion's crown. Pierre rallied his old friend and Saint Laurent faithful Diana Vreeland, who was by now rising eighty and special consultant at the Costume Institute of the Metropolitan Museum of Art in New York, and in 1983 a major retrospective of Yves Saint Laurent opened there. It was the first time a living designer had been honoured with a retrospective at the Metropolitan. It was remarkable not just because Yves was still alive, but also because he was still so young, aged forty-seven. The exhibition, 'Yves Saint Laurent – 25 Years of Design', comprised 243 pieces that were drawn from every stage of Yves' career – the Dior days through to the Broadway collection – and it was an astounding evocation of Yves' power and reach. Yet at the same time it had all the cold marble connotations of a mausoleum. Yves' life, work and dreams were encased behind glass; there were memories on mannequins and sweet eulogies. Yves seemed dazed by the very idea of it. 'I'm afraid to even think about it,' he said just before getting on the plane to New York for the opening gala night. 'All those people, all those parties, all those journalists. And then, of course, there's the biggest worry of all. What will I do afterwards?' Afterwards Yves Saint Laurent – the couturier and his couture house – became an act of remembrance. Over one million visitors went to see the Saint Laurent exhibition in New York. But the retrospective did not end with the closing of the exhibition doors in August 1984. It travelled the world to Beijing, Paris, Moscow, St Petersburg, Sydney and Tokyo and dragged on for an incredible seven years.

This was a decade dominated by major clinical depressions for Yves Saint Laurent. Victoire remembers Yves being hospitalised for an alcohol-induced coma during 1985. There were long periods at the American Hospital in Neuilly, as well as in a private psychiatric clinic west of Paris.

Not surprisingly the pace and intensity of Yves' creativity slowed considerably. 'I have become a monk,' he said in 1982. 'Going out is my idea of torture. I want to stay at home. When I'm in my bed with a great book, I feel as if nothing else matters.' He cut himself off from reality and it showed in his work. The Saint Laurent shows and clothes became a fairy tale of a lavishly dressed, rich and consummately bour-geois woman. It was as if the sixteenth-*arrondissement* woman that Helmut Newton had imagined as the personification of what he loved to photo-graph had grown up into a 45-year-old divorcee whose vice no longer manifested itself in her afternoon sexual dalliances but rather in how much financial damage she could inflict on her ex-husband by totting up couture bills at the house of Saint Laurent. The clothes Yves imag-ined during the 1980s were overtly extravagant: a huge taffeta fuchsia skirt worn with rich black silk velvet jacket soft enough to lay your head on, movie-star voluptuous furs, a panther-printed trench coat enveloped in the syrupy scent of his new perfume Paris, launched in 1983. These clothes did indeed reflect the booming wealth of the indus-trialised world of the 1980s, with bull markets and the *nouveau riche* and their highly demonstrable wealth, but they did not communicate the Saint Laurent subversive chic and edge of old.

There was a palpable disappointment at his shows, both with his clothes and significantly with him. It was as if the audience could not give up the hope that he would redeem them all by delivering genius once again. The repetition within his collections was even more apparent once Christian Lacroix burst upon the couture scene as designer at Jean Patou. By 1985 the press, and in particular the American couture clients, were enraptured by Lacroix's stupendous colour, puff and sense of eigh-teenth-century coquetry. Hebe Dorsey, fashion editor of the *International Herald Tribune*, wrung her hands at the sight of suit after suit on the

Saint Laurent catwalk. 'He is such a giant that I wonder if we are not asking too much of him. I wonder if he is bored. He's not working, he's not caring, something is broken there. He is just making the pretence,' she said in an interview. 'Now we don't have a leader. What Saint Laurent did was unbelievable – the range of things and the creativity. At one time, everybody had something of his – from the smallest little secretary with a scarf, to the boots and the jackets. Now what do we have? Little suits.' Interestingly, when prompted to come up with a replacement for Yves she initially named Karl. 'Karl is fantastic, and, if anybody could replace Saint Laurent, Karl could do it. He is a non-stop worker.' But then minutes later she retracts her suggestion. 'I don't think anybody could ever replace Saint Laurent. Karl is like a chameleon – one minute he is Fendi, one minute Chanel and another KL. He is too prolific, and he needs editing.'

When Yves did reappear in public, it was as a changed man. He limped, he slurred his speech, his lips trembled, he had difficulty controlling his jaw muscles, he was hunched over and he stumbled. He had put on vast amounts of weight; the pencil-stroke silhouette of the 1970s was gone. When he came out to receive his ovation at the end of a show, he clung from one model to the next, staggering to make his way down the runway. Bergé made sure that he was constantly surrounded, aided and instructed by bodyguards, with a clutch of doctors standing backstage. Saint Laurent was undergoing intense psychoanalysis, with daily visits to his Paris psychiatrist. He supplemented his visits to the psychiatrist by taking sedatives, which unfortunately he often chose to knock back with alcohol, a habit remarked upon by a *Time* Paris correspondent when he went to interview Yves at home in Rue de Babylone in 1983.

According to Christophe Girard, who worked at the house of Saint Laurent alongside Bergé from 1977 to 1997, 'Bergé's real strategy from the 1980s onwards was to get Saint Laurent into the museums. And it was very much a strategy, chosen and decided by him alone. Bergé was the one who had the idea for the retrospective and proposed it to Diana Vreeland, then negotiated with the Metropolitan so that it should happen. After the Metropolitan, it was museums all the time. I think Pierre Bergé was scared for Saint Laurent's health; from the 1980s onwards Saint Laurent was not in good physical shape, and I think that Pierre was very fearful.

So there was this need to fix the name in eternity, I think this was the reaction of someone extremely worried. It was a strategy that paid off.'

The retrospective was the cornerstone of this process, for it represented the official recognition of Yves not only as the greatest living designer, but as an artist. After New York, Pierre organised an endless cycle of anniversary dinners, tributes, retrospective fashion shows and smaller exhibitions. There was a celebration dinner to mark the twenty years of the house of Saint Laurent, held at the Lido in 1982, with Catherine Deneuve and the whole staff of the couture house choked by tears and emotion. There were exhibitions of the Russian themes of Saint Laurent's collections held at the Musée Jacquemart-André in Paris and Saint Laurent's Indian-inspired dresses in New Delhi. In 1992 there was a celebration to mark the thirty years of the couture house with a huge retrospective show at the Opéra Bastille, at which Catherine Deneuve and the whole staff of the couture house were once more choked by tears and emotion.

Along with the exhibitions, Pierre invited stars of the French literary establishment – Marguerite Duras, Françoise Sagan, Bernard-Henri Lévy – to write about Yves in a series of books, catalogues and monographs that Pierre organised. They poured out their prose in homage to Yves' fashion and addressed the issue of Yves as artist in a manner that at times seemed less than spontaneous. In 1985 Yves was made a Chevalier de la Légion d'Honneur in a ceremony conducted by François Mitterrand.

This was also the decade in which Pierre started to live out his own personal ambitions. It started with a friendship with Jack Lang, the new Mitterrand-appointed Minister of Culture and perhaps France's first Minister of Culture to be seen out at night dancing at Le Palace. Lang was characteristic of the new face of French socialism, the so-called *gauche caviar* (a French equivalent of the champagne socialist), with his Saint Germain good looks, winter suntan and high ideals of state-subsidised culture. He perceived fashion as a marvellous means of communicating France's peerless sensibility of beauty and taste, as well as a terrific source of export revenue. Bergé was still president of the Chambre Syndicale at the time and together the two men came up with a plan to move the ready-to-wear shows, previously held out in an exhibition centre in the draughty outskirts of Paris, into tents to be erected during show-time, bang in the centre of Paris, in the central *cour carrée* of the Louvre.

Bergé, a man who had voted for the conservative Raymond Barre in 1981 and had watched the results of the election at the Hôtel Lambert as a guest of Marie-Hélène and Guy de Rothschild, became a high-profile patron of the socialists, and then an intimate of François Mitterrand himself. This happened in what Bergé described to *The New Yorker* as a 'stupefying' moment at an after-rally dinner where Bergé was talking of his admiration for obscure Breton poet René-Guy Cadou and Mitterrand stood up and spontaneously recited a Cadou poem. It was another classic episode in Bergé's epic voyage of life: the fateful encounter across the sweeping and heroic tumult of French liter-ature. They met for weekly Sunday lunches at the resolutely French restaurant L'Assiette and went for walks along the Seine afterwards and talked of Zola. Bergé's friendship and considerable generosity to the Left's coffers were recognised in 1988 when he was appointed the director of the Paris Opéra. This was the pinnacle of his success and influence and a logical progression in Bergé's childhood avowal to be close to the *faiseurs de feu*, the fire-makers. He had progressed through literary heroes; he had explored the limits of fashion, which he had always regarded as a minor art with the obvious and unique exception of Saint Laurent. Now, aged fifty-eight, he wanted a shot at the real political power-brokers. 'It was at this moment that I said to myself, *bon*, the house of Saint Laurent is a done thing. I had not finished my job, but I had done a lot and I could take a step back both from Yves and from the house and it is in this way that I started to apply myself to artistic things. I started to have a different professional life, separate to the house,' says Bergé with a sudden, theatrical change of tone (*subito forte*) to denote his gathering importance. 'It is in this way I became president of the Opéra of Paris. It is in this way I entered into the realms of political support. It is in this way that I became involved with the press, newspapers, a whole roster of things that were completely apart from the house of Saint Laurent.' And it is in this way – Bergé dearly hoped – that he would be remembered for being something more than just the man who made Yves Saint Laurent.

★

Karl was settling into his new and glorious status as couturier at Chanel. He had arrived and he wanted the world to know. 'Lagerfeld wants to reign over fashion,' read the headline to a highly controversial interview that Karl gave in 1984 to *Actuel*, a French magazine that cross-bred contemporary culture, music, fashion and clubbing with world current affairs. The lengthy interview was conducted for the most part in question-and-answer format. Karl started with some verbal darts slung in the direction of Chloé before firing off a catalogue of insults against Yves Saint Laurent. He dragged up the Yves and Jacques affair. 'I had an assistant who people took to be my boyfriend, but I don't care if they thought that. When he started out in this milieu it was totally new to him and he wreaked havoc. They thought that I wanted to break them up . . . At the beginning of the '70s he brought another style that was different to the *babas cools* and hippies. All of a sudden it was a look that was *bon chic bon genre, bcbg* . . .' There is a short diversion into the merits or otherwise of the hippie period before the interviewer asks what sort of havoc Jacques wreaked and Karl replies, 'Yves Saint Laurent fell in love with him. His partner too . . . They even thought that I was trying to break them up in this way.'

It is not surprising that Yves' affair with Jacques eleven years earlier was still a source of immense bitterness and rancour for Karl; it always would be. However, what is startling about this exchange is the way in which Karl speaks of Jacques and his refusal even to acknowledge Jacques by his name or admit to him being anything more than an 'assistant'. Whether or not Jacques was Karl's boyfriend, he was certainly never Karl Lagerfeld's fashion assistant. The unwillingness to recognise Jacques that Paloma Picasso had remarked on at the very outset of their relationship was still an obstacle between them, eleven years later in 1984.

Karl then went on to insist on his friendship and admiration for Yves even as his speech rattled with resentment. 'Yves doesn't see many people these days . . . he only speaks about his health, it is extremely dull all that. But he is someone that I like a lot. Really. Who has sides to him that are touching. But I like what he does less. As soon as he starts talking in public, I don't like what he says; I find him extremely conventional . . . it is the apotheosis of the commonplace. That particular Yves I don't like because I know another one. He is one of the funniest people alive, with an incredible sense of humour, who can do

unbelievable impressions . . . who loved to use swear words and loved
anything scatological . . . who was really very funny. It is an absurd idea
when he says that he didn't have a youth. I knew him myself when
he had one, but he only had one desire at the time . . . to be rich and
famous.'

The interviewer interjected to say that was precisely the moment
Yves met Pierre Bergé. 'The day he met certain of his friends, it
changed his life . . . He was made to succeed. The first time I saw him
I said to myself, that is someone who is going to make it, he has a
kind of genius that is sure and certain. It came to him very quickly,
at the time of his last collection at Dior, in 1961, before he got himself
fired with that story of military service as a pretext. It was one of the
best collections of his life . . . He has invented a style that is modern
and easy to wear, which doesn't date and which corresponds to a
certain image of a bourgeois elegance that is accepted today.' Accusing
Yves of pulling the military service as a pretext for getting himself
fired from Dior was a heavy allegation to make. And later in the interview Karl could not resist a parting strike: 'He is very middle-of-the-
road French . . . He is very *pied-noir*, very provincial.' *Français moyen*,
pied-noir, *province*, they are all words that conjure up regional accents,
inferiority complexes and a lace doily hanging on the back of a faux-
tapestry armchair. Indeed they are words specifically intended to denote
the antithesis of Paris, capital, urbane, polished, sophisticated. And most
importantly they are words intended to express the antithesis of fashion,
which can only truly be created in Paris and worn by Parisians. This
is of course a myth, and one which fashion historian Valerie Steele
discusses with ironic bite when she writes, 'Paris is the capital of civil-
ization, the place where all the refinements of civilized life reach their
fullest expression – including the concepts of fine language and elegant
fashion. Certainly foreigners and provincials may *wear* Paris fashion –
even recognize its superiority – but they never wear it quite the same
way, and are utterly incapable of creating anything as good themselves.'
Steele says it with tongue firmly in cheek, but this is what Paris fashion
actually believes, and by accusing Yves of being a little *pied-noir* from
the provinces Karl was thrusting a dagger into the heart of Yves' taste
and chic.

Not surprisingly the story in *Actuel* provoked a violent backlash against Karl, earning him the sobriquet of Katty Karl, as fellow couturiers and the press flew to the defence of Yves, whom everyone knew was ill, depressed, down and out. Karl claimed he hadn't intended these comments for publication and that they had been quoted out of context. The journalist replied saying he had all the tapes, should anyone wish to verify, and that they contained much worse that he had been unable to print, which is presumably the reason for the use of ellipses throughout the published text.

Characteristically there was no reply from the wounded Yves himself. Instead Pierre Bergé pounded back in the press. 'The poor boy has a psychological problem. He is just a German designer who wants to be a Saint Laurent. He should see a psychiatrist. He needs help.'

What his words in *Actuel* make clear is that Karl's relationship with Yves started out as admiration, from that moment when Karl saw him as a natural and monumental talent, a man who was sure to succeed at a time when he, Karl, was perhaps less sure of his future path. Perhaps Yves was a kind of fixation for Karl – back in the days when he hung a sketch by Yves above his fireplace in the Rue de Tournon apartment, in the years when he saw Yves every night and they drove up and down the Champs-Elysées in high spirits in Karl's car and Yves decided where they should dine. And wasn't Karl in awe, just as they all were – Anne-Marie Muñoz, Victoire, Fernando, Jean-Pierre Derbord, Edmonde Charles-Roux, Pierre Bergé – when they first encountered Yves' sketches and felt the force and conviction of his line?

'Yves was born with a star over his head and there was nothing anyone else could do about that,' says Loulou de la Falaise, describing Yves' non-negotiable glory from the very beginning. 'It started from school. He always got more attention, the models were always more in love with him, and everybody would always pick him up – "how are you?" or "poor thing" – or they would mother him or look after him. I think that it shone out of him that he had talent. And it's enraging for people who are in the same trade and it's inexplicable in a way.'

Karl's ensuing envy was due to Yves' phenomenal, precocious success, but there was more to it than just that. Yves represented something that Karl could never be, Yves Saint Laurent whose whole creative process was a series of overreaching highs and cataclysmic lows, of giving his all in a frenzy of expression and emotion. Yves Saint Laurent whose work shimmered with emotion – 'the love letter to women', as Irene Silvagni so aptly describes it. He poured his whole being into his fashion: sexual energy, neurosis, tears. 'Oh yes,' Yves said in a French documentary of his life, *Le Temps Retrouvé*, in 2002, 'my sexuality has been very important to my creativity.'

This was the absolute contradiction of Karl's approach to creativity. For Karl there was no outpouring of emotion. Instead Karl creates by productivity, using his never-ending nervous energy, industriousness and knowledge and combining all that with other people's pasts and other people's emotions. 'Karl has always had the talent of finding the hip people that would feed him,' says former fashion schoolmate Fernando Sanchez. 'When he has finished with them he will [Sanchez flicks his hands to motion disposal of] and new people come in. Karl is brilliantly intelligent, brilliantly cultivated and he knows how to read, he knows how to decipher and he knows how to surround himself with what is happening. Great talent.'

This design process is a source of immense strength for Karl because it means there is constant renewal and therefore he will never be left behind by fashion. Not for him the fate of all those designers who express themselves, their vision, and then watch as their style, what they stood for, what they had created, falls from fashion, or, even more heartbreaking, realise that they have nothing more to express. This will never happen to Karl because he will never reveal himself, as he said in 1986. 'What do I stand for? The reflection of the spirit of the time – whatever season it is. Or more simply, fashion opportunism.' And fashion opportunism will never be *démodé*.

Instead Karl moves irrepressibly onwards. Arie Kopelman, former president of Chanel for nineteen years, remembers his first-ever Chanel show when he joined the company as president in January 1985. He went backstage to congratulate Karl on his collection and Karl brushed away his compliments with the words: 'No congratulations. It's already history, what counts is the next collection.'

'Karl's world is all about the next,' says Kopelman. 'It's very important for Karl to always take things to new levels. Who is more *branché* than Karl Lagerfeld? He loves being on top of what is going on in music, literature, film, he is so curious, so learned; this is his life, he has many, many interests beyond fashion, it is one big productive stew.'

It takes a lot of effort and determination to stay hip in your seventies.

Indeed Karl frequently describes himself as a 'fashion machine'. In 1983 he said, 'I'm like a computer who's plugged into the Chanel mode,' and his seemingly inhuman capacity for work and endurance, his ability to design for so many brands at the same time, has the never-ending efficiency and yield of a production line. But where is Karl the human in all this productivity and renewal, and where is Karl's emotion in his work? Hidden away, far, far away, out of touch, and out of reach from hurt and human pain. For isn't Karl's denial of human emotion inherently a denial of human suffering too?

When he talks of his relationship with fashion and life Karl uses powerful images of repression. Looking back at the 1970s and '80s Karl reflected in 2002, 'I have always been a horrible puritan Calvinist. But that is not as a result of my education, it is my profound nature. At the end of the day I have allowed myself very little and that is the reason I am still here today. There are people who are made to survive and I fear I am a part of that group; I am not particularly amusing with myself. I am an auto-fascist!' And when he talks about his endless fashion collections and his pitiless striving, he chooses a strange metaphor. 'I'm never totally pleased,' he said in 1984. 'I'm a kind of fashion nymphomaniac who never gets an orgasm. I'm always expecting something from the next time.'

The perpetual work pattern, the myriad contracts, the decoration of houses, the photography, the publishing house, all the productivity and labour, none of these seem to fulfil or assuage Karl's sense of dissatisfaction. On the contrary: 'Once he's finished,' says Patrick McCarthy of his eternal interiors projects, 'a little bit of the pleasure is gone.'

And yet he continues in the pursuit and hyper-activity, caught up in a quest for the elusive state of satisfaction or perhaps quite simply not daring to stay still. 'You don't dedicate yourself to the life he has without some kind of suffering going on. There is a reason you have to keep moving like that,' says Patrick McCarthy. 'Karl suffers, but instead of moaning and groaning, rather like Monsieur Saint Laurent, he just goes on with it and uses it to make himself stronger. And Karl finds his salvation through work.'

Karl has never discussed how he might have suffered. Rather by continually changing and embroidering his life history he throws up a screen between himself and the past – whatever its humiliations and disappointments might have been. 'I bleach my past,' he said in 2003. When asked about his childhood in 1979, Karl replied, 'Thank God there isn't anybody left to remember that any more! And I've forgotten it all myself.'

There was the exclusion he lived in as a child but there was also a wider context of potential suffering, and that was the day-to-day reality of being a small boy aged six when the war broke out and then living through the war and Nazi Germany, although this too Karl has consistently denied. In the *Actuel* interview of 1984 Jean-François Bizot asked him if he had experienced the war and Nazism and Karl replied, 'I didn't even notice that it happened . . . In the north, nothing happened there, there were no bombardments. Other than in Hamburg, where I was born, but I was no longer there.' In 2004 he was still insisting, 'I was lucky; I escaped everything. I saw nothing of the war.'

Karl's family had moved back briefly to central Hamburg in 1939, when Karl was aged six and at a time when Otto Lagerfeld felt his daily commute between Hamburg and Bad Bramstedt had become too dangerous. But Hamburg was not only a strategic German trade port; it was also a centre of ship- and submarine-building and Otto Lagerfeld must have feared the possibility of bombing there, for he moved his family back out of the city and away again to the relative safety of Bad Bramstedt, thereby avoiding the devastating Allied bombardments of the summer of 1943.

Bad Bramstedt did not suffer from direct bombing, but no one avoided the reality of the war or Nazi Germany and its totalitarian grip on life. Young Karl was very frightened by the Allied planes flying overhead. 'We were all scared walking to school in the morning,' remembers Karl's former next-door neighbour Karl Wagner, 'then we would get to school and the sirens would go and we had to go home again. At the end of the war in the last three months there were low-flying aircraft and they shot at anything that moved, horse or person; they didn't even stop at Red Cross vehicles.'

There were extreme shortages of food and anyone with any land was under orders to grow crops – turnips in the Lagerfeld's case – for the war effort. The Lagerfeld family muddled through the war just as others in Bad Bramstedt who grew their own vegetables and had some live-stock. 'We had the advantage that we were producing things ourselves,' remembers Wagner. 'Sometimes a cow died, it would then be hidden in the straw – of course you couldn't say it in those days, but we hid it and then we had something to eat again. They counted the cows, so we had to get rid of it before they came to count, or sometimes the man who did the counting "missed" one and then he got a bit of it too. The war made people very inventive.'

The Lagerfelds had the advantage of money. Otto Lagerfeld turned sixty in 1941 and was still working at Glücksklee, although the factory had already stopped producing tinned milk by the beginning of the war. The company belonged to the American Milk Products Corporation and was therefore deemed enemy assets, and according to Neustadt local newspaper *Ostholsteiner Nachrichten* Otto Lagerfeld was appointed as the administrator. During the war the Neustadt Glücksklee factory produced butter and skimmed milk that was processed to form powdered milk.

At the end of July 1943 the Allied bombing campaign targeted the city of Hamburg and afterwards there were the homeless, who arrived in Bad Bramstedt by train or on foot, escaping the blistered devasta-tion. Towards the end of the war, from 1944 onwards, there was also an influx of refugees into Bad Bramstedt from the east, Germans such as Hans-Joachim Bronisch and his mother, who were fleeing the advancing Red Army. Refugees came from East Prussia, Poland, Pomen, Breslan and Danzig and were billeted with families. There were also soldiers retreating west. The Pimpfen, who were the young Hitler Youth, helped distribute supplies around the fields full of soldiers. The population of Bad Bramstedt, which had been 3,300 in 1939, had swelled to 7,000 by 1945.

At the end of the war, in May 1945, the British arrived. The Lagerfelds' house was requisitioned by the British army. According to Karl Wagner the Lagerfeld barn was used during the war as a 'store room for the organisation TOT, which was an army administrative network supplying blankets and tents', and the British tended to take over any existing administrative arrangement. They entered the house and ordered the family at gunpoint to hand over any firearms, cameras and binoculars. Karl was twelve. Then the family was given three days to vacate the house and move out into the cowshed next door, where they lived for a year in two makeshift rooms. The family was not alone in the cowshed; there were two girls from the Ukraine, as well as turnips and grain.

It was a year of considerable hardship for the Lagerfeld family, who suffered, as so much of northern Germany, from the dire shortage of food and cramped, miserable conditions. 'Food was extremely scarce,' confirms Bad Bramstedt local historian Manfred Jacobsen. 'Living conditions were bad: the population had doubled, the production had dwindled – fields were not being properly ploughed, farmers had died in the war – there was very little milk as cows were being used for meat. And there was a great scarcity of housing. Even in the 1950s there was an average of only five metres square living space per person in Schleswig–Holstein and that included the animal dwellings.' Thinking about where your next meal was coming from became a grim and obsessive anxiety. At the nadir of their fortunes the Lagerfeld family had just two pieces of bread left to eat, one for Karl, another for his sister Christel. This was not the land of plenty that Karl would later conjure up. Indeed seen in this light the protestations of grandeur and luxury take on a particularly poignant note. 'I remember huge luncheons and dinners during the war at our country estate. We had a great many Polish and Russian servants. Germans weren't available. As my father was Swedish, they considered themselves in a foreign land,' Karl said in 1983, and then again later in 1992 he said, 'There were never any shortages of food. The moment the war was over, as my father was not German, we had everything again.' Ten years later he would claim, 'In 1945 I had six bicycles with which to ride to school.'

The Lagerfeld family stayed in Bad Bramstedt for another three or four years after the end of the war. Then the family moved back to Hamburg. Karl has said of postwar Germany, 'I wanted to get out as soon as I could.' And he did. He left for Paris in 1952, at the age of nineteen, having finished his secondary education. Christel left Germany in 1957; she was aged twenty-six and she went to live in Seattle before marrying an American and moving east.

If Karl Lagerfeld chose to forget what he had lived through, he was not alone in doing so. As early as 1968 the postwar phenomenon of collective denial and repression of what Germans had lived through and its far-reaching effects were recognised by Alexander and Margarete

Mitscherlich in their study of group behaviour, published under the title *The Inability to Mourn*. Professor Detlef Junker, a world authority on German–American relations in the twentieth century who happens to have gone to school in Bad Bramstedt (though later than Lagerfeld), explains the nation's beleaguered state of mind at the end of the war. 'From 1943 onwards the German population increasingly suffered from the effects of the war, from mass expulsion and the terror bombardment of the western allies. Those who survived the unconditional surrender of the German Armed Forces had only one thing in mind: to forget about the past and go on with life. Few wanted to remember the last thirteen years. The whole emphasis was on the future, on rebuilding the economy and a stable democracy. The denazification process [immediately after the war], however, forced them to think about the Nazi past. Therefore, almost anybody who was involved in the denazification process felt threatened.' And with this national sense of guilt and victimisation came a period of stifling the past.

It is only recently that self-reflection has been able to emerge in the German collective consciousness, instigated in part by a younger generation curious to investigate their parents' and grandparents' past.

Denying his own past must have had some effect on Karl's creative process. For a fashion designer the childhood so often represents the wellspring of his or her visual iconography. For many it is also their first fantasy kingdom and their ceaseless longing to recapture its loss lies at the heart of the unattainable idealism integral to fashion. In this way a designer's mind, while digesting all around them in the present, is drawn backwards to the magnetic pole of their childhood. The childhood is always there: it is there in Saint Laurent blinking in the sunlight of colonial Oran with its naval officers dashing in their summer uniforms, its shoeshine boys barefoot and calling. It is there in John Galliano in the collision of immigrant child and Peckham childhood and his memories of standing outside his first Communion dressed in a frilly white shirt as all around him the south London high street shuffles by. Even Chanel, whose childhood did not fit with the ideal of a fantasy kingdom, hence her lifelong denial of it, founded her aesthetic and style on the visual foundations of that childhood, in the austere uniforms of her convent orphanage.

The apparent and understandable impossibility for Karl to mine his

own visual memories perhaps goes some way to explaining his preference for creating through a combination of proxy and Zeitgeist. It
was one thing for photographer Helmut Newton, a German Jew who
fled Berlin in 1938, to skewer the menace of Nazi Germany with black
humour, black leather and blonde models, but how could Karl, as a
German, ever permit the visual aesthetics of his childhood into his
work?

It would also explain why Karl appears to have moved his own
magnetic pole to the period before his own birth. He hankers with
a longing and wistful romanticism for what he perceives as a golden
age of old Europe, pre-Nazi Germany. In 1986 he said, 'I had this
feeling that my parents had lived fabulous lives between the wars and
that I had been born too late in a lousy period.' The stiff white high
collars and black ties that he favoured for both himself and Jacques as
well as for his own more recent fashion collections are pulled from
Prussian Germany and, more specifically, his mother's political heroes
such as Walther Rathenau, a German Jewish industrialist and Foreign
Minister in the Weimar Republic who was assassinated by two far-
right army officers in 1922. Karl's palette of black and white, his preference for a certain formality, his jewelled tiepins, these are the only
style constants that Karl will admit to – not necessarily for his own
fashion but at least for his own personal sense of style – and they are
the style mannerisms of his parents. Later in the 1990s Karl tried hard
to recapture that pre-war Germany when he returned to Blankenese
and bought a house high up on the banks of the River Elbe, which
he then spent nearly seven years renovating. 'I imagined the protected
world of my parents in the late '20s and early '30s. They always talked
about how marvellous life was then: how pleasant, how luxurious, how
divine.'

The house was a neoclassical villa built in 1922 and lay about ten
minutes' walk from his parents' home in Baurs Park, Blankenese, the
home they had moved to when they were first married in 1930 and
the home where Karl lived as a baby. It was grander and more statu-
esque than the original family home, with a façade marked by columns
and towering statues on top of the roof. But it had the same poetic
view out over the river, and when the container ships passed by it
seemed they were so close that you might reach out and touch them.

Karl furnished the house with northern European decorative arts and furniture, Georg Jensen candlesticks from the 1920s, Swedish bronzes that had been made for the 1925 Exposition des Arts Décoratifs in Paris and a marvellous 1919 Max Lieberman painting of Berlin's Brandenberg Gate. 'The first sounds I remember were the horns of the ships on the river, and my first memory in life was sheer tulle curtains at the windows blowing in the wind,' he said, and so there were the same tulle curtains blowing in the wind of this house. He called it 'an abstract house – a pure vision of the mind'. He transported paintings from Paris, statues from his home in Monte Carlo. He photographed the house and published a book of the photographs. But Karl only ever spent a matter of days in the house before leaving it, selling up, walking away, disillusioned once more. 'It's really my farewell to Germany,' he said at the time. 'When I finished, I realised this Germany doesn't exist any longer, couldn't exist any longer. But for me, it would have been the only Germany I could have lived in. It's divine to have had the idea, but I don't want to live there.' And there is something deeply mournful about this confession: the sense of being born in the wrong age, the longing to recapture the time immediately before his own birth and the aching sense of emptiness when he does attempt to do so. It was an impossible act of remembrance for an irredeemable age, one that he had never known. It was an aesthetic ideal behind net curtains while outside in reality a suburban housewife jogged by.

Although the *Actuel* scandal blew over, it remained in people's memory as an example of Karl's propensity to wound. Attacking Yves has been one of Karl's few major errors in his fashion career. But it seems the need to do so is stronger even than his considerable powers of judgement, for he has done it repeatedly. He has attacked him covertly for his stagnating creativity: 'But your way has to be updated. When you listen to the same operas in the studio for twenty-five years, there's a chance you'll get the same dresses too. I am not sure that fashion can be only based on Proust, Callas, Verdi, Bérard and Cocteau,' said Karl in 1991, listing every single one of Yves' hallowed references.

He has criticised him openly. In 1991, when asked about Yves Saint

Laurent, Karl snapped, 'His clothes to me all look the same. He should forget his past in a way. The problem of Yves was that it was too much from the beginning, the Trapèze at Dior when he was still so young. Things should rise slowly, not a sudden jump to fame in your youth and then you float up there. That's very dangerous and unhealthy.' Eleven years later, when questioned whether he thought as Proust and Saint Laurent did that the most beautiful paradise is one that is lost, Karl replied, 'I detest revivals, I only like the present moment and the future, today and tomorrow. The best way of surviving in the present is forgetting the past, to permanently recreate one's paradise. If you start referencing your own past, you are heading for trouble. Moreover, they [Proust and Saint Laurent] were both heading for trouble . . . Saint Laurent professes to have invented the modern woman, but has he ever really read Proust?'

It seemed that Karl could not get Saint Laurent out of his mind. During fashion weeks in the 1990s Karl would call through to the Chanel studio from home the morning after the Saint Laurent show to ask that Suzy Menkes' *International Herald Tribune* review of Yves' collection be read out to him over the telephone. In 1993 he allowed his portrait to be used in an advertising campaign with the high-street fashion chain Kookaï in which they showed billboards of designers, including Karl and Saint Laurent, commenting on Kookaï. 'They used more of me, you know, than the ones of Yves and Sonia Rykiel,' Karl could not resist telling one reporter. 'Really, the people there told me.' 'This is what is so difficult,' says Paloma Picasso. 'Karl might do a fabulous collection one season which was quite extraordinary and better than anybody, but still Yves was always the one at the top and there was never the space to have two at the top at the same time. He [Karl] always felt that he had to be grappling to get there.'

Unfortunately the incessant verbal criticism earned him a reputation for bitchiness that would last throughout the 1990s as well as souring several friendships. Paloma Picasso finally dropped Karl in the 1980s when she felt that his comments about Yves became excessive and, in Paloma's words, 'certain things appeared in the press that were really quite unacceptable'.

It is true that Karl did know another Yves. The scatological, witty, mimicking Yves that Karl knew was the same Yves who pulled faces about a model behind her back because he thought her thighs were too fat, the same Yves that commented after one black model left his studio, 'Mmmm, a little too Museum of Mankind.' It was the same Yves who, when discussing silicon penis implants with Andy Warhol and Pierre Bergé in 1977, said how he hoped everyone would have one, so then he could design new trousers. Karl wanted to rip Yves out of the holy myth in which he was encased and show the world this other Yves existed.

But what Karl failed to appreciate was the special place that Yves Saint Laurent occupied in the public imagination – and not just the public, but the client and the journalist, the *vendeuse* at the perfume counter, Diana Vreeland, the tea lady at the couture house and the *petites mains* stitching upstairs in the workrooms. For all of them Yves Saint Laurent 'the suffering *artiste*' was the very essence of their fashion fantasies.

The couturier suffering for his art, suffering for us women and for our wardrobes, was an extraordinarily potent message at this time in France. For twenty-five long years Yves had been telling all those around him how he would love to stop this fashion, give it all up and instead design for the theatre, write novels, paint – anything but this fashion and this anxiety. But he continued suffering because he had a responsibility to his house, his ateliers, his staff, his studio. The emphasis was always on martyrdom. 'Without a doubt one has to be anguished to be inspired. The more I work, the more I suffer. And the more I suffer, the greater the success,' he said. 'The closer you get to a *métier*, the more resources you have to draw on, the more agonising it is. In the beginning, when one is young, one is insouciant. At my age, it's terrible. A millimetre can change everything.' Even at the end of his career in 2002 he was still talking about the anguish, indeed it is his principle topic of conversation in the French documentary of his life *Le Temps Retrouvé*. 'When I draw I torture myself,' he says with a cigarette hanging from his lips, a tombstone of ash waiting to fall. 'I hurt myself; I am always in a state of fear when I am creating. It really is pretty terrible what I go through.'

In 1991 he told *Elle* magazine that he fantasised about picking out the largest bronze in his collection and tying it round his legs and plunging to his watery death in the Seine. Yves Saint Laurent did suffer, but perhaps that suffering had more to do with his manic depression than simply his making of dresses. His anguish has been romanticised, both by Yves and Pierre. Romanticised by Pierre to sell perfumes and neckties, romanticised by Yves perhaps for its connotations of artistic genius, or perhaps, as Betty Catroux suggests, because 'it means he can get away with doing anything he likes'.

Throughout the 1980s and onwards the affliction, the alcohol and the loneliness were all turned into symbols of the couturier's passion on the long road to the Calvary of his art. 'He likes to be remembered for his depressions, his alcoholism, his addictions,' said Loulou. 'He always tells the darkest side of himself.' The music of the shows, tragic arias of Callas, the literary references within the couture collections, quotes from Apollinaire *tout terriblement* and Aragon's 'Sun I am black inside' embroidered on the back of jackets, all contributed to the overwhelming tragedy of Yves and the stage drama of his career.

And there was another reason behind the power of Yves' role as suffering *artiste*. The international contemporary art scene had long since packed its bags and moved to New York and London. There was no Picasso, no Braque, no Cocteau and no Dalí any more; Warhol was but a breathless tourist when he came to visit Paris and by 1987 he too was dead.

Instead there was Yves Saint Laurent with a dining room of Goya, Matisse and Mondrian paintings, making Picasso dresses, Braque dresses, dresses inspired by Warhol and satin coats quoting Apollinaire that one might wear to a gala dinner at the Elysée Palace in the presence of President Mitterrand. For a generation of consumers Yves *was* the visual artist of Paris. *Artiste*, that magical word that in the French language and the French imagination conjures up a heavenly circle of painters, poets and writers with furrowed brows and tragic destinies consumed alive by the flames of their creativity. Yves was the very first couturier to be admitted into the great pantheon of *artistes* by the French consciousness. Not even Gabrielle Chanel, with all her intimacy with artists, the financial patronage of Diaghilev, the affair with writer Pierre Reverdy, not even she managed to swing that change of status, nor would she have dared imagine she might. From dressmaker to artist was a mighty leap and says as much about the society of the time as it does about the resolve of Pierre Bergé and the talent of Saint Laurent.

Elevating Yves to the status of artist had always been Pierre's objective,

even back in the early years when Saint Laurent was still young, rebel-
lious and insisting, 'I detest couturiers who confuse their work with art.'
By the 1980s and the onset of middle age Yves' protests against the artist
label were rather less vociferous and he graciously allowed Pierre to
bring about the final elevation.

Chapter 19

1989

Despite the hopes raised by every new drug – suramin, AZT and later ribavirin – seemingly nothing and no one could stop the ruthlessness of the HIV virus. AIDS killed and fashion was at the front line of the disease. It struck at every level of the industry, obliterating talent, desire, creativity and next year. 'It was like living through a war,' says Ariel de Ravenel. 'Half the people we are talking about aren't here any more.' It seemed as if all the charisma and joy were being wrung out of fashion.

Antonio was diagnosed with the virus early on. By the mid-1980s he was still working and living out of his Union Square studio, where he was being looked after by Juan and Paul Caranicas. Juan too was HIV positive. Antonio worked throughout his illness, in part to fulfil his creativity but also in order to pay for his medical treatment. He had no medical insurance and he was running out of money. He began his last major work, to illustrate a book of *Tales from a Thousand and One Nights*, in 1985. This was a truly courageous undertaking as he was struggling to find energy and inspiration, and by now he was weak and suffering from acute respiratory problems linked to the illness. Antonio died in 1987 at the age of forty-four. Juan would die eight years later, aged fifty-three.

Antonio had been the Pied Piper of glamour, dancing his way through Paris and New York, beckoning all to follow in his kohl-eyed, Cuban-heeled wake, but his legacy was so much more vital than that implies. He fused a highly personal and erotic vision of femininity with a multitude of changing images and influences, high art, thumping sexuality, butch boys and street culture. In doing so he not only forged one of the key visual strands that defined this epoch in fashion, but he also left a legacy of both work and attitude that would influence fashion's direction for generations to come.

It was brutal that an age that had begun in so much insouciance should end in so much death and loneliness. 'It was a world of illusions,' says Diane de Beauvau-Craon, 'a very beautiful world, but a very rough world: it cost lives.' It had been an extraordinary period to live through, but one fraught with dangers. Perhaps Paris, beneath its unflinching splendour and classical proportions, is a dangerous city. 'Paris has always been this *ville de lumière*, a city of light that attracts people to it,' says Thadée Klossowski. 'Either you get burnt or you become a Parisian, I suppose.'

For some there was a means of escape. Loulou gave birth to a daughter, Anna, in 1986; she and Thadée had a life to look after. Pat Cleveland had lived as a model for fourteen years, she had been through star boyfriends Warren, Ryan et al., she had personified the fantasies of designers and audience, but now she knew she had to get out. She was in love: 'I had someone to save me.' She turned down the Chanel advertising campaign that Karl asked her to do. She returned to Le Palace for the last time, back to the lasers of light dancing over yearning, upturned faces. 'I had on blue jeans, I had cut my hair. I was watching from the balcony and down below on the stage there were people swaying under drugs and André was there and he whispered to me, "You're free now." I said goodbye to everybody: "I'm going away." It was so hard to leave, but there was too much night, too many people dying.'

In Paris many of those suffering from HIV and AIDS took their leave of the Flore and their friends without a word. They went back home, back to the place from which they had escaped all those years before. Or they chose to die anonymous and alone in a hospital room in Paris. For those not ill, the pain was in what they had to witness, as all around them lovers and friends were dying. Corey Tippin was living in New York and says of these years, 'I know I have seen hell. I felt it in those moments, towards the end, when there was no grace present, only dark.'

These early years of the disease involved a cruel and added burden of shame. People were denying they were ill for fear of losing their jobs, their friends and their insurance. The French media was finger-pointing and naming AIDS sufferers, often incorrectly. Actress Isabelle Adjani was falsely identified as suffering from it and eventually she appeared on television to deny the rumours. Then Yves Saint Laurent was named, again inaccurately. Pierre Bergé denied the rumour, saying, 'Everyone knows that [Saint Laurent] has psychological problems, that he takes too many tranquillisers, which make him seem a little confused, but I declare on my honour that he doesn't have cancer, that he doesn't have AIDS – he hasn't even tested positive. What can I do? Yves Saint Laurent's illness didn't begin yesterday. People have been talking about it for fifteen years.'

In the Saint Laurent group it was Joël Le Bon who was ill. His role as madcap jester in the house of Saint Laurent belied a real importance as inspiration and catalyst. His drug habit had slid from the recreational to the dire. Kim d'Estainville was also suffering, as was Kenzo's boyfriend Xavier de Castella. Jacques, like so many, sought to keep his illness hidden. The Lagerfeld entourage was not supposed to know. Jacques rarely saw Renaud or Christian during the second half of the 1980s and neither friend was ever informed or knew of Jacques' illness. Renaud continued to receive the traditional New Year greetings cards from Jacques, which from 1985 onwards bore images of Jacques drawn by Karl Lagerfeld. For January 1985 there was a card showing an impeccable Jacques in profile, wearing a Tyrolean jacket and tie, with hair slicked back and something of the exiled Habsburg prince about him. The following year was a card featuring an illustration by Karl of a woman in a black strapless party dress and huge black hat, standing alongside a man dressed as Father Christmas with red bonnet, coat and boots trimmed in white fur. He wears black sunglasses and has a white beard and full red lips. The picture is signed 'Karl '85'. The large black sunglasses worn in all weathers presumably symbolise Karl, and there is something of Karl in the square shape of the head and the mouth. But the slim and elongated silhouette of the man, his height and slender fingers all belong to Jacques. There is a certain overlap of identity, the partial eclipse of one by the other. It was at this period in their lives that both men were talking openly of a plan for Karl to adopt Jacques. It was a plan that came to nothing and was perhaps more an indication of the transformation in their relationship whereby they now viewed each other as 'father' and 'son'. And yet at the same time, in contrast to this adoption plan, there was Karl's reluctance to put a name to Jacques, as witnessed in the *Actuel* magazine interview of 1984.

Jacques' illness accelerated throughout 1987 and 1988. When he was low and ravaged by it he returned home to La Berrière for a three-week 'cure' — away from the eye of Paris. His sister Anne cooked for him. He slept in his bedroom on the first floor of the château with a small balcony overlooking the courtyard, the 'chambre de roi' bedroom as his sister calls it with a sad smile. Then in 1988 he returned home for months on end, during which time Anne nursed him and he slept in his late grandmother's bedroom. It was at night that the panic over-took Jacques. He couldn't sleep, he couldn't breathe; the terror was at his throat. He kept a loaded shotgun in the bathroom adjoining his bedroom.

Anne insists that in his illness Jacques found a lucidity and honesty in the assessment of his life and choices that he had not known before, accepting responsibility for the decisions that he had taken. He talked of his father obsessively. 'He rejected my homosexuality and that destroyed me,' he said, over and over again. For years before his illness Anne had feared a phone call that would tell her there had been an overdose, an accident, his death. 'There was such ambivalence to Jacques. He did not resolve the contradictions deep within himself,' she says. 'He could not reconcile these two worlds.' But perhaps Jacques could never reconcile these two conflicting worlds for as long as he remained in fashion, for the very nature of fashion keeps you suspended within the illusion. 'He was living with some kind of private tragedy,' says his brother Xavier, 'and I don't know what that was.'

In January 1988 Jacques was admitted to Bichat hospital in the eight-eenth *arrondissement* in the north of Paris. His sister Elisabeth visited him there daily. Anne telephoned Diane de Beauvau-Craon to explain that Jacques was asking for her. This was the first Diane knew of Jacques' illness; there were many others that were never told. Diane went to see Jacques and for the next eighteen months accompanied him through his illness.

Karl visited Jacques every day, and when his workload prevented him, he liaised with Diane constantly. Karl provided all the means possible for Diane to be by Jacques' side daily, not least a car and a driver.

According to Diane, Karl was constant and unlimited in his support of Jacques and his treatment. 'He was totally devastated by what was happening to Jacques,' says Diane de Beauvau-Craon. 'He was wonderful to Jacques at this time.' They changed hospital, moving Jacques to Raymond Poincaré hospital in Garches to the west of Paris in June 1988. They changed specialist, they changed drugs; like all those fighting disease they were desperate to explore every possible hope.

Some days Jacques was allowed home to his apartment on the Rue de Rivoli. He wrapped up his frail body in overcoat and scarves and walked out alone under the arcades, past the Tuileries and the empty chairs of winter days. He headed for the local café on the Place du Marché Saint-Honoré, where he sat outside and drank his espresso in the tearing wind. From his table he could see across into the fire station and he watched the firemen exercising, fit and careless with all the insolence of health.

In January 1989 Renaud received the last New Year greetings card from his old friend Jacques. By now Jacques was living the advanced stages of AIDS. On the front of the card was an illustration by Karl, a black pen line-drawing against a red and cream background. It is the portrait of a beautiful, dandy musketeer, Jacques de Bascher, defender of the Vendée and the monarchy, raising his beribboned hat in the air with a gesture of grand bravura. He is wearing breeches and thigh boots, he has a black beard and black hair, he wears a white wing-collar and white bow-tie and just beneath is pinned the red cross and red heart of the Vendée. He wears a black jacket that is buttoned down the side of each lapel and a thick white sash that is wrapped around his waist and tied in a large bow.

Jacques was dying but the Jacques of the portrait is immortally glamorous and swashbuckling, virile and victorious. It is signed 'Karl Lagerfeld '88' and inside, printed on the left-hand side, is the line 'Jacques de Bascher vu par Karl Lagerfeld', which literally translates as 'Jacques de Bascher as seen by Karl Lagerfeld'. There is a printed New Year's message of good wishes and greetings in Vendée slang from Jacques, and at the end he has added by hand, 'Get out your white sash and your black tie. Why don't we meet up for the mass of Louis XVI?' Even at the end Jacques could not give up his bid for grandeur. The mass for Louis XVI is celebrated every year on 21 January to commemorate the execution of the king on this day in 1793. It is a service attended by the die-hard monarchists of France and some rather melancholy aristocrats still scratching at the scar of lost privilege. Renaud did not attend the mass. He could not reach Jacques by telephone; he could never find him.

By May 1989 Jacques' lungs were under assault and he needed oxygen to assist with his breathing. Xavier remembers visiting his brother in hospital early that September and being utterly distraught at Jacques' deterioration. 'He said to me very sweetly, "Listen, OK, I'm going to die young but don't be sad; if you live until you are one hundred you still wouldn't experience the half of what I have. So it's as if I have lived to be eighty."' They were brave words of comfort offered to a man facing the death of his elder brother.

While the true nature of the bond between Karl and Jacques is hard to understand, what is clear is that it *was* a bond and that it was infinitely more complex and indelible than simply that of keeper and courtesan. There was a mutual fascination between the two men. Jacques was captivated by Karl's learning, his expanse of knowledge and brilliance and what he, Jacques, could learn from that. 'Jacques was himself someone highly intelligent and cultivated; the attraction that he felt for Lagerfeld and the way in which their relationship developed relied on there being a real dialogue between the two men,' says Christian Lvowski. 'Whenever Jacques spoke of Karl it was an admiring tone, to say, "Karl has done this" or "Karl has done that" or talk of the wonders of Karl at Chanel. You got the idea that Jacques considered Karl an exceptional man. It was a good association whereby each one found something that could complete the other.'

They shared the passion of two aesthetes and, crucially, each man held the key to the aesthetic of the other. Karl was captivated by Jacques' Frenchness, background and culture, by his nineteenth-century physiognomy and allure, just as Jacques was passionate about Karl's Teutonic culture and in particular the whole crashing romance, tragedy and ecstasy of nineteenth-century Germany. It leads one to speculate – and speculation is all that it is – that if there was one person in Paris who knew the truth about Karl and his background and childhood in Germany it was Jacques.

'It was a communion,' says Jacques' younger brother, Xavier, 'an encounter that was extremely complementary. There was a kind of mirror image between the two men. Jacques represented everything Karl would have wanted to be in terms of birthright and body, and then there was Jacques' own fascination for Germany, for the Wagnerian hero and the incredible myth of Ludwig, a man who personified all Jacques' own dreams of dandyism lived to the extreme. Ludwig was Jacques' absolute hero, a man who burnt through his entire fortune building his castles, a man who literally built his dreams.'

Jacques was an ideal for Karl: an aesthetic ideal, a cultural ideal but also crucially a living ideal. 'He was everything I could not be, would be, should be,' said Karl in 2002. There was, and still is, so much longing attached to this ideal, not so much a longing of the flesh as a longing to be. There is an almost audible sigh to Karl's highly romanticised images of Jacques, the sketches of Jacques as a 1920s beau, photographs of Jacques as a *fin de siècle* salon hero. The portraits of Jacques by Karl and the many, many, photographs that Karl took of him throughout their relationship call to mind something that Karl said about his concept of a relationship later in 2002: 'And although in the past I said that my dream of a relationship with another person was to create a frame and then put the image into it, sadly this romantic notion was soon overtaken by reality.' But Jacques was not just Karl's sepia ideal; he was also the conduit by which Karl could experience life. Jacques was intent on burning himself up alive, on feeling every volt ricochet through his body in an attempt to numb the pain of his soul, and there watching it all was Karl. For Karl Jacques was a way out of himself and his own rigid self-exigency. Jacques' brother Xavier reflects on the nature of their creative exchange: 'People looked at Jacques and thought he does nothing, he just gads around. But they didn't realise to what extent Jacques and the trips and voyages he made, the people he met, how much all that fed Karl. Karl is a man who hated going out, who doesn't drink, doesn't smoke, doesn't do drugs, doesn't have sex. He needed feeding and all these experiences of Jacques were material for him. So I don't know how you would describe that in terms of a job, but I would say that Jacques was highly qualified.'

Karl was Jacques' financial support, but that does not explain the complexity or longevity of their relationship. Jacques with his dash and charisma could have found protectors everywhere and indeed did. 'Jacques was never interested in money in terms of building up a fortune,' says friend and journalist Dominique Brabec. 'Jacques only wanted money to blow through it.' Patrick McCarthy agrees: 'I never got the sense that Jacques was hanging around waiting for the francs to be handed out. Anyway Jacques was someone to whom you could give an unlimited budget and he would exceed it; you know, he was one of those people who could spend money on anything.'

'Karl allowed him to live his life like he wanted to, this sort of lightness of being,' says Xavier de Bascher. 'Jacques needed money, needed time and no constraints to be the dandy he dreamed of. I think Jacques made his pact with the Devil – God bless Karl – whereby Karl gave him what he needed materially and Jacques gave his soul, his spirit.' Christian Lvowksi perceives it in similar albeit less Faustian terms. He believes that Jacques was propelled towards beauty and that it was fashion, 'above all at this moment in fashion and at this level in fashion, that allowed him to achieve the kind of life he desired'.

But there was more to it for Jacques than just the aesthetic high. Jacques also sought the reassurance of a paternalistic figure and it was not the first time he had done so in his life. It was there in the friendship with Bertrand, the English teacher ten years his senior, when he was aged seventeen. They too had experienced an overlap in identity in the growing similarity of their dress code, in the merging of their signature. This process was taken to greater heights of fantasy with Karl. Jacques' sister Anne maintains that it was their father's 'veto against Jacques' homosexuality' which precipitated her brother on his search for a paternal figure in opposition to his own.

Being in Karl's world was a way for Jacques to leave behind all that was provincial, mediocre, *petite noblesse*, bourgeois and anonymous. Karl had created for himself a highly original and erudite world of lustrous possessions. And just as once Eugène de Rastignac had encountered the *monde* and the gilded salons of Faubourg Saint-Germain he could never go back, so Jacques once he had encountered Karl and the glamour of fashion could not turn away. 'The more Eugène enjoyed of the pleasures of life in Paris, the less he wanted to remain obscure and poor,' wrote Balzac in *Le Père Goriot*.

But in the endless prism of reflections of ideal and identity between these two men, it cannot be forgotten that there was also friendship, companionship and love. 'Karl relied on him,' says Patrick McCarthy. 'He gave Karl emotional support. They were really good friends; Jacques made Karl laugh, they had the same sense of humour.'

'I think he brought a lot of joy into Karl's life,' says Rose-Marie Legallais, who worked alongside Karl for fifteen years at the house of Chloé. 'It brought a lot of pleasure to Karl, who is someone so rigorous, to have Jacques and his lightness of life around him.' Florentine Pabst-Schober says simply, 'Jacques is the love of his life.'

If Jacques was the love of Karl's life he was also one of the few to understand the boundaries and limitations of that love. 'Karl prefers Coca-Cola and chocolate cake to love,' Jacques told writer Gerry Dryansky in the 1980s. 'They're his, they're there in the refrigerator and always accessible.'

As Karl suggested when he talked of his ideal of a relationship being the frame in which he could place the image, his idea of love was more bound up with 'Geist', the intellectual and aesthetic, than flesh and reality. He has frequently repeated his resolve to live life solo. 'I realised at fourteen that I was born to live alone. I live in a set, with the curtains of the stage closed and with no audience – but who cares,' he said in 1997.

There was a kind of enforced solitude and rational control to Karl's life. It calls to mind writer Thomas Mann, a fellow North German scion of a Hanseatic trading family, when he explores the idea of self-isolation through the voice of Felix Krull: 'I either avoided such contacts entirely or took care that they never became intimate; for in early youth an inner voice had warned me that close association, friendship, and companionship were not to be my lot, but that I should instead be inescapably compelled to follow my strange path alone, dependent entirely upon myself, rigorously self-sufficient.' Felix Krull then goes on to explain the deep-rooted fear that should he become familiar: 'I should literally do violence to some secret part of my nature, should, so to speak, thin the vital sap and disastrously weaken and reduce the tension of my being.'

Karl Lagerfeld is no Felix Krull, but there are parallels to be drawn in his resolve for solitude and in the strong element of dread that characterises Karl's approach to friendship. Many were those who mistook their role in the entourage to mean that they were intimate with Karl

Lagerfeld. This was an error that was usually followed soon after by their downfall. And yet Karl in some ways encouraged this confusion by his own behaviour, his extreme generosity, his crush to see you, all of which pulls you to him. There is a strategy of insistent seduction; there are endless presents: books chosen to delight your literary tastes, handwritten notes accompanying the baskets of heavenly scented sky-blue hyacinths delivered from La Chaume. There is the offer to design your wedding dress and the plane tickets to fly you over for your dress fittings, and then since Karl's career stakes have been raised there are the offers to host your wedding, the Concorde flight tickets, the Fabergé diamond pins, the wardrobe of Chanel jackets and bags, the full-length Fendi fur coats, the suite at the Ritz, all offered with such seemingly ingenuous charm.

And at the time of Karl's giving there is some genuine sentiment attached to these acts of generosity. He is not just some sort of designer flytrap, gobbling up people and their inspiration. Karl is not the black-caped pantomime villain. The interplay of his motivation and compulsions is more complex and painful than that. Even those who have suffered by his hand recognise that. 'He has these extraordinary infatuations, and in that moment he really is sincere and incredibly kind because for that moment he becomes serene again, he is calmed, he is almost consoled that everything is OK, that he has found a kindred soul,' explains one friend. And people feel and respond to not only the kindness in him but also the vulnerability that they sense there, which only makes the ultimate fall all the harder to bear.

'I loved him. I really loved him. I still love him,' says Ralph Toledano, his former managing director at Karl Lagerfeld and then Chloé. 'When I think of Karl I think of the brain and the culture. It was a huge privilege to work with him. Of course if I see him in the street now he won't be nice, but we were family, that company [Karl Lagerfeld] was really a family.' Frédéric Mitterrand, a friend of Karl's for some fifteen years before being cast out, reflects, 'It is cruel. One becomes attached to him.' And Karl to you too, but sooner or later, six months into the friendship or perhaps fifteen or twenty-five years later, he must rid himself of you. 'There is a hecatomb of casualties on his path,' observes a friend. Anna Piaggi, Patrick Hourcade, Gilles Dufour, Gaby Aghion,

Kitty d'Alessio, Inès de la Fressange, Jeremy Scott, Claudia Schiffer, Eric Wright – these are just some of the people who no longer exist for Karl. 'He throws you out once he has played with you enough,' says one who knows. 'Out!'

Is it that he has played with you enough or is it when he feels he has divulged too much? Is it when he feels the threat that intimacy will in some way weaken 'his vital sap' or is it that he constantly fears betrayal? Only Karl knows. Inès de la Fressange pinpoints the disintegration of their friendship to the moment she chose to speak of Karl's vulnerability in public. 'He sometimes had his complexes, a side to him that was touching,' writes Inès de la Fressange in her autobiography, describing his loathing for his hands caused by his mother and how he always wore long sleeves to try to hide them. She then recalls telling an American newspaper how she found that part of Karl 'attendrissant' meaning tender or touching. The day after the article appeared, Inès turned up at the Chanel studio to find a furious Karl Lagerfeld. 'Karl said to me, "So, you're the *petite psychanalyste* are you now?" I realised that he was extremely upset. He threw the newspaper in my face. I understood from then on that you always had to stay on the light side, never make interpretations, and never reveal anything.'

Gaby Aghion believes that this serial breaking-up is 'a form of freedom. He doesn't want to be constrained by friendship; he wants to be free as the air. He can do what he wants because he is not attached to people.' Perhaps, although that does not explain the invective with which Karl rids himself of these people. There is something self-mutilating about his repetitive destruction of these friendships, and yet defensive as well, as if afraid of being struck he strikes to pre-empt pain. 'I think it's actually sad for Karl not to have been able to find another way of relating to people other than by owning them or destroying them,' says Paloma Picasso. Surely his behaviour can only be explained in the context of his own pain. 'He is an *écorché vif*,' says de Beauvau-Craon, which means a tormented soul, although the words literally translate to a flayed soul. 'Karl could be an absolutely beautiful person if he would like himself. He was always seeking something, as certainly I was in that phase, but at a certain point you must become adult and accept yourself and then all the good comes out. Karl is so unhappy, he is in such conflict.'

'Karl did not know how to love,' says one casualty of long-term friendship. 'There is no place for affection in Karl's life. He refuses affection, he is in constant flight before affection.' And so instead Karl encourages, cultivates these relationships based on dependency, on financial interest or on favour, as if to deny the value of true affection, or to stunt its potential growth. And yet at the same time in the insistent giving there is a bid to surround himself with affection, to buy loyalty, to console himself and, perhaps, to relieve the pain. 'His need for approval is incredible, impossible to ease,' says a friend. 'It will never be eased because his anxiety is too great.'

In 1988 Yves' father died. He died in Monte Carlo with Brigitte, his youngest daughter, by his side. Brigitte called Yves to tell him the news of the death, but as so often happened she could not reach him. Instead she had to leave the message with Albert, the maître d'hôtel. Later that day she received a message to go and pick up Yves from the airport: 'Monsieur was on his way.' He arrived in a private plane and was escorted by a member of the Saint Laurent staff. He was in a terrible state. He had not seen his father for three years. Brigitte remembers her brother crying out at the sight of his dead father, 'Papa. Papa.' He rearranged his father's silk handkerchief in his pocket. 'He lived Papa's death as a revelation,' says Brigitte. 'I suppose he had always thought, not that Father didn't love him, but that he must blame him for being homosexual. They never had conversations on the subject.' However, Brigitte does say that Yves had told his father of his homosexuality before his death and that Yves' father had replied, 'My son, that changes nothing.'

In the two years that followed his father's death, Yves veered dramatically between lucidity and depression. There was a well-received beautiful couture collection in January 1990 and then he went plummeting down again. Pierre was preparing for the opening of the Opéra Bastille, which was a huge commitment and responsibility for him. The building of the new Opéra was one of Mitterrand's *grands projets* and cost the French state $400 million dollars. It was surely hard for Yves to accept that Pierre Bergé's attention could be taken up by something other than himself.

By March 1990 Yves was ill and drinking again. He was depressed and behaving in a highly irrational way in Marrakech. He was painting the walls, had cut his hair to look like a soldier and was hard at the whisky. For once Pierre could not go to pick up the pieces as he was too busy with the Opéra and so Yves' sister Brigitte was asked to go and bring Yves back. He refused to return to Paris with Brigitte until finally he was brought back by private plane and taken to a private clinic in Garches, where he was admitted against his will for detoxification. He entered hospital on the very day that the Opéra Bastille opened to the public. After, Yves described the hospital as a 'clinic with bars', his stay there as an 'incarceration' and he remembered shouting 'assassins' up and down the corridors. Later Bergé said, 'I locked him up against his will, but after a day or two he entered into the cure with his full cooperation.' Yves stayed for three weeks.

A year later Yves Saint Laurent talked openly of his illness and hospitalisation in an interview with *Le Figaro* that ran in two parts, in which he referred to his health problems both as 'detoxifications' and 'depressions'. In the first instalment of the interview Yves said 'I have just come out of two consecutive depressions and they have changed my character. No doubt Pierre Bergé was right when he said that I was born with a nervous breakdown. I am very strong and very fragile at the same time.' Days later, in the second instalment, he reiterated, 'The two depressions that I have had one after the other have done me a lot of harm. I was extremely unhappy and very badly treated. The first was at the Hospital Labrousse. Then a year ago I fell into another depression that was so bad that they had to treat me for delirium tremens. They put me in a psychiatric hospital for three months; it was terrible.'

Perhaps just as revealing as Yves' depiction of his mental torment is the text he wrote for *Le Figaro* to appear alongside the interview, which is entitled 'La Gloire': 'I love glory. Glory is celebration. I love celebration. It is gay. It shines. It sparkles. *Coupe de champagne*. Gold of chandeliers, gold gilt of pannelling, gold of medals. Glory only comes in gold. Gilded in gold leaf. It is old, it is secular. It makes a noise, a lot of noise. It explodes. It strikes. It doesn't care about anything. It walks all over everyone. It disturbs. Glory, I wanted it. It strengthens me. It cleanses me, purifies me and embalms me. I am an effigy crucified on the breast of this heroine, half goddess, almost queen, called glory.'

This strangely operatic text contains the threads of megalomania,

masochism, rage and melodrama that weave throughout Yves' life and
career. 'He wants to prove every time that he is beyond competition,'
says Betty Catroux. 'He doesn't just address himself to rivals, but to
everyone, the whole world. He is extremely megalomaniac and with
reason because he is a genius.' He had crucified himself for his art and
for his own glory and now he ascended on high into the pantheon of
national icons, while Pierre busied himself on earth with the necessary
wrangling to ensure the continuation of their considerable personal
fortunes.

Over the next thirteen years Bergé performed all manner of canny
and brilliant deals and share manoeuvrings, buying back the perfume
division, taking the company public in 1989 and selling Yves Saint
Laurent to Sanofi for $650 million in January 1993. During the previous
summer Bergé had sold $18 million of his and Yves' YSL shares privately
in Switzerland. Then in September 1992 he had announced disappointing first-half results, warning of a further fall in profits for the
second part of the year. The transactions made during the summer
precipitated an investigation that ended in 1994 with Pierre being fined
3 million francs, later reduced on appeal to one million francs, by the
French stock-market authorities for insider trading and contravention
of the rule of selling shares outside the Paris market. And all this time
the chasm between the Avenue Marceau couture house – with its
rarefied atmosphere of *grain de poudre* shoulders being lifted one and a
half millimetres higher – and the real world of insipid ready-to-wear
and licences being sold all over the world in the name of Saint Laurent
grew ever wider. The ready-to-wear had fallen into faceless repetition
and from 1989 Bergé spoke openly of his desire to find a designer to
take it over. The slew of YSL clothes licences – which included a diffu-
sion line called Yves Saint Laurent Variations, two menswear lines signed
with Bidermann in America plus a host of licences in Japan – were all
farmed out to be designed; the collections bore no relation to Saint
Laurent's creativity, beyond some vague and diluted interpretation of his
style and the fact that his name was sewn into the inside collar.

Christophe Girard remembers these years as a period when 'Bergé
was aggressive to everyone. He said everyone else was making rubbish.
For twenty years I heard that every other designer was rubbish, I heard
les horreurs said about Jean Paul Gaultier, Karl Lagerfeld, Christian Lacroix

and then later on John Galliano. They were all useless. It is just another way of saying Saint Laurent is the only one. Saint Laurent is the only one and the message sticks. It's a marketing technique and it is true that Saint Laurent,' and here Girard's voice changes from one of dry bite to dreamy nostalgia, 'makes the most magnificent dresses; that is undeniable.'

Yves was right when he said the depressions had changed him. The thrill had gone. As he withdrew from his dancing partners – 'no alcohol, no drugs, no naughtiness and no chocolate' – he became, he said, 'so alone'. The numerous falls over the years weakened his right arm and his power to sketch and his drawings became less prolific. Often for the couture collections Yves would pull out old sketches from years gone by and then pick new fabrics, new embroideries and new colour schemes to rejuvenate the outfits. He concentrated on the perfection of his line, which had always been his overriding concern. In a way it was during these final years in his career, when innovation had all but disappeared from his work, that Yves' indomitable strength really showed. Even during the 1990s when people started to cough and fidget during the Saint Laurent shows, when people spoke of 'bourgeois', 'irrelevant' and 'nothing new to say', still Yves Saint Laurent would not budge and would not compromise his fashion identity. He never did change to suit the whims of fashion. 'Yves is much stronger than people give him credit for,' says Patrick McCarthy. 'He's sad and at times pathetic, but he is *very* strong; you don't produce collection after collection and stick to your guns the way he did, when people were pushing him: "Oh Yves, get modern! Yves, change your look! Yves, follow what's going on in the streets; Yves, look what's going on elsewhere on the runway!" It requires a real strength of character to resist that.'

Yves' force was never more apparent than in his work and belief in himself as a couturier. He possessed the kind of absolute conviction that comes with worldwide success at the age of twenty-one. 'Premature success gives one an almost mystical conception of destiny as opposed to will-power – at its worst the Napoleonic delusion,' wrote F. Scott Fitzgerald in 1937 of his own early success. 'The man who arrives young believes that he exercises his will because his star is shining.'

Yves has always believed he was the one, the true path. Now he was more self-righteous and self-absorbed than ever. In 1991 he revealed his thoughts on fashion and himself in a controversial interview for French arts magazine *Insensé* which caused a storm at the time: 'In truth there are very few great couturiers, very few brilliant couturiers . . . Even less than very few. To be precise, I would say there are two, only two: Givenchy and me. The rest, the others, they are the mob, *c'est l'horreur*. They are precisely "la mode". Nothingness . . . Nothingness, I tell you. Since the time when Balenciaga and Chanel confronted each other, nothing more, really nothing more, except for Givenchy and me. People think there are still couture houses, but I, I know that there are none. Yes, of course you could roll off some names that I myself don't even dare to pronounce, but these names don't exist. They are a misunderstanding. No point in talking about them.'

The interviewer interjects to say that the newspapers at the time of the collections are of course obliged to recognise the existence of these other designers, an idea that throws Yves into a fit of even greater pique. 'Waste of time! Absolute waste of time! Journalists need to believe their own lies, their own errors of taste. They have to fill their articles up, they have to blacken their pages. Moreover these journalists make me laugh: they get in a fluster over a bare breast, when it was me that revealed the breast fifteen years ago. Open your eyes and take a look: fashion has become a kind of village fête, a little ridiculous spectacle where each person comes with their own bad taste and sets up their tent. *L'horreur*. And where is the talent in this? The genius? The art? The colours? The fabric? The light? What I love, above all, is to behave as if I could sculpt light. To choose a fabric, submit myself to its lines, give it light, master its mystery . . . At that moment it is as if I was a painter, a writer.'

It was ironic that Yves would end as he swore in 1968 he would not: a couturier. And as Yves entered the last decade of his career, he did so without a thought for a successor. Unlike Chanel, who had spoken of Yves as her successor; unlike Dior, who had named Yves as his successor: there was no *dauphin* at the house of Saint Laurent. Nor would Yves recognise the talents of anyone else as being able to continue couture. No one was being trained to inherit his secrets. There would be no heir to inherit his crown; when he died Saint Laurent was adamant that couture died with him. He claimed the end of the dynasty, *la fin de race*, as the ultimate expression of his egoism. 'I am the last couturier,' he said in 2002, 'the last couture house. Only I remain.' This was one more glory that Yves wanted for himself: haute couture would end with him.

Jacques died in the hospital at Garches on the morning of 3 September 1989. The utter loneliness of his life is nowhere more apparent than in his death and its aftermath. He was thirty-eight years old when he died and he asked to be placed in his coffin with his teddy bear Mischka by his shoulder. Anne arrived from La Berrière, bringing her dead brother five white roses from her garden at home to represent the five brothers and sisters.

Jacques had asked that he be cremated, which is an unusual choice in France and for someone of the Catholic faith. The hearse waited outside the hospital to take him to Père Lachaise for the cremation. Anne had called the funeral company before to request that she sit with her brother in the car. They set off from the hospital and Anne had the fleeting, fierce desire to take Jacques home back to La Berrière right there and then, to get him out of Paris and out of fashion, but that was not what had been arranged. She could not do that but she did tell the driver to head to Neuilly, and in doing so she diverted the cortège that was following behind. She took Jacques back to say goodbye to his childhood, past their family home where he had grown up on the Boulevard du Commandant Charcot, past his primary school and past the wooded park and pond of the Bois de Boulogne, where they had walked together, older sister and her beloved favourite brother Jacquot.

After that the car turned back and headed east, crossing the city of Paris before climbing up to the cemetery of Père Lachaise. The coffin was removed from the hearse and most of the cortège returned to their cars and left the cemetery. Elisabeth and Gonzalve waited outside the crematorium, while Anne stayed with the coffin to accompany their brother on this last stage of the cremation.

At the end there were two urns of ashes; this was as Jacques had requested. He had instructed that the body of his ashes be divided in two, that half should be given to his mother and the other half to Karl Lagerfeld. Even in death Jacques would be divided.

Karl held a service for Jacques in the village chapel next to Le Mée, his manor house just outside Paris. It was the house where Jacques and

Diane used to go for the day when Jacques was well enough to leave the hospital. The chapel was filled with white lilies and scent; Karl and Diane stood in the front row behind the ashes, Jacques' mother and family stood behind them. It is a decision that Diane now regrets. Anne refused to attend the service.

Ten days later the De Bascher family held their own service. Anne cleared the paths and pruned the alley of hornbeam trees that leads to the small family chapel beside the house. She called Bernard de Boissière, a priest and old friend of her father, to ask if he would lead the service and he took the train from Paris to Nantes to do so.

In the days before the mass the urn was placed in the salon on the Louis XIV console, which was covered with the family's best tablecloth. A candle was placed on either side of the urn to burn night and day. The service was for Jacques' family, brothers and sisters, nieces and nephews and the small retinue of staff from the château. No one else was invited.

When the time came Anne picked up the urn from the table and handed it to her eldest brother to begin the procession. He walked out of the salon and over the slatted wooden bridge that spans the moat and leads to the parkland at the back of the house. He returned the urn to Anne and she walked a short way with Jacques before passing the urn to her sister Elisabeth. In this way the family walked Jacques through the park, handing the urn from one to the next, from adult to child, sibling to nephew, and then at last to his mother, Armelle de Bascher, who walked her son to the steps of the chapel. She handed the urn to the priest, who took it from her and turned to walk into the chapel for the mass of commendation. And in this way Jacques de Bascher, that part of Jacques that could be, was laid to rest.

Epilogue

For Karl, the years that followed Jacques' death were polarised between private devastation and the phenomenal fashion success he was generating at Chanel. He had cut Inès de la Fressange out of his life in 1989, two months before Jacques' death, in what seemed like a cruelly self-inflicted blow. His justification was that Inès had agreed to pose as Marianne – the incarnation of the French republic displayed as a photograph or a bust in town halls throughout France – while she was under exclusive contract with Chanel. Yet this reasoning did not tally with Chanel's initial delight at the Marianne news, which was an enormous publicity coup for the house. Even more so since it was the bicentenary of the French Revolution and therefore two hundred years since Marianne had first appeared with her Revolutionary bonnet and bared breast. Certainly the contempt to which she was subjected suggests a more personal reason for her banishment. Inès herself believes it had more to do with her growing fame and her falling in love with Luigi d'Urso than with any contractual constraints. For five years she had been by Karl's side, in the studio with him every day, all day long up until 2 a.m., when they would leave to go and meet Jacques at Le Voltaire on the *quai* for a cold supper. Karl perhaps sensed that a man in her life would make her less available to him and less dependent on him. 'Lots of people told me that Karl was jealous of my fame, but I didn't believe it . . . Perhaps I was too naive . . . I think above all he was convinced that I would be less faithful from the moment I got married. He thought he would lose me. I wasn't thinking ahead. I was so sure of our friend-ship that I didn't think he could feel abandoned.' Fearing betrayal he broke off their friendship with considerable animosity, accusing Inès in the press of money-seeking and, according to Inès, sending letters to fashion editors. 'There is behind this irresponsible behaviour of hers a story about money and nothing else. As the German proverb goes, Inès is after money, like the devil is after the soul,' Karl told *Paris Match* in a three-page interview that focused entirely on their fall-out. A few days before Inès herself had given an interview in *Le Figaro* entitled 'What I think of Lagerfeld', in which she told her side of the story: 'He is perhaps a little jealous of my success. His German origins resurface from time to time – that is his "Kaiser" side.' Karl's reaction was caustic: 'I wish her all the luck in the world just as long as I don't have to see her any more or hear her spoken about. Forgetting purifies and I know how to be an amnesiac.'

Karl and Diane de Beauvau-Craon clung to each other in the early years after Jacques' death. Diane was drinking heavily. She was there with Karl at the Chanel studio every day and they spent weekends together at the house in Le Mée. There was talk of Diane as Karl's new muse. It was an intense partnership of grief, which, according to Diane, is why it was finite. 'Karl looked at me and saw Jacques. I looked at Karl and saw Jacques, which is why it could not go on. We simply parted.'

During the years of Jacques' illness and in the aftermath Karl put on considerable amounts of weight. He no longer wore his bespoke busi-ness suits but instead started wearing loose-fitting dark suits by Yohji Yamamoto. His hair turned grey and he started powdering it. He was never seen without his dark glasses. It was after Jacques' death that he bought the house in Blankenese; he said it was to be a shrine to Jacques. He changed the house's name, calling it Villa Jako, which was his name for Jacques. He named a perfume after Jacques and launched it at the villa in 1992, shortly before selling the house.

It was on one of these trips back to Hamburg that Karl returned to Bad Bramstedt. He drove out to see his childhood home of Bissenmoor. Karl Wagner's brother still lived in a house to the rear of the Lagerfeld's former home and saw the car arriving. Karl did not get out but watched from his car window as his driver drove him around the outside of the house. The villa had been turned into a

restaurant and then an old people's home, and by the time Karl revisited it had been abandoned due to beetle in the timber. Wagner and
locals in Bad Bramstedt took Karl's reconnoitring to be a sign that he
would buy the house and restore it. But that was not Karl's intention
and the house was knocked down a few years later, so that now all
that is left is woodland.

The loneliness of his private life contrasted with the overwhelming
noise and population of his working days at the Chanel studio. He was
making news and pushing sales figures, designing biker gear – black
leather peak caps, black leather jackets and studded belts – and mixing
it up with exquisite meringue puffs of long taffeta skirts. He put underpants on the runway and branded them with the black double 'C' Chanel
logo. He sent Linda Evangelista out wearing a pair of black lycra pedal-
pushers and a plain white shirt, made Chanel-like by the mass of costume
jewellery and gilt chain belts jangling with logos piled on top. At one
point in the 1990s it seemed as if Karl was deliberately pushing the
clothes to the furthest point of banality in order to produce a creative
tension to blow up all those long-held, authoritarian Chanel dictates –
style over fashion, less is more – and make the house his own.

Karl's irreverent manipulation of the Chanel *œuvre* drove Yves Saint
Laurent to distraction. One of the few times Yves criticised Karl's work
in public was when he said, 'Today this profession [couture] is in regres-
sion. I don't understand it. At Chanel they put chains everywhere, leather
straps. That poor woman must be turning in her grave. I see things that
are appalling, sado-masochistic.'

But Karl's Chanel vision was perfectly pitched for the new MTV generation and a decade that spawned a new race: the supermodel. Claudia
Schiffer, Linda Evangelista, Christy Turlington, Helena Christensen and
Naomi Campbell held fashion in their thrall with their shiny-limbed
glamour. They possessed a movie-star status tracked by paparazzi and
celebrity magazines that made Jerry Hall look like a Texan *ingénue*. For a
while the supermodel became more important than the actual clothes.
Karl employed all the supermodels for the Chanel shows, but claimed
Claudia as his own and as the new face of Chanel. And the sight of
Claudia wending her way down the Chanel runway in a pair of pale pink
tweed hot pants and tweed cropped Chanel jacket had a spectacular effect
on sales. The atmosphere in the Chanel studio throughout these years was

electric. 'It was like being at an Oscar party it was so heady,' says Natasha Fraser-Cavassoni, who was working in the studio at the time. 'In the days leading up to the show there would be all these powerful editors coming in to see Karl and all so excited to be there. Linda was unbelievably beautiful, Victoire would be running round with trays of bracelets and necklaces, and Gilles was popping camellias on shoulders. Sylvester Stallone dropped by. No one wanted to leave. Downstairs in the boutique they couldn't keep the clothes on the store mannequins. It was euphoric and it was Karl that generated all that excitement and glamour. It all emanated from him. He was the ringleader.'

The supermodels were commanding $25,000 a show. It was a time when a model like Naomi could make $400,000 from runway fees during Milan fashion week alone. Helmut Newton, who had started in Paris in the late 1960s getting paid 250 francs a day for French *Vogue* with a beer and baguette thrown in, was by now commanding 10,000 francs a photo for the same magazine. But all of this moneymaking, not surprisingly, was to the detriment of creativity. Now that luxury groups such as Louis Vuitton Moët Hennessy and Dunhill Holdings or pharmaceutical companies like Sanofi were buying up fashion houses, their managers wanted to control fashion and its results. The mad, crazy spontaneity of fashion design that had characterised the 1970s was vanquished. Branding was the buzzword. Once people started describing clothes as 'product' it was clear that commerce had gained the upper hand over invention.

In contrast to his achievements at Chanel, Karl Lagerfeld's own line was less successful. Despite Bidermann investing considerable amounts of money, the Lagerfeld line never fully ignited. In 1987 relations between Bidermann and Lagerfeld were highly antagonistic and Bidermann sold the house to Cora-Revillon. Ralph Toledano, managing director of the Karl Lagerfeld line at the time, insists that for the ensuing five years the Karl Lagerfeld line was successful. 'By the early 1990s we had business of $14 million wholesale in the US, which is not bad at all.' Then in 1992 Dunhill Holdings, which had recently bought the house of Chloé from Gaby Aghion and Jacques Lenoir, also bought Karl Lagerfeld from Cora-Revillon, although their rationale for doing so was principally to persuade Karl to go back to work for the house of Chloé, which he did, rather than a real commitment to Karl's own line.

Karl's own brand never did become a global success and it never generated the press coverage or the excitement of any of the other lines he worked for. It finally went under in 1997 with a 100-million-franc deficit, having run at a considerable loss for five years. Financially Karl was not greatly wounded; he had never invested any of his own money in the line, although he had received royalties. But it was a significant loss of face for Karl. The failure of his own line has given rise to the criticism that Karl is a kind of design mercenary who can succeed designing for other houses but cannot make a success of his own house. In fact Karl could never give his own line the time, concentration and devotion it needed. He spread himself so thin. Much of his energy and creativity were spent on Chanel. 'I'm sure he could have built a huge house [with KL] but he was not ready to abandon the comfort of Chanel, all this exposure that Chanel was giving him and all the money,' says Ralph Toledano. 'If you decide to start Lagerfeld, you become an outsider. When you are at Chanel you can compete with all the top people, ensure you are the best.'

Karl needed Chanel. He needed the power-base from which he could conquer fashion. He needed the financial package: his salary there paid for his increasingly sumptuous lifestyle, which now included a three-floor villa in Monaco – that had cost a rumoured $14 million to renovate – and his newly rented larger apartment within the Hôtel Soyecourt on Rue de l'Université. Money, according to many who have worked with him, is a decisive motivating factor in Karl's career decisions. 'His relationship with money is really very simple,' says one former friend. 'Money, money, money. He is willing to sacrifice everything for money.'

Although Karl has honed a highly productive synergy with the Chanel style, there are perhaps times when her indestructible legacy must surely haunt him. For if there is stimulation from working within another designer's framework, there is also dependency. 'Karl is a designer who works on the variations of a theme: Chanel,' says Edmonde Charles-Roux. Karl is reliant on Chanel as the base, even if it is a base against which he kicks and rebels. Perhaps that is why there were times during the 1990s when it seemed as if Karl was overawed by his own alter ego at Chanel. Diane de Beauvau-Craon remembers going to the Karl Lagerfeld boutique on the Rue du Faubourg Saint-Honoré and picking out clothes for herself there. Karl was both surprised and touched when she told him what she had done. 'He couldn't quite believe that I would prefer Karl Lagerfeld to Chanel,' says Diane.

In 1998 Yves Saint Laurent gave up designing ready-to-wear at the age of sixty-two. It was a highly symbolic retreat for the man who placed such great pride in his ready-to-wear and what he had done when he opened his first Rive Gauche boutique, making high-fashion design available for the first time to so many. Alber Elbaz, an Israeli-born designer, was hired to design the house ready-to-wear collection, and although he stayed only a year in the position he attracted considerable media attention. According to someone who worked in the press office at the time, the excitement about YSL ready-to-wear, after so many years of stagnation, provoked considerable jealousy in Yves.

In 1999 Sanofi, who owned YSL, sold the company to François Pinault, French self-made retail titan, for $1 billion. Pinault then sold it to the Gucci group, who were in the process of building a stable of luxury fashion houses that might rival LVMH. Bernard Arnault, Louis Vuitton Moët Hennessy chairman, was also lobbying hard to buy YSL, which, despite its years of licences and Variations, was still perceived as the jewel in the Parisian fashion crown. The Pinault buy-out left Bergé and Saint Laurent in control of the couture house with a settlement of $70 million and an annual fat-cat salary of $6.6 million each, but the corporate marriage was far from amicable. For although Yves Saint Laurent still headed up and designed his own haute couture, there was now a new idol in the house of Yves Saint Laurent: Tom Ford.

Texan-born and full of charisma, Tom Ford had already miraculously turned around the fortunes of the house of Gucci in the 1990s with his sexy and supremely commercial style, all of which owed a huge debt of inspiration to the work of Yves Saint Laurent, and more specifically the work and mood of Yves Saint Laurent from Paris in the 1970s. Ford, an adolescent in the 1970s, was unashamedly steeped in nostalgia for this period and belonged to a generation fascinated by the seeming weightlessness of pre-AIDS life and the heady maelstrom of fashion, sex and society.

For his first show Tom Ford chose Betty Catroux as his muse. He created the whole collection around Betty, basing it on the trouser suit shown in black and white and restyled for the new generation. He presented the collection in a huge purple perspex box that he had constructed in the gardens of the Rodin Museum, less than five minutes' walk from Yves' home. There was a phalanx of male ushers strung out on the steps of the Rodin Museum, bare-chested beneath their smoking jackets, to greet guests. Ford sat Betty and Bianca on the front row. But although that first collection generated massive press coverage and buzz, it was not a creative hit and it demonstrated that the complexity, scale and sheer power of the Saint Laurent style could not be reduced to a lowest common denominator. Over the next three years at the house, Tom Ford revisited all Yves' 1970s blockbuster collections and themes – *chinoiseries*, androgyny, opium and Carmen, all the obsessions of the Yves Saint Laurent glory years.

Yves, somewhat inevitably, disliked Tom Ford's interpretation of his work and his lack of traditional technique. He criticised him for failing to capture the spirit of Saint Laurent. 'I think he has a lot of talent, for, what do you call it, for marketing,' he told one journalist. To another he sniped, 'He does what he can – poor guy.' Fashion design was almost unrecognisable from the days when Yves began with his portfolio of sketches and passionate love affair with fabrics. Nowadays when Tom Ford edited the ready-to-wear collection days before his Yves Saint Laurent show, he did so by walking alongside the racks of clothes, pulling off those he didn't want in the show and simply letting them slide to the floor.

Despairing of this new reality of fashion, Yves Saint Laurent chose to retire. In January 2002, forty years after his first YSL couture show, a press conference was called and journalists and television cameras crushed into the potted-plant tension of the Avenue Marceau couture salon. In the front row sat his loyal and loving friends: Loulou de la Falaise, Anne-Marie Muñoz, Betty Catroux; three women who had stuck by him from the day they met him. On the small stage Pierre Bergé sat and wiped away tears as Yves Saint Laurent announced his departure. 'I have today decided to bid farewell to the world of fashion I have so loved,' he said. He paid tribute to those who supported him, had faith in him and, perhaps most of all, loved him. He surveyed his career with pride and deemed his contribution considerable. 'In many ways I feel that I have created the wardrobe of the contemporary woman and that I have participated in the transformation of my era,' he said. 'I utterly reject the fantasies of those who seek to satisfy their egos through fashion. Unlike them, I wanted to put myself at women's disposal. That is to say, to serve them, to serve their bodies, their gestures, their attitudes, their life. It was my wish to accompany them in that great movement of liberation that occurred during the last century.'

Saint Laurent also chose this moment to speak openly about his mental illness and struggles with addiction and depression. 'Every man needs aesthetic phantoms in order to exist. I have hunted mine out, pursued them, tracked them down. I have grappled with anguish and I have been through sheer hell. I have known fear and the terrors of solitude. I have known those fair-weather friends we call tranquillisers and drugs. I have known the prison of depression and the confinement of hospital. But one day, I was able to come through all of that, dazzled, yet sober. It was Marcel Proust who taught me that "the magnificent and pitiful family of the hypersensitive are the salt of the earth". I, without knowing it, was a part of that family. It is my own. I did not choose this tragic descent, but through it I was able to rise to the heavens of creativity, where I came across the fire-makers that Rimbaud spoke of, discovering myself and understanding that the most important encounter in one's life is that with oneself.'

As soon as his farewell speech was over, Yves left the stage and disappeared with a Garboesque sense of drama, into the waiting car and home to Rue de Babylone, while Pierre Bergé stayed to field questions. Among the Saint Laurent faithful there were tears, but mostly there was relief that they could stop playing this game of make-believe that they had been playing for so long now – the obsessing over fantasy clothes to be worn by just a handful of women in the world. They were free. 'They shed a tear for a minute because an era was over,' says Fernando Sanchez, 'but mostly they were thinking "Alleluia" to be rid of it.'

Anne-Marie Muñoz has retired now; she no longer spends her days tending to Yves Saint Laurent but still the reflex, the instinct to please him, remains. 'I should go to see Yves this week,' says Madame Muñoz, touching her hair with the self-conscious gesture of a young girl, 'but I will wait until I have been to the hairdresser.' Betty Catroux remains an object of fashion fascination. She is muse to both Tom Ford and Hedi Slimane, menswear designer at the house of Dior, as well as grandmother in black leather and dark glasses. She has remained the closest to Yves. They are joined by their past. Unlike Yves, Betty has moved beyond hers. It cannot all have been 'divine' for Betty. She went through a detoxification programme at the American Hospital in Neuilly at the same time as Yves, where they passed notes back and forth via a tame nurse. She later described the treatment with characteristic Betty coquetry as 'a dream stay'. And yet she admits now it is only since the year 2000 that she has been at peace with herself. 'I feel reborn, newborn,' she says, 'it's very, very strange.' Asked about François Catroux's role in the aftermath of the heady 1970s, Betty is candid: 'He saved me. We lived through a very difficult moment. Thank God he didn't let me fall.'

After Saint Laurent retired, Loulou de la Falaise imagined her future might be that of genteel gardening at her house in the country. But then the fashion instinct outwitted her reason. With Thadée's support and aged fifty-two, she invested the Saint Laurent pay-off and opened her own fashion house and boutique in Paris, selling her inimitable sense of fantasy and colour pulled into focus with a trenchant chic.

Karl and Yves are the great survivors of fashion, with careers that span forty-seven years in the case of St Laurent and fifty-one years and still counting in that of Karl Lagerfeld. They survived it all, the brutal changes and perilous expectations of fashion as well as the collapse of the epoch that was theirs. They survived because of their talent, ambition and the ruthless pursuit of their dreams. For whatever sacrifice the pursuit neces-sitated, both men, in very different ways, were prepared to make it.

Karl survived by his miraculous capacity to anticipate fashion and to regenerate himself. He refused to be bound or defined by his epoch and reinvented himself to take on the next, each time shedding a skin to renew himself. He has gone from being a 1950s boy of sketches and longing to master of the fashion universe in the Internet, marketing, digital-imagery and global-branded age. He drives fashion on with his relentless curiosity and he has never become stuck in the luxury of his life and its trappings. During the 1980s he started taking photographs and he now works prolifically as a photographer of fashion and celebri-ties, for editorial as well as photographing his own advertising campaigns.

He has opened a bookshop and started a small and energetic publishing imprint within the German publishing house of Steidl, publishing books that catch his interest. When his own line went bust in 1997 he bought the brand name from Vendôme for a symbolic franc, picked himself up and started it again. He renamed it Lagerfeld Gallery and, for the first time in his long career, invested some of his own money in his own fashion. In December 2004 Karl sold his trademarks Karl Lagerfeld, Lagerfeld Gallery and KL to Tommy Hilfiger for $30 million. Hilfiger has grand plans for the business, as does Karl, who has bought himself an apartment in the Gramercy Park Hotel as a place to stay when he is in New York working on the collection. Just one month before selling his brand Karl had designed a capsule collection for Swedish chain store H&M, posing himself for a lifesize billboard campaign. The collection featured black skinny trousers at $50 a pop and caused in-store riots when the clothes hit the shelves.

His creative approach and mental resources are the envy of both designers and photographers alike. 'He's like a living library,' says art director Donald Schneider, who worked with Karl on the H&M advertising campaign. 'He uses cultural history as an instrument but then he reshapes it in a modern context. And we are not talking just simple references from fashion magazines; he goes way back in history. He knows what colour Catherine the Great liked for her bedroom.'

Was it merely coincidence or did Yves Saint Laurent's retirement in 2002 finally release Karl from the rivalry in which he had been confined? Now that Saint Laurent was removed from the Paris stage, it seemed as if Karl could breathe at last. He didn't have to try and beat Saint Laurent; he could be Karl Lagerfeld and enjoy it. How to explain the extraordinary weight loss that took place at the time? How to explain his re-emergence into social life having lived as a recluse beyond work since Jacques' death? Or perhaps it was that after more than ten years of mourning Jacques he felt ready to come back.

He cut off the ponytail, he quit the fan habit and lost over six stone in weight. He did so, he says, in order to fit into the clothes designed by Hedi Slimane, who is not only the menswear designer for the house of Christian Dior, but also a close friend of Karl's since 2001. Slimane began his career at the house of Yves Saint Laurent designing menswear in 1997. He is intense, uncommonly shy, tall and introverted with a driving will-power. In his startled appearance and ambition he bears a resemblance to the Yves Saint Laurent Karl knew in the 1950s.

After Karl lost weight he threw away the Japanese suits that covered his sadness and anxiety for all those years and now, over seventy, is to be seen at every party, every opening in town, in jeans and fingerless black leather gloves. He is delighted to be the grand old man of fashion and behaving like a teenager. He claims he has the body he had when he was seventeen. He takes tango lessons at home in the ballroom and dances with Hedi Slimane and, on one momentous occasion, with Oscar de la Renta.

Significantly it is in the last years that Karl has produced some of his greatest couture collections for the house of Chanel. He has left behind the anecdotal and released a gorgeous flurry of gossamer fragility, scintillating pattern and romance into his collections. *International Herald Tribune* fashion editor Suzy Menkes called his 2003 summer collection, marking twenty years at the house of Chanel, 'the most beautiful collection he has done for the house' and a 'magical blend of the fresh and the precious'. 'Karl is like a great wine,' says Chanel vice-chairman Arie Kopelman, 'he just keeps on getting better.' As do Chanel sales. Karl's fashion is the motor that drives the company sales to a conservatively estimated figure of $2.2 billion worldwide in 2005.

As well as shedding his weight, Karl purged himself in other ways. In 2000, after lengthy and extensive tax investigations, Karl sold off property and possessions. The whole eighteenth-century collection of 150 paintings and 400 items of furniture was sold at Christie's for some $29 million. A lesser collection of art-deco furniture was also sold. After all those years living in historic wonderland, he now lives in a pared down, gilt-free interior of plasma screens and multiple iPods. He no longer rents the eighteenth-century *hôtel particulier* on the Rue de l'Université; after thirty years there he has moved on to live in a glass-fronted apartment on the Quai Voltaire, overlooking the Seine. The country house of Le Mée was sold to Princess Caroline of Monaco and the Château de Penhoët was also sold. 'It's the place I prefer most in the world,' Karl once said, but he chose not to return to Penhoët for the last time. Instead a removal lorry was sent with one of Karl's administrative staff. In their haste, they left scraps of his country life behind: the model of the house he commissioned all those years ago, when he and Jacques shared extravagant dreams, sits abandoned on the floor in the chapel at the entrance to the house, along with magazines and forgotten fashion sketches by Karl, a memory from another life.

And yet in all the purging, Karl still keeps his childhood around him, not through people – he has only sporadic contact with his sister Christel through telephone calls and letters – but through possessions. In a down-stairs room of his former apartment on the Rue de l'Université, Karl reconstructed his childhood bedroom with the original furniture from his parents' home: a small, narrow, painted wooden bed, a chair and a child's desk. There is nothing remarkable about the design of the furni-ture – that is to say it was not kept for its value or charm. What is the significance, then, of this nursery furniture to a man past the age of seventy?

Yves Saint Laurent survived in fashion on the strength of what he created. He invented a style and, when there was no more to invent, he set about perfecting it. He also survived by his immense, immovable will. 'I do not believe that I have betrayed the adolescent who showed his first sketches to Christian Dior with such unshakeable faith and conviction. That same faith and conviction has never deserted me,' he said in his retirement speech. He had a vision from which he would not be deflected.

He has an unbending resistance to change that is integral to his internal contradiction of strength and vulnerability. The Rue de Babylone home has remained unchanged for over thirty years. Each time one of Yves' French bulldogs dies, he mourns it, buys another and calls it Moujik. Brigitte Bastian's husband took a photo of Yves standing on his terrace talking to his new puppy Moujik in 2005. He then manip-ulated the picture on computer, adding all the other Moujiks from Yves' life, so that Yves is surrounded by a colony of black and white bull-dogs. There is something about that photo that summons up the tragic unreality and looming claustrophobia of Yves' life: he has bound himself between the dependency of childhood and old age.

He wanted all those around him to stay the same. He wanted Pierre to stay, Loulou, Anne-Marie, Betty, all the people in the couture house; he needed all their reassurance, love and care. Back in 1967 Yves was interviewed for *Dim Dam Dom*, a television show that was France's first timid foray into popular culture. They asked the couturier the favourite 'Proustian' questionnaire. What is your greatest fault? 'Shyness,' he replied. What is your greatest strength? 'Will.' And what do you appreciate most in others? 'Indulgence.' He needed their indulgence and he got it. As Jacques Grange says, 'He was a genius and so we allowed it all.' They still do. 'For a long time it's been getting worse and worse. He is completely shut off from normal life,' says Thadée. 'It's very hard to find a topic of conversation. He talks about his dog vaguely. Loulou and I, we love him dearly but mostly it's a bit distressing because we can't imagine how he's ever going to get over this dreary mood he's in.' Yves invited Fernando, his oldest friend, on holiday to Tangier and saw him only twice throughout the stay, complaining daily that he felt too fat, too depressed, too tired, too miserable, his hair not quite right, to see Fernando. 'We are ready to forgive him for being so unhappy,' says Thadée. 'It is one thing that Karl hates him for, being so unhappy; I guess for him it's one of the things Yves has no right to be, to go whimpering when he's been so successful and rich and handsome.'

Yves always thought it was fashion that caused this anxiety, fashion that imprisoned him in angst, but then he retired and realised it was a part of him. 'Outside of my collections,' he said in 1991, 'I live in total absence.' And this was how he would live after his retirement. Without the support and vitality of his couture house around him, he retreated into the Rue de Babylone, where he lives now with his house staff. He does not read. He rarely sketches. He does not write. His post is opened and read for him. He watches television. He sees Betty for dinner. A driver takes him and his dog the short drive to the Champs de Mars and he gets out and walks Moujik on the grass. His friends despair of his depression. 'He is miserable,' says Betty, 'but he was always self-destructive and this is just another part of that.'

For a time even after his retirement he still went to the studio at Avenue Marceau, arriving in the afternoon to spend time quietly sketching. But in 2004 the couture house was made into a museum. The artist's journey was complete. It is now called the Pierre Bergé – Yves Saint Laurent Foundation and it is a place of exhibitions, research and archives. Upstairs is a library and archive room intended for students, writers and members of the public. In the couture salon where once the clients came to discuss their wardrobes and their husband's bypass operation, now there are exhibitions of Yves' dresses and his sketches for theatre and fashion. It is the sketches that retain their vitality. The dresses hang on mannequins, yet while clearly demonstrating the extraordinary legacy of Yves in the line and iconic style, there is nothing quite so sad and lifeless in fashion as seeing a beautiful dress without the woman inside.

Perhaps Saint Laurent's legacy is strongest and at its most dynamic when it carries on influencing and reappearing on other catwalks and in other collections. Marc Jacobs, Tom Ford, Viktor and Rolf, and Ralph Lauren are just some of the designers who have referenced Yves in their work and who owe a huge debt of inspiration to his *œuvre*. That is the way Saint Laurent's work lives on, resurfacing elsewhere.

Upstairs his studio remains intact, although he rarely goes there now. The studio is empty but for Catrine Gadala, who once recorded all the fabrics and dresses of the haute couture and who now sits alone, waiting at her desk should Monsieur Saint Laurent come. There is no chat, no laughter, no movement any more. Just a bright light reflected off the building next door and the huge mirrors reminding you of your reflection. 'You feel your ugliness,' says Catrine Gadala. There are Yves' 'aesthetic ghosts' – as the press office calls them – a wall of inspiration in front of which Yves Saint Laurent once sat and sketched. The portrait of Yves as a young man by Bernard Buffet is in the centre, there is a postcard of Proust as a child, a photograph of Loulou's daughter Anna as a child with wild hair and her mother's eyes, and a photo of Prince William looking handsome in black tie torn from *Vanity Fair* magazine.

Along the corridor Pierre Bergé is at work in his office. He is an old man now, as active and implicated in life as ever. He is still gilding the legend, organising exhibitions at the foundation as well as an exhibition in Saint Petersburg. The dream may be over, but history is assured. He has bought an auction house, he has written his memoirs, he has bought a caviar restaurant and still he looks after Yves.

Pierre never abandoned Yves. He stuck through the drunken years and manic depression. He stuck through the 150 cigarettes a day, the bouts of aggression and violence, the terrifying phases when as one friend of the couple observes, 'Yves was at the limit of a kind of murderous madness.' Did he do it for himself, for his own need for reassurance, for his own rapacious desire for power and possession? Perhaps it was for all these reasons, but it was also for love. A strange, compulsive and ruthless love, but it was love nevertheless. 'There was a total passion between them,' says François Catroux. 'There still is. Perhaps at this age you don't call it passion, but in any case it is love, that's for sure. They are a couple without a doubt, with all the pettiness of their old age, with all the caprices that Yves pulls, the theatrics to grab Pierre's attention, still, even now at the age of sixty-seven. Every time Yves goes to Tangier on holiday he will fall down the stairs at least four times on purpose so that Pierre must come, take the plane and save him. And Pierre is the same: if all of a sudden Yves said, "I'm flying to Istanbul tomorrow," Pierre wouldn't know what to do with himself – the fact that Yves had made a decision without him. Pierre adores Yves. Of course there is also a matter of his own posthumous glory, but there is always this idea to raise Saint Laurent up to this towering figure that the others are not. And Pierre will carry on doing that until he dies.'

'I don't know that he falls on purpose,' replies Pierre when asked if this is what happens, 'but he falls and I go. Even today I am more of a prisoner than Yves. Yves is someone who lives in Paris and does not want to leave his home. Therefore I don't go away at the weekends because I don't want to leave him alone. Yes, but that is the very least I can do. I go away when I really have to, but otherwise I stay in Paris and I have lunch with Yves every Saturday. Of course it's love; it's not anything else, is it? Naturally it is love. Absolutely and with all the forms that love may take.'

All this talk of love is enough to make one believe that Pierre Bergé, at seventy-five, has mellowed in his dotage. But mention the name Karl Lagerfeld and the old Bergé wrath rises again. 'Talking about Yves Saint Laurent and Karl Lagerfeld is like talking about Maria Callas and a friend she had at the *conservatoire*. One went off to become Maria Callas and the other, well, it's not quite the same thing,' he says, warming to his theme. 'Karl Lagerfeld is someone who does a very good job at Chanel, who is a very good stylist in that he can make a style and mix the [existing] codes. Unfortunately he is not a creator. If he was a creator he wouldn't have waited until he got the job at Chanel to succeed; if he was a creator he would not have failed at everything he has done under his own name. Karl Lagerfeld was a minor designer working in second-rate houses, Jean Patou and others, while Yves Saint Laurent was successor to Christian Dior. When Yves Saint Laurent opened his own couture house, Karl was working for a house that was called Chloé. And so it continued. Saint Laurent has always stuck in Karl Lagerfeld's gullet. He has never digested Yves Saint Laurent's success and he never will. So he can try and have a sip of water here, have some success there, be applauded here and there, but he will never be Saint Laurent and he knows it. Yves Saint Laurent turned his epoch on its head, he invented his epoch, he created it; Karl Lagerfeld has illustrated his. And sadly it is an epoch that bears more resemblance to the principality of Monaco and *Gala* magazine than a period that is really about fashion and creativity. But apart from all that, I find Karl Lagerfeld is someone very intelligent and very cultivated. But, my God, what a shame that he did not keep up with the success of Yves Saint Laurent; I always think that the success of others never bothers you, unless you don't have enough talent yourself to accept it.'

Not so mellow after all. When you remove the theatrics and hyperbole of that diatribe – after all, Yves Saint Laurent might have expressed his epoch, may even have defined it, but he can hardly be credited with having invented it – there are accusations to be addressed. Surely it must be recognised that a man has the right to find success at any age, not just twenty-one. And even if Bergé is right that today's epoch is more about celebrity magazines than fashion, Karl Lagerfeld must be credited with having the intelligence and sheer courage to lead an epoch in fashion that is not, in terms of age group and generation, rightfully his own.

The difficulty in digesting Saint Laurent's success has been a factor in Karl Lagerfeld's life and past choices. But one also needs to recognise that Karl has succeeded in moving beyond that now. He is quite simply not the man he was twenty years ago; after all, neither is Yves Saint Laurent. And surely out-working Yves Saint Laurent has been a most effective kind of digestion for Karl. The fact that Karl is still creating, still partaking, still a media obsession and, most important of all, still relevant in fashion – isn't that the sweetest victory that he could have hoped for? Isn't the fact that he is still striving the most creative of acts? He has transformed himself once more, to take on the world. 'He is happy. He has become the star he always wanted to be,' says Victoire fondly. Victoire is a mother of two sons, a grandmother and married to painter Pierre Doutreleau. When in Paris she lives in a *pied-à-terre* on Rue de l'Université, in the very same building where Karl lived thirty years before when Warhol shot *L'Amour*. In her apartment she keeps the sketches that Karl and Yves once dedicated to her. There is the wispy, Bérard-style sketch of Victoire dressed in a Dior cocktail dress designed by Yves, signed Yves Mathieu-Saint-Laurent and dedicated to 'the woman who wears my dresses so well'. And beside it is the sketch by Karl showing Victoire through the ages, wearing a historic array of six dresses from Second Empire to flapper girl, not one of them Karl's own.

Victoire is right: Karl is a star now. He parties with Nicole Kidman, he is in every magazine you open, on every people page. He is on celebrity shows; he has cameo roles in movies. He has published a best-selling book of his own diet. When he goes to Japan he is mobbed by teenage fans filming him on their mobile telephones. 'He says he's not a marketing guy, but the truth is he has done a brilliant job of projecting his image. He has become a rock star. He has a presence far beyond most designers. He makes the magical headline,' says Arie Kopelman, before adding the essential retail truth, 'and all of that funnels into helping leverage the [Chanel] brand.' Karl recognises that the fashion world is now a place 'where life became a special effect' and so he has made himself a performance artist to take on that age. He knows the endless cynicism of the fashion world and he can match it, hence his ability to beat it. When asked if he would have received the kind of attention he gets now a few years back, his response was sanguine: 'No, it's only since I've become this kind of marionette.'

When he turned up late for Delphine Arnault's wedding service at the cathedral of Saint-Jean-Baptiste de Bazas, his high heels ringing out on the cobble stones of the French provinces, the crowd let out a cheer of approval and applauded him. At last, the French love Karl. It is his time in the sun. In 2004 he held an exhibition of his photographs at the Pierre Passebon gallery in Paris. His great friend Princess Caroline of Monaco was there with her husband and daughter Charlotte. Bernadette Chirac was there, dressed in Chanel tweed and heard to be saying, 'Of course I had to come for my Karl.'

Perhaps Karl's legacy will be less about the body of work he leaves and more about the direction he led fashion in and the irrepressible daring and inquisitiveness with which he does so. He invented the blueprint for breathing life into a moribund fashion house, and all those who have come after – Tom Ford, John Galliano, Marc Jacobs and Nicolas Ghesquière at Balenciaga – have emulated his formula in some way. He calls himself a 'professional hit man' and that is what dominates fashion now, designers working in a house not bearing their own name. 'I'm not sure that the new Armani or the new Ralph Lauren will be possible in the future. I think designers now have gotten used to putting themselves behind the label, the way Tom [Ford] has. It doesn't have to be "my house, my name, my label, it will die with me". That's not modern,' said Karl recently. His legacy will be more in the attitude than the line, something he recognised long ago.

There is commotion on the street in Paris as it is 9 p.m. on a weekday and Karl is leaving for a *dîner mondain*. It is a scene worthy of the star he is. A blue Jaguar moves out into the road. Its windows are dark and smoky, but transparent enough that you can see right into the light-filled interior. Inside Karl sits bolt upright; he is wearing thick tan foundation, a high white collar, black sunglasses and gloves with a mass of silver jewels at the collar. Revving hard is a huge, anti-terrorist-type jeep with floodlights and enormous bumper barrier that has trouble making the turn out of the gateway. There is much gear-changing and frustrated reversing. But Karl's Jaguar doesn't wait; there is never a moment to waste. It sweeps off into the night and finally the anti-terrorist, floodlit vehicle makes the turn and zooms off to catch up. The goodly bourgeois residents of the seventh *arrondissement* stare. After the dinner is over Karl will go on to the Flore. For after so many years of absence Karl is to be found there again; night after night he sits at the café, alone at his table or surrounded by those younger than him. Behind dark glasses, Karl watches the door to see who will step in.

INTERVIEW LIST

The two names missing from the list below are those of Yves Saint Laurent and Karl Lagerfeld. When I interviewed Karl Lagerfeld for a magazine article I was working on during the early stages of my research for this project, I told him about my book and asked if he would speak with me. He said yes and gave me his private fax number to contact him on. I did so and heard nothing. Over five years I sent many letters and faxes to Karl Lagerfeld but did not receive any replies.

Trying to get an interview with Yves Saint Laurent involved years of suspense and neurosis. Betty Catroux introduced me to Yves Saint Laurent at a party at Loulou de la Falaise's new shop. He was charming. I said I would write a letter and he said wonderful, we would speak. I wrote the letter. Betty Catroux, whom I had already interviewed, entered into a campaign on my behalf in which she, using her words, 'harassed him daily' for about two years. No interview materialised. Letters, postcards, faxes, emails, phone calls followed. Rather surreally, I bumped into Yves Saint Laurent on my street one day. Most unusually he was out walking alone. I stopped him and reintroduced myself. 'Yes,' he said, 'I have not been able to do the interview, but next week. I promise you.' That was in May 2003.

Unless otherwise indicated in the footnotes, all quotes/quoted material come from interviews with the author.

There are a handful of people interviewed by the author who did not wish to be named below.

Gaby Aghion, Paris,18 and 24 June 2002, and 3 September 2002
Charlotte Aillaud, Paris, 10 December 2002
Kitty d'Alessio, by telephone, 14 December 2005
Norbert and Lydie Alvérola, Niort, 29 September 2005
Anouschka, Paris, 17 January 2001
Javier Arroyuelo, Paris, 13 November 2002
Claude Aurensan, Paris, 21 November 2001
Anne de Bascher, Paris, 30 September 2002 and La Berrière, 18 and 19
    May 2004
Xavier de Bascher, Paris, 17 September 2002
Brigitte Bastian, Toulon, 26 September 2005
François Baufumé, Paris, 24 January 2002
Renaud de Beaugourdon, Paris, 16 April 2004 and 16 February 2006
Diane de Beauvau-Craon, Paris, 21 October and 7 November 2002, and
    7 July 2003
Pierre Bergé, Paris, 31 May 2005
Christine Bergström, Paris, 30 July 2002
Jean-Pascal Billaud, Paris, 17 June 2003
Billina, New York, 3 December 2002
Manolo Blahnik, London, 3 April 2002
Jean de Bodinat, Paris, 4 April 2005
Marc Bohan, Paris, 19 February 2004
Dominique Brabec, Paris, 20 February 2003
Hans-Joachim Bronisch, Bad Bramstedt, 19 September 2005
Joan Juliet Buck, Paris, 23 February 2002
Stephen Burrows, New York, 31 January 2002
Patrice Calmettes, Paris, 14 October 2003
Paul Caranicas, New York, 1 February and 6 December 2002
Betty Catroux, Paris, 21 November 2002
François Catroux, Paris, 28 September 2004
Edmonde Charles-Roux, Paris, 2 April 2002
Pat Cleveland, Stresa, 28 February 2002
Doctor Scott Coffey, by telephone, 8 December 2004
Madison Cox, New York, 1 December 2002

John Crawley, Paris, 10 January 2001
Francine Crescent, Paris, 18 January 2001
Guy Cuevas, Paris, 20 December 2001
Gérard Danet, Grand-Champ, 18 March 2003
Bernard Danillon, Paris, 15 November 2001
Davé, Paris, 11 January 2001
Claude Deloffre, Paris, 1 July 2002
Jean-Pierre Derbord, Saint Cloud, 14 September 2004
Louise Despointes, Paris, 11 February 2002
Nicole Dorier, Paris, 12 September 2002
Jimmy Douglas, Paris, 9 February 2004
Victoire Doutreleau, Paris, 3 October 2002 and 20 October 2005
Gerry Dryansky, Paris, 6 March 2002
Gilles Dufour, Paris, 12 November 2002
Jean Eudes, Paris, 14 November 2002
John Fairchild, London, 4 April 2002
Loulou de la Falaise, Paris, 12 January 2001, 2 April 2003; by telephone
    19 January 2006
Maxime de la Falaise, St-Rémy, 25 June 2003
Judith Fayard, Paris, 23 January 2001 and 29 January 2003
Robert Ferrell, Paris, 8 November 2002 and 12 December 2004
Natasha Fraser-Cavassoni, Paris, 3 June 2005
Diane Von Furstenberg, New York, 6 December 2002
Philippe Garner, London, 3 April 2002
Christophe Girard, Paris, 14 November 2002
Tan Giudicelli, Paris, 6 June 2002
Pamela Golbin, Paris, 21 December 2001
Jacques Grange, Paris, 25 November 2002
Florence Grinda, Paris, 23 January 2001
Didier Grumbach, Paris, 11 December 2002 and 12 February 2003
Anna Harvey, Paris, 22 January 2002
Jim Haynes, Paris, 7 November 2001
Philippe de Henning, Paris, 20 June 2002
Steve Hiett, Paris, 15 January 2002
Patrick Hourcade, Paris, 17 October and 21 November 2002
Irié, Paris, 21 November 2001
Manfred Jacobsen, Bad Bramstedt, 19 September 2005

Donna Jordan, New York, 4 December 2002
Professor Detlef Junker, by telephone, 6 April 2004
Kirat, Paris, 22 October 2002
Michel Klein, Paris, 17 October 2002
Thadée Klossowski, Paris, 13 October 2003
Arie Kopelman, by telephone, 6 June 2005
Lorna Koski, New York, 30 January 2002
Christel (née) Lagerfeld, USA, 21 June 2005
Kurt Lagerfeld, Neustadt in Holstein, 17 and 18 February 2003
Valérie Lalonde, Paris, 1 October 2003
Emile Laugier, Paris, 27 May 2002
Rose-Marie Legallais, Paris, 26 November 2002
André Levasseur, Paris, 5 December 2003
Roxanne Lowit, New York, 30 January 2002
Hélène de Ludinghausen, Paris, 23 October 2002
Christian Dumais-Lvowksi, Paris, 30 September 2002 and 16 April 2004
Guy Marineau, Paris, 19 December 2001
Patrick McCarthy, New York, 5 December 2002
Pat McColl, Paris, 15 March 2002
Marian McEvoy, New York, 3 December 2002
Eric Mension-Rigaud, Paris, 20 April 2004
Frédéric Mitterrand, Paris, 8 February 2003
Xavier Moreau, Paris, 16 January 2002
Jean de Mouy, by telephone, 4 December 2003
Anne-Marie Muñoz, Paris, 22 May 2003
Helmut Newton, Monte Carlo, 11 December 2001 and 29 August 2002
Florentine Pabst-Schober, Paris, 13 November 2002
Paquita Paquin, Paris, 22 November 2002
Lucien Pellat-Finet, Paris, 5 February 2003
Anna Piaggi, Paris, 21 January 2003
Jean-Jacques Picart, Paris, 28 October 2002
Paloma Picasso, Paris, 4 April 2003
Andrée Putman, Paris, 19 November 2002 and 28 January 2003
Ariel de Ravenel, Paris, 15 January 2001
Alexis de Redé, Paris, 3 October 2003
Joaquim Reuter, Paris, 20 November 2002
Marc Rioufol, Paris, 23 January 2001

Vincent Risterucci, Paris, 24 September 2002

Guy de Rothschild, Paris, 5 December 2001

Kal Ruttenstein, by telephone, 2 April 2002

Clara Saint, Paris, 16 January 2003

Janie Samet, Paris, 29 November 2002

Fernando Sanchez, New York, 1 February and 4 December 2002

Sao Schlumberger, Paris, 27 November 2001

Donald Schneider, Paris, 20 November 2005

Charles Sebline, Paris, 6 December 2003

Irene Silvagni, Paris, 21 November 2002

Donald Tait, Paris, 29 January 2003

Kenzo Takada, Paris, 9 December 2002

Daniel Templon, Paris, 16 March 2002

Corey Grant Tippin, New York, 2 December 2002, 17 December 2004 and 17 November 2005

Ralph Toledano, Paris, 6 November and 20 December 2002

Susan Train, Paris, 10 January 2001

Eija Vehka ajo, by telephone, 8 November 2002

Karl Wagner, by telephone, 11 September 2003, Bad Bramstedt, 19 September 2005

Holly Warner, Paris, 27 February 2002

Isabelle Weingarten, Paris, 4 March 2002

Eric Wright, by telephone, 1 December 2005

Susi Wyss, Paris, 29 January 2001

Renata Zatsch, Paris, 23 November 2002

ABBREVIATIONS

KL = Karl Lagerfeld
YSL = Yves Saint Laurent
PB = Pierre Bergé
AD = Alicia Drake

BF = Bibliothèque Forney, Paris
CDA = Christian Dior Archives
EA = *L'Express* Archive
FA = Fairchild Archive
FVA = French *Vogue* Archive
FPB-YSL = Fondation Pierre Bergé–Yves Saint Laurent
LFA = *Le Figaro* Archive
LPA = *Le Point* Archive
NYPL = New York Public Library
NYTA = *New York Times* Archive
TA = *Time* Archive
UCAD = Bibliothèque de la Union Centrale des Arts Décoratifs, Paris
WWD = *Women's Wear Daily*

NOTES TO THE TEXT

Chapter 1

To research this chapter I interviewed Brigitte Bastian, YSL's youngest sister, about Yves' childhood and background.

Understanding what being a *pied-noir* meant at this time and getting a feel for life in French colonial Algeria is quite a challenge, particularly if you are not French. I tracked down a series of delightfully obscure books entitled *Oran of My Youth* which are full of people's old snapshots of school choirs and champion swimming-teams. I also interviewed Lydie and Norbert Alvérola, both of whom lived in Oran at this time and conjured up the cherished colonial life there.

For YSL's years at Dior, I had access to the archives of the house of Christian Dior in Paris. The archive library of the weekly magazine *L'Express* was another important source for YSL's first seasons at Dior. Interviews with former Dior employees Victoire, André Levasseur and Tan Giudicelli were particularly helpful in reconstructing life at the house of Dior in the 1950s.

4   **already on the road** Bernard Lafay, president of the Conseil Municipal of Paris, on handing out the prizes to the three winners, 7 January 1955.
5   **Elegance is a dress** Janie Samet, *L'Echo d'Oran*, 7 January 1955.
6   **Our world at the time** YSL in 1983, appeared in *Yves Saint Laurent par Yves Saint Laurent* (Editions Herscher: Paris, 1986) p. 15.
7   **I think he made** *New York Times*, 3 June 1971.
8   **a revelation for Yves** Ibid.
    Theatre was all Ibid.
12 **Maman, it won't** As told to AD by Anne-Marie Muñoz during interview.

12 **Fernando Sanchez remembers** being at the Ecole Chambre Syndicale de la Couture Parisienne with Karl Lagerfeld. Fernando started in the Spécial Supérieur B in October 1954. KL was in a different class to Fernando and YSL.

13 **Contrary to what** YSL letter from the private collection of Victoire Doutreleau.

15 **Balmain made me** G.Y. Dryansky in *Connoisseur* magazine, December 1985.

16 **My first day** Margit Mayer, 'King Karl', *WWD*, 20 November 1991 (FA).

Detail on 1950s Paris homosexual life can be found in the essay 'Folles, Swells, Effeminates, and Homophiles in Saint-Germain-des-Prés of the 1950s: A New "Precious" Society?' by Georges Sidéris, in Jeffrey Merrick and Michael Sibalis, *Homosexuality in French History and Culture* (The Haworth Press, Inc.: New York, 2001).

19 **the woman that** Sketch by YSL in Victoire Doutreleau private collection.

Lucienne Mathieu-Saint-Laurent tells of her meeting with Dior and his naming YSL as heir in *Yves Saint Laurent, Le Temps Retrouvé*, a film written and directed by David Teboul (Canal+/Movimento/INA Entreprise/Transatlantic Vidéo, January 2002).

21 **I was in a state** Franz-Olivier Giesbert et Janie Samet , 'YSL: Je suis né avec une dépression nerveuse', *Le Figaro*, 11 July 1991.

little-girl dresses Eugenia Sheppard, *New York Herald Tribune*, 31 January 1958 (CDA).

22 **I never saw a better** Ibid.

YSL and the Dior balcony stunt: John Fairchild, *The Fashionable Savages* (Doubleday & Company, Inc.: New York, 1965), p. 24.

23 **YSL – *le nouvel enfant triste*** *L'Express*, 6 February 1958 (EA).

studious schoolboy *Yves Saint Laurent, Le Temps Retrouvé*, op. cit.

Chapter 2

The Christian Dior archives were particularly useful for photographs from Saint Laurent's collections for the house. These collections have tended to be described in street-style terms unrealistic for the period, so it was essential to be able to see the sketches and photographs of the clothes.

L'Express archives were a valuable source in documenting the Algerian War: at the time the newspaper (now a magazine) conducted a fierce campaign against the war and government.

Marc Bohan was a key source for reassessing the ousting of YSL at Dior. Bohan's discretion over the years concerning this subject contrasts with Bergé's dominance of the story, and meant that Bohan's chronology of events and the fact that he was on the Dior payroll from 1957 – hired by Dior himself – and then kept as a back-up plan, should YSL not work out, was never widely known.

25 **I began uniquely** Gerry Dryansky, *WWD*, 19 January 1968 (FA).

26 **were not exactly** Madame Bergé interview in *Globe, edition spéciale*, 14 November 1990.

He never bent Ibid.

lazy and undecided Ibid.

27 **Life revolved around** Pierre Bergé, *Les Jours s'en vont je demeure* (Editions Gallimard: Paris, 2003).

I had been Ibid.

28 **strange, shy boy** Lesley White, 'The Saint', British *Vogue*, November 1994.

Everything I didn't YSL in *Yves Saint Laurent, Le Temps Retrouvé*, op. cit.

This quarrel has Matthieu Galey, *Journal 1953–1973* (Editions Grasset & Fasquelle: Paris, 1987), p. 174.

Is this the insensitivity Ibid, pp. 174–5.

an amusing digression Ibid, p. 176.

29 **As for Pierre** Ibid, p. 177.

her dress was J. F. Bergery, 'Jours de France', 13(?) November 1958 (CDA).

32 **It was a terrible** YSL to Franz-Oliver Giesbert, Janie Samet, *Le Figaro*, 11 July 1991.

33 **It was horrifying** Ibid.

35 **There is no** As told by PB *Yves Saint Laurent, Le Temps Retrouvé*, op. cit.

36 **No, we haven't** Interview with Victoire, *Paris Match*, 6 February 1992.

37 **Everyone wanted this** Patricia Peterson, 'YSL in debut on his own', *New York Times*, 20 January 1962 (NYTA).

39 **But that is not** As told to AD by Victoire.

41 **The word seduction** *Dim Dam Dom* television programme (ORTF, 1967)

Detail of Andy Warhol and Pierre Bergé's cock ring, diary entry of Sunday, 4 September 1977 in *The Andy Warhol Diaries*, ed. Pat Hackett (Warner Books, 1989), p. 66.

Chapter 3

I used the *Women's Wear Daily* archives in New York as a source throughout the book. As the industry daily newspaper it was invaluable to me as it recorded not only an uncommon level of detail on the workings of the burgeoning industry, but also its intrigues and scandal, so dear to John Fairchild's heart. The friendship between John Fairchild and PB and YSL meant that *WWD* reporters were allowed unusual access to Yves Saint Laurent, particularly in the first half of the 1970s.

Many people spoke to me of the Marrakech years, but it was Thadée Klossowski and Fernando Sanchez who marvellously evoked the feeling of wild, sweet bliss at the end of the 1960s. Unlike many, they still recalled the details and were willing to share the memories.

I researched Paris 1968 by working on the archives of *L'Express* and French *Vogue*, as well as through interviews and reading referred to in the bibliography. Jim Haynes, who founded the sexual-liberation newspaper *Suck* in the early 1970s in Paris, gave a valuable account of the freedom and excitement of sex and sexuality at this time.

47 **When I knew** Yves Saint Laurent talks to Bianca Jagger, *Interview* magazine, January 1973 (NYPL).

50 **Oh, I woke** As told to AD by Thadée Klossowski in interview.

52 **I owe to** '*Naturellement l'opium reste unique et son euphorie supérieure à celle de la santé. Je lui dois mes heures parfaites*', Jean Cocteau, *Journal d'une désintoxication* (Stock: Paris, 1930).

I just hate As told to AD by Thadée Klossowski in interview.

just what I 'The Saints Come Marching In', *WWD*, 13 September 1968 (FA).

53 **We were supposed** *Interview* magazine, April 1975.

54 **Let's do crazy** *WWD*, 13 September 1968 (FA).

55 **Je l'adore** Ibid.

56 **Yves, I think** As told to AD by Anne-Marie Muñoz.

Which fashion show As told to AD by Anne-Marie Muñoz.

58 **It is strictly** '*Il est strictement interdit d'interdire Loi du 13 mai 1968*', a notice at the Sorbonne, photographed in *L'Express*, 20 May 1968 (EA).

60 **Recent political events** *WWD*, 3 July 1968 (FA).

61 **I do not** Ibid.

attacked my liberty *WWD*, 19 January 1968 (FA).

One thing you Ibid.

We will return 'The Lotos Eaters', Alfred Tennyson (1833).

I feel in Helen Lawrenson, *Esquire* magazine, June 1970.

62 **Real fashion today** *WWD*, 3 July 1968 (FA).

63 **I have never** Ibid.

is based on Ibid.

The difference between Ibid.

Chapter 4

Researching Karl Lagerfeld's early life required two trips to Germany. The first trip in 2003 was primarily to interview Kurt Lagerfeld, Karl's cousin, who was aged eighty-nine at the time and died eight months later. He lived in Neustadt, Holstein, and we discussed his own life as well as that of Karl and Karl's father. He showed me photo albums and an important family document that Karl's father, Otto, had written about his life and work. On that first trip I also spent time in Blankenese, Hamburg, and made a brief excursion to Bad Bramstedt to find

Bissenmoor. I returned two years later to Bad Bramstedt for further research. By this time I was in touch with some of Karl's former schoolmates and was able to interview Karl Wagner, next-door neighbour to Karl as a boy. He showed me Karl's school and the site of the house where KL lived as a child, and he walked me round Bissenmoor and pointed out where they had played, the tree Christel used to climb, and described the layout of the house and garden. I also interviewed Hans-Joachim Bronisch, who sat behind Karl at senior school.

For information on KL's work at Chloé the most valuable source was Gaby Aghion, whom I interviewed on several occasions. She was able to evoke the industriousness of KL and the brilliance of his collections there. I used the Chloé archives, which are sadly depleted due to the changing fortunes and owners of the house of Chloé during the 1980s. There are images from advertising campaigns, but there is little editorial coverage of these years and no sketches or actual clothes.

It was a joy to find the film *Top Ten Designers in Paris*, made by Software Productions in 1979, that not only showed the collections of ready-to-wear designers such as KL, Kenzo and Tan Giudicelli, but also featured interviews with each designer discussing their work and world. The interview with KL from the film was a great source drawn upon throughout the book.

I travelled to the USA three times for research purposes. In 2002 I interviewed Paul Caranicas, Corey Grant Tippin and Donna Jordan in New York to discuss the arrival of the Americans in Paris and their effect. Paul Caranicas allowed me access to the immense archive of Antonio and Juan, comprising all their illustrations, photographs, photographic albums, journals and paintings from these years. He was also a key source in understanding the nature of their life in Paris and their working relationship.

Other sources in this chapter include the New York Public Library, for *Interview* magazine archives.

65 **I was not ambitious** Karl Lagerfeld and Jean-Claude Houdret, *Le Meilleur des régimes* (Robert Laffont: Paris, 2002).

   I came to François Wimille, 'King of the Collections Karl Lagerfeld', *Interview* magazine, May 1979 (NYPL).

   It was my dream *Top Ten Designers in Paris*, film made by Software Productions, 1979, loaned to AD by Jean-Jacques Picart.

68 **None of them** KL, 'All White and Spheres', *Home Furnishing Daily*, 26 July 1968 (FA).

   KL's age is a subject of some debate. For many years Karl has given his birth date as 1938, which would have meant he was sixteen when he won the IWS competition. Yet at the time of the competition his age is given as twenty-one in a number of publications, including *L'Aurore*, 14 December 1954. KL's cousin, the late Kurt Lagerfeld, also confirmed KL's age at the time of the IWS competition as being twenty-one. Kurt Lagerfeld said that KL was born on '10 September 1933'. Karl's next-door neighbour Karl Wagner was born in 1934 and remembers Karl as his contemporary as a child, when they played together aged five and six. Kurt Lagerfeld gave me a photo of Karl as a young boy with his sister Christel and Kurt's own daughter, Margrit. KL is a young boy, dressed in lederhosen, white shirt and scarf knotted at the neck, standing with his hand on a chair. On the back of the photo there is a handwritten identification of Karl and his sister with the date marked as 19 May 1940. Hans-Joachim Bronisch went to school with KL at the Jürgen Fuhlendorf Schule that begins at the age of ten/eleven. Says Herr Bronisch: 'I arrived in Bad Bramstedt in 1947 and I went into the seventh grade; I was aged thirteen and this was senior school, and Karl was certainly not nine as he would have had to be according to his calculations.'

German law does not allow access to birth certificates for people who are not members of the family. However, a German newspaper has published a copy of KL's birth certificate in which his date of birth is marked as 1938; the date of birth is written by hand. KL's baptism record is held at a Catholic church in Hamburg. In 2003 a journalist from *Bild am Sonntag* referred to this baptism certificate and wrote a story saying that KL's real year of birth was 1933. I contacted the priest of the church and then travelled to Hamburg to view the baptism certificate myself. On arrival in Hamburg I was told that the priest was travelling. Many frustrating and rather absurd telephone conversations ensued between myself and the priest: call me back tomorrow, call me back later, I can't hear you, I'm in my car, etc. On the morning that I was due to depart I called the priest one last time, where-upon he informed me that he had faxed KL on his personal fax number to ask permission to show me the record. He said KL did not reply to the fax. I was not allowed access to the baptism record.

KL has not responded to my requests for an interview and so I have not heard him directly on this subject. However, having seen the private family document written by Otto Lagerfeld, KL's father, which Kurt Lagerfeld showed me, and having seen the school photos, dated family photos and interviewed those close to KL as a child in Bad Bramstedt, I took the decision to stick with the date of the year in which I believe KL was born and that is 1933.

73 **As a child** KL to Sven Michaelsen and Stephanie Rosenkranz, *Der Stern*, 24 October 1996.
78 **Antonio wanted everybody** KL, *Sunday Telegraph* magazine, 12 January 2003.
This was in Ibid.
My mother to me *Interview* magazine, August 1973 (NYPL).
79 **I never saw** *Sunday Telegraph*, op. cit.
That is the most *Interview* magazine, op. cit.
80 **my assistant** *Interview* magazine, op. cit.
Both he and Juan Paul Caranicas, *Antonio's People* (Thames & Hudson: London, 2004), p. 8.

Working a pocket describes the old-fashioned way of modelling when a girl would saunter down the runway, hand placed nonchalantly in pocket, elbow held just so for triangular perfection with perhaps the other hand used to swing her jacket jauntily from one shoulder.

Chapter 5

In November 2002 I met up with Corey Grant Tippin in a Chelsea (NY) diner and he told me his remarkable life story, from Connecticut prep school to Andy Warhol Factory and back. The interview began at 2 p.m. and lasted five hours. That evening I went with Corey to see a private showing of *L'Amour* with Jay Johnson and Paul Caranicas. I interviewed Corey many times for the book and, as well as his memories, he also provided press cuttings, photos and letters to help with my research. The day after interviewing Corey, I met with Donna Jordan in another diner on Tenth Avenue. Donna now lives in New York State, is studying English literature at university and has scant regard for her Paris fashion past, although her daughter has followed her mother's example and become a model.

In 2002 I travelled to Lake Stresa in Italy to interview Pat Cleveland, who lives there with her photographer husband and two children. Interviewing Pat was a unique experience, as she tends to act out her memories, becoming whichever character she is describing and adding a voice-over of memory. Down in the basement of her house, she was a heavy, panting Antonio, tongue wrapped around his lips as he sketched; she was Jerry Hall curving down a catwalk; and she was herself, walking into La Coupole for the first time on her first night out in Paris, waiters cheering, arms flying. A year later I met up with Pat again at the Flore – she was in Paris for the weekend, as by this time her daughter Anna had been discovered and was modelling – along with Pat – in the Chanel show for KL and being photographed by French *Vogue*.

I interviewed Loulou de la Falaise on several occasions for the book. I also interviewed her mother Maxime de la Falaise, who was key not only to understanding Loulou's background but also to gaining insight into the context of fashion and society at this turning point. I went to stay with Maxime in Saint Rémy and happened to arrive in time for her eighty-first birthday party, where I was able to witness the Falaise talent for partying.

83 **Corey, take this** As told to AD by Corey Tippin, in interview.
84 *Le pays de* Jean des Cars and Jean-Paul Caracalla, *Le Train Bleu* (Editions Denoël, 1988).
86 **Like a divinely** *WWD*, 8 September 1970 (FA).
  who stops traffic Ibid.
  Established Saint-Tropez Ibid.
90 **indecent luxury** Bevis Hillier used this splendid phrase to conjure up modernism's dim view of art deco in his lecture 'Art Deco Revisited', delivered at the conference The Art Deco World at the V&A, 27 April 2003.

92 **Here, my dear** As told to AD by Corey Tippin, Donna Jordan and Pat Cleveland.

95 **Inasmuch as I** Chanel to Paul Morand in his book, *L'Allure de Chanel* (Hermann: Paris, 1976); English translation from *Chanel and Her World*, Edmonde Charles-Roux (Weidenfeld & Nicolson: London, 1981).

I read that *WWD*, 14 July 1970 (FA).

98 **You are the** As told to AD by Maxine de la Falaise in interview.

L'Amour, 1972. Story and direction Paul Morrissey, producer Andy Warhol, camera Andy Warhol and Jed Johnson, from the archive of the Andy Warhol Museum, Pittsburgh, PA.

Donna Jordan cover and shoot by Guy Bourdin appeared in French *Vogue*, November 1970 (UCAD).

Chapter 6

Material for this chapter was drawn predominantly from interviews. Corey Grant Tippin, Loulou de la Falaise and Betty Catroux all had vivid memories of the YSL-PB party. Corey was able to compare Andy Warhol and YSL's genius for wielding control within an entourage, having experienced both first-hand.

It is rare to discuss this time in Paris without an interviewee wanting to talk about Le Sept. The nightclub has now been transformed into a small Japanese restaurant, the downstairs dance floor is gone and in its place are the restaurant loos and storeroom. The description of the club is derived from many people's accounts of nights spent there. Claude Aurensan and Guy Cuevas both worked there and evoked the spirit of the nightclub.

107 **I can shit** As told to AD by Loulou de la Falaise in interview.

109 **I'd like to sleep** YSL in *Dim Dam Dom*, 1967, op. cit.

YSL, who can *WWD*, 29 November 1974 (FA).

Oh yes, absolutely YSL talks to Bianca Jagger, *Interview* magazine, January 1973 (NYPL).

The decrease in the number of haute-couture houses is to be found in Didier Grumbach's *Histoires de la Mode* (Editions du Seuil, 1993) p. 191. Grumbach also points out that in 1971 Saks and Bergdorf Goodman did not send their buyers to the haute-couture shows in Paris, a sure sign of disinterest in couture.

114 **completely hideous** Eugenia Sheppard, *New York Post*, quoted within *Time*, 15 February 1971.

nauseating *Daily Telegraph*, quoted within *Time*, 15 February 1971.

petty, narrow-minded reactionaries *New York Times*, 19 February 1971.

Fashion is the Ibid.

the Occupation aspect *WWD*, 29 January 1971 (FA).

114 **A retrospective of** Ossie Clark at the V&A in 2004 reaffirmed the English designer's influence on fashion and on YSL, as well as revealing him as the pioneer of the 1940s trend. See Judith Watt, *Ossie Clark 1965–74* (V&A Publications, 2003).

115 **These are clothes** As told to AD by Loulou de la Falaise in interview.

118 **I was looking** Antonio Lopez and Christopher Hemphill, *Antonio's Girls*, edited by Karen Amiel (Congreve Publishing Company: New York, 1982), p. 9.
I couldn't believe Ibid.

119 **If it's not** As told to AD by Pat Cleveland in interview.

Chapter 7

The first part of this chapter was sourced through interviews with Paul Caranicas, Corey Grant Tippin, Billina, Donna Jordan, Pat Cleveland and Eija. Other sources included the archive of Antonio's work, books written on Antonio (cited in the bibliography) and a question-and-answer interview with Antonio published in *Interview* magazine that I found at the New York Public Library.

For research into the childhood of Jacques de Bascher, I was able to interview both his sister Anne and his younger brother Xavier. Anne, a novelist, invited me to stay at La Berrière, where she lives in a house next to the château. Renaud de Beaugourdon was also an important source for Jacques de Bascher, not only in his verbal memories but also in his written records. He kept a diary and noted dates of trips and meetings, as well as factual details such as the name and class of ship on which Jacques did his military service. Renaud de Beaugourdon kept all the correspondence he received from Jacques de Bascher over a twenty-two-year period and he generously allowed me to work from this correspondence.

To get a grip on the French nobility, I interviewed Eric Mension-Rigau, *maître de conférences* in history at the University of Paris-Sorbonne (Paris IV), who was able to explain the divisions and distinctions between the layers of nobility. Rigau's book *Aristocrates et Grands Bourgeois. Education, Traditions, Valeurs* (Plon: Paris, 1994) was also an enlightening source. Comte Jean de Bodinat, member of the Association d'Entraide de la Noblesse Française, unearthed the two historical references for the date of the ennoblement of Jules Bascher.

130 **vampirising** As told to AD by Florentine Pabst-Schober in interview.
I am a sort *People* magazine, 5 May 1975.
Tu es très, très chic As told to AD by Corey Tippin in interview.

135 **I remember the** André Leon Talley, 'Karl Lagerfeld in a cloud of Chloé', *Interview* magazine, June 1975. This quote is not a translation. Jacques was speaking in English at the time of the interview, hence the occasionally unusual syntax and vocabulary.

137 **Off we go** The postcard belongs to the private correspondence of Renaud de Beaugourdon.

Information on the De Bascher genealogy was found using the library of the Association d'Entraide de la Noblesse Française in Paris. There are two separate sources for information on the ennoblement of the family: H. Beauchet-Filleau et Feu Ch. de Chergé, *Dictionnaire Historique et Généalogique des familles du Poitou*, Tome Premier (Imprimerie Oudin et Cie: Poitiers, Juillet 1891); and Gustave Chaix d'Est-Ange, *Dictionnaire des Familles Françaises Anciennes ou Notables, à la fin du XIXe siècle* (first published by Evreux in 1903; republished by Editions Vendome: Paris VIe, 1983). Both dictionaries cite Jules Bascher as the member of the family ennobled in 1818; he had two sons, one of whom was killed in the Vendée insurrection of 1832. The other son's only son, Joseph-Alfred Bascher, died without an heir.

Chapter 8

For this chapter I interviewed Pierre Bergé and all the Saint Laurent entourage, as well as many Saint Laurent staff from the couture house. I used archives of *Interview* magazine found at the New York Public Library, and I also worked from archive material at the house of Saint Laurent. *Women's Wear Daily* was essential for following the business and financial details of these years, and Alice Rawthorn's biography of YSL was a valuable source for cross-referencing Bergé's restructuring of the house.

Information on the provenance of furniture in the Rue de Babylone home is drawn from numerous sources, including the two magazine articles that appeared in American *Vogue* and *Connaissance des Arts* listed below. Other sources included interviews, in particular with decorative-arts expert Philippe Garner, who drew my attention to the importance of the art-deco period to both YSL and KL and their contrasting approaches to the style. I researched the decorative period through reading, in particular the V&A's comprehensive book, *Art Deco 1910–39*, and Philippe Garner's revised and edited editions of Martin Battersby's *The Decorative Twenties* and *The Decorative Thirties* (both revised editions, Whitney Library of Design: New York, 1998). Edouard Sebline's lecture on the collection of Jacques Doucet entitled 'Le goût d'un couturier: Jacques Doucet and the decorative arts, 1912–1929', delivered at the V&A during the conference *The Art Deco World* in April 2003, was an informative study on Doucet's taste and patronage.

141 **Braless and backless** *Newsweek*, 27 November 1972.
   Aren't there qualities *Interview* magazine, January 1973 (NYPL).
   No, because ultimately Ibid.
143 *Ah, voilà* As told to AD by Nicole Dorier in interview.

146 **I just want** *Interview* magazine, March 1973 (NYPL).

147 **It won't last** G.Y. Dryansky, *WWD*, 10 June 1974 (FA).

149 **When I don't like** Jane Kramer, 'The Impresario's Last Act', *The New Yorker*, 21 November 1994.

151 **I'm an aesthete** *Interview* magazine, op. cit.

153 **It is the late** 'Oasis in Paris', American *Vogue*, November 1971.

154 **great big poodles** Philippe Jullian, 'Les années 20 revues dans les années 70 chez YSL', *Connaissance des Arts*, 1973 (BF).

155 ***La vilaine Lulu*** By Yves Saint Laurent (Claude Tchou, Editeur: Paris, 1967).

156 **one dull Thursday** Ibid.

    Comme c'est amusant 'Oh how amusing'. Ibid.

    The author warns Ibid.

    Quel bel enfant 'What a beautiful child'. Ibid.

    the lack of Ibid.

157 **Of course, it** Ibid.

    She understood then Ibid.

Chapter 9

To attempt to understand Jacques de Bascher, his hopes and ambitions, I interviewed many who knew him, not all of whom wished to be named when quoted. The memories of Jacques' sister Anne, his brother Xavier and his friends Christian Dumais-Lvowski, Renaud de Beaugourdon and Diane de Beauvau-Craon were all fundamental to this chapter. I also attempted to reconstruct Jacques' life during these years from numerous press cuttings and society pages. It was Philippe Garner who drew my attention to certain magazine articles from these years recording the style and décor of KL's Saint Sulpice apartment.

Over a period of five years I have conducted many interviews with those who have worked with Karl, been close to Karl or grew up with Karl, again not all of whom wished to be named.

Information on the Beauvau-Craon family is sourced from Gustave Chaix d'Est-Ange, *Dictionnaire des Familles Françaises*, op. cit.

160 **I do not take** As told to AD by Diane de Beauvau-Craon in interview.

161 **'Revival of a Dandy'** Article on Jacques de Bascher appeared in *L'Uomo Vogue*, October 1973.

    Carita moustache-trimming detail cited in *Vogue Hommes*, March 1973 (FVA).

162 **I have played** As told to AD by Anne de Bascher in interview.

    The origin of the attempt to join the name De Beaumarchais to De Bascher can be found in Gustave Chaix d'Est-Ange, *Dictionnaire des Familles Françaises*, op. cit. '. . . Pierre-Paul Bascher, born in Nantes in 1790, who played an active role in the uprising of the Vendée in 1815 and in 1832 and who became owner of the château of Beaumarchais, near to the Sables-d'Olonne, by his marriage in 1814 with Marie Lenfant de Lanzil, daughter of a demoiselle Lemoyne de Beaumarchais. The son of this one [Pierre-Paul], Théophile Bascher, born in Nantes in 1829, married in Paris in 1862 to Mademoiselle Guillaume, and his children were known by the name of the de Bascher de Beaumarchais; following difficulties with the family Delarue de Beaumarchais, Théophile Bascher and his son, Louis-Joseph, born in Nantes in 1868, asked on 26 October 1890 the authorisation to officially join to their name that of: DE BEAUMARCHAIS; but their request was not authorised.'

Detail on KL's Saint Sulpice apartment is drawn from interviews and the following articles: 'Karl Lagerfeld', French *Vogue*, November 1973; 'The Art Deco Life', American *Vogue*, September 1974; *Connaissance des Arts*, November 1975; 'A Designer Bids "Adieu" to his Art Deco', Patricia McColl, *New York Times*, 27 November 1975.

166 **They show off my** American *Vogue*, September 1974.

168 **Those types of beds** André Leon Talley, *Interview* magazine, June 1975 (NYPL). **I never fall** Ibid.

169 **He learned to** *WWD*, 21 June 1984 (FA).

I sold more *Actuel*, March 1984.

Episode of KL sketching collections in the style of other designers told to AD by Ralph Toledano in interview.

170 **From the beginning** *WWD*, 21 June 1984, op. cit.

171 **the same year Mozart was born** François Wimille, *Interview* magazine, May 1979.

It doesn't look As told to AD by Patrick Hourcade in interview.

André Leon Talley writes in American *Vogue* of March 1995, '. . . and one grand, Versailles-wannabe spread in Brittany, called Grand-Champ, which is the French translation of his Swedish family name.'

country estate *Interview* magazine, April 1983 (FA).

172 **near to the Danish border** Rosamond Bernier, American *Vogue*, December 1992.

huge luncheons and *Interview* magazine, op. cit.

At five, I André Leon Talley, *WWD*, 2 March 1978 (FA).

his early childhood Kennedy Fraser, American *Vogue*, September 2004.

My mother, a *Interview* magazine, op. cit.

Chapter 10

The importance of Helmut Newton to the visual landscape of this period was paramount, and I was fortunate to interview him twice during my research. The last interview took place at his beach club in Monte Carlo just over a year before his death. Newton, aged eighty-three at the time, made for a tricky if highly entertaining interview. He produced a stream of amusing repartee amid incessant phone calls and Leopold von Sacher Masoch asides, and he was extremely cagey about what he would divulge, not least because at the time he was awaiting publication of his own autobiography ('No, no, no, no! That is a long story that doesn't concern you!'). When I asked him about his aesthetic, smoke started puffing gently from his ears and he fumed about the pretension of fashion photographers today. He was, however, delighted to reminisce about Paris, its bosomed fashion editors and their tight black leather skirts.

Newton and Bourdin were the great photographic bastions of French *Vogue* and I interviewed several people close to Bourdin (he died in 1991), including Holly Warner, his former girlfriend and also a stylist on his shoots. I also interviewed Joan Juliet Buck, who worked as Bourdin's stylist in the early 1970s, and Bourdin model Isabelle Weingarten.

I went twice to the Château de Penhoët in the south of Morbihan. As it is privately owned and was at the time undergoing extensive renovation, I was unable to visit the interior of the main house, although I did visit the small chapel and the gardens and grounds. On the first trip I interviewed historian Gérard Danet, who provided several texts on the château and its history as cited below. On the second trip I interviewed locals who lived on and off the estate and were there during KL's tenure of the house.

175 **Did you ever** April in Paris Special, *Interview* magazine, April 1975.
176 **Maddeningly sexy** *Queen* magazine, March 1969.
 Helmut Newton's portraits of Paloma Picasso appeared in French *Vogue*, November 1973 (UCAD).
177 **Where are you?** Notes left by Clara and Thadée as told to AD by Corey Tippin in interview.
178 **You do it** As told to AD by Patrick Hourcade in interview.
179 **I want to know** Bernadine Morris, 'Lagerfeld: Fashion's Statesman', *New York Times*, 19 October 1988 (NYTA).
180 **le village** As told to AD during interviews with residents on the Penhoët estate.
 Detail of the picnic on Erdeven beach, clothes and crystal comes from Anna Piaggi's book, *Karl Lagerfeld: A Fashion Journal* (Thames and Hudson: London, 1986).
 Photo of birthday party: French *Vogue*, November 1973 (UCAD).
182 **No, no, no** As told to AD in interview, name withheld.
 Les Années 30 dinner mentioned in *WWD*, 8 January 1974 (FA).

183 **Exhibition** *David Hockney* *dessins et gravures*, 15 April – 24 May 1975 at Galerie Claude Bernard, 5, 7, et 9, Rue des Beaux-Arts, Paris 6.

186 **Yves really loved** As told to AD by Diane de Beauvau-Craon in interview.

187 **I wish I** Oscar Wilde, *The Picture of Dorian Gray* (1891).

Chapter 11

For this chapter I conducted extensive interviews, although very few people wished to be quoted directly within the text.

Discovering the question–and–answer interview that André Leon Talley conducted with KL, Jacques and José in New York was an important find. It is one of the rare occasions on which Jacques' actual words were reported and it is the only time that José's words can be found, hence its importance throughout the chapter.

KL's sketches of Anna Piaggi at this time were published in a book in 1986. These sketches were central in reconstructing the movements of KL and his entourage during this summer of 1975 and in describing the ambiance of their days at Penhoët.

My investigation into the death of José took me to Vannes on two research trips. It also required lengthy correspondence with the Procureur of Vannes and the gendarmerie.

190 **$3,500 for surplus baggage** André Leon Talley article in *Interview* magazine, June 1975 (FA).

blanched and boiled food Ibid.

Karl Lagerfeld, the Ibid.

191 **Subdued José de** Ibid.

In this country Ibid. Jacques de Bascher was speaking English; this quote is not translated.

Joris-Karl Huysmans, *Là-Bas* (1891).

The Marquis de Quote from Terry Hale's English translation edition of *Là-Bas*, *The Damned* (*Là-Bas*), (Penguin Books: London, 2001), p. 46.

194 *le petit hameau* *Interview* magazine, op. cit.

guests and somebody Ibid.

I am going Ibid.

The death certificate of José Maria Bazquez-Sarasola is held at the town hall of Saint-Avé in Morbihan.

The Procureur of the Tribunal de Grande Instance of Vannes called a search for documents concerning the death. No such documents were found, as after fifteen years have passed after a suicide any such documents may be destroyed. The gendarmerie of Vannes also reported that all documents are destroyed after twenty years has passed.

Discovery of the body appeared in *Ouest France*, 27 August 1975.

196 **'Les Matinées de Grand-Champ'** This sketch appears in Anna Piaggi's book of Lagerfeld sketches of her: Anna Piaggi, *Karl Lagerfeld: A Fashion Journal*, op. cit.

197 **That's it** As told to AD in interview, name withheld.

198 **This Minet from** *La vilaine Lulu*, op. cit.

199 **a skein of** Marcel Proust, *Du côté de chez Swann* (1913). This quote is taken from C. K. Moncrieff and Terence Kilmartin's English translation, revised by D. J. Enright (London: Vintage, 2000).

Chapter 12

This chapter drew on many interviews with those close to YSL, not least Pierre Bergé, but also with members of his entourage and those people who worked alongside YSL for over twenty-five years and remember the Opéra couture and Carmen ready-to-wear collections so vividly. The majority of interviews with YSL staff were conducted after YSL's retirement. Looking back I think this was an advantage, as it meant that they could breathe at last and view YSL with an objectivity that they did not possess whilst still toiling in the hothouse of 5, Avenue Marceau.

For both the Opéra and Carmen collections I drew on archive press reports and photographs, sourced from the PB-YSL foundation as well as Fairchild, French *Vogue*, *Le Point*, the *New York Times* and UCAD. I also interviewed couture clients. I was given colour photocopies of pictures of the Carmen collection taken on the runway and this was the most incredible resource with which to visualise the flagrant energy and sexiness of the show.

200 **3 March 1976** Laurence Benaïm, *Yves Saint Laurent* (Bernard Grasset: Paris, nouvelle édition 2002) p. 275.

Henceforth we are *Globe* édition spéciale, 14 November 1990.

201 **I am the man** Laurence Benaïm, *Yves Saint Laurent*, op. cit.

202 **Unbearable. He needed** *Globe*, op. cit.

Pierre Bergé told biographer Laurence Benaïm that YSL was using alcohol, cocaine and tranquillisers: *Yves Saint Laurent*, op. cit., p. 275.

Details on sales figures for YSL business comes from Andreas Freund, 'The Empire of Saint Laurent', *New York Times*, 8 August 1976 (NYTA).

206 **I am sick** *Le Point*, 6 December 1976, no. 220 (LPA).

207 **Yves saw himself** Benaïm, *Yves Saint Laurent*, op. cit., p. 275.

I needed a violent Marian McEvoy, *WWD*, 2 August 1976 (FA).

Like a painter *People*, 23 August 1976.

For several months *Le Point*, op. cit.

208 **spinning with ideas** YSL to *People* magazine, op. cit.

208 **The clothes incorporated** Bernadine Morris, *New York Times*, 29 July 1976.

209 **It is as if** Barbara Schwarm and Martine Leventer, *Le Point*, 25 July 1977, no. 253 (LPA).

Detail of YSL discharging himself from hospital comes from *People* magazine, op. cit.: 'Finally I left against my doctor's orders and came back to put the collection together.'

211 **art appliqué** Anthony Burgess, 'All about Yves', *New York Times* magazine, 11 September 1977.

Everyone started to *People* magazine, op. cit.

It is as stunning Bernadine Morris, *New York Times*, op. cit.

These are not *New York Times* magazine, 11 September 1977, op. cit.

212 **The collection was** YSL to Marian McEvoy, *WWD*, 29 October 1976 (FA).

214 **I wanted to show** *Le Point*, 6 December 1976, op. cit.

It is a personal Ibid.

face haggard, undone Ibid.

Saint Laurent was *WWD*, 27 October 1976 (FA).

The fact that JdeB gave the letters from YSL to KL was confirmed in several interviews conducted by AD; also KL himself said that he was in possession of the letters in an article that appeared in the *New York Times* on 24 December 2000, when he told journalist Cathy Horyn that the letters were kept in boxes in his (KL's) house. 'We keep them sleeping,' he said.

216 **I am in the** *W* magazine, 7 February 1975 (FA).

God, when I Patrick McCarthy, *W* magazine, 1 January 1982 (FA).

217 **We talked of the** Anthony Burgess, *New York Times* magazine, 11 September 1977.

218 **Designing fashion for** Ibid.

For the last two *Le Point*, 25 July 1977, op. cit.

219 **I saw Jacques** As told to AD in interview, name withheld.

Chapter 13

The memories of Christian Dumais-Lvowski and Renaud de Beaugourdon were key to this chapter.

Christian Dumais-Lvowski recounted the detail of Jacques de Bascher's party in his Saint Sulpice apartment to AD.

222 **I was at the gym** Karl Lagerfeld and Dr Jean-Claude Houdret, *Le Meilleur des Régimes* (Robert Laffont: Paris, 2002), p. 22.

It does not correspond *Actuel*, March 1984, op. cit.

Garderoben Gesetze Text by Freiherrn H. von Eelking, illustrated by Ernest

Ludwig Kretschmann (Verlag Finckenstein und Salmuth: Berlin, Bielefeld, Heidelberg, 2003), from 1923 original manuscript.

Decorative detail of Jacques' apartment comes from the accounts of Christian Dumais-Lvowski and Renaud de Beaugourdon.

224 **Lanz in Salzburg** KL and Jacques de Bascher went annually to this shop to buy Austrian outfits for JdeB and Tyrolean jackets for KL.

227 **As a child** Interview with KL in Christie's Monaco catalogue for the sale of Collection Lagerfeld, 29 April 2000.

228 **This is the purpose** Dennis Thim, *W* Magazine, 17 October 1988 (FA).

All that has François Wimille, *Interview* magazine, May 1979.

229 **a real German baron** André Leon Talley, *WWD*, 2 March 1978 (FA).

Lunch detail at KL's house comes from *Interview* magazine, May 1979, and Anna Piaggi, *Karl Lagerfeld: A Fashion Journal*, op. cit.

230 **When I was four** *WWD*, 2 March 1978, op. cit.

My mother made KL interview with Bernard Pivot, *Double Je* (Equipage-RFO-TV5-2003), broadcast 27 February 2003.

Nabokov detail from Anthony Lane, *The New Yorker*, 7 November 1994.

Was I an only Rosamond Bernier, American *Vogue*, December 1992, op. cit.

231 **When I hear** *WWD*, 2 March 1978, op. cit.

His considerate manners Rosamond Bernier, American *Vogue*, December 1992, op. cit.

I walked out Ibid.

235 **It's not very** *Top Ten Designers in Paris*, op. cit.

236 **Lagerfeld has turned** *WWD*, 2 March 1978, op. cit.

My style is more François Wimille, *Interview* magazine, op. cit.

I have no opinion *WWD*, 2 March 1978, op. cit.

Chapter 14

I interviewed both Loulou de la Falaise and her husband Thadée Klossowski on the subject of their marriage and wedding party. I also read Joan Juliet Buck's story on the wedding ball for British *Vogue*, Hebe Dorsey's story for French *Vogue* and the *Women's Wear Daily* coverage, all of which provided details of the party which unfortunately many of the wedding guests could no longer recall.

I used *Le Palace* magazines from this time to evoke the atmosphere of the club, as well as studying the photographs of Paris fashion and night-life photographer Guy Marineau.

I interviewed all YSL's 'women' – Loulou, Betty, Paloma, Clara, Anne-Marie – with the exception of Marina Schiano. She fell out with YSL and PB in the 1990s and declined to be interviewed as she is writing her own book.

237 **It's all from** 'The Four-minute Bride', *WWD*, 16 June 1977 (FA).

I've never seen Marian McEvoy, *W* Magazine, 24 June – 1 July 1977 (FA).

238 **I think to be** James Reginato, *W* Magazine, February 2000 (FA).

The book appeared under the title *Renaud Barrault, Paris, notre siècle, conception et réalisation Joël Le Bon avec la collaboration de Thadée Klossowski* (Editions de Messine/Pierre Bergé: Paris, 1982).

Joan Juliet Buck, *Daughter of the Swan* (Weidenfeld & Nicolson: London, 1987).

244 **What lovely lampshades** *WWD*, 5 July 1977 (FA).

248 **Younger, more cynical** Alexis Bernier and François Buot, *L'Esprit des Seventies* (Editions Grasset & Fasquelle: Paris, 1994).

Jacques was photographed in 'L'œil de Vogue', French *Vogue*, December 1977 (UCAD).

249 **unbelievable** KL to Thierry Ardisson in television programme *93, Faubourg Saint-Honoré*, Paris Première, 28 June 2005.

250 **I must say** *WWD*, 2 March 1978, op. cit.

The marvellous decorative details of the Opium launch party in New York come from an article written by Andy Port in *W* magazine, 13 – 20 October 1978 (FA).

Sleeping under the pattern-cutting table is a reference to John Galliano, who when he first came to Paris as a penniless designer bursting with talent did just that. Now John Galliano is the designer at Dior, lives in an *hôtel particulier* in the Marais, has a driver, holidays in Saint-Tropez and is a global fashion force.

253 **I like money** Maxime de la Falaise McKendry, *Interview* magazine, December 1975.

Italian designers were featured in a story entitled 'Les Stylistes de Milan' that appeared in French *Vogue*, August 1977 (UCAD).

254 **Italians don't make** As told to AD in interview with Patrick McCarthy, present at the lunch.

255 **It is completely** Brice Couturier, *Une scène jeunesse* (Editions Autrement: Paris, 1983).

totally clean, beautiful Ibid.

If that is elegance Ibid.

Detail on the Palace nights and staff comes from interviews, Le Palace magazines, and private archive collections of Claude Aurensan and photographer Steve Hiett.

258 **Le Palace has** *Façade*, no. 8, 1980; also quoted in *L'Esprit des Seventies*, op. cit.

I wouldn't be Patrick O'Higgins, *Town & Country*, November 1978 (FPB-YSL).

260 **Loulou told us** Andy Warhol, 11 February 1980, Zurich, in *The Andy Warhol Diaries*, op. cit.

I don't know Judy Fayard, 'Breadth of a Salesman', *WWD*, 30 May 1978 (FA).

Chapter 15

It took me two years and about fourteen faxes to secure an interview with Italian fashion editor Anna Piaggi. After months of silence she rang me out of the blue and asked if I could be at the Flore in fifteen minutes. We were shown to a table on the ground floor and the interview began. I was interested in Anna's former great friendship with Karl, as well as her fondness for Jacques de Bascher, and I also wished to talk about how she perceived her role as Karl's inspiration, the daily sketching and the summers spent at Penhoët. But I was not to find out, for just then the door to the Flore opened and in walked Pierre Bergé, who was shown to the table next to ours. Bergé famously disliked Anna Piaggi during the 1970s, although surely it was not Anna he disliked but her proximity to KL. They greeted with politeness and profound *froideur*. PB lunched alone within elbow's length of us. He sat taking notes on a biography of Juliette Gréco. There was no possibility of conducting the interview I had planned under these close-knit conditions. Although I tried to contact Anna regularly over the next three years, sadly she did not reply to my faxes, telephone messages and letters.

Fortunately the book that Anna published – of KL's hundreds of sketches made of her over a fifteen-year period and his handwritten captions – proved a rich source for examining their friendship and the fashion ties that once bound them.

Details of Anna Piaggi's outfits at Paloma's wedding come from Anna Piaggi, *Karl Lagerfeld: A Fashion Journal*, op. cit. The day suit was designed by Piero Tosi for Luchino Visconti's *L'Innocente* and was borrowed from Umberto Tirelli's theatrical costume house in Rome.

263 **What is this** André Leon Talley, *W* Magazine, 26 May – 2 June 1978 (FA).
  haven't been on Ibid.
  We all used Ibid.
  And what I Ibid.
  Karl is someone Ibid.
264 **We are not bourgeois** Ibid.
  I made a dress Ibid.
  This whole scene Ibid.
    Anna Piaggi's dress for the evening was a 1923 gown by the Callot Sisters, in silver fabric trimmed with raspberry-coloured ostrich feathers. The helmet was from the play *Orlando Furioso*, directed by Luca Ronconi, details from Anna Piaggi, *Karl Lagerfeld: A Fashion Journal*, op. cit.
    Elisabeth Lagerfeld, née Bahlmann, born 25 April 1897, died on 14 September 1978.
265 **I talked a lot** Christa Worthington, 'Keeping up with Kaiser Karl', *WWD*, 21 February 1986 (FA).
266 **I never saw** American *Vogue*, September 2004, op. cit.
267 **You don't like** Ibid.
267 **Illness – I don't** *Der Stern*, 24 October 1996, op. cit.

Top Ten Designers in Paris, 1979, op. cit.

KL's letter to Anna Piaggi published in *Karl Lagerfeld: A Fashion Journal* (op. cit.) is dated 1 December 1976 and reads: '*Chère Anna, j'ai trouvé ce petit corselet fait pour* Vogue *et retiré de la collection quand St. Laurent en avait fait pour la couture* . . .' This translates to: 'Dear Anna, I found this little corset top made for *Vogue* and removed from the collection when YSL did them for couture . . .'

269 **He never did** Victoire Doutreleau, interviewed in *Paris Match*, 17 January 2002.

In the end Loulou de la Falaise to Tim Blanks, *Sunday Telegraph* magazine, 6 March 2004.

272 **I speak very** *Le Figaro*, 15 July 1991, op. cit.

274 **You know what** Ibid.

276 **Get that gigolo** As told to AD in interview, name withheld.

So, I see This episode and Diane's reaction to Pierre was told to AD by Diane de Beauvau-Craon in interview.

Men like women *W* Magazine, 31 March – 7 April 1978 (FA).

It's too disgusting Ibid.

277 **that Italian who** The rivalry between Chanel and Schiaparelli is well documented by Edmonde Charles-Roux in both her biography of Chanel, *L'Irrégulière* (Bernard Grasset: Paris, 1974), and *Chanel and her World* (Weidenfeld & Nicolson: London, 1981). 'That Italian who makes clothes' is an oft-repeated quote of Schiaparelli's, although Dilys E. Blum's *Shocking! The Art and Fashion of Elsa Schiaparelli* (Philadelphia Museum of Art in association with Yale University Press, 2003) records that Chanel referred to her as 'that Italian artist who's making clothes'.

278 **That is all** André Leon Talley, *Interview* magazine, October 1980.

I think the base Jonathan Moor, *Daily News Record*, 23 February 1981 (FA) **Today, the street** Patrick McCarthy and Christa Worthington, *WWD*, 23 November 1983 (FA).

279 **I've always hated** Patrick McCarthy, *W* Magazine, 1–8 January 1982 (FA).

pure YSL *W* magazine, 27 March 1981 (FA).

recreate the ambiance John Richardson, 'Yves Saint Laurent's Château Gabriel: a passion for style', American *Vogue*, December 1983.

281 **We never separated** Janie Samet, 'Pierre Bergé: "Ma plus grande qualité? – la mauvaise foi"', *Le Figaro* 4 January 2003 (LFA).

282 **they look great** Patrick McCarthy, *W* Magazine, 14–21 January 1983 (FA).

'RICH RICH RICH' Patrick McCarthy, *WWD*, 30 April 1982 (FA).

283 **Determining Karl Lagerfeld's** Ibid.

I'm like Mr Gulbenkian G.Y. Dryansky, *Connoisseur*, December 1985. KL refers here to Calouste Sarkis Gulbenkian, 1869–1955, who was a financial and economic advisor to the Ottoman embassies in London and Paris, formidable negotiator, philanthropist and collector with a major painting collection that includes portraits by Rubens, Rembrandt and Gainsborough. He was a 15-per-cent shareholder in the Turkish Petroleum Company founded in 1912 to exploit the rich oil fields in

Iraq. Later, with the break-up of the Ottoman Empire, he played a decisive role in the Red Line Agreement of 1928, which conciliated the petroleum interests that the major powers – namely the USA, France, Holland and Anglo-Persia – had for the oil fields there. Subsequently Gulbenkian held 5 per cent of the shareholding of the newly renamed Iraq Petroleum Co. Ltd. (the former Turkish Petroleum Company), which earned him both a fortune and the nickname of 'Mr Five Percent'.

Chapter 16

Diane de Beauvau-Craon agreed to be interviewed several times for the book. Diane's mannerisms, *ton*, speech pattern and general sense of the dramatic are eighteenth century in inclination.

I was able to interview Doctor Scott Coffey, Associate Professor at the Department of Psychiatry and Human Behavior at the University of Mississippi Medical Center. He talked to me about the co-occurrence of borderline personality disorder and substance-use disorders as well as substance use in general; he also sent me research papers on the subject that provided background to this chapter and the book in general.

286 **the dinosaurs** *W* Magazine, 29 January 1982 (FA).
  The old order Ibid.
287 **delirium** *Le Palace* magazine, no. 1, January 1980.
  Louis XVI and the *Autrichienne* Ibid.
  Empty landscape, empty Alain Pacadis, *Libération*, 9 April 1978.
  totally European scene Fabrice Emaer, 'Pourquoi j'ai fait Privilège', *Le Palace* magazine, January 1981.
288 ***Totalement interdit*** Totally forbidden to women, *Le Palace* magazine, no. 1, January 1980.
289 **He just might** *People* magazine, 24–31 December 1979.
  Kenzo figures for turnover and later the drop in turnover from 240 million to 180 million francs in one season of 1987 were remembered by François Baufumé, former *directeur général* of the house.
292 **I, the undersigned** Xavier de Bascher kept this note and showed it to AD during interview.
292 **I rove, drift, float** Henry James, *The Tragic Muse* (1890).
293 ***Views-interviews*** Advertising film for the launch of KL's perfume for men called Lagerfeld. A promotion describing the shooting of the film and featuring a photo of Jacques de Bascher credited as scriptwriter appeared in French *Vogue*, March 1978 (UCAD).
296 **I will marry** As told to AD by Anne de Bascher in interview.

297 **Will you spare** The French wording of the postcard is '*Auras-tu une petite pensée pour nous?*'; from the private archive of Renaud de Beaugourdon.

The information on the house of Chanel comes from a variety of sources, including interviews, the many biographies written about Chanel cited in the bibliography, and numerous articles, including Phyllis Berman with Zina Sawaya, 'The Billionaires behind Chanel', *Forbes*, 3 April 1989.

299 **artistic orientation** The statement released by the house of Chanel said: 'The life and imagination of Chanel's haute couture collection will be benefited by the artistic orientation of Karl Lagerfeld beginning in January 1983.' This statement was published in *WWD*, 16 September 1982 (FA).

Poor Yves didn't Lynn Langway with Scott Sullivan, 'The Bad Boy of High Fashion', *Newsweek*, 2 May 1983.

302 **He had the inherent** *Connoisseur*, December 1985, op. cit.

In a question-and-answer interview with KL published in *Le Palace* magazine, the interviewer asks KL where his houses are and he replies: 'I have one in Paris, one in Switzerland and a château in Brittany that I inherited from my mother.' *Le Palace* magazine no. 6, February 1981.

The most arresting Edmonde Charles-Roux, *L'Irrégulière, ou mon itinéraire Chanel*. This quote is taken from the English edition of the biography, published under the title *Chanel* and translated by Nancy Amphoux (Collins Harvill: London, 1989).

Chapter 17

I did not use the house of Chanel archives for this book, as doing so necessitates granting the house a right of review and approval on what is written. Instead I researched the house of Chanel through interviews and my own archive research. I travelled to New York to see the Chanel exhibition in 2005, which was an interesting encounter between the work of Chanel and that of KL for the house. The exhibition and its catalogue were sponsored by Chanel, with additional support by Condé Nast. KL had hand-coloured the faces and bodies of the women in the catalogue, which was then printed and bound by Steidl Verlag in Germany, a publishing house of which KL's own 7L is an imprint. President of Chanel Maureen Chiquet wrote a mission statement in the first pages of the catalogue that ended with the words: 'We are pleased that our support now enables the Costume Institute to present this exciting exhibition on the remarkable, ever-evolving world of CHANEL.' The sponsor's proactive involvement in the exhibition prompted a heated debate into the state of museum objectivity in an age of corporate sponsorship and branded exhibitions.

304 **Karl says he came** Reviews at the time of the show reported that KL went

with his mother to see Chanel's comeback show in 1954, and over the years the story became fact. Melissa Richards, *Chanel Key Collections* (Hamlyn: London, 2000), p. 121.

I hear he's lost KL told reporters before the show that he had lost twenty-two pounds through acupuncture; see Etta Froio, *WWD*, 8 December 1982 (FA). Less than a year later he was on another new diet; this time he said he had lost thirty-seven pounds thanks to Paris nutritionist Dr Pierre Richand. *W* Magazine, 23 September 1983 (FA)

Lagerfeld sputters *WWD*, 26 January 1983 (FA).

305 **grabs at the** Ibid.

He's got a feeling Marie-Hélène quoted in *WWD*, 26 January 1983.

306 **You want our advertising** Many people that I interviewed – including photographer's agent Xavier Moreau, John Fairchild and Helmut Newton – spoke of the transition during these years from editorial objectivity to advertising-led fashion coverage. John Fairchild called the 1970s 'the last age of creativity without any of the hiccoughs of promotion', while Helmut Newton described the transition with characteristic bluntness: 'At one stage the editor-in-chief and the art director were god in the magazine; now the god is what they call the publisher, who's in fact just the word-space salesman. The lowest form of animal life on a magazine was once the guy selling the ads. And when they became powerful and the art director became just somebody to paste down the pictures, that's when things changed.'

I like to work *WWD*, 19 January 1983 (FA).

307 **Fashion is also** Karl Lagerfeld, 'Le Style de Chanel', an essay included in the exhibition catalogue accompanying the exhibition *Chanel* at the Metropolitan Museum of Art, 5 May–7 August 2005.

Detail on Inès de la Fressange's relationship with KL taken from Inès de la Fressange, *Profession Mannequin, Conversations avec Marianne Mairesse* (Hachette Littératures: Paris, 2002).

310 **I'm working like** *WWD*, 19 January 1983, op. cit.

An ideal evening out Lynn Langway with Scott Sullivan, *Newsweek*, 2 May 1983.

I have my spies '*J'ai quand même des espions . . .*' *Actuel*, March 1984.

311 **They called me** '*On disait que . . .*' Inès de la Fressange, *Profession Mannequin*, op. cit., p. 95.

In the beginning '*Au tout debut . . .*' Ibid., p. 95.

312 **altering horrible dresses** *Actuel*, March 1984, op. cit.

some poor East 'Lagerfeld backs bid by Bidermann', *WWD*, 17 October 1983.

312 **I know. I know** As told to AD by Anne de Bascher in interview.

not creating anything As told to AD by Renaud de Beaugourdon in interview.

316 **They say she's** *Newsweek*, 5 November 1990.

316 **A house without** Patricia McColl, 'Renegade Décor', *New York Times* maga-

zine, 14 August 1983.

Frankfurt hotel concierge Ibid.

Fran Lebowitz detail on heroin comes from Natasha Fraser-Cavassoni and William Middleton, '70s Paris: The Party Years', *W* magazine, March 1997. Lebowitz says: 'Heroin was only taken privately in New York, while in Paris, people took it openly.'

Chapter 18

The information on conditions during the Second World War in Bad Bramstedt comes from a variety of sources, some unnamed, including interviews with Bad Bramstedt local historian Manfred Jacobsen and Karl Wagner. I also drew upon information in Wolfgang Platte's book *Bad Bramstedt in 20. Jahrhundert* (Stadt Bad Bramstedt, 1985). I interviewed Professor Detlef Junker, who happened to go to school in Bad Bramstedt (although not in the same period as KL) and is a world authority on German-American relations in the twentieth century and a professor at the Heidelberg Center for American Studies (HCA). Doctor Ortwin Pelc of the Museum für Hamburgische Geschichte in Hamburg answered my queries on the Allied bombings of Hamburg and its environs.

The exhibition *Yves Saint Laurent – 25 Years of Design*, December 1983 – August 1984, was organised by Diana Vreeland at the Costume Institute at the Metropolitan Museum of Art, New York.

322 **I'm afraid to** Patrick McCarthy and Christa Worthington, Saint Laurent Retrospective, *WWD*, 23 November 1983 (FA)

The exhibition then continued to the China National Museum of Fine Arts, Beijing, May – October 1985; Musée des Arts de la Mode, Paris, May – October 1986; the Central House of Artist, Moscow, December 1986 – January 1987; Hermitage Museum, St Petersburg, February – March 1987; Art Gallery of New South Wales, Sydney, May – July 1987; Sezon Museum of Art, Tokyo, November – December 1990.

323 **I have become** Patrick McCarthy, 'YSL: 20 years of couture', *W* magazine, 1-8 January 1982 (FA).

324 **He is such a giant** Reported by Susan Alai, *W* magazine, 6 October 1986 (FA).

YSL's habit of taking pills with alcohol was thus reported: '[YSL] takes a regimen of "calmant pills", which he unwisely chases with alcohol on occasion.' William Blaylock, 'The Designer at Home', *Time*, 12 December 1983 (TA).

326 **stupefying moment** Detail of the René-Guy Cadou encounter comes from Jane Kramer's brilliant portrait of Pierre Bergé, 'The Impresario's Last Act', *The New Yorker*, 21 November 1994.

327 **Lagerfeld wants to reign** Jean-François Bizot, *Actuel*, March 1984.
I had an Ibid.
babas cools 'Les babas' is the French term for hippies.
Yves Saint Laurent fell in Jean-François Bizot, *Actuel*, op. cit.
Yves doesn't see Ibid.

328 **The day he met** Ibid.
He is very middle Ibid.
Paris is the capital Valerie Steele, *Paris Fashion: A Cultural History* (Oxford University Press, 1988), p. 5 of revised and updated paperback edition printed in 1998.

329 **The poor boy** Susan Alai, *WWD*, 17 September 1984 (FA).

330 **Oh yes** *Yves Saint Laurent, Le Temps Retrouvé*, op. cit.
What do I KL in *W* Magazine, 3 December 1982 (FA).
No congratulations As told to AD by Arie Kopelman in interview.
branché I have kept the word *branché* as although Arie Kopelman was speaking in English he chose to use this French term to describe KL, meaning plugged-in and hip.

331 **fashion machine** Patrick McCarthy, 'Fall Notes', *W* magazine, 8 October 1982 (FA).
I'm like a computer *WWD*, 19 January 1983, op. cit.
I have always *Paris Match*, 20 June 2002.
I'm never totally Jay Cocks and Dorie Denbigh, 'Monte Karl on a Roll', *Time*, 24 September 1984.

332 **I bleach my past** Miles Socha, 'Karl's Reign at Chanel', *WWD*, 22 January 2003 (FA).
Thank God *Interview* magazine, May 1979, op. cit.
I didn't even *Actuel*, March 1984, op. cit.
I was lucky American *Vogue*, September 2004, op. cit.
Requisitioning of KL house and the ensuing conditions for the Lagerfeld family comes from an unnamed source.

334 **I remember huge** *Interview* Magazine, April 1983, op. cit.
There were never American *Vogue*, December 1992, op. cit.
In 1945 I had Interview with KL by Bernard Pivot, *Double Je*, February 2003, op. cit.
I wanted to get out Ibid.

336 **I had this feeling** Christa Worthington, 'Keeping up with Kaiser Karl', *WWD*, 21 February 1986.

336 **I imagined the** William Middleton, 'Heavenly Hamburg', *W* magazine, September 1996.
The first sounds Ibid.

337 **an abstract house** Ibid.
It's really my Ibid.

337 **But your way** Margit Mayer, 'King Karl', *WWD*, 20 November 1991 (FA).

338 **His clothes to** Ibid.

I detest revivals *Paris Match*, 20 June 2002, op. cit.

They used more Kevin Doyle, 'The Gospel According to Karl', *W* magazine, February 1994.

339 **Mmmm, a little** As told to AD in interview, name withheld.

Penis silicon implants and YSL's reaction can be found in *The Andy Warhol Diaries*, op. cit., diary entry of 4 September 1977, p. 66.

Without a doubt *WWD*, 23 November 1983, op. cit.

The closer you Ibid.

When I draw *Yves Saint Laurent, Le Temps Retrouvé*, op. cit.

340 **He likes to** *Sunday Telegraph* magazine, 6 March 2004, op. cit.

341 **I detest couturiers** YSL quoted in Felicity Green, 'Left Bank Couture', from Ruth Lynam (ed.), *The Great Designers and Their Creations* (Michael Joseph Ltd: London, 1972).

Chapter 19

The information on the last years of Jacques' life is drawn from interviews with Anne de Bascher and Xavier de Bascher, Renaud de Beaugourdon, Christian Dumais-Lvowski, Diane de Beauvau-Craon and Marc Rioufol.

344 **Everyone knows that** Robert Murphy and Mort Sheinman, 'Closing the Door', *WWD*, 7 January 2002.

345 **He rejected my** As told to AD by Anne de Bascher in interview.

The detail of Jacques and the café comes from Lucien Pellat-Finet's memory of the last time he saw Jacques.

348 **He was everything** Cathy Horyn, *New York Times*, 24 December 2000.

And although in KL quoted in Marc Kayser, 'Ich habe einen Traum', *Die Zeit*, 17 October 2002.

349 **The more Eugène** Honoré de Balzac, *Le Père Goriot*, op. cit., p. 170.

350 **Karl prefers Coca-Cola** G.Y. Dryansky, *Connoisseur*, December 1983, op. cit.

I realised at André Leon Talley, 'Master of the House', American *Vogue*, March 1995.

I either avoided Thomas Mann, *Confessions of Felix Krull, Confidence Man (The Early Years)*, first published in German in 1954 under the title *Bekenntnisse des Hochstaplers Felix Krull: Der Memoiren erster Teil*. This quote is taken from the edition translated from the German by Denver Lindley (first Vintage International edition: London, 1992, copyright Alfred A. Knopf, Inc.).

All the details of KL's gifts, flights and clothes are drawn from AD's interviews.

352 **He sometimes had** Inès de la Fressange, *Profession Mannequin*, op. cit.

353 **Monsieur was on** As told to AD by Brigitte Bastian.
   Papa, Papa As told to AD by Brigitte Bastian.
   My son As told to AD by Brigitte Bastian.
      The detail of painting walls and cutting hair: Laurence Benaïm, *Yves Saint Laurent*, op. cit., p. 411.
354 **clinic with bars** Ibid.
   I locked him Edmund White, 'The Last Emperor', *Sunday Times* magazine, 9 October 1994.
   I have just *Le Figaro*, 11 July 1991 (LFA)
   The two depressions *Le Figaro*, 15 July 1991 (LFA).
   I love glory *Le Figaro*, 11 July 1991, op. cit.
356 **no alcohol, no drugs** *Focus* magazine, 3 February 1997.
   so alone Ibid.
   Premature success gives F. Scott Fitzgerald, 'Early Success', (first published 1937, copyright Estate of F. Scott Fitzgerald 1937) in *The Crack-Up and other Stories* (Penguin: London, 1965).
357 **In truth there** 'La Passion selon Saint Laurent', *L'Insensé*, November 1991.
   Waste of time! Ibid.
   I am the last *Yves Saint Laurent, Le Temps Retrouvé*, op. cit.

Epilogue

I was present at YSL's retirement press conference. It took place in 2002, during the early days of my research for this book. At the time YSL was still regarded in fashion terms as a living god. What has been extraordinary to watch is how quickly fashion has forgotten YSL. His *œuvre* is referenced constantly and yet does the customer recognise the originator behind the ideas?

There is a new generation for whom the name Yves Saint Laurent is a brand, not a man. Equally significant is the transformation that has taken place in people's attitude to KL during the same time frame. When I first started researching and interviewing there were regular gossip items in fashion newspapers predicting the arrival of Marc Jacobs at Chanel. In 2001 I was at a restaurant in Paris and happened to sit next to an American fashion buyer for the Midwest; we got talking and she told me she had been at the Chanel studio the day before and she thought KL was finished at Chanel: the clothes weren't selling. Five years later KL is every bit the 'master and commander' at Chanel and 'the Boy Prince of Fashion'. The research press file that I have gathered for KL for the four years since his draconian diet and weight-loss is larger than for any other decade of his career.

360 **Lots of people** Inès de la Fressange, *Profession Mannequin*, op. cit.

361 **There is behind** Pepita Dupont, 'Chanel La Guerre en Dentelle', *Paris Match*,
10 August 1989.

What I think *Le Figaro*, 27 July 1989 (LFA).

I wish her *Paris Match*, op. cit.

362 **Today this profession** Laurence Benaïm, *Le Monde*, 29 January 1992.

366 **I think he** Robert Murphy, 'Saint Laurent Speaks his Mind', *WWD*, 27 February
2004.

He does what YSL to Godfrey Deeny, European Editor of www.fashionwire-
daily.com, July 2003.

I have today YSL retirement speech, delivered at a press conference on 7
January 2002; translation from the house of YSL.

In many ways Ibid.

Every man needs Ibid.

367 **A dream stay** Betty Catroux in Laurence Benaïm, *Yves Saint Laurent*, op. cit.

370 **the most beautiful** Suzy Menkes, 'The exquisite lightness of Chanel',
International Herald Tribune, 22 January 2003.

It's the place American *Vogue*, March 1995, op. cit.

Architect's maquette of the château, magazines and sketches were seen by
AD on a visit to the Château de Penhoët in 2003.

371 **I do not believe** YSL retirement speech, op. cit.

372 **Outside of my** *Le Figaro*, 15 July 1991, op. cit.

375 **where life became** André Leon Talley, 'Stylefax', American *Vogue*, July 2000.

No, it's only since Cathy Horyn, 'The Rootin' Teuton', *New York Times*, 20
February 2005 (NYTA).

Of course I Witnessed by AD at the exhibition opening for KL's photographs.

377 **a professional hit man** *New York Times*, 20 February 2005, op. cit.

I'm not sure Cathy Horyn, 'A designer at his peak without a label', *New York
Times*, 2 June 2002 (NYTA).

BIBLIOGRAPHY

Abadie, Louis, *Oran de ma jeunesse, 1935–1962, tome 2* (Editions Jacques Gandini: Nice, 2000)

Agins, Teri, *The End of Fashion: The Mass Marketing of the Clothing Business* (William Morrow and Company, Inc.: New York, 1999)

Amiel, Karen (ed.), text by Christopher Hemphill, *Antonio's Girls* (Congreve Publishing Company: New York, 1982)

Balzac, Honoré de, *Le Père Goriot* (Hodder and Stoughton: London, 1967; first published 1834–5)

Balzac, Honoré de, *Lost Illusions*, translated by Herbert J. Hunt (Penguin Books: London, 1971; first published in three parts 1837–43)

Banier, François-Marie, *François-Marie Banier* (Gallimard: Paris, 2003)

Banks, Brian R., *The Image of Huysmans* (AMS Press: New York, 1990)

Battersby, Martin, *The Decorative Thirties*, revised and edited by Philippe Garner (Whitney Library of Design: New York, 1988)

Battersby, Martin, *The Decorative Twenties*, revised and edited by Philippe Garner (Whitney Library of Design: New York, 1988)

Benaïm, Laurence, *Yves Saint Laurent, biographie* (Bernard Grasset: Paris, 2002; nouvelle édition)

Bender, Marylin, *The Beautiful People* (Coward–McCann, Inc.: New York, 1967)

Benton, Charlotte, Tim Benton and Ghislaine Wood (eds.), *Art Deco 1910–1939* (V&A Publications: London, 2003)

Bergé, Pierre, *Les jours s'en vont je demeure* (Gallimard: Paris, 2003)

Bernier, Alexis, et François Buot, *L'Esprit des seventies* (Editions Grasset & Fasquelle: Paris, 1994)

Birkett, Jennifer, *The Sins of the Fathers: Decadence in France 1870-1914* (Quartet Books Ltd: London, 1986)

Bizot, Jean-François, *Underground: L'Histoire* (Actuel/Denoël: Paris, 2001)

Blum, Dilys E., *Shocking! The Art and Fashion of Elsa Schiaparelli* (Philadelphia Museum of Art in association with Yale University Press: New Haven and London, 2003)

Bony, Anne, *Les Années 70* (Editions du Regard: Paris, 1993)

Brubach, Holly, *A Dedicated Follower of Fashion* (Phaidon Press Ltd: London, 1999)

Callahan, Temo, and Tom Cashin (eds.), *Jed Johnson: Opulent Restraint* (Rizzoli: New York, 2005)

Caranicas, Paul, *Antonio's People* (Thames & Hudson: London, 2004)

Cars, Jean des, and Jean-Paul Caracalla, *Le Train Bleu et les grands express de la riviera* (Editions Denoël: Paris, 1988)

Carter, Ernestine, *The Changing World of Fashion* (G.P. Putnam's Sons: New York, 1977)

Chaleyssin, Patrick, *La peinture mondaine de 1870 à 1960* (Bibliothèque de l'Image: Paris, 1999)

Chanaux, Adolphe, and Léopold Diego Sanchez, *Jean-Michel Frank*, (Editions du Regard: Paris, 1997)

Charles-Roux, Edmonde, *Chanel and Her World* (Weidenfeld & Nicolson: London, 1981)

Charles-Roux, Edmonde, *L'Irrégulière, ou mon itinéraire Chanel* (Bernard Grasset: Paris, 1974)

Cleveland, Pat, *In the Spirit of Grace* (Pearl Publishing: Italy, 2001)

Colacello, Bob, *Holy Terror: Andy Warhol Close Up* (Cooper Square Press: New York, 2000)

Cotton, Charlotte, and Shelly Verthime (eds.), *Guy Bourdin* (V&A Publications: London, 2003)

Delgado, Fernando, and Samuel Bourdin, *Exhibit A: Guy Bourdin* (Editions du Seuil: 2001, Paris)

Doutreleau, Victoire, *Et Dior créa Victoire* (Robert Laffont: Paris, 1997)

Dwight, Eleanor, *Diana Vreeland* (William Morrow: New York, 2002)

von Eelking, Freiherrn Herrmann-Marten, *Garderoben-Gesetze*, illustrated by Ernst Ludwig Kretschmann (republished by Finckenstein und Salmuth: Berlin, 2003)

Fairchild, John, *The Fashionable Savages* (Doubleday & Company, Inc.: New York, 1965)

Faucigny-Lucinge, Jean-Louis de, *Fêtes mémorables, bals costumés, 1922–1972* (Editions Herscher: Paris, 1986)

Floquet, Charles, *Dictionnaire des châteaux et manoirs du Morbihan* (Yves Floch: Mayenne, 1991)

Francis, Mark, and Margery King (eds.), *The Warhol Look: Glamour Style Fashion* (Little, Brown and Company: New York, 1997)

Fressange, Inès de la, *Profession Mannequin: Conversations avec Marianne Mairesse* (Hachette Littératures: Paris, 2002)

Furstenberg, Diane von, *Diane: A Signature Life* (Simon & Schuster: New York, 1998)

Galey, Matthieu, *Journal 1953–1973* (Editions Grasset & Fasquelle: Paris, 1987)

Gandini, Jacques, *Oran de ma jeunesse, 1945–1962* (Editions Jacques Gandini: Nice, 1997)

Gildea, Robert, *France since 1945* (Oxford University Press: Oxford, 2002; second edition)

Goldsmith, Lady Annabel, *Annabel: An Unconventional Life* (Weidenfeld & Nicolson: London, 2004)

Grumbach, Didier, *Histoires de la mode* (Editions du Seuil: Paris, 1993)

Hackett, Pat (ed.), *The Andy Warhol Diaries* (Warner Books: New York, 1989)

Harrison, Martin, *Appearances: Fashion Photography since 1945* (Rizzoli: New York, 1991)

Haye, Amy de la, and Shelley Tobin, *Chanel: The Couturiere at Work* (V&A Publications: London, 1994)

Haynes, Jim, *Thanks for Coming!* (Faber and Faber: London, 1984)

Heiting, Manfred (ed.), *Helmut Newton. Work* (Taschen: Cologne, 2000)

Herald, Jacqueline, *Fashions of a Decade: The 1970s* (B.T. Batsford Ltd.: London, 1992)

Hockney, David, *David Hockney by David Hockney: My Early Years* (Thames & Hudson: London, 1988)

Huysmans, Joris-Karl, *The Damned (Là-Bas)*, translated by Terry Hale (Penguin Books: London, 2001; first published in 1891)

James, Henry, *The Tragic Muse* (Penguin Classics: London, 1995; first published by Macmillan in 1890)

Jullian, Philippe, *Robert de Montesquiou: un prince, 1900* (Librairie Académique Perrin: Paris, 1965)

Kochno, Boris, *Christian Bérard* (Editions Herscher: Paris, 1987)

Kurlansky, Mark, *1968: The Year that Rocked the World* (Ballantine Books: New York, 2004)

Lagerfeld, Karl, and Dr Jean-Claude Houdret, *Le meilleur des régimes* (Robert Laffont: Paris, 2002)

Leon Talley, André, *A.L.T.: A Memoir* (Villard Books: New York, 2003)

Lowit, Roxanne, *Moments – Roxanne Lowit – Photographs* (The Vendome Press: New York/Paris, 1993; Editions Assouline: Paris, 1992)

Lowit, Roxanne, *People* (Editions Assouline: Paris, 2001)

Ludwig, Arnold M., *The Price of Greatness: Resolving the Creativity and Madness Controversy* (The Guilford Press: New York, 1995)

Lynam, Ruth (ed.), *Paris Fashion: The Great Designers and their Creations* (November Books Ltd: London, 1972)

Madsen, Axel, *Chanel: A Woman of Her Own* (Henry Holt and Co.: New York, 1990)

Mann, Thomas, *Confessions of Felix Krull, Confidence Man: The Early Years*, translated by Denver Lindley (Vintage International: New York, 1992)

McIntosh, Christopher, *The Swan King: Ludwig II of Bavaria* (Taurisparke Paperbacks: London, 2003)

Mension-Rigau, Eric, *Aristocrates et grands bourgeois: Education, traditions, valeurs* (Plon: Paris, 1994)

Merrick, Jeffrey, and Michael Sibalis (eds.), *Homosexuality in French History and Culture* (The Haworth Press, Inc.: New York, 2001)

Metelmann, Henry, *A Hitler Youth: Growing up in Germany in the 1930s* (Caliban Books: London, 1997; revised edition published by Spellmount Ltd, Staplehurst, 2004)

Mitscherlich, Alexander and Margarete, *The Inability to Mourn: Principles of Collective Behavior*, translated by Beverley R. Placzek (Grove Press, Inc.: New York, 1975)

Morand, Paul, *L'allure de Chanel* (Hermann: Paris, 1996)

Newton, Helmut, and Alice Springs, *Us and Them* (Scalo: Zurich-Berlin-New York, 1999)

Newton, Helmut, *Autobiography* (Nan A. Talese: Doubleday, New York, 2003)

Newton, Helmut, *World Without Men* (Xavier Moreau, Inc.: New York, 1984)

Newton, June, and Walter Keller (eds.), Helmut Newton, *Pages from the Glossies: Facsimiles 1956–1998* (Scalo: Zurich–Berlin-New York, 1998)

Paquin, Paquita, *Vingt ans sans dormir, 1968–1983* (Editions Denoël: Paris, 2005)

Piaggi, Anna, *Karl Lagerfeld: A Fashion Journal* (Thames & Hudson: London, 1986)

Platte, Wolfgang, *Bad Bramstedt im 20. Jahrhundert* (Stadt Bad Bramstedt, 1985)

Pochna, Marie-France, *Christian Dior* (Editions Flammarion: Paris, 1994)

Polhemus, Ted, *Street Style* (Thames & Hudson: London, 1995)

Prange, Carsten, *A Journey through Hamburg's History* (Hamburg: M. Glogau Jr Verlag, 1990)

Proust, Marcel, *A la recherche du temps perdu*, edited by J.-Y. Tadié (Bibl. de la Pléiade: Paris, 1987–1989)

Ramos, Juan Eugene, *Antonio – 60, 70, 80* (Schirmer/Mosel: Munich–Paris, 1994)

Rawsthorn, Alice, *Yves Saint Laurent* (HarperCollins: London, 1996)

Réage, Pauline, *Histoire d'O* (Société Nouvelles des Editions Pauvert: Paris, 1954)

Réthy, Esmeralda de, and Jean-Louis Perreau, *Monsieur Dior et nous, 1947–1957* (Anthèse: Arcueil, 1999)

Richards, Melissa, *Chanel Key Collections* (Hamlyn: London, 2000)

Richardson, Joanna, *La Vie Parisienne 1852–1870* (Hamish Hamilton: London, 1971)

Richardson, Joanna, *The Courtesans: The Demi-Monde in 19th-Century France* (Weidenfeld & Nicolson: London, 1967)

Rothschild, Guy de, *Les surprises de la fortune*, (Editions Michel Lafon: Neuilly-sur-Seine, 2002)

Rous, Lady Henrietta (ed.), *The Ossie Clark Diaries* (Bloomsbury: London, 1998)

Sainderichin, Ginette, *Kenzo* (Editions du May: Boulogne, 1989)

Saint Laurent, Yves, *Images of Design 1958–1988* (Alfred A. Knopf: New York, 1988)

Saint Laurent, Yves, *La vilaine Lulu* (Claude Tchou, Editeur: Paris, 1967)

Saint Laurent, Yves, *Yves Saint Laurent par Yves Saint Laurent* (Editions Herscher: Paris, 1986)

Scarry, Elaine, *On Beauty and Being Just* (Gerald Duckworth & Co.: London, 2000)

Schlesinger, Peter, *A Chequered Past: My Visual Diary of the 60s and 70s* (Thames & Hudson: London, 2004)

Sebald, W. G., *On the Natural History of Destruction*, translated by Anthea Bell (Random House: New York, 2003)

Sebbar, Leïla (ed.), *An Algerian Childhood* (Ruminator Books, 2001)

Seeling, Charlotte, *Fashion: The Century of the Designer, 1900–1999* (Könemann: Cologne, 1999)

Steele, Valerie, *Fifty Years of Fashion: New Look to Now* (Yale University Press: New Haven and London, 1997)

Steele, Valerie, *Paris Fashion: A Cultural History* (Oxford University Press: Oxford, 1988)

Tadié, Jean-Yves, *Proust: La cathédrale du temps* (Gallimard: Paris, 1999)

Teboul, David, *Yves Saint Laurent* (Harry N. Abrams, Inc.: New York, 2002)

Thiébaut, Philippe, *Robert Montesquiou ou l'art de paraître* (Editions de la Réunion des musées nationaux: Paris, 1999)

Vreeland, Diana, *D.V.*, edited by George Plimpton and Christopher Hemphill (Da Capo Press: New York, 1997; note, this is an unabridged republication of the edition published in New York in 1984)

Walden, George, *Who's a Dandy? Jules Barbey D'Aurevilly, Dandyism and Beau Brummell* (Gibson Square Books: London, 2002)

Wallach, Janet, *Chanel: Her Style and Her Life* (Nan A. Talese, Doubleday: New York, 1998)

Watt, Judith, *Ossie Clark 1965–1974* (V&A Publications: London, 2003)
Wilde, Oscar, *The Picture of Dorian Gray* (Penguin Books: London, 2000; first published in 1891)

Films

Double Je, Karl Lagerfeld interviewed by Bernard Pivot (Equipage/ RFO/TV5: Paris, broadcast 27 February 2003)
Helmut by June, director Alice Springs (Eyestorm: London, 19 March 1999)
Top Ten Designers (Software Productions: Paris, 1979)
Yves Saint Laurent, Le Temps Retrouvé, director David Teboul (Canal+/ Movimento/INA Entreprise/Transatlantic Vidéo: Paris, 2002)
Yves Saint Laurent, 5 Avenue Marceau 75116, director David Teboul (Canal+/Movimento/INA Entreprise/Transatlantic Vidéo avec la participation de la WDR: Paris, 2002)
Celebration, director Olivier Meyrou (2001)

Audio

'La grande histoire et les petites histoires des bas quartiers d'Oran', speaker Emile Serna (conference of 4 January 2002, organised by A.O.C.A.Z and A.L.L.O; CDs 1 and 2, from the private collection of Monsieur Norbert Alvérola)

Catalogues

'Chanel, The Metropolitan Museum of Art, New York', Harold Koda and Andrew Bolton (The Metropolitan Museum of Art: New York, 2005)

'Collection Lagerfeld, Volume 1: Important Mobilier et Objets d'Art' (Christie's: Monaco, 29 April 2000)

'Collection Lagerfeld, Volume 2 : Important Mobilier et Objets d'Art' (Christie's: Monaco, 29 April, 2000)

'The Lagerfeld Collection, Volume 3: Old Master Pictures' (Christie's: New York, 23 May 2000)

'Collection Karl Lagerfeld: Arts Décoratifs du XXe Siècle' (Sotheby's: Paris, 15 May 2003)

'Sixties Mode d'Emploi: Collections du Musée de la Mode et du Textile' (Union Centrale des Arts Décoratifs: Paris, 2002)

'Yves Saint Laurent: Dialogue avec l'Art' (Fondation Pierre Bergé–Yves Saint Laurent: Paris, 2004)

ACKNOWLEDGEMENTS

I would like to thank everyone who I interviewed over the course of the last five and a half years, who gave of their time and shared their memories of what was a euphoric period in which to live and yet a strangely melancholic one to look back upon. In particular I would like to thank Gaby Aghion, Charlotte Aillaud, Lydie and Norbert Alvérola, Xavier de Bascher, François Baufumé, Marc Bohan, Joan Juliet Buck, François Catroux, Edmonde Charles-Roux, Pat Cleveland and her husband Paul Van Ravenstein, Madison Cox, John Crawley, Jean-Pierre Derbord, Victoire Doutreleau, Gerry Dryansky, John Fairchild, Judith Fayard, Christophe Girard, Tan Giudicelli, Jacques Grange, Patrick Hourcade, Thadée Klossowski, Roxanne Lowit, Hélène de Ludinghausen, Marian McEvoy, Xavier Moreau, Lucien Pellat-Finet, Paloma Picasso, Andrée Putman, Marc Rioufol, Guy de Rothschild, Fernando Sanchez and Ralph Toledano.

I am extremely grateful and would like to express my thanks to Paul Caranicas, who graciously allowed me access to Antonio's archive as well as answering my questions and allowing me to use Antonio's pictures inside the book. Thank you to Corey Grant Tippin for his patience and powers of recall in responding to my many queries. I am grateful to Betty Catroux for her tenacious lobbying of Yves Saint Laurent. Anne de Bascher stood firm and fair throughout our many conversations about her brother's life and I am extremely thankful to her. Brigitte Bastian's memories enabled me to imagine her brother's childhood. Many thanks go to Christel for her wry wit and hospitality. I am indebted to Patrick McCarthy, who gave me permission to work on the Fairchild archives as well as allowing me to use Fairchild pictures inside the book. Thank you to Christian Dumais-Lvowski for his willingness to be interviewed many times, and for offering me insight, Normandy day-trips and allowing me to see another side of Jacques. I am grateful to Renaud de Beaugourdon, who generously allowed me to work and quote from his private correspondence, as well as responding to all my queries and theories with remarkable objectivity. I wish to thank Philippe Garner for his decorative enlightenment and Diane de Beauvau-Craon for her frank account of these years. Thank you to Loulou de la Falaise for withstanding my questioning and to Maxime de la Falaise for her hospitality and acute observations. I am grateful to Guy Marineau, who allowed me access to his extensive picture archive of this time and who worked so hard to come up with the relevant pictures for the inside of the book.

I am indebted to the following for their expert knowledge: Associate Professor Scott F. Coffey of the University of Mississippi Medical Center; Professor Dr h.c. Detlef Junker of the Heidelberg Center for American Studies (HCA); Doktor Ortwin Pelc of the Museum für Hamburgische Geschichte; Manfred Jacobsen, town historian of Bad Bramstedt; Gérard Danet, national heritage historian; Eric Mension-Rigau, *maître de conférences* in history at the University of Paris-Sorbonne (Paris IV) and member of l'Institut universitaire de France; and Comte Jean de Bodinat of the Association d'Entraide de la Noblesse Française. I am also grateful to Hugo Vickers, Cecil Beaton's literary executor.

I spent a year writing the first draft of the book in the library of the Union Centrale des Arts Décoratifs and I would like to thank all the staff for their kindness and for turning a blind eye to my Thermos flask of coffee. I wish to thank the archive staff of Fairchild Publications, including Merle Thomason (now retired), whose clippings books contain many marvels, Margaret Skeeter, for answering my fact checks, and Delano Knox. I am grateful to all those archivists who helped with my queries and research: to Philippe Le Moult, corporate relations manager, and Soizic Pfaff, archivist, at the house of Christian Dior; Antonya Tioulong, head of archives at *L'Express* magazine; Gérald Chevalier of the Ecoles de la Chambre Syndicale de la Couture Parisienne, and school director Monsieur François Broca. I would like to mention Pascal Sittler of the Fondation Pierre Bergé–Yves Saint Laurent, and Jean-Christophe Laizeau, press officer for Loulou de la Falaise, both of whom assisted me with unfailing courtesy. I am grateful to Anne Crowther of the Bradford Textile Archive; Helga Dupuis, bureau chief of *Der Stern* in Paris; Ruth Viebrock at *Die Zeit*; Madame Lévy at *Le Point*; Gilles LeRoux at *Le Figaro*; and Aurélie Poulain at Equipage.

For my research into Karl Lagerfeld's childhood in Germany I would like to express my thanks to Rosemary Kluth, for her exceptional translation skills as well as for accompanying me with such tireless enthusiasm on my interviews and for the extra research and reflections that she shared with me. I am grateful to Chantal Zakowski for translating during my first telephone interview with Herr Wagner and later for her welcome in Bad Bramstedt, and to Anne Vogelpohl for her help with research in Hamburg. Thank you to Lucy Richardson, Amalia-Bianca Agelopoulos, Tim Scales, Anusch Cutujian, Jasper Neidel and Mareile Kirsch for drawing my attention to the significance of the Hanseatic identity. I would like to thank Herr Josef Riepl of Glücksklee in Neustadt, who so kindly arranged the interview with the late Herr Lagerfeld. Thank you too to Herr Lagerfeld's daughter, Margrit Greune, for her welcome, and to Malte Betz of *Bild am Sonntag*.

I would also like to thank friends, writers and members of the fashion industry who gave me valuable advice, introductions, help and assistance with queries, articles and people searches: Isabella Capece, Melissa Comito, Godfrey Deeny, Aliona Dolestkaya, Pamela Fiori, Pamela Golbin, Chantal Goupil, Anna Harvey, Lorna Koski, Vinny Lee, Tina Lignell, Suzy Menkes, Robert Murphy, Janet Ozzard, Ian Phillips, Alice Ryan, Gloria Sheahan, Jenny Weil, Ron Wilson. So many people helped me in diverse and crucial ways: I am grateful to Steve Hiett, Jean Eudes and Claude Aurensan, who loaned me publications from this period. I am grateful to Patrick Swirc, Madame d'Artagnan, Robert Fonteneli, Rachel Caunt for her stoic photocopying, Tasha Pike, Sophie Dumont Ader, the Reverend Peter Watkins, Tran Huu Nghia, as well as Thien Tran, Max Desbrosses and Alex de Olveira, who rescued both me and my computer many times. May I express my gratitude to Maître Christophe Ayela, Monsieur Chassot, le procureur de la République de Vannes, Madame Le Hen, Maître Karl Hepp de Sevelinges, Maître Jean-Pascal Bus and Albena Iordanova for her kindness. I would like to thank Jodie Hutchins-Godon for moving my office and my family three times during the course of the book and bringing administrative order and optimism to seething chaos.

I am grateful to all those friends who supported me: Alev Aktar, Ruth Benoit, Nick Birts, Laurent Buttazzoni, Xavier Chaumette, Amanda Foreman, Rachida Kadaoui, Prosper Keating, Lulu Lytle, Aléssia Margiotta-Broglio, Sally Mayhew, Anna Maxted, Roseline Mercier, Darrell Moos, Sarah Raper-Larenaudie, Phil Robinson and Donald Schneider. Great thanks go to Charles Sebline for sharing both his knowledge and a fashion dialogue over these years, and to Robert Ferrell for his innate understanding of the fashion industry and his willingness to answer my questions, any time, any place.

Thank you to my agent Lizzy Kremer for her commitment and voice of reason throughout. I wish to thank my publishers: Alexandra Pringle at Bloomsbury for her unceasing encouragement to follow the story I had to tell, and Judy Clain at Little, Brown for her dynamism and belief in the book. Profound thanks go to my Bloomsbury editor Victoria Millar, who has been brilliant and approached the book with such sensibility and dedication. I am grateful to Andrea Vazzano at Little, Brown in New York, as well as Molly Messick, Claire Smith, Emily Sweet for her deft touch and copy-edit, and Maggie Traugott for her constructive comments. Thank you to lawyers Maddie Mogford in London and Linda Cowen in the USA for their thorough legal reports. Many thanks go to Ed Victor, who started me out on my marathon.

I would like to thank the following people for their precious gift of friendship: Lucy and Mark Cornell for their marvellous support, Alice Scales, Rozelle Webster, and Marie-Laure Dauchez for her persuasive letters and powers of analysis. Thank you to Frédéric Venière for his beautifully crafted letters. I thank Khadija Chafiqui for her devotion to our children and her generosity to our family, and Rosalina Enriquez for her loving care. I would like to express great thanks to Yvette Citoleux for her wisdom and insight.

I would like to thank my readers who not only offered valuable and thought-provoking comment on the manuscript but also kept me going throughout: Henrietta Courtauld, a true friend who offered astute observation and constant support; Natasha Fraser-Cavassoni, who introduced me to Ed Victor, drew my attention to this period when I was intent on avoiding it and has been unfailingly generous and wise in her judgement and advice; Claudia Shear, who had me to stay in New York, offered expert opinion and wrote emails that got me through the night; Sarah Turnbull, from Paris to Papeete, whose direction and encouragement have been uplifting, essential. I wish to express my thanks to my dear parents George and Charlotte Drake and to my sisters Louise Bartlett and Sarah Drake, all of whom have been by my side every step of the way. And I also thank my parents-in-law, Rosamund and Edward Reece, for both practical and moral support.

To my darling children, Lily, Hathorn, Peony and the twinkle inside: 'Go on Mummy, you can do your book' − you got me to the end. Thank you, thank you.

And to Rupert, my husband, my reader, who has given me love, wisdom, comfort and sweet inspiration throughout. This book is dedicated to you with endless love and thanks.

Paris, 21 May 2006

List of Illustrations

Plate section

The prizewinners of the 1954 International Wool Secretariat competition: Karl, Lagerfeld, Yves Saint Laurent and Colette Bracchi. © KEYSTONE-FRANCE

Yves Saint Laurent in September 1961.© KEYSTONE-FRANCE

Karl Lagerfeld, in around 1960, working on a couture outfit at the house of Jean Patou. © KEYSTONE-FRANCE

Betty Catroux pictured in the Place Vauban garden in 1968 with Yves Saint Laurent, Pierre Bergé and François Catroux. Photograph by Mary Russell/*Women's Wear Daily* © Fairchild Publications, Inc.

Loulou de la Falaise. Photograph by Patrick Sauteret © *Vogue* Paris

Yves Saint Laurent in Marrakech, 1976. Photograph by Guy Marineau

Donna Jordan, Corey Tippin and Antonio Lopez in Saint-Tropez. Photograph by Juan Ramos from the Antonio archive, property of Paul Caranicas

Pat Cleveland in a Rive Gauche bar in Paris. Photograph by Juan Ramos from the Antonio archive, property of Paul Caranicas

Karl Lagerfeld in Saint-Tropez, with Juan Ramos. Photograph by Antonio Lopez, from the Antonio archive, property of Paul Caranicas

Antonio Lopez in the Jardin du Luxembourg, 1971. Photograph by Juan Ramos from the Antonio archive, property of Paul Caranicas

Yves Saint Laurent surrounded by models from his 1940s collection of 1971. © Bruno Barbey/Magnum Photos

Dinner at La Coupole. Photograph by Max Scheler, Scheler Estate, Hamburg, Germany

David Hockney, *Jacques, Paris, April 1974*, coloured pencil on paper, courtesy of The Museum of Contemporary Art, Los Angeles. Photograph by Brian Forrest

Jacques de Bascher, *L'Uomo Vogue*, Italy, October 1973. Photograph by Alex Chatelain

The Opéra collection of autumn/winter 1976. Photograph from the Fondation Pierre Bergé-Yves Saint Laurent

The Opium collection of autumn/winter 1977. © Pierre Vauthey/ CORBIS SYGMA

The Broadway collection of spring/summer 1978. Photograph from the Fondation Pierre Bergé-Yves Saint Laurent

Saint Laurent after the October 1976 Carmen ready-to-wear show. Photograph by Guy Marineau/*Women's Wear Daily* © Fairchild Publications, Inc.

Loulou de la Falaise and Thadée Klossowski's wedding celebrations. All photographs by Guy Marineau/*Women's Wear Daily* © Fairchild Publications, Inc.

Bianca Jagger and Yves Saint Laurent at Loulou and Thadée's wedding ball. Photograph by Guy Marineau/*Women's Wear Daily* © Fairchild Publications, Inc.

Yves Saint Laurent, Loulou de la Falaise and Betty Catroux in 1978. Photograph by Guy Marineau

Paloma Picasso and Rafael López-Sánchez on their wedding day in May 1978. © Alain DeJean/Sygma/CORBIS

Inès de la Fressange wears a black evening dress from Karl Lagerfeld's first haute couture collection for the house of Chanel in January 1983. Photograph by Chris Moore

Model Shalom Harlow walks the runway in the Chanel spring/summer ready-to-wear show of 1995. Photograph by Guy Marineau

Jacques de Bascher and Karl Lagerfeld at night in Paris, 1978. Photograph by Guy Marineau

Yves Saint Laurent, Loulou de la Falaise and a model in the final stages of preparation for the spring/summer couture show 2001. © Françoise Huguier/RAPHO

Yves Saint Laurent and Pierre Bergé on the terrace of the Château Gabriel, 1983. Photograph by Guy Marineau

Karl Lagerfeld and model Devon Aoki at the end of the autumn/winter couture Chanel show in July 2000. © by GAMMA

Karl Lagerfeld kisses Nicole Kidman at the Chanel spring/summer 2005 ready-to-wear show. © BENAINOUS-ROSSI/GAMMA

Yves Saint Laurent with Laetitia Casta and Catherine Deneuve at the retrospective fashion show of 2002, held at the Centre Pompidou. Photograph by Simon-Stevens © by GAMMA

Yves Saint Laurent and Karl Lagerfeld at Le Palace in March 1983. © Roxanne Lowit

Illustrations in the text

Page 10: Yves Saint Laurent as a teenager on the tennis courts of Oran. Photograph from the private collection of Madame Lucienne Mathieu-Saint-Laurent, loaned by the Fondation Pierre Bergé-Yves Saint Laurent, Paris

Page 24: Bernard Buffet's drawing of Yves Saint Laurent, courtesy of the Fondation Pierre Bergé-Yves Saint Laurent, Paris

Page 71: Karl Lagerfeld as a young schoolboy with fellow pupils of the Jürgen-Fuhlendorf-Schule in Bad Bramstedt. Photograph from the private collection of Jans-Joachim Bronisch

Page 157: La vilaine Lulu meets her fate in Saint-Tropez. Illustration from *La vilaine Lulu* by Yves Saint Laurent, first published by Claude Tchou, Editeur, Paris, 1967; republished by Tchou, Editeur in 2003

Index

A NOTE ON THE AUTHOR

Alicia Drake writes regularly for a variety of publications, including the *International Herald Tribune, Travel and Leisure, W* magazine and British *Vogue,* for which she was a contributing editor. She has lived and worked in Paris for the last ten years.